# Dollars for Terror
## The United States and Islam

# Dollars for Terror
*The United States and Islam*

Richard Labévière

Translated by Martin DeMers

Algora Publishing
New York

Algora Publishing, New York
© 2000 by Algora Publishing
All rights reserved. Published 2000.
Printed in the United States of America
ISBN: 1-892941-06-6
Editors@algora.com

Originally published as *Les Dollars de la Terreur, Les Etats-Unis et les Islamistes* © Éditions Bernard Grasset, 1999.

Library of Congress Cataloging-in-Publication Data 00-008415


Labévière, Richard.
    [Dollars de la terreur. English]
    Dollars for Terror: The United States and Islam / by Richard Labévière; translated by Martin DeMers.
        p. cm.
    ISBN 1-892941-06-6 (alk. paper)
    1. Terrorism—Government policy—United States. 2. Terrorism—Kenya—Nairobi. 3. Terrorism—Tanzania—Dar-es-Salaam. 4. Bin Ladin, Osama, 1957- 5. Terrorism—Islamic countries—Finance. 6. Taliban—Finance. I. Title.
HV6432 .L3313 2000
303.6'25'0882971—dc21

Algora Publishing
wishes to express its appreciation
for the assistance given by
the Government of France
through the Ministry of Culture
in support of the preparation of this translation.


New York
www.algora.com

# TABLE OF CONTENTS

MAPS

The Cold War Continues. . .

What's happened since the bloody bombings of the American embassies in Nairobi and Dar es Salaam in August, 1998? Frankly, not much. At least 263 were killed and 5,000 more were wounded; the retaliatory bombing of a chemical plant in Sudan and of logistics and training bases in Afghanistan two weeks later had little effect. How could such counterattacks address the terrorist actions of an international nebula with strong ties to many countries? Fifteen people were indicted; only five of them are currently in American prisons. The FBI investigation is still underway. The State Department has offered a $5 million reward to any person having information leading to the capture of Osama bin Laden or any other suspect.

But fundamentally, the State Department is not exerting any real pressure on the Taleban to "catch" the Saudi billionaire who is happily whiling away his days in Afghanistan. More pro-Islamist than ever, the CIA still plays down the criminal misdeeds of its former agent and maintains the same supportive policy toward the Islamists and against Russia and China. The Saudi secret service, too, hardly seems eager to neutralize (much less arrest) its old acquaintance bin Laden, who bank-rolled the "holy war." Saudi Arabia, through its "Wahhabi associations"[1] and other armed religious fanatic organizations, is making its influence felt more than ever throughout the Arab-Muslim world (and especially in South Africa and Central Asia). In short, the objective alliance, the convergence of strategic and economic interests between the

American government and Sunni Islam is doing just fine — in spite of the new geopolitical reality.

Between 1994 and 1997, Bill Clinton was happy to allow Pakistan and Saudi Arabia to support the Taleban, seeing them as a useful counterbalance to Iran's influence; but today, in the long term, time is working against God's Afghan madmen. Indeed, Russia, Iran and India have ended up joining forces to destroy the religious Utopia of Kabul before it contaminates the whole area. The Russians have not forgiven the massacres of Communists in Kabul, symbolized by the hanging of former President Najibullah, and they fear the invasion of nearby Tajikistan. The Iranians cannot sit idly by while Shiites are persecuted and the Hazaraja lose their autonomy. India, finally, has decided to carry over into Afghanistan the open war that the Pakistani army wages against them daily. The Pakistani morass and its profound strategic implications for all of Central Asia have become one of the most alarming and chaotic scenes on the planet. As one of the most strategic areas of the next millennium slips into a criminal state, Uncle Sam looks on with cynicism (if not benevolence).

"The policy of guiding the evolution of Islam and of helping them against our adversaries worked marvelously well in Afghanistan against the Red Army," explains a former CIA analyst. "The same doctrines can still be used to destabilize what remains of Russian power, and especially to counter the Chinese influence in Central Asia." In a certain sense, the Cold War is still going on. For years Graham Fuller, former Deputy Director of the National Council on Intelligence at the CIA, has been talking up the "modernizing virtues" of the Islamists, insisting on their anti-Statist concept of the economy. Listening to him, you would almost take the Taleban and their Wahhabi allies for liberals. "Islam, in theory at least, is firmly anchored in the traditions of free trade and private enterprise," wrote Fuller.[2] "The prophet was a trader, as was his first wife. Islam does not glorify the State's role in the economy."

This edifying statement, obligingly broadcast by the official newspaper of a certain stratum of the French intelligentsia, partially explains the American government's laxity in Central Asia. Parallel to the astonishing ideological convergence between the Parisian ex-Leftists and certain former CIA analysts, there is a perceptible propagation of Sunni Islamism (in varying degrees) from Chechnya to Chinese Xinjiang, and it affects all the Muslim republics of the former Soviet Union. With the active support of Saudi Arabia, the United Arab Emirates and other oil monarchies and with the benevolence of the American services engaged in these areas, we can expect a "Talebanization" of Central Asia, particularly in Chechnya.

Following a series of terrorist attacks in Moscow during the autumn of 1999, the Russian army launched a series of operations in Chechnya and Dagestan. This new war in Chechnya came on the heels of a series of grave events ascribable to the Sunni Muslims, whose networks are still expanding from the Caspian Sea to the gates of China. Aslan Maskhadov, the Chechen president, had sought to unify his country via Islam; in the end, threatened by militants who want to establish an Islamic State in Chechnya similar to that of the Taleban in Afghanistan.

After the withdrawal of the Russian troops in 1996, incidents between Islamists and the police force escalated dramatically. An emir of Arab origin, who wanted to found an Islamic State covering the whole of the Caucasus, raised an army of 2000 men. On July 15, 1998, conflicts between 1000 Islamic combatants and the security forces killed more than 50 people in the town of Gudermes, 23 miles east of Grozny. Shortly after these clashes, Chechen President Maskhadov called on the population and the local religious authority to resist the "Wahhabis and those who are behind these misled insurrectionaries." He affirmed his intention to excise from Chechnya "those who are trying to impose a foreign ideology on the population." On July 31, 1998 he barely escaped an assassination attempt attributed to Islamic activists.

On December 12, 1998, the Chechen authorities announced the arrest of Arbi Baraev, a Wahhabi militant. He had proclaimed a "Jihad against the enemies of the true religion," and was implicated in the murder of the four Western engineers (three British and one New Zealander) whose severed heads were found on December 10, 1998. He also admitted participating in the kidnapping and the detention of Frenchman Vincent Cochetel, a delegate from the U.N.'s High Commission of Refugees. Cochetel disappeared in Ossetia; he was released on December 10, 1998, after 317 days in captivity. The Islamists, in addition, acknowledged kidnapping the Chechen Attorney General Mansour Takirov, on December 11, 1998. And on March 21, 1999, the Chechen President escaped a second bombing, right in the center of Grozny.

While Aslan Maskhadov proclaims his determination to eradicate Wahhabi Islamism in his country, he is opposed by several members of his government who protect the religious activists. Thus Movadi Uklugov, a member of the Chechen government, wants to establish diplomatic relation with the Taleban of Afghanistan. The Chechen Vice President Vakha Arsanov called for reprisals against the United States after the August 20, 1998 bombing of Sudan and Afghanistan. One year later, Chechnya was cut in two by the Russian forces; 170,000 women and children headed for exile in Ingushetia, another Islamic sanctuary. The pressure of refugees fleeing the war in Ossetia is growing and the entire area is slipping into a civil war mode, like Afghan — just what Maskhadov wanted to avoid. But "Talebanization" is gaining ground in Dagestan, Tatarstan, Uzbekistan, Kyrgyzstan and the fringes of China as well.

In May 1997, in Dagestan, Wahhabi militants wielding automatic weapons clashed with representatives of local Sufi brotherhoods. Two people were killed, three others wounded and eighteen Wahhabis were taken hostage by the Sufis. On December 21, 1997, three units of former volunteers from the Afghan resistance attacked a Russian military base in Dagestan. These combatants, coming from Chechnya, Dagestan, Ingushetia, Uzbekistan and Kyrgyzstan, assassinated several dozen Russian soldiers and officers, and then set fire to some three hundred vehicles. Before retiring to Chechnya, these Islamists handed out leaflets proclaiming, among other things, that new military training camps would be opened in Chechnya to prepare additional combatants "who will teach the impious Russians a lesson."

In August 1998, the Wahhabi communities of three Dagestani villages proclaimed "independent Islamic republics," recognized *Sharia* as the only law valid in the state, and sought to leave the Russian Federation to join Chechnya. Lastly, August 21, 1998, the mufti of Dagestan, Saïd Mohammad Abubakarov (who had urged the authorities to react firmly against Wahhabi terrorism) and his brother were killed when his residence was bombed. The chaos caused by this attack led the country to the brink of civil war.

In Tatarstan, the authorities see the development of a radical Islamist movement as a serious threat to the country's stability, since the appearance of "religious political organizations" endangers the coexistence of the Russian and Tatar populations. In March 1999, Mintimer Chaîmiev — President of Tatarstan — denounced "the action of emissaries from Islamic countries who recruit young people in Russia, and give them military training abroad, leading to terrorist actions." During 1999, several Pakistani, Afghan and Saudi "missionaries" were expelled from the country for proselytism intended to unleash a "holy war."

The Ferghana Valley in Uzbekistan has long been the site of an Islamist education and agitation center with close ties to Pakistan and the Saudi Wahhabi organizations. In 1992, after an uprising in Namangan, the biggest town in the Ferghana Valley, President Islam Karimov (the former head of the Uzbek Communist Party) ordered a series of arrests against the Islamist agitators while seeking to promote an official form of Islam through the International Center of Islamic Research financed by the State. In December 1997, several police officers were assassinated by Wahhabi activists. On February 16, 1998, the Uzbek Minister for Foreign Affairs blamed the Islamist organizations in Pakistan and accused them of training the terrorists who conducted these assassinations. According to his information services, more than 500 Uzbeks, Kirghiz and Tajiks were trained in Pakistan and in Afghanistan before returning to their home lands in order to propagate a holy war against the "impious authorities."

Between July 1998 and January 1999, a hundred Wahhabi Islamists were tried and sentenced to three to twenty years in prison. On February 16, 1999, six explosions ripped through Tashkent, the Uzbek capital, killing 15 and wounding some 150. The first three charges exploded near the government headquarters; three others hit a school, a retail store and the airport. Shortly after this lethal night, the Uzbek authorities denounced acts "financed by organizations based abroad" and reiterated their intention to fight Wahhabi extremism. On March 18, 1999, some thirty Wahhabi militants (suspected of involvement in the February 16 attacks) were arrested in Kazakhstan. According to Interfax, the Russian press agency, they were holding airplane tickets for the United Arab Emirates, Pakistan, Chechnya and Azerbaidjan.

In Kyrgyzstan, in February 1998, the Muslim religious authorities launched a vast information campaign to counter Saudi proselytism and the propagation of Wahhabi ideology. On May 12, the Kyrgyzstan security forces arrested four foreigners, members of a very active clandestine Wahhabi organization. This group was training recruits from Kyrgyzstan in military boot camps linked to Afghanistan and Pakistan. The police also seized Afghan and Pakistani passports, a large sum in U.S. dollars, video cassettes summoning viewers to a "holy war," and other propaganda documents. The authorities announced a series of

measures against those who were using religious instruction "to destabilize the country." In May 1998, the Kyrgyz authorities, who had already arrested and extradited eight Uzbek activists in 1997, signed two
agreements on anti-terrorist cooperation with Uzbekistan and Tajikistan.

China has not been spared. Xinjiang (southern China), has a
population that is 55% Uighur (a turkophone Sunni ethnic group); it
has been confronted with Islamist violence since the beginning of the
1990's. Created in 1955, Xinjiang (which means "new territory") is one
of the five autonomous areas of China and is the largest administrative
unit of the country. The area is highly strategic at the geopolitical
level — Chinese nuclear tests and rocket launches take place on the
Lop Nor test grounds — as well as from an economic standpoint, since
it abounds in natural wealth (oil, gas, uranium, gold, etc.). Against this
backdrop, attacks have proliferated by independence-seeking cliques,
all preaching "Holy War."

Some are acting in the name of Turkish identity, while others are
fighting in the name of Allah (especially in the southern part of the region). As in the rest of Central Asia, in Xinjiang we are witnessing the
rising influence of Wahhabi groups and the increasing proselytism of
preachers from Saudi Arabia, Afghanistan and Pakistan. Traditionally
allied with popular China, Pakistan is nevertheless trying to extend its
influence to this part of China, using the Islamists as it did in Afghanistan. For this reason Beijing closed the road from Karakorum, connecting Xinjiang to Pakistan, between 1992 and 1995. Since 1996, the fre-
quency of the incidents has skyrocketed. In February 1997, riots exploded in Yining (a town of 300,000 inhabitants located to the west of
Urumqi, near the Kazakh border). This violence caused ten deaths,
according to Chinese authorities, and the Uighurs have counted more
than a hundred victims.

Every week in 1998 saw a bombing or an attack with automatic
weapons. The region's hotels, airports and railway stations are in a
constant state of alert. In April, Chinese authorities in the vicinity of
Yining seized 700 cases of ammunition from Kazakhstan. In September, the Secretary of the Xinjiang Communist Party declared that "19
training camps, in which specialists returning from Afghanistan edu-
cate young recruits in the techniques of terrorism, with the assistance
of the Taleban," were neutralized. In January 1999, 29 activists implicated in the February 1997 riots were arrested. On February 12, violent

clashes between the police and groups of Uighur militants wounded several dozen people in Urumqi. Two hundred people were arrested. In early March, 10,000 additional soldiers arrived at Yining to beef up security, while in Beijing, the Uighur Islamist organizations took credit for several bomb attacks.

This Asian test-bed is supporting the emergence of a new type of radicalism. Sunni-ite and ideologically conservative, it is supranational in its recruitment and in its ideology. It does not emanate out of scissions in the great Islamists organizations, but from a radicalization of the Afghan Talebans, from their sanctuaries and their ties with small terrorist and mafia groups, marginalized and radicalized by repression (as in Egypt and Algeria), in a context of economic and financial globalization, as well as from the circulation of militants who have lost their territories. The principal characteristic of these networks (except in Central Asia and Egypt) is that they recruit, establish their bases, and act at the margins of the Arab-Muslim world. In addition to the Egyptians, Pakistanis, Sudanese, Yemenites, and Filipinos, recently there has been a wave of immigration to Great Britain and the United States. Operations take place in Egypt, certainly, in Algeria and Central Asia, but also in the east and the south of Africa, in Yemen, Bangladesh, New York, etc.. The favorite "holy wars" are Kashmir, Afghanistan, Chechnya, the Caucasus and, now, China.

Taking advantage of economic liberalization, many former chiefs of the "holy war" have now transmuted into businessmen. They make up an "Islamo-business" world that has colonies in various sectors: Islamic financial institutions, Islamic garment industries, humanitarian and benevolent organizations, private schools, and so on. As political scientist Olivier Roy says, "Today's Islamic actors are working for liberalism and against state control." They represent a globalization of Islam, de-territorialized, in an approach that ahs been uncoupled from the Middle East. A striking Westernization of Islamism is taking place or, more precisely, of the traditionally infra-state networks; tribes, Koran schools, etc. are linking up with worldwide networks that function in an extremely modern way and outside the control of any State authority. This evolution results from a history that began long ago. . .

Richard Labévière
Ferney-Volaire
October 11, 1999

Footnotes

1. An austere and puritanical fundamentalist movement founded in the 18th century by Mohammed bin Abdulwahhab; since then it has dominated Arabia as a result of the Saud dynasty's influence. The Wahhabis consider those who do not subscribe to their dogma to be heretics and apostates.

2. *Le Monde diplomatique*, September 1999.

# PREFACE

A specter haunts the world — the specter of religious fanaticism. Against a backdrop of economic and social woes, theocratic ideologies have declared a cold war on the democracies. Fanatical Christian, Jewish and Muslim cults are proliferating, along with related associations and criminal organizations. Those endowed with faith have a common goal: to end the separation of the Church and State, politics and religion, belief and citizenship. They have a horror of the Republican exception. In the name of "the dialogue between cultures" or "the right to be different," these fanatical movements favor the community over the subject and they preach ideologies of non-integration. The Islamists have become masters in this art of manipulation. In the Arab-Muslim world, and elsewhere, they are seeking to found a new apartheid between believers and nonbelievers; and their totalitarian ideology is sowing death. On February 13, 1994, my friend Ali S. was killed in a small city in western Algeria. An Islamist organization claimed responsibility for his assassination. His wife and three little daughters still live in Algeria. A printer, an intellectual Arabist and a French-speaker, my friend was profoundly Muslim but was savagely opposed to the Islamists, who are "mutilating their religion and betraying their country," as he used to tell anyone who would listen. I began this investigation to try to understand this unjust and absurd death. In Geneva, I found the traces — almost by chance — of several members of the organization that had taken responsibility for the assassination. The latter easily obtained asylum in Switzerland, from where they continue their political activities thanks to the protection and the money of Saudi benefactors. Saudi money became, in spite of me, the common thread that weaves throughout this investigation.

On November 17, 1997, 62 people were assassinated in a temple in Luxor by an Islamist commando. Inquiring into the motives and the supporters of this massacre for the magazine *Temps Présent* (affiliated with Switzerland's French-speaking television station), my research invariably led me back to Saudi Arabia. Many times over, American, European and Arab diplomats and public officials advised me to follow the trail of "the dollars of terror." Indeed, by reconstructing the financial circuits of terrorism, one has a better chance of understanding the true nature of Islamist ideology. Every time, I was brought back to both the official and the secret structures of Saudi finance. Every time, I stumbled on the fraternity of the Muslim Brothers. The representatives of this cult, with Saudi Arabia's assistance, are financing influential associations in Egypt — but also in Africa, in Asia and in Europe.

In the United States and in several European countries, representatives of the Muslim Brothers speak in the name of Islam and of the entire Muslim community. The confusion between *Islamism* and *Islam* is based on a triple ruse. Under cover of a spiritual quest, these agents of influence try to legitimate outright attacks on human rights, the bases of the republic. Under cover of transcendence, they gradually undermine the separation of the political and the religious, which is one of the bases of democracy. Under cover of tolerance, they work to propagate a fascistic, if not fascist, ideology.

Where does the money for this dangerous proselytism come from — the money that finances mosques and Koran schools, supports Islamist organizations, orchestrates the fight against the "impious" regimes of the Arab-Muslim world, and organizes the activism of certain Muslim communities of Europe? Since the ayatollahs came to power, all our suspicions have turned toward Iran and its Shiite revolution. However, four years of research have established that the real threat lies elsewhere: in Saudi Arabia and other oil monarchies allied with the United States. The greatest world power is fully aware of this development. Indeed, its information agencies have encouraged it. In certain parts of the world, the CIA and its Saudi and Pakistani homologues continue to sponsor Islamism.

Written on the basis of a hundred interviews and numerous journalistic investigations and after having consulted many national and
organizational archives, this book outlines an unfinished journey trail-
ing "the dollars of terror." Riyadh, Islamabad, Cairo, Khartoum, Sanaâ,
Mogadishu, Washington, London, Zurich, Geneva: this course, guided
by discreet inquiries, deconstructs the generally accepted idea of America as a lighthouse of democracy for the world. It attempts to show
how America's imperial intention is fed by a "Lebanization" of the
world, and is extended through the introduction of State-based, authoritative and moralistic theological-political orders. Bound together
by the United States, this objective alliance with the Islamists is
masked by the new worldwide circuits of organized crime and a transnational hybrid of business and politics.

Ultimately, this is the cause for which Ali, the printer, was assassinated. I dedicate this investigation to his memory, to the future of his
wife and his daughters; and I hold in my thoughts Jean-Claude L., Ma-
rina Vargas Henriquez and Thierry Masselot as well.

# Chapter I
## The Nairobi and Dar es Salaam Attacks

> "Superstition is the surest means of controlling the masses. Under the banner of religion, it would be easy sometimes to make men adore their kings as gods, and sometimes to make them hate them and curse them as permanent plagues of the human species."
>
> Spinoza

Nairobi, Friday August 7, 1998.

It was 10:35 when a violent explosion ripped through the business district of the Kenyan capital, between the city hall and the railway station. Black smoke engulfed the entire downtown area and the great Uhuru park.

At the intersection of Haile-Selassi and Moï avenues, it was war! Silhouettes staggered about, or stood petrified at the edge of pools of blood; others fled, uttering shrieks and undecipherable cries. The rear wall of the tower housing the United States embassy was demolished and a small adjoining building was reduced to a smoking heap of concrete.

The shock was so great that every window within a radius of 1000 feet was shattered. In the embassy parking lot, the hulks of cars continued burning. Around an enormous crater blasted into the pavement, stupefied witnesses were repeating, "car bomb, car bomb . . ."

The Kenyan Red Cross arrived immediately. The howls of sirens blended with the metallic rotations of the army helicopters that followed one after another. Apocalypse!

Mrs. Prudence Bushnell, the Ambassador of the United States, exited the building, supported by two young men, her suit spattered with blood. Marines armed with machine guns deployed themselves around the embassy. Some survivors were extracted from the debris but the corpses piled up, before being carried away in Red Cross trucks. The first tally counted about sixty victims. It would go up, in fact, to 263 fatalities, including 12 American nationals plus more than 5,500 wounded.

Precisely four minutes later, some 500 miles away, the same scenario was replayed on a street in the embassy district of Dar es Salaam, the capital of Tanzania. A tank-truck that had pulled up alongside the building housing the American representatives exploded, obliterating the building's façade. The toll: ten dead, a hundred wounded. Unlike in Nairobi, none of the victims was American; but the total body count was still the highest since the suicide attack against the quarters of the American troops in Beirut in 1983, in which 241 marines were killed.

As always in such a case — and it is strange that the press is astonished by this every time — the attacks appeared to have been perpetrated by an unknown group. According to the Arab daily newspaper *Al-Hayat*, its Cairo office received an anonymous call on Saturday, August 8, claiming the two explosions in the name of an "Islamic Army for the Liberation of Muslim Holy Places."

The same claim was transmitted to the office of an international press agency in Dubaï. By telephone, the anonymous interlocutor specified that one attack was carried out by "a son of Saudi Arabia," and the other by "a son of Egypt."

The day before the two attacks, the French Press Agency office in Cairo had received an statement (dated August 4) from the Egyptian armed Islamist organization "Jihad," saying that, "The American government, in coordination with the Egyptian government, has arrested three of our brothers in an Eastern European country and extradited them to Egypt. One of the three is called Tarek. He was arrested while he was with his Albanian wife in an Eastern European country known for its hostility toward the Muslims. This crime comes less than two months after the arrest of four Egyptian brothers in Albania. We want to inform the Americans that we have received their message and that we are preparing the response. Be well advised, we will write it, with the assistance of God, in the language that they understand."

Independently of the facts that the FBI's investigation would establish, the harsh reactions and the various explanations that were hastily suggested underscored the United States' embarrassment over the rise to power of a threat that they themselves had unleashed at the end of the Second World War. This policy was at its height during the

Afghanistan War (1979-1986), when the Red Army was faced with a myriad of underground groups that the Western press hastily baptized "freedom fighters." With the assistance of the Saudi and Pakistani secret services, the CIA armed and trained Afghan resistance fighters who would prove to be the most radical Islamists[1] in the world.

Obsessed by their confrontation with the Soviets, the Pentagon strategists would bet without any hedging on the Islamic religion, and would invent a fearsome war machine against the Red Army: armed Islamism. The sentence "In God We Trust," inscribed on the dollar bill — emblematic symbol of global capitalism — recalls that the lay founders of the American Republic were never shy to seek divine protection for the success of their companies. U.S. diplomacy is in the habit of using religious movements against Communism and any other obstacle to its hegemonic objectives.

After the collapse of the Soviet empire, this policy persisted without any major setback until the Gulf War. Mainly intended to safeguard the American oil supply, that police action caused a great trauma in the Arab-Muslim world. Armed Islamism then started to question the guidance of its protective father. The fatal bomb attack perpetrated right in the center of New York on February 26, 1993, sounded the hour of truth. Other violent incidents would be targeted against the American military presence in Yemen, Somalia and Saudi Arabia.

The attacks in Nairobi and Dar es Salaam are part of the ongoing "blow-back" effect. Shortly after the Gulf War, armed Islamism turned against its principal creator who, in spite of all, did not give up his paternalistic reflex. Indeed, although in the uncomfortable position of the attacker attacked, the United States still continues unabated its policy of supporting the multifarious explosion of an ascendant Islamism, its terrorist excesses and its business networks that are extremely ramified (if not entirely melded into the circuits of the legal economy).

Without suggesting that the CIA's hand is behind every acceleration of the historical process, without succumbing to the paranoiac view of "the great conspiracy," our research continually ended up pointing more or less directly to American responsibility, to more or less convergent interests and to a more or less controlled utilization, in many theatres, of Islamist operations.

A consequence of a foreign policy that is increasingly privatized — where one can no longer be sure who exerts the real decision-making power — American responsibility can be detected, at the same time, in the obdurate war that has been going on between the Islamists and the Egyptian power since 1992; in the fatal advance of the Algerian Armed Islamic Groups (AIG) and their attacks in France during the summer of 1995; in the establishment of Islamist sanctuaries in Bosnia, in Chechnya, Albania and the Philippines; but also in new hotbeds like Madagascar, South Africa, and Brazil.

Other Nairobi's and Dar es Salaam's, unfortunately, will undoubtedly take place, but the conversion of the Islamists' business networks within the international structures of organized crime is still more dangerous to the world order. Here again, the Islamist strategies converge with the interests of imperial America, which feeds on both a globalization of the liberal economy and a fragmentation of territorial sovereignties.

The United States has given its unconditional support to the kingdom of Saudi Arabia (one of the most reactionary regimes on the planet) since its foundation in 1932; and it has recently expressed again a strange tolerance for the delirious regime of the Taleban, those students in Muslim theology who are the new Masters of Afghanistan. With the attacks in Nairobi and Dar es Salaam, the American sponsorship of Islamism has reached one of its ultimate heights.

After these two attacks, the White House spokesman declared: "Given the simultaneity of the two explosions and the nature of the targets, it is reasonable to consider that they are terrorist actions and that they are connected." A few hours after this official statement, the United States embassy in Uganda would be closed and the security reinforced around the American embassies in every capital in the region.

Later on, following new threats, the embassies in Islamabad, Sanaâ and Tirana would be evacuated; and the one in Cairo would be transformed into a fortified camp. the State Department at once raised several analogies between this terrorist operation (which it considered to have been well-coordinated and well-planned), and the explosion that killed seven Americans in a Saudi military training center in Riyadh, in November 1995.

But the June 24, 1996 attack against the American base of Khobar — also in Saudi Arabia — was the most disconcertingly similar to the events of Nairobi and Dar es Salaam. Parked near the perimeter of the base, a truck full of explosives blew up the military quarters, costing nineteen American soldiers their lives.

After the incident, the Saudi authorities did not show a great determination to collaborate with the FBI investigators who were dispatched on the spot. Almost casually, they announced that they had arrested all the culprits: four opponents to the monarchy who, after a confession recorded on national television, were quickly decapitated before the American investigators could interview them...

In their televised confessions, the four convicts admitted to having acted deliberately against "the monarchy that had sold out to the evil empire." They were grateful to inscribe their actions in the history of the "holy war" declared on the United States by Osama bin Laden, the famous Islamist chief living in exile in Afghanistan. From his refuge in Kandahar, in the heart of the zone controlled by the Taleban, bin Laden denied any direct implication in these attacks (although he rejoiced that they had taken place).

If the State Department's suspicions, relayed by editorialists worldwide, converged on Osama bin Laden, it is also because he had recently renewed the threats against U.S. interests that he has regularly uttered since the Gulf War. "If Allah so wishes, our next victory will make American forget the horrors of Vietnam and of Beirut.... I predict a black day for America, and the end of the Union as the United States breaks into separate entities and withdraws from our holy ground, gathering up the bodies of their children to take them back home," he prophesied to a team from ABC-TV, on May 28, 1998, from his Afghan stronghold.

Who is this man who suddenly became Public Enemy Number One of the United States, and therefore of the whole world? The son of a family of Yemeni origin that made a colossal fortune in construction and public works in Saudi Arabia, Osama bin Laden has become an essential contact for most of the Islamist movements in the world since the war between Afghanistan and the Russians. Trained by the CIA, he was one of the top agents recruiting Arab volunteers for the great crusade against the Communist invaders.

A pure product of the American secret services — in full agreement with their Saudi and Pakistani homologues — he used money from his family (which had settled in Saudi Arabia) and from the monarchy to arm and train these Arab volunteers, the famous "Afghans" of the CIA that one finds today within the armed Islamist groups in Algeria and Egypt, and also in Yemen, Sudan and the Philippines.

After Afghanistan's first war against the Russians, he continued to furnish "Afghan" weapons and "soldiers" to the Taleban militia, always with the triple approval, discreet but quite real, of the Pakistani, Saudi and American services. Taking advantage of his family's many business connections, his various channels currently allow the Taleban to export the morphine base that today accounts for 80% of European heroin consumption.

In Yemen, Osama bin Laden controls the principal routes of qât, the hallucinogenic leaf consumed in the Horn of Africa and the southern part of the Arabic peninsula. Lastly, in Sudan, his money is thriving in various highway construction and infrastructure programs, agricultural establishments and real estate projects. Today he is sitting on a personal fortune of three billion dollars. . . which has earned him the nickname, "Banker of the Jihad."

Although he officially forfeited his Saudi nationality in 1994, he continues to maintain — according to the Egyptian and British information services — regular relations with his Saudi family in Jeddah, with the various financial companies that the family controls worldwide, and with the Saudi and Pakistani secret services. Lastly, bin Laden maintains friendly relations with his Afghan host, the all-powerful Mullah Omar, chief of the Taleban. The two men now have family ties, since one of the Afghan leader's sisters has become bin Laden's sixth wife.

In an interview published by the Pakistani daily newspaper *The News*, shortly after the Nairobi and Dar es Salaam attacks, Mullah Omar exonerated his friend and brother-in-law, asking: "How can a man living as a refugee in Afghanistan organize bombings in remote Africa?" The same day, the spokesman for the religious militia, Abdul Hai Mutmaent, declared to the Agence France Presse that "any suggestion aiming to establish the implication of Osama bin Laden is a matter of groundless propaganda, with the intention of defaming the Taleban's 'guest.'"

Saudi Arabia, one of the three states with Pakistan and the United Arab Emirates to recognize the Taleban regime, reacted very timidly to the attacks. Riyadh published a statement containing only a formal denunciation of terrorist violence. During the Council of Ministers on August 10, the crown prince Abdallah condemned terrorism "wherever it comes from and whatever the circumstances." This official Saudi declaration was accompanied by a call for the American and Israeli governments to intensify their efforts to establish an equitable and global peace in the Middle East.

The Saudi press made much of the spectacular magnitude of the incidents and the scope of the support that must have been behind them. It mentioned bin Laden only by allusion, without mentioning his extremely wealthy and powerful Saudi family. The claim by the "Islamic Army of Liberation of the Holy Places" was quoted only by the newspaper *Al-Sharq Al-Awsat*, whose editorialist concluded: "The United States, as the premier world power, must prevent such acts and try to contain better the problems that affect the world, instead of obscuring them. . ."

Only the Afghan and Saudi responses so distinctly minimized bin Laden's role. Abruptly elevated to the dignified position of public enemy number one, in just a few days the Saudi became a media phenomenon all around the planet, recalling the Carlos effect of the 1970's and 1980's when governments and the media blamed Carlos for every terrorist attack in the world.

According to the Emergency Response and Research Institute (ERRI), a terrorism research center based in Chicago, in June 1998 bin Laden went to Peshawar, Pakistan to take part in an assembly of Egyptian, Palestinian, Jordanian, Lebanese and Saudi armed Islamist organizations. At this meeting, intended to build an operational "Islamist Internationale," bin Laden supposedly declared — according to the same institute — that the anti-American attacks of recent years were no longer sufficient and that it was time now to start "the real battle."

The existence of a "bin Laden trail" and of armed Islamist networks in several countries does not mean that this "organization" is like an actual "*Internationale*," designed along the same model as the legendary Komintern, a pyramidal organization functioning as the nerve center of all terrorist activities. This fantasy of a central command organizing all the attacks very often coincides with that of the Iranian bogeyman that is brandished every time a bomb explodes anywhere and we have no other explanation.

*Foreign Report*, the London bulletin published by Jane's, quoted a source from one of the Middle East counter-espionage services on August 13 and indicated that bin Laden is supposed to have concluded an anti-American pact in February 1998 with a top leader of the Iranian "Revolutionary Guards." The *Wall Street Journal* of August 11 considered that "in spite of the attention paid to the moderate Iranians and to the thaw of Irani-American relations, it is completely plausible that Iran could be behind the latest anti-American attacks. Legitimately, these explosions could be the action of the Iranian radical wing that is firmly opposed to the openness currently proposed by the new president Mohammed Khatami." Several capitals, including Tel-Aviv, also accused Iran, speculating that the events were related to the confrontation between the radicals and the moderates. Always inclined to see the hand of Tehran when an attack is made anywhere in the world, the U.S. State Department also officially considered this hypothesis, which had already been advanced at the time of the anti-American attacks in Saudi Arabia.

Since the ayatollahs came to power in 1979, all suspicion inevitably turns toward Iran and toward Shiite fundamentalism whenever terrorism rears its head. However, the principal threat lies elsewhere, particularly among the solid allies of the United States: Saudi Arabia, Pakistan and the Taleban of Afghanistan.

Among its many consequences, the Afghanistan War confirmed Sunni Islam in its claim of hegemony — especially out of distrust for the heretic Shiites — over all the Arab-Muslim world. All those who have subsidized or carried out terrorist actions since the beginning of the 1990's are of Sunni persuasion, and invariably have ties to the networks of veterans of the "holy war" of Afghanistan.

Trained by the CIA, the "Afghans" have been successively implicated in the bombing of the World Trade Center in New York (1993), in the destruction of Egypt's embassy in Islamabad (1995), in the attempted murder of Egyptian President Mubarak in 1996 in Addis-Ababa, in the various attacks on hotels and tourist sites in Ethiopia and Eritrea, as well as in the abominable slaughter at Luxor in November 1997.

What are the Sunni "Afghans" trying to accomplish? Their main goal is to increase the destabilization of every country they have penetrated, especially of Egypt, epicenter of the Arab-Muslim world. Solidly based on their infiltration of the West and supported by the Taleban in the East, they seek to attack from both sides the Saudi monarchy — self-proclaimed guardian of the holy places of Islam and struggling with King Fahd's failure to clarify the succession. Pakistan is the third bridgehead of this war of liberation.

The "Islamic Army for the Liberation of Muslim Holy Places," which claimed the Nairobi and Dar es Salaam attacks, has Jerusalem in mind for the long term but, in the immediate future, is focused on the two holy mosques of Mecca and Medina in Saudi Arabia. Saudi Arabia, in the psyche of the "Afghans," represents the heart of the Caliphate. Reconquering this political and religious birthplace would constitute the first stage of the restoration of the *Oumma*, the community of believers.

In this configuration, Kenya and Tanzania are enemies on two accounts: not only are both states traditionally allied with Israel, out of fear of Arab expansionism, but they are used as an undercover base for the animist movements of southern Sudan — which is in rebellion against the Islamist regime of Khartoum, a friend and host of the "Afghans." The United States is directly involved in supporting this armed rebellion.

Indeed, the trail of the Nairobi and Dar es Salaam attacks leads to Sudan. The Islamist regime of Khartoum is going through its most serious political crisis since it was established in 1989. Religious and military clans, tribal and mafioso cliques are vying to control the business channels, where one finds so many representatives of bin Laden. In this low-intensity war, the Sudanese security services are all-powerful.

But before we can reconstruct the mechanism by which the "convincing attacks" on Nairobi and Dar es Salaam were carried out, we must examine the context. Why did the United States and Saudi Arabia sponsor Sunni Islamism and its most radical factions, before the CIA's "Afghans" had penetrated nearly all the terrorist networks of the Middle East?

Their banker, bin Laden, deserves close attention. Indeed, how does this "Most Wanted," trained by the CIA, still in touch with the Saudi and Pakistani services and living under the protection of the Taleban, stay out of reach of his former bosses?

How can we understand the contradictions of Uncle Sam, victim of the religious fanatics that he himself armed? This question touches on more than the attacks in Nairobi and Dar es Salaam. Do the contradictions mask further subterfuges, or it is simply a matter of defending economic and strategic interests?

Between the United States and Saudi Arabia there was, in 1945, a pact that sealed political and economic relations. The feudal monarchy bought its legitimacy as ruler of the holy sites by financing most, if not all, of the Sunni Islamist groups. We will analyze the geopolitics of the house of Saud, its diplomatic priorities and its methods of influence based on money. Saudi money is heavily invested in Egypt, in particular, where religious violence bears the hallmark of the fraternity of the Muslim Brothers. We will see how the headquarters of the contemporary Islamist movements is also conducting the "holy war" through its banking and financial relations, not only in the Arab-Muslim countries but also in Europe.

Given the expansion of Islamism, how should we assess the attitude of the premier world power? Between the options of the Pentagon and the CIA, the State Department, the White House and Congress, who controls its foreign policy? Who decides? Ultimately, is there a pilot at the helm of the American aircraft?

The political inconsistencies of U.S. foreign policy are particularly salient in Central Asia, theater of a new "grand jeu" between the great powers. Since the Soviet withdrawal from Afghanistan, the American services have supported the Taleban tyranny; the mercenaries of the big oil companies make the law there, seeking to control the old "silk road," the royal highway that leads, no doubt, to the gates of China.

On November 17, 1997, 62 people were massacred by an Islamist commando in a temple in Luxor, in Upper Egypt. Bin Laden' "Afghans" were behind this new massacre, and they were prepared from London a month before, right under the nose of the British police.

Between their Egyptian redoubts and their Taleban stronghold, the "Afghans" have established sanctuaries in new territory. Through fluid, privatized networks, the "new Afghans" are inventing the terrorism of tomorrow: an Islamist moneymaking enterprise that is secularized in the transnational channels of organized crime and finds sanctuary in the world's tax havens.

The voyage that we are about to begin will arrive at one conclusion: Islamism is soluble in the market economy. The theological-political order that is promoted by the Islamist ideology is perfectly in tune with the requirements of American capitalism. The imperial intention of the United States feeds on any weakening of the sovereign and territorial principles of organization that buttress our national political entities. This loss of political jurisdiction heralds the unilateral reign of uncontrollable globalization, in the hands of business mafias and religious fanatics.

Footnotes

1.  Maxime Rodinson defines "Islamism" as "a political current inspired by Islam, intended to answer every social and political problem by means of religion and, simultaneously, to restore all the dogmas."

Chapter II

AN AMERICAN FRIEND AT THE PALACE OF NATIONS

> "The United States very quickly understood that Islamic rebellion would be a secret Afghan hornet's nest that the Russians would not recover from."
>
> Alexandre Del Valle

They called it the "Snake Bar" because of its sinuous length. There, the delegates of 53 member states and a few hundred representatives of the major nongovernmental organizations were waiting for one of the last meetings of the night, as the 50th Session of the U.N. Commission on Human Rights came to an end on April 18, 1997. For nine years, I had been following the Commission's work assiduously, not only because it is the most powerful evidence of the United Nations' work in Geneva, but also because it constitutes a gathering of diplomats, lawyers, representatives of nongovernmental organizations, heads of liberation movements, human rights activists, men and women who are experts of every kind, unique in the world.

This session confirmed the traditional chasm that exists between the countries of the North — laying more emphasis on civil and political rights — and those of the South — more eager to strive for the right to development. The Commission was drawing to a close, as was the day. The various groups had completed their final negotiations and the deal-making on the side was winding down, each party considering that as much as possible had been gained, while the essentials had been preserved. People relaxed, knowing that there would be no more changes as the moment approached for the vote on a draft resolution condemning such and such government, and sparing such and such other.

Obsessed by Cuba (as they are every year), the American delegates understood that, this time, they were about to experience a historic reversal. Their resolution, which had regularly succeeded in condemning Fidel Castro's regime for more than 30 years, was going to be rejected in just a few minutes. The first councilor of the Permanent Mission of the United States to the U.N. had just given his ambassador the latest calculation of the anticipated vote: 19 countries vs. 16 would reject the American text, and the remaining 18 would abstain. A triumph for the *Lider maximo*, a snub for Uncle Sam!

Within the American delegation there was an atmosphere of resignation, halfway between incomprehension and the usual anti-European resentment. I knew that I could approach Greg,[1] the special councilor for the Arab world, as he sat drinking his double scotch. A very well-informed Arabist, he had worked as a CIA analyst for many years. And although he claims not to have any further contact with them these days, he still maintains the "culture of the big house." "Certainly, we're losing face on Cuba, but once again we've avoided the worst for our Saudi friends who are under investigation in confidential proceedings. . . . Sure, as far as violating basic human rights, the keepers of the oil wells are guiltier than our old Cuban adversaries. . . . Business is business."

Night had fallen an hour since on the park surrounding Lake Geneva, which we surveyed through the big picture windows of the new wing of the Palace of Nations. I pointed out to Greg that America's unconditional defense of Saudi interests meant that, in fact, they were providing cover for the principal supporters of Islamist terrorism. "One day, they will end up selling you the rope to hang yourselves." "That's Lenin's theory," Greg answered cheerfully. Like most Harvard alumni, he likes historical-ideological references.

Why do the same thing with the Egyptian Islamists? How could Sheik Omar Abdel Rahman, spiritual guide of Gama'a islamiya, quietly make his way to the United States while he was being sought actively by all the police forces of Egypt and the Middle East? Officially a diplomat, the political councilor uncrossed his legs and adjusted his blazer before twirling the ice cubes in his glass three times.

"By the most legal means in the world, dear boy, with an entry visa delivered by my country's embassy in Khartoum, where the blind old sheik was staying at the time!" Greg paused for effect. "We are always loyal to our allies. Sometimes they are sons of b_'s, but they are *our* sons of b_'s. That's the game! Gama'a and their spiritual guide gave us a big hand with the Soviets during the Afghanistan War. What could be more natural than to return the favor in some small way? Besides, the State Department thought, at that time, that the old sheik would be more dangerous and more harmful stewing in the Sudan. This trade-off was just the lesser evil. . ."

The fatal attack on New York's World Trade Center was also only a trick of history for Greg, who wonders — as a number of my *confrères* have done — whether Sheik Abdel Rahman is indeed the mastermind who sponsored the attack.

"According to my information," Greg added, the "World Trade Center bombing was planned and carried out by militants from a group of 'the Egyptian Islamic Jihad,' who wanted to break the ties that had existed between the Gama'a and the American administration since the Afghanistan War."

But now the Afghanistan War is finished. The withdrawal of the Soviet army and then the fall of the Berlin Wall definitively ended the Cold War, so why persist in maintaining relations with most of the Islamist movements in the world, if not for obvious economic reasons?

"Precisely!" smiled Greg, before being cut short by the bell that indicated the meeting's resumption. Emptying his glass in one draught before joining his ambassador who, like thirty other delegations, was about to vote against Sudan — accused of "summary and extra-judiciary executions, arbitrary arrests, forced displacement of populations, torture and slavery," Greg promised me we'd continue this conversation, telling me simply: "This complicity with the Islamists is an old story."

This "old" — and oh, so dialectical — story can be summarized in three critical moments: the Afghanistan War, or how the United States turned Islamism against the Soviet army; the oil rush, or how the United States supported Islamism to guarantee its energy needs; and the fall of the House of Nasser, or how the United States channeled Islamism against Arab nationalism. These three trends are still playing out their effects. The end of the East-West confrontation did not render them obsolete, but it has released "fluid wars" against a background of globalization where any means of attack is permitted, especially when big American corporations use certain Islamist factions as watchdogs to protect the new economic reality.

A few days later, Greg left the United States Mission to the U.N. for the American embassy in a country on the Arabian peninsula, to work there on one of his preferred assignments: the difficult succession of King Fahd of Arabia.

We would pick up this interrupted conversation one year later, in the Yemeni capital, at an international meeting on the security of the Arabian peninsula. The discussion naturally turned to the revelations of the former CIA director, Robert Gates. In his memoirs,[2] Gates admitted that U.S. special services had been active in Afghanistan alongside the local mujaheddin . . . six months before the Soviet intervention! This revelation was confirmed to *Le Nouvel Observateur*[3] by Zbigniew Brzezinski who, at the time, was advising President Carter on security issues. "Yes, according to the official version of the story, the CIA's assistance to the mujaheddin began during 1980, i.e. after the Soviet army had invaded Afghanistan on December 24, 1979. But the reality, kept secret until the present, is quite different. It was on July 3, 1979 that President Carter signed the first directive on clandestine assistance to those opposing the pro-Soviet regime of Kabul. And that day, I wrote to a note to the president, in which I explained to him that in my opinion this assistance was going to lead to a military intervention by the Soviets."

The stage was set. The first Afghanistan War provided the backdrop for America's creeping support of the Islamists. In Afghanistan, the United States reused the old prescription that had succeeded so well for them in Saudi Arabia in the 1930's: to accommodate tribalism, religious fanaticism and oil interests.

The end of the Cold War and the post-war period of the Gulf did not give way to the heralded "new international order." The American will for exclusive control of questions of defense, energy and the Israeli-Palestinian conflict went nowhere. Respect for international law and human rights did not progress, terrorism did not disappear and the world was rocked by the most insane commercial competition that it had ever seen. In this context of economic war where all's fair, the United States devotes most of its foreign policy to the conquest of new markets. Priority is given to commercial and financial investments over any other consideration; and this is a central tenet in the policy that uses radical Islamists as a subcontractor for the American influence in the Mediterranean, Central Asia and the Far East. This approach, which worked wonders in Afghanistan during the "holy war" against the Communists, was invented in the 1930's in Saudi Arabia. The pact sealed on board the *Quincy* between President Roosevelt and King Ibn Sa'ud was already an exchange of oil for security and political protection. From that point forward, the Americans and Saudis would play Islamism and all other forms of religious fanaticism against secular and progressivist forms of Arab nationalism. Still today, the Islamists are working, consciously or not, toward the establishment of a *pax americana* that feeds on a "Lebanization" of the world.

The Afghanistan War offered the United States a historical opportunity of the type that does not come along twice in a century. It enabled the U.S. to deflate the specter of the "Great American Satan" decried by Islamists the whole world over since the Iranian Revolution, and to forge with yesterday's enemies a "new alliance" that would be almost planetary in scope. This outrageous reversal, that the most facetious of Pentagon strategists never would have dared to imagine, does not mean, however, that the United States could count on an "Islamist *Internationale*" organized like a kind of "Green Orchestra" (the color of Islam) that might intervene in a homogeneous and coordinated way at all points across the planet.

My American friend always warned to me against these two misconceptions: that of an Islamist Comintern, so beloved by systematic minds, and the very French myth of a monolithic American foreign policy, a kind of "malignant genius" of international relations. On this last point, Greg (and several enlightened diplomats) used their science to explain why, when it comes to external decision-making, the American executive branch is like the layers of an indigestible baklava pastry: the White House, Congress, the National Security Council, special interest groups, the CIA, NSA, big private firms, etc.. The lowest common denominator to these various entities would appear to be guided more by the laws of commercial competition and the conquest of new markets than by the intention to define a new Wilsonian vision or, conversely, a final concerted isolationist retreat.

Therefore, *a priori* there could be no American plot, nor a green

*Internationale!* After one of his visits to the University of Vincennes, ge-ographer Yves Lacoste gave me pretty much the same view. "Although nostalgic for the *Oumma* (the community of believers), the Arab-Muslim world is worked over by various Churches, and not only those of the different Sunni or Shiite forms of Islam — and besides, the latter have highly hierarchical clergies — but also by those of various brother-hoods whose networks extend in many countries. The same holds true for the various Islamist groups, whether of Sunni or Shiite faith. In fact, there are quite different Churches, clandestine or already recognized (depending on the states) that each have their international networks and their holy sites, or that dispute the most important of them."[4]

This essential review of the facts, which should prevent the resur-gence of any "essentialist" hypothesis (according to which the very na-ture of Islam, its founding texts and its teachings ineluctably would produce the conditions of Islamism and of terrorism), does not prevent us from putting into perspective the goals, both short- and long-term, of these Islamist groups.

"It is known that these groups aim to impose the *sharia*, Koranic law, as the only legal code in all the Muslim (or considered as such) states," notes Lacoste,[5] "and especially, they are fighting to achieve an enormous geopolitical plan, to regroup all the Muslims, a billion men and women, in spite of their very great linguistic and cultural diversity, into the same political unit. Then it would be possible to restore the authority of the caliphate (abolished by the Kemalist revolution in 1923) or to place it under the leadership of a college of scholars, all of whom would be both political leaders and theologians. The desire to abolish the borders (that are blamed on European colonialism) separat-ing the Muslim states from each other is only one aspect of the Islamist groups' geopolitical strategy. They also intend to support the expan-sion of Islam in every country, including in those where it is presently very much a minority, and they oppose by various means the integra-tion of Muslims émigrés and their children into non-Muslim societies." Reactivated through the "holy war" of Afghanistan, in its ideological as well as logistical dimensions, this twofold strategy happens to accord with the interests of the United States.

Here again, we must guard against a hasty, mechanistic interpre-tation that would suggest the existence of a hidden plot. We will see how "a trick of history" has produced a convergence of interests that we call the "new alliance," contracted in Afghanistan.

Sealing Uncle Sam's reconciliation with the Islamists, this "new alliance" is highly effective since it coordinates three different types of causality. The first is the most obvious, since it classically reproduces the logics of confrontation of the Cold War. Still traumatized by their humiliating rout by the Vietnamese, and to give the Soviets a taste of their own medicine, the Americans lured the Russian bear into the Afghan hornet's nest that would precipitate the collapse of the Communist camp.

Internal to the Muslim world, the second area of causality rests on the ancestral confrontation between the Sunni universe and the Shiite minority. As guardian of the holy places of Islam, Saudi Arabia has done everything in its power to counter the Iranian influence that was growing since the 1979 Islamic revolution. Iran and Saudi Arabia are playing a high-stakes Islamist game, where the winner will embody the political future of the "true Islam." The game is played by supporting any movement likely to help "the cause." Iran, however, has confined itself to forms of assistance that it can, to some extent, control, whereas the oil monarchies have given and are still giving without counting, and without requiring any accounting. "Aid to Islamist movements," notes Lacoste, "comes on the one hand from the organization Rabitat ul-alam al-islami,[6] and on the other hand from Islamic banking syndicates, including Faysal Finance and al-Baraka. This aid, which started in the 1970's, accelerated in the 1980's with backing from the United States, which used it as an antidote for Communist subversion. Since the collapse of the Soviet Union and the Gulf War, this aid is intended above all to counter the influence of the Iranian revolution."[7]

Pakistan, finally, is trying to seize the opportunity to secure its western flank in order to concentrate the bulk of its military clout on the confrontation with India, especially in Kashmir. With the assistance of the all-powerful Pakistani special services, ISI (Inter Service Intelligence), the Americans are arming and training the most radical Islamist factions, in particular that of Gulbuddin Hekmatyar, a Pashtun, to the detriment of the moderate Massoud Ahmed-Shah, who is Tajik. With backing from the American special services, ISI chooses to promote the Pashtuns because the same ethnic group dominates the government, the army and the Pakistani secret service.

In 1989, when the Soviets were packing up their bags, the "holy war" against the infidels quickly turned into an ethnic confrontation. The Gulf War increased these tensions. Hekmatyar, the Americans' man, sided with the Iraqi camp against the Arab-Western coalition. Anxious to perpetuate the Pashtun solidarity that protects its western border, Pakistan quickly proposed to the Americans a way to replace him. The ISI enrolled thousands of students in the "medressehs," the region's Koran schools, and there provided the training and the military logistics necessary for a new holy war. Trained by the same American-Pakistani duo, the Taleban thus made their entry onto the Afghan stage, fired up with a puritanism that commands them to keep women from going out, children from flying kites, and birds from singing. This rigor delights the guardians of *Wahhabi* orthodoxy and keeps the taps of Saudi financial assistance flowing.

These theology students, who now control almost three quarters of the country, have appeared at the crucial moment when the American oil companies are confirming that the Central Asian zone surrounding the Caspian Sea will become the principal strategic area of the next millennium. It contains sizable energy reserves, at least as great as those of the area around the Arabian-Persian Gulf.

With the end of the Cold War and in spite of the disappearance of the Communist threat, the "new alliance" with the Islamists thus gained a second wind. The American calculation is simple: the energy route (gas and oil pipelines) from this new *eldorado* must inevitably pass through Afghanistan, and the Taleban will be its guardians. The convergence between American interests and the Islamists thus survives the fall of the Berlin Wall, thanks to the god, oil.

Back to square one! Indeed, it all started with oil. Betting on the young Saudi monarchy's distrust for the old colonial powers, in 1933 Standard Oil of California obtained the first oil concession in the eastern area of Saudi Arabia for a payment of 50,000 pounds sterling, for a period of 66 years. The company obtained a new concession in 1939, for the same duration, for a unit representing more than 744,000 square miles in the eastern part of the country. Meanwhile, Standard Oil of California allied itself with Texaco in 1944 to form a consortium dubbed Aramco (Arabian-American Oil Company). In 1948, Mobil Oil (Socony) and Standard Oil of New Jersey took a 40% stake in Aramco, thus finalizing its capitalization. One cannot insist enough on the importance of oil in the foreign policy choices made by the United States:

a "New Alliance" maybe, but an old story!

The Second World War demonstrated oil's vital importance to the operation of the Allies' war economy. The American forces were haunted by the notion that their energy reserves might be exhausted before the end of the conflict; this would remain an obsession of the American leaders of the post-war period. The modern economy, redeployed through the Marshall Plan, would be accompanied by the pursuit of war by other means. This effort would appear all the more vital since, at the Yalta Conference, February 4, 1945, the Americans and the Soviets had just divided the world into two zones of influence. An obsession in times of war, an obsession in times of peace, oil is one of the major elements of the United States economy. Americans represent only 5% of the planet's population today, but they consume almost a quarter of world production. The oil bill alone accounts for more than a third of the American trade deficit; oil irrigates the infrastructure of the country's economy. Prospecting, extraction, transport, refining and distribution are translated into econometric equations, which in turn evolve into domestic issues (if not national security issues).

But while this may be "economically reckless," oil has become "a total social fact" of American society. "The transport sector in 1990 absorbed more than 60% of consumption, including 42% for private cars alone (the U.S. has the lowest gas prices in the entire industrialized world)."[8] This consumption colors the everyday worldview, the culture; and it is a source of pride and national unity. Like the conquest of the West, the control of this "black gold" is enjoyed and publicized like the epic tale of a "new frontier" that is being relentlessly pushed back. It produces its own legends, its westerns and its heroes.

In the Pantheon of those who "made America," President Roosevelt occupies a unique position, since he played the role of the father of the great oil adventure. A few weeks before the Yalta Conference, the president read with the greatest attention Senator Landis's report on American interests in the Middle East. Fundamentally, this text (which became the White House bible on Arab affairs) predicted the imminent break-up of the "sterling zone" and the establishment of direct relations between Washington and the Arab countries. On his way back from Yalta, Roosevelt — who made a stopover in Egypt — asked the American consul in Jeddah to organize a meeting with the King of Saudi Arabia. The meeting took place on February 14, 1945, on board the *Quincy*, a cruiser anchored in the great lake Amer between Port-Saïd and the mouth of the Suez Canal. We owe the most detailed account of this interview to an expert on the Arab-Muslim and Turkish worlds, Jacques Benoist-Méchin.[9] The meeting put an end to what had been, for a century and a half, a private hunting preserve for His British Majesty. With all the honors due to the head of an important state, Ibn Sa'ud boarded the cruiser. A shade of fine white muslin was stretched across the bridge to allow to king to sleep in the open air during the crossing of the Red Sea. Very sure that this hospitality would not fail to have its effect on the old Bedouin, Roosevelt extended both his hands and exclaimed,

"So glad to meet you . . . What can I do for you?"

"But it is you who asked to see me," retorted the old warrior, adding, "I suppose that it is you who have something to ask of me!"

After this rather rough start, the two men talked for several hours in the shade of the artillery on the upper bridge. King Ibn Sa'ud remained inflexible on the future fate of the Jews of Palestine. Roosevelt asked him to accept this infusion of population while pointing out to him that it would constitute only a very small percentage of the total population of the Arab world. The president returned two or three times to the subject by different routes, but each time encountered a total and absolute rejection.

Attempting to relax the atmosphere, Roosevelt tackled a second subject, the American high command's need for harbor infrastructures in the Arab-Persian Gulf. The king was more conciliatory, although he asked for much in return. Lastly, the president broached the most important question, which he had kept for the end: oil. He wanted the kingdom to grant the United States a monopoly on the exploitation of all the oil-bearing layers discovered in Saudi Arabia.

Ibn Sa'ud, who had carefully prepared for the interview, negotiated hard on each American request. Finally, the discussion would lead to an agreement that has been baptized the "*Quincy* Pact." It is articulated around five sets of themes that still apply:

1) The stability of the kingdom is in the "vital interests" of the United States. In and of itself, the kingdom holds 26% of the world's proven oil reserves. Its importance as an essential supplier became clear to the Americans during the Second World War, when other sources of supply were cut off by the Japanese occupation. Tradition-

ally choosing a policy of moderate prices, the kingdom guarantees that the bulk of America's fuel needs will be met. In return, the United States ensures unconditional protection against any possible external threat. In 1991, American engagement in the second Gulf War constituted a spectacular illustration of "*Quincy* Pact." Ibn Sa'ud did not lose an inch of territory. The concessionary companies are to be tenants only. The duration of the concessions is to be sixty years. "Upon the expiry of the contracts, i.e. in the year 2005, the wells, the installations and the material are to return entirely to the monarchy's possession. The premium paid to the king is to go from 18 cents to 21 cents for every oil barrel exported from Arabia. The Aramco concession is to be extended to a territory covering 930,000 square miles."

2) By extension, the stability of the Arabian Peninsula is also in the "vital interests" of the United States. Indeed, American support of the kingdom is based not only on its capacity as oil supplier at moderate prices, but also on hegemonic power over the Arabian Peninsula. The United States thus jointly controls the priority task of the House of Saud's "Arab diplomacy": to guarantee the stability of the Peninsula and more generally of the entire area of the Gulf. "Since the first wells were beginning to be exploited," one oil expert specifies, "Aramco, the American governmental oil company, ensured the kingdom all kinds of legal, even military, aid in the dispute between the Sauds and the other emirates of the Peninsula." While it now takes other forms, this assistance is still topical.

3) An almost exclusive economic, commercial and financial partnership continues to link the two countries since the adoption of "*Quincy* Pact." The United States increases its oil purchases in exchange for more and more substantial deliveries of American weapons. Shortly after the Gulf War, the United States signed the largest contracts (and on exclusively political criteria) to the detriment, of course, of other members of the anti-Iraqi coalition. This preferential treatment of American contractors does not apply to the weapons sector alone. One may cite the example of the contract for modernizing the Saudi telephone network, allotted to an American firm in 1994, on the basis of a simple phone call from President Clinton, whereas other partners were objectively much better positioned. Because of pressures from the American government, the contract for refurbishing Saudia Airlines airliners in 1995 was given to Boeing and McDonnell Douglas, a prefer-

ence that was both technologically and economically unfounded. In return, experts estimate that some $350 billion (public and private) in Saudi funds are directly invested in the United States, especially in Treasury bills. One might easily think that the kingdom is maintaining this "American preference" as an insurance policy.

4) American non-interference in questions of Saudi domestic politics is the flip side of the American preference in economic, financial and commercial matters. Usually so prolix any time the question of human rights comes up anywhere in the world, the American government here observes a muteness that is both constrained and absolute. "The most powerful liberal democracy in the world is indeed allied with an absolute monarchy by divine right," comments a European diplomat, "a monarchy that is, on social and political matters, one of the most obscurantist regimes on earth." The United States government is unable to close this question, which constantly threatens to put it in an embarrassing position vis-à-vis the public opinion that is so quick to flare up over whatever indignities the media selects. "Indeed, the Saud monarchy is, today, hardly more justifiable than the Pahlavi one was in Iran, just before the Islamic revolution," adds the diplomat. Being unable to provide an adequate justification on this significant subject, the American government tries to minimize, if not to deny, the question that regularly comes up in "confidential proceedings" at the U.N. Commission on Human Rights. In addition, one is obliged to note that the American mass media, usually so attentive to these problems, do not get particularly agitated over these cases.

5) The only dark area in the "Quincy Pact" is the Palestinian question. This marks the limit of the American-Saudi partnership. Indeed, whereas President Roosevelt was not able to extract from King Ibn Sa'ud any agreement on the increase in Jewish immigration to Palestine, the kingdom never could obtain from Washington the least flexibility with regard to its policy of unconditional support for the State of Israel. While the American administration completely supports the House of Saud in its hegemonic rule over the Arabian Peninsula, it leaves it very little room for maneuver in the Israeli-Palestinian process. It is, however, within the narrow confines of this corridor that the Islamist movements are financed.

The discussion then turned to the construction of a Trans-Arabian pipeline, a tube some 1240 miles long, intended to connect the oil-producing region of Hasa to a port on the eastern Mediterranean. And Jacques Benoist-Méchin concludes that "In spite of the slightly rough turn that the conversation had taken at its beginnings, Roosevelt and Ibn Sa'ud were left enchanted with each other. They both had the impression that they had made an excellent deal."

An excellent deal, an unfailing alliance and an "old story," the pact sealed on board the *Quincy* marked a decisive break in the history of the international relations of the post-war period. Nothing would be the same any more. By evicting the British influence, this pact establishes the United States as the dominant partner in the Middle East game, to the detriment of the European states. Lastly, it ratifies a bargaining method that persists and continues to be used as the model for other agreements of the same type, especially in Central Asia.

This historical bargain would prove to have many consequences: black gold for the security, survival and continuity of what is one of the most reactionary religious dynasties in the world and, moreover, guardian of the holy places of Islam.

This last reason, too, is strategic on two accounts. By circumscribing the emergence of lay Arab nationalism, this protection also makes it possible to ensure the security of the state of Israel. These two requirements may, however, seem contradictory. We will see, on the contrary, how they connect the two sides of the same process whereby Islamism constitutes a common thread. On board the *Quincy*, the American president and the king of Saudi Arabia not only concluded an "excellent deal." They also secured an unfailing alliance that would lead them, one and the other, and their successors as well, to becoming the godfathers of Islamism.

## Footnotes

1. Fictitious name.

2. *From the Shadows*, Simon and Schuster, New York, 1997.

3. No 1732, January 15-21, 1998.

4. Interview on February 12, 1993.

5. Herodotus, "Churches and Geopolitics," *La Découverte*, 1st trimester 1990.

6. The World Islamic League, founded in 1963, which received funds from Aramco; the oil company was gradually nationalized between 1974 and 1980.

7. *Dictionnaire géopolitique des Etats 98*, Flammarion.

8. Louis Blin, *Le Pétrole du Golfe, guerre et paix au Moyen-Orient*, Maison-Neuve & Larose, 1996.

9. Jacques Benoist-Méchin, *Fayçal roi d'Arabie*, Albin Michel, 1975.

10. Jacques Benoist-Méchin, *Ibn Séoud ou la naissance d'un royaume*, Albin Michel, 1955.

# Chapter III
## ISLAMISM VERSUS ARAB NATIONALISM

> "The vast clandestine movement of the Muslim
> Brotherhood has many branches; no one knows for
> sure how many, but the sympathizers (who fluctu-
> ate) are certainly innumerable. It is difficult to assess
> the different factions that must exist within the lead-
> ership of this organization. But the one that domi-
> nates is a kind of archaïcizing Fascism, by which I
> mean the will to establish an authoritative and totali-
> tarian state whose political police would savagely
> maintain the moral and social order."
>
> Maxime Rodinson

Early in the 1950's, the Middle East was shaken by the forceful takeover of "free Egypt" by military officers and by Colonel Gamal Abdel Nasser's accession to power. Positioned as a geographical hyphen between Black Africa and Asia, at the maritime crossways between the Orient and the Occident, with the Suez Canal (the bridge to the Indies), Egypt — which was the first to be emancipated from the Ottoman yoke in 1805, has always been seen as the epicenter of the Arab-Muslim world.

It is precisely in connection with Egypt, at the time of the Suez incident, that the United States donned (and continued to wear until the last Gulf War) the uniform of gendarme of the Middle East. By halting the Franco-British intervention against the nationalization of the Suez Canal on November 1, 1956, they succeeded in ousting London and Paris from the Near-Eastern scene. On November 2 at 4:18 AM, the General Assembly of the United Nations, in an extraordinary meeting, adopted by a crushing majority the American resolution condemning the intervention and asking for the withdrawal of all the troops engaged. Washington's initiative won 64 votes, including that of the USSR. In addition to Great Britain and France, only Australia, New Zealand and Israel voted against. The international community got the message.

London and Paris pulled out. The United States wanted to show the Arab world that it is a better ally than the Soviet Union could ever be. At that time, and since the overthrow of King Farouk, Nasser enjoyed unlimited support from the CIA, in particular thanks to Kermit Roosevelt, Vice President of Gulf Oil and a former information agency liaison. In February 1958, Nasser created the ephemeral United Arab Republic (a fusion of Egypt and Syria), the first glimpse of Arab nationalism that was beginning to make itself felt on the international scene.

At first this emergence of Arab nationalism was welcomed by President Kennedy, who maintained a regular correspondence with Nasser. Washington has always delighted in defying the vestiges of European colonialism. As a former British colony, it always lends a hand to support the people's right to self-government. . . But this friendship would decline when the U.S. refused to help in constructing a high dam on the Nile at Aswan, and with Johnson's arrival at the White House.

Wishing to return to the bases of America's policy in the Middle East — in the spirit of the *Quincy* Pact — the new president's advisers were wary of Nasser's initiatives and chose to consolidate the alliances made with those oil monarchies considered to be more stable, and especially more economically profitable. The new king of Arabia, Fayçal, was invited to the United States in June 1966. He solemnly warned Johnson against Nasser's pro-Soviet inclinations, as Nasser was turning more and more to Moscow (not only for the construction of the Aswan Dam, but for weapons and for military aid for the Yemeni republicans since autumn 1962).

In September, a revolution led by the Yemeni colonel Sallal overthrew the Imam Badr, who had just succeeded his father in Sanaâ; this entangled Egypt in a bitter war that would drag on for five years. Nasser immediately joined the fray on the side of the insurgents who were proclaiming a republic, while Saudi Arabia armed and financed the royalists. In June 1967, some 68,000 Egyptian soldiers were still engaged in Yemen. This was the first time that the Egyptian army had fought against Muslims. At this point, Nasser clearly affirmed his desire for hegemony over all the Arab world. This confrontation between marxistic republicans and royalists, who were indebted to the oil monarchies of the Peninsula, sped the flight of "Arab nationalists" into the socialist camp.

The Arab world had its revolution and it established secular states and national institutions in opposition to the conservative regimes, not only in Egypt, but in Iraq, Syria, Tunisia and Algeria. "Initially, Nasser spoke of fighting the Arab reactionaries, of liquidating the imperialist bases in the Middle East and the economic influence of the Western owners, of the imperialist seizure of Arab oil, of unifying the Arab world and establishing socialism. Nothing in what Nasser had done for eleven years would have led anyone to believe that he was going to attack Israel. On the contrary, he seemed to have deferred indefinitely 'the liberation of Palestine.' In fact, the Israelis preferred to talk with the Arab conservatives," explains Eric Rouleau.[1]

For the third time in less than twenty years, the Jewish state and its Arab neighbors had a military clash at the beginning of June 1967. The Israeli army's victory was so sudden and so complete that it has almost made us forget how the war began, how it unfolded, and the various adventures that constituted this war. The trauma is such that exorcism and anathema supplant the rare attempts at political analysis.

The Islamists made their explosive entry onto the Arab political scene by claiming that the secular models imported from the West were to blame for the memorable defeat that was the Six-Days War, opening the way for Arab nationalists and pitting the East against the West. An Islamist ideology was then resolutely expressed in terms of a response to specific facts of Arabic nationalist developments, although in fact it was based on a considerably longer history.

Most contemporary Islamist movements, associations, factions and groups are linked to the fraternity of Muslim Brothers — al-Ikhwan al-Muslimin. This was founded in March 1928, in Ismaïlia in Lower Egypt, by two teachers, Hassan al-Banna (1906-1948) and Sayed Qotb (1906-1966). Striving to create a great party that would be an instrument of social and political battles to be based on principles originating in Islam, al-Banna and Qotb founded their movement on a radical unification of politics and religion, based on the principle of the *tawhid*, implying that religious law and civil law are one. This view led to the call for a strict application of the *Sharia*, a non-negotiable application of the "revealed" divine law, setting the Islamist concept diametrically opposite to all the humane, contractual and democratic inventions of the political philosophies that have inspired the nation state and the "state of law," in other words, the will to live together in a pluralistic and open society.

In several books, Sayed Qotb has elaborated the Brotherhood's strategy, in particular its refusal to collaborate with the established powers that it considers to be impious, as well as its choice of resorting to "legitimate violence." With Saudi Arabia's financial support, the Brotherhood set up a clandestine armed branch — the "Special Order" — and then, starting in 1954, the year Nasser ordered a great repression against the Brothers, formed an international branch directed by Saïd Ramadan from Munich, and from Geneva after 1961.

From the very start, this initiative enjoyed subsidies by King Fayçal of Arabia and the assistance of various American intelligence services, who considered that it was necessary to support this "war machine against Nasser and the Arab nationalists." Besides its European "bases," the Brotherhood now has numerous connections in Arab-Muslim countries: Sudan, Jordan, Yemen, Syria, Palestine, Afghanistan, Tunisia, Algeria and Morocco. It remains the "headquarters" of most of today's Islamist movements, including in Latin America, Black Africa and Southeast Asia.

The Muslim Brothers' ideological paternity of most of the Islamist movements has ended up creating a very heterogeneous movement. Generically, three types of organizations are grouped together by Islamist ideology. They include reformist organizations (classified in the so-called "salafist" contingent and striving to reinvigorate the bases of Islam as viable solutions to the problems of the Arab-Muslim societies), various ultra-conservative groups focusing their efforts on the law and on Islamic morality (dress and gastronomical codes, sexual and family rites, ethical questions, etc.), and communities of the faithful that function either as religious cults or through various forms of political violence and terrorist activity.

During the Cold War and until the end of the war of Lebanon in 1989, these various incarnations of the Islamist ideology endeavored to develop specific national variants, aimed at thwarting specific regimes, in Syria, in Egypt or Afghanistan. Since then, they have become more limited operations, localized either within the sphere of influence of a great family or within the territories of such and such warlord or, finally, within transnational ethnic configurations.

These various forms of "Islamism" give way, generally, to territorial recombinations that aim to dismantle the existing political spaces. Outside of rare exceptions like the Algerian "djazarists" of FIS and the Turkish "Refah," Islamist ideology does not propose any alternative national territories, unless through sheer tactical opportunism. The current states of the Arab-Muslim world, a heritage of the old European colonial powers, are thus stripped of any legitimacy. As a result of the *nahda* (the renascence), a reformist movement that was very much influenced by the philosophy of the Enlightenment, Arab nationalism embodies, through its various expressions, the absolute eradication of Islamist ideology.

Thus Kemalism, Nasserism and Baasism are like magic spells and curses to be listed in the damnable archives of "anti-Muslim plots," from the Crusades to the Six-Day War, including the *Reconquista*. As many founding Islamist texts affirm, the very idea of the nation is "impious" and is regarded as a diabolical invention of the "infidels" to break up the unity of the Oumma, the community of believers. Aside from very rare exceptions, the territory of the Oumma is never claimed as such in its entirety; thus its ideal representation is more ontological than overtly cartographical.

This does not mean that the Islamists have not given much thought to geography. Their answers vary widely, but here we are touching on a central question of Islamist ideology: its geopolitical dimension.. Insofar as the Oumma does not relate to a precise cartography, how can the conundrum of power and sovereignty arise? The question of territory is not only central, but vital. Not being able to assume, theologically, the heritage of arbitrary borders, in most cases the Islamist concept of sovereignty goes hand in hand with an ongoing temptation to partition and divide territories. These, in turn, will support the emergence of so many new markets for American investors, spaces whose economic future offers triple benefits: the provision of raw materials, the guarantee of a zone of exponentially growing demand for consumer goods, and finally, the impossibility that any new competing hubs will emerge.

The British were the first to understand how much they could gain from this centrifugal force. When India achieved national independence in 1947, they supported the secession of Pakistan and Bangladesh, mainly populated by Muslims. Clearly intended to weaken the young Indian state, this denominational partition met two goals at the time: to avoid losing the jewel of the Empire, just as it was, and to ensure the future of the British presence in the sub-continent. "The policy of 'divide and conquer,' based on the lever of Islamic identity, was a constant of British diplomacy since the middle of the 19th century. The Foreign Office encouraged the creation of one of the largest Islamic states in the world. It was going to become one of the main pillars of support for the international Islamist movement, which today threatens global geostrategic equilibrium and has managed to compromise the development of the Islamic world."[2]

As a worthy successor to this imperial logic, the United States would take up the same policy at the end of the Second World War. Washington would rely on Pakistan, Saudi Arabia and Turkey as the bases of its strategy of containment of the Communist expansion, and this would reinforce the development and the global influence of the Islamist ideology; this strategy would culminate in the "holy war" of Afghanistan. In spite of the Soviet army's withdrawal and the collapse of the Eastern bloc, this strategy is enjoying its second wind today with "Eurasia," defined by Zbigniew Brzezinski[3] as the United States' main interest for the next millennium; it is an area very rich in raw materials, extending from Western Europe to China, via Central Asia.

Consequently, the American strategists intend to continue pursuing their doctrine of containment in order to put a stop not only to the advance of Communism but to Russian access to warm water ports, as well as to a possible partnership with the nations of the European Union. This containment strategy is based on the consolidation of the zones of Turkish, Saudi and Pakistani influence, and on the expansion of Islamist ideology, which Brzezinski interprets as a "more pronounced Islamic identity."

Thus there would be an inescapable alternative between the assertion of this "more pronounced Islamic identity" and chaos. "Actually, it is a question of choosing between a subtle regional balance that would make it possible gradually to integrate the region into the fledgling world economy, while the states would probably pursue and adopt a more marked Islamic identity, and an ethnic conflict, a political fragmentation and, undoubtedly, an open war along the southernmost border of Russia. To arrive at a balance that would allow for consolidation must be the major objective of American global geostrategy in Eurasia."[4]

Brzezinski is the father of the "Islamist doctrine" that is still

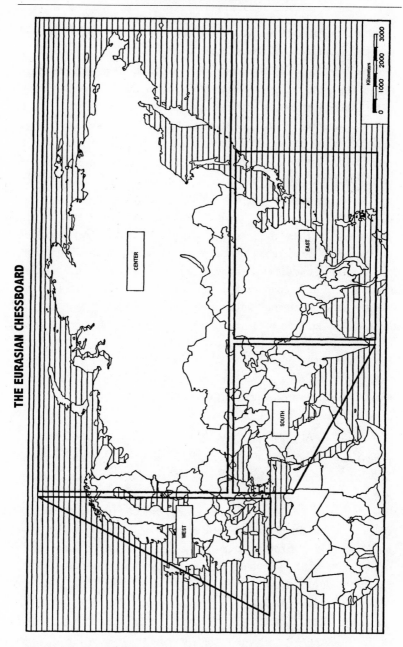

THE EURASIAN CHESSBOARD

promulgated today by some in the American administration. Called "the Polack," as president of the National Security Council (NSC) in 1978 he was responsible for setting up (in collaboration with the CIA, and the Saudi and Turkish intelligence services) Islamist propaganda networks intended to infiltrate the Muslim nationalist organizations of the Soviet republics of Central Asia.

Weapons and Korans printed in the Gulf monarchies were introduced into Uzbekistan, Tajikistan and Turkmenistan in great quantities. Except for the implications of the Afghan crisis, geopolitics experts are unanimous in recognizing that "the great game" of the next millennium will be tied to this area where not only the Russian, American, Saudi, Turkish and Pakistani influences meet, but also those of Iran and China.

By actuating the "Islamist lever" once more, the United States thus generates a new zone of political instability that renders their presence, then their arbitration, necessary in Eurasia. This will open the "new Silk Road," the object of so much covetousness. Lacking an active national middle class, the countries along this new axis of development have little chance, in the short or the long term, of asserting themselves as emergent "partners," future exporters of products with high added value. In short, there is no immediate danger of making them into competitors. In summary, Islamism is soluble in capitalism; Islamism is an antidote to nationalist temptations; and finally, Islamism is a rampart against the ever-present threat of a return of socialism. In short, Islamism is an essential ally of the neoliberal revival.

In his book, *Jihad vs. McWorld — Globalization and Fundamentalism Against Democracy*, Benjamin R. Barber wrote, "The Jihad and the McWorld have one thing in common: they are both at war against the sovereign nation-state and they undermine its democratic institutions. They scorn civil society and reduce democratic citizenship, without creating any alternative democratic institutions. Their common point is their indifference toward civil liberty. The Jihad forges communities of blood, founded on exclusion and hatred, which reduces democracy to the benefit of a tyrannical paternalism or a consensual tribalism. The McWorld forges global markets founded on consumption and profit, giving up the public interest and the common good (so recently in the hands of the citizens and their vigilant democratic governments) for the "invisible hand," a concept that should be considered questionable or even completely fictitious."[5]

## Footnotes

1.    Eric Rouleau, Jean-Francis Held, Simonne and Jean Lacouture, *Israel et les Arabes, le 3e combat*, Le Seuil, 1967.

2.    Alexandre Del Valle, *Islamisme et Etats-Unis, une alliance contre l'Europe*, L'Age de l'homme, 1997.

3.    Zbigniew Brzezinski defines "the Eurasian chessboard" as a space that extends from Lisbon to Vladivostok, and is composed of four subspaces: Central (Russia); West (Europe); South (the Middle East and Central Asia); East (Southeast Asia). See Map No. 1.

4.    Zbigniew Brzezinski, *Le Grand Echiquier — L'Amerique et le reste du monde*, Editions Bayard, 1997.

5.    *Jihad vs. McWorld*, New York, Time Books, 1995.

Chapter IV

THE MERCENARIES OF GLOBALIZATION

> "The Americans don't realize the deplorable ways in
> which the Saudis use the money that they give them.
> This money . . . is employed throughout the Middle
> East to encourage subversive operations against the
> West. Thus it serves Soviet objectives, which is in-
> tolerable, and it is annoying that Washington does
> not want to accept that."
>
> Anthony Eden

5:00 PM, Geneva, May 18, 1998. On the eve of the 50th anniversary of the World Trade Organization, the delegations of the 132 member states settle themselves in the prestigious Assembly Hall of the Palace of Nations. In this historical chamber, the end of the Afghanistan War was negotiated, the Iran-Iraq conflict was resolved, and preparatory talks were held that led to a referendum on self-determination for the Western Sahara, so it is not by chance that today's event commemorating the liberalization of world trade should take place in this temple of political multilateralism, at the very heart of one of the U.N.'s most memorable sites.

At 7:15 PM, Air Force One touches down, bringing the American president to the airport of Geneva-Cointrin. For 18 hours all the intersections have been blocked, the broad avenues evacuated. Completely brought to a stand-still, the international city at the end of Lake Geneva awaits President Clinton. "Globalization is not a choice, it is a fact. But we are all faced with an alternative. At a time when, for the first time in the history of mankind, most people have a government that they themselves have chosen, when the discussion is closed on the question of whether free enterprise or state socialism is better, when the people of every continent wish to join the system of free markets, those among us who have benefited from this system and have been the leaders cannot turn our backs on them. For my part, I am determined to adopt a vigorous strategy of opening the markets in every area of the world. . ." His speech went on for thirty minutes; then he headed back to Washington.

By 10:00 PM, in downtown Geneva, a few groups of teenagers had been breaking windows and plundering hundreds of shops for several hours already, wedged between two contingents of police, amidst clouds of tear gas. For days, the People's World Action (AMP), which had invited delegations from every continent, had been orchestrating popular protests, acts of civil disobedience and conferences against the rich man's globalization. Behind this globalization, a *fait accompli*, the logics of commercial war prevailed, with no holds barred. Consequently, regional conflicts no longer have the same effect and their intensity no longer makes much impact. The religious, ethnic and identity conflicts have revealed new economic risks and opportunities and given a new strategic importance to "a weakened world order."[1] In this context, fluid wars — having neither fronts nor laws, doctrines nor armies, and taking place in neither space nor time — have supplanted the conventional tools of domination. The United States (which is seeking to enhance its dividends as the principal victor of the Cold War), is devoting most of its foreign policy efforts to the conquest of new markets by these means. The imperial apparatus feeds on the "continuous fragmentation" of the world and on military activities that are, according to Max Weber, "economically directed;" and the priority given to commercial and financial investments over any other consideration occupies a central place.

Thus, although he is the anointed cheerleader for planetary free-trade, it was the same Bill Clinton who signed the Helms-Burton law on March 12, 1996, intended to penalize every American and foreign enterprise that might take it into its head to invest in Cuba. In spite of the demise of the Soviet threat, this "law" reinforces the economic embargo that the United States has imposed on Cuba for 34 years. On August 5 of the same year, the White House also gave its imprimatur to the D'Amato-Kennedy law, which establishes sanctions for any American or foreign company that might invest more than $40 million dollars in Libya or Iran, in particular in the hydrocarbon sector. Very ironically, these measures — which were unilateral and written without paying the least heed to international law — were adopted in the name of the international fight against terrorism. But which "terrorism" are we talking about? In this case, more than anywhere else, the end justifies the means; and by default the difficult question of defining "terrorism" finds a formulation that is as necessary as it is unilateral.

Most meetings and international conventions on anti-terrorism stumble on the precise definition of their subject. It is quite difficult, indeed, to spell out what is "international terrorism," and to specify what is "Islamist terrorism." As economic and financial globalization progress, terrorism too reconfigures its objectives, its methods and its sources of finance. These new forms of terrorism do not play a marginal role; they are actors completely outside the economic and social transformations that are upsetting the world order, the spectacular and pandemonic aspect of a silent loss of direction. Is this the last round before we are swallowed up in a majority of silent and distressed consumers? By installing state-led theological-political orders, the geopolitical face of Islamist ideology is taking full benefit while its heroes, the guardians of the (nearly completed) neo-liberal globalization, have become subcontractors of the American influence in the Mediterranean, the Middle East, Central Asia and the Far East. Islamism played a central role in the fall of Suharto, and Islamist organizations now dominate the Indonesian political scene.

This vast construction project requires local project superintendents, financiers, Mafias, private security companies and mercenaries engaged in Algeria, in Bosnia, in Chechnya, Afghanistan and the Philippines, experimental laboratories that thrive, as Olivier Roy says, in "the de-territorialized space at the margins of Islam." At the dawn of the 21st century, new hotbeds of Islamist agitation are developing in Niger, Madagascar and Zanzibar and, through the proliferation of armed gangs, in South Africa as well as in Brazil.

There are many transnational networks detached from any national and or state roots, set up on a temporary basis around any Islamic causes to be defended here and there. The Algerian Armed Islamic Groups (GIA) fulfill an emblematic role in the emergence and the assertion of these new forms of terrorism. Engaged in the infernal spiral of violence that wipes whole villages off the map, minor local delinquents — self-proclaimed "emirs" — make no distinction between religious fanaticism and banditry. This alliance is aimed less at the contested state apparatuses than at the civil society — artists, journalists, intellectuals, trade unionists, unveiled women — chasing them out and then backing up their conquests with theft, racketeering and a wild take-over of territory. Focusing inward on the defense of their systems of emoluments from the oil and gas and the import-export sectors, the leaders of the security forces have given over the campaigns to private militia, so many vigilante groups that, likewise, end up pursuing their own particular interests. "These three protagonists — the GIA, the army and the private militia — gradually have become complementary enemies who, each in his own way, contributes to a profound transformation of Algerian society," says Luis Martinez,[2] author of a remarkable dissertation that he defended in Paris in June 1997. This is not so much a religious struggle as a fight to the death for power, money and honor. Whitewashed with a more or less calculated religious alibi, this broad-based criminality leads to privatized violence that becomes the principal instrument of new means of accumulating riches and social stature.

The parallelism, if not the superimposition, of the privatization of violence and the privatization of the economy has become paradigmatic. Thus, apart from any religious purpose, the "Jihad" is gaining ground as a profitable activity. It becomes liable to all the mafioso devolutions, and sinks then into pure banditry. In many cases, Islamist ideology is used as a wonder-worker to paper over banditry in all its forms.

The terrorist logic of the Algerian GIA also prevails in Afghanistan, where the Taleban act in the guise of private security companies protecting the big American petroleum companies that are anxious to secure the Central Asian drilling zones and the routes of their future oil and gas pipelines, through Afghanistan and Pakistan to the detriment of Iran and Russia. The United States gives today's coloring to the old Saudi recipe from the Quincy, while simultaneously playing with Islamism, tribal fragmentation and hydrocarbons.

Afghanistan is one of the poorest countries in the world. Producing some 2,800 tons of opium in 1996, it surpassed the greatest producers on the planet, specifically those of the famous "Golden Triangle" of Southeast Asia. According to data from the United Nations Program for International Drug Control, based in Vienna, 180,000 acres are devoted to growing *papaver somniferum*, "the soporific poppy," from which opium is extracted, then morphine-base, then heroin. Interpol estimated that Afghan production would reach 5,000 tons in the year 2000;

that is more than the global production of 1994. Heroin has once again taken center stage in the drug problem worldwide, overtaking cocaine, the preferred drug of the "golden boys." 90% of the land reserved for poppy cultivation, covering some 250 square miles (about the size of Rhode Island), is controlled by the Taleban, providing a living for 1.4 million farmers — a spectacular statistic when we consider that approximately 80% of the heroin consumed in the European countries comes from Afghanistan. Overall, the Taleban take between 15 and 20% of the opium profits. "While it is absolutely prohibited to consume opium in the territories that they control, and is forbidden to any Muslim, the Taleban encourage opium production intended for the youth of the 'infidel world,' as another means of waging holy war against irreligious people," reports a U.N. official. Without being directly implicated in this "death trade," the promotion of which is supervised by their Pakistani allies, the American and Saudi special services have preferred to turn a blind eye, in order to preserve this means of financing the Taleban militia. Opium has become increasingly important in the financing of the Afghan civil war that shapes the economic future of all of Central Asia.

The most violent expressions of contemporary Islamist ideology penetrate economic programs and military actions not only in Algeria and Afghanistan but throughout the world, thanks to the leaders of the international Jihad. The most famous of them, Saudi billionaire Osama bin Laden, proclaimed the advent of "the world Jihad where everything can be bought and everything is for sale." He lives in Afghanistan, under close protection by the Taleban and the Pakistani secret service.

But, beyond the mystery with which he is surrounded, beyond the journalistic legend that he himself initiated and promoted, Osama bin Laden is the perfect embodiment of the "privatization" of Islamist terrorism. He enjoys a solid credit rating in the highest realms of international finance, where he controls a patrimony of more than $3 billion; the funds circulate between various companies based in the United States, Europe and the Middle East. These profitable relationships enjoy the benevolent protection of great and honorable international banks. Bin Laden has directly financed the construction of roads, airports, mosques and military infrastructures in Sudan. Funds from his organization support numerous training camps for the "warriors of Islam" in Somalia, Yemen, southern Afghanistan and in South Africa.

"Via bin Laden's transnational organization," explains a diplomat, "new forms of terrorism are evolving into a kind of mercenaries' exchange that is governed by the laws of the market and with Islam as the best alibi." The crime cartels constitute "the highest stage and the very essence of the capitalistic mode of production," according to Jean Ziegler.[3] "They benefit tremendously from the deficiency of the leaders of contemporary capitalist society. The globalization of the financial markets weakens the state of Law, its sovereignty, its capacity to respond. The neo-liberal ideology that legitimates — or worse, that 'naturalizes' — the unified markets, defames the law, debilitates the collective will and deprives men of the freedom to dispose of their own destiny."

Do the new forms of terrorism actually embody the highest stage of capitalism? There is a disconcerting convergence between Islamist ideology and certain economic networks in the process of being globalized. Seeking to understand the bases of economic development, Max Weber clarified Protestantism's historical contribution to the rise of capitalism. It could be that today not only Islamism but the return of the religious to the political scene is supporting the new expansion (if not the globalization) of capitalism.

The straw men of the bin Laden Organization's subsidiaries are very well received by the business lawyers of Wall Street and the Bahamas, by the wealth managers of Geneva, Zurich and Lugano, and in the hushed salons of the City of London. Indeed, in London bin Laden quite tranquilly conducts a wide variety of financial, religious and political activities via a perfectly visible association. London . . . where bin Laden flies, from time to time, by private jet, to visit his friend the financier Khaled al-Fawwaz and his partners. The bin Laden enigma lies in the fact that the central question of how Islamist terrorism is financed crops up more and more frequently, but as soon as the question is raised, it gets lost in the sands of transnational financial networks that are beyond any control, any legislation, and any statistical knowledge. "To fight effectively against these criminal organizations, one must cut the terrorists' supply lines, i.e. by breaking their financial conduits," President Hosni Mubarak recommended to delegations from nineteen countries who met at the Egyptian resort of Sharm el-Sheik on March 13, 1996, to reinforce international anti-terrorist cooperation.

Dubbed the "meeting of the peace-builders," this summit, as novel as it was weird, presented a façade of unanimity that scarcely disguised the contradictory, if not irreconcilable, geopolitical interests of the Europeans and the Americans. Faithful to their concept that terrorism mainly emanates from a few specific countries, every year the United States draws up a list of the worst pupils (rogue states), upon which they impose a policy of economic sanctions that they try to get endorsed by the U.N. Security Council. Established more on the basis of political and economic priorities than on universal ethical principles, this list primarily condemns Iran, Iraq and Libya.

The treatment of the Hafez el-Assad regime is a case in point. Condemned on a regular basis, Syria suddenly became acceptable after having chosen to join the Western coalition before the Gulf War was unleashed in January 1991. Suffice it to say that "state terrorism" and its classifications remain fuzzy categories, encumbered by ulterior motives and incipient economic conflicts. The Europeans contest this notion of singling out individual nations, especially Iran, with which the European Union intends to continue its policy of dialogue. European security leaders, especially the French, prefer to view terrorism as a "transnational" phenomenon, particularly in regard to its financial networks and its Mafia-like tendencies, as well as its communications and computer-based networks.

The 22 members of the Arab League signed the first anti-terrorist convention on April 22, 1998; the signatories, Ministers of Justice and of the Interior, insisted, likewise, on fighting against the international sources of financing. The Algerian Justice Minister, Mr. Mohamed Adami, pointed out that it is "imperative to do everything possible to stop the associations linked with the Gulf countries from financing these Islamist groups." Lastly, at a summit in Birmingham, May 15 and 16, 1998, the G7 countries examined a French proposal for "a universal convention to fight the financing of terrorism," a proposal due to be discussed by the General Assembly of the United Nations. During the debates, the majority of the Europeans, like most of the Arab countries, found themselves in agreement with this relatively new idea: that it is imperative to fight against the financial and commercial networks related to terrorism. It is imperative to cut the money pipelines that allow the CIA's "Afghans" to organize their international networks.

Since the beginning of the 1990's, most anti-terrorist investigations have converged on these circuits. Their affiliation with drug trafficking and illegal arms deals, their banks and their offshore companies, make the CIA's "Afghans" into the principal actors of Sunni Islamist terrorism. This burdensome heritage of the Cold War is one of the bases of contemporary organized crime.

Footnotes

1. *L'Ordre mondial relâché*, under the direction of Zaki Laïdi, Presses de la Fondation national des sciences politiques, 1993.

2. Conversation with the author on May 15, 1996. *La guerre civile en Algerie — 1990/1996*, Institut d'études politiques de Paris.

3. *Les Seigneurs du crime — Les nouvelles mafias contre la démocratie*, Le Seuil, 1998.

4. ARC (Advice and Reformation Committee). London office: BM box 7666, London, WC 1N. 3XX, the U.K. Director: Mr. Khaled A. al-Fawwaz.

## Chapter V

## THE CIA'S "AFGHANS" AND THEIR NETWORKS

> "Believers fight for the cause of God. Non-believers
> fight for the cause of Satan. Therefore, fight the parti-
> sans of Satan for, in truth, their machinations are very
> weak."
>
> The Koran — IV, 76

The United States financed, armed and trained the most radical Islamists of Afghanistan to defeat the Red Army. They did not realize that one day they would have to pay dearly for this victory. On November 13, 1995, an Egyptian diplomat was assassinated by a faction of Afghan veterans. Six days later, the same organization took credit for a bombing attack on the Egyptian embassy in Islamabad. These acts of reprisal were intended to avenge the disappearance of a very special envoy, the liaison officer for the various bases of the CIA "Afghans" throughout the world. The Islamist trail leads from the "Bosnian laboratory" to Afghanistan, where the religious fanatics all hail one man: Abdullah Azzam, the real precursor of the "Afghans" and mentor of Osama bin Laden, himself ringleader of the Afghan-Pakistani sanctuary. The CIA gave them ground-to-air missiles that were supposed to equip the American army and NATO troops exclusively. This was the beginning of the Stinger scandal. After the Red Army withdrew, the "Afghans" settled in the Horn of Africa and brought in Sudanese factions. Khartoum became their new headquarters. Political Islam was stymied and the "Afghans" converted part of their forces into business pursuits. Others went to organize new bases in Yemen and there they began a war for the reunification of the country. From 1995, they were

63

militarily redeployed between Yemen and Sudan. "If you liked Beirut, you'll love Mogadishu," joked a diplomat to the American troops departing for the Somali capital.

**Geneva.** The automatic garage door unit is broken again. This is the third time this month. The "super" is really delinquent, says Alaa el-Din Nazmi as he hauls himself out of his green BMW 318 with the diplomatic plates identifying the Permanent Mission of Egypt to the United Nations in Geneva.

It is pitch dark outside. He has trouble finding, among all his keys, the one that he so seldom has had to use in order to get to the first basement of this elegant building in the international district. The damp cold chills him to the bone, and reminds him of the joke his Chilean colleague made about the weather: "Geneva has nine months of winter and three months of taxes." And November is the worst time of the year. Moreover, he usually arranged to be back in Cairo at this season. This time he couldn't, because he had to prepare for an extraordinary meeting of UNCTAD (the U.N. Conference for Trade and Development) that would be held in a few days in Morocco. Since his little daughter Nadia was born — six months ago — Alaa el-Din Nazmi was coming home by 9:00 PM. As usual, his wife would have prepared dinner, and perhaps the vivacious account of her day would make him forget his heavy responsibilities.

When the door finally closed again behind him, the light in the parking lot failed to come on automatically as it was supposed to every evening. Definitely, nothing was working anymore in this building. Thus he had to turn on the headlights again before he could park properly in his reserved space, duly marked with the inscription of his diplomatic plate. He had hardly closed the car door again and was automatically selecting the key to lock it when a sharp, sudden pain in the left shoulder literally knocked him off his feet. Gasping, and with an effort that appeared to him superhuman, he got up again. But at once and almost in the same place, a second shock accompanied by a dry metallic sound reached him, before he collapsed from pain. A third explosion rent his ears. It occurred to him that someone was shooting him, from above.

With the fourth shot, he understood that they wanted not only to wound him but to kill him. Six shots in a few seconds ... "Think about your daughter," he repeated to himself, trying not to faint, crawling in the direction of the elevator. Too late. Alaa el-Din Nazmi, 42 years, diplomat, commercial attaché of the Egyptian Mission, died on November 13, 1995.

Alerted by the sound of the gunshots, a tenant called the super, who lived near the building. Noting in his turn that the timer on the garage door was not working, the latter went back home before starting out again, this time with a flashlight. He discovered traces of blood leading to the elevator, then the lifeless body of the Egyptian. He immediately telephoned the police, who arrived on the spot at 11:00 PM. Once the formalities were completed and the body removed, the men from the homicide squad conducted their first investigation. They found six 9-millimeter casings and a SIG P.210 Parabellum gun, apparently the killer's weapon, abandoned in the staircase. The gun was wrapped in a styrofoam cover to muffle the sound of the shots. "The work of a real professional," recognized the inspector. Taking the victim's keys, he and three of his men then went to Mr. Alaa el-Din Nazmi's office and went through the piles of folders concerning the economic and financial activities that are "normal" for a diplomatic mission. Their visit over, in the wee hours of the morning, they telephoned the station chief, Egyptian Ambassador Egypt Mounir Zahran, who was furious to be informed so tardily and especially after his colleague's office had been searched.

The public ministry of the Swiss Confederation tackled the case. The following day, in a press statement dated November 14, 1995, Bern announced it was opening a criminal investigation for murder. And to show Ambassador Zahran that Bern was not taking the matter lightly, Mrs. Carla del Ponte, Attorney General of the Swiss Confederation, went directly to the site before issuing the statement that they would "not favoring, for the moment, any one possibility." However, the Ambassador of Egypt was not placated. Despite his denials and the meticulous description he gave investigators of this highly skilled colleague, married and a young father, who attended the mosque every Friday, the police officers stubbornly directed their investigation in the direction of sordid assumptions, gaming debts, woman trouble and other dubious dealings. The investigators then chose the theory of mistaken identity and a settling of accounts between rival Kurdish factions: the assassins might have confused the diplomat with another

person living the building, the leader of a political organization opposed to the PKK (Kurdish Communist Party). An arrested suspect
was soon released.

There remained the political track, which the investigators
seemed deliberately to want to avoid in spite of Ambassador Zahran's
insistence. Following a murder attempt on President Hosni Mubarak
in Addis-Ababa, June 26, 1995, the Egyptian authorities had accused
several European countries, including Denmark and Switzerland, of
sheltering leaders of radical Islamist groups. An Egyptian delegation
had just gone to Bern to address the question with the Swiss authorities, in particular the case of Ayman al-Zawahiri, military chief of the
armed organization of the Jihad. The Egyptian special services claimed
that he lived in Switzerland under a false identity, which the Swiss authorities formally deny.

On Wednesday, November 15 in Cairo, two days after the assassination, a heretofore unknown Islamist organization faction, "Gama'a
International Justice," took responsibility for the diplomat's assassination. "Yes, we killed him pursuant to the law of retaliation, for a death
sentence was pronounced against him and the battalion of the martyr
Abdallah Azem carried out the sentence by shooting him," specified a
typed press release, undated, that arrived by fax office at the British
press agency Reuters. Abdallah Azem, a Palestinian considered to be
the founding father of the first Arab groups of the *mujaheddin*, the
"soldiers of the faith" fighting in Afghanistan against the Soviet army,
was killed in 1989. His name was appropriated by many armed Islamist
organizations. The text of the statement was entitled, "Press release of
Gama'a International Justice concerning the execution of the Egyptian
diplomatic attaché in Switzerland."

"Other death sentences have been pronounced and will be carried
out against other people implicated in the witch hunt against *ulemas*
(Muslim scholars) and the sons of the Islamic movement," continued
the text. "These people have incited the governments of the countries
where they reside to act against the sons of the Islamic movement by
accusing them of terrorist activities. We make a point of reassuring
those members of the Egyptian diplomatic missions abroad who are not
implicated in these odious deeds that have made it possible to throw
young Muslims into prison where they are tortured before being condemned to death by military tribunals. . . . Our duty is to put an end to

the injustice that strikes Muslims whatever their origin, everywhere in the world and against any authority that attacks the Muslims," the statement concluded. It was the third time in 1995 that an Egyptian armed organization took credit for an incident abroad. Gama'a Islamiya had put its name, to the attempted murder of President Mubarak in Ethiopia, in June, and then to a car-bomb attack in Croatia in October.

**Islamabad.** November 19, six days after the assassination of the diplomat, two explosions destroyed Egypt's embassy in Islamabad. The author of the attack drove a van up to the gate at around 11:00 (local time). A first explosion blew in the gate and its security device. The vehicle then advanced about 150 feet. A second explosion, extremely powerful, then blasted a crater 10 feet deep and 15 feet in diameter. The entrance of the building and its main wing were shattered. The combustion, which was heard all over the Pakistani capital, killed 15 people and wounded dozens more. "Gama'a International Justice" immediately claimed the suicide-attack in the name of "the brigade of the martyr Khaled Islambouli," by a typed text that was similarly sent to the Reuters office in Cairo. (Khaled Islambouli was one of the authors of the assassination of Egyptian President Anwar al-Sadat in 1981.)

This was the first time that such a large attack had been made in Islamabad. Home of most of the chancelleries as well as the seat of the presidency and the Parliament, the international district is regarded as the most secure in the Pakistani capital. Expressing fears of a wave of violence against Egyptian interests abroad, Cairo demanded security reinforcements for its embassies in fifteen countries, including Great Britain, Germany, Italy and France. In Switzerland, the public ministry was still observing the greatest discretion with regard to the assassination of Alaa el-Din Nazmi. However, on November 21, it proceeded with two investigations — one at the mosque in Geneva, property of Saudi Arabia, and the other, in the same city, at the Islamic Center, a listening post for the fraternity of the Muslim Brothers. A passport was seized, along with a license plate and a list of telephone numbers.

According to various sources close to the investigation, the Egyptian diplomat had been handling several sensitive files relating precisely to the financial resources of the Muslim Brothers, of which $200 to

$500 million was managed by various financial organizations between Geneva and Tessin (in the Italian canton of Switzerland). By carefully re-examining the papers from Alaa el-Din Nazmi's office, the investigators established that the diplomat had played a major part in an attempt to recover these funds. One of the dossiers followed by the diplomat related to a financial company based in Lugano, registered in the Bahamas, that turned out to be nothing less than the Muslim Brothers' bank.

This bank is very interesting for three essential reasons. By financing various organizations through humanitarian programs in several Arab countries, it occupies a strategic position in the international Islamist constellation. In addition, it reveals the critical importance of Saudi capital in these financings. Lastly, its history and that of its founders constitute the essential link in how the Muslim Brothers established themselves in Europe. By reconstructing this history, to which we will return later on, one understands better the Muslim Brothers' attempt to take over all of the Islamic organizations of Europe, with the political and financial support of Saudi Arabia.

To these four anti-Egyptian operations carried out between June and November 1995, we must add the series of attacks perpetrated in France that same year, from July to September, and claimed by the Algerian Armed Islamic Groups (GIA). French investigators, too, would bring to light the existence of several international connections in Belgium, Italy, Switzerland, Sweden and Great Britain; the investigators established Saudi businessman Osama bin Laden's direct involvement in financing the London logistics of the GIA, leading to the preparation of the French bombings. While they answer to their own logic, these two series of attacks also confirm the existence of "new forms of Islamist terrorism," the Sunni prevalence, and the role of the military and paramilitary structures of the "Afghans." These attacks are thus often linked to the same logistical networks, to the same financial backers and to the same transnational agents.

**Zagreb.** One can approach this constellation by reconstructing the itinerary of certain characters who have no identity, no fixed residence, and no nationality. The arrest of a man carrying a passport in the name of Ibrahim Yaacoub as he arrived in Zagreb on September 12, 1995, opens one path. Apprehending him at night, right in the downtown area, at the home of friends from a "humanitarian organization" who were putting him up, the Croatian police knew very well that they had just caught the Egyptian Gama'a chief of foreign operations.

This man, Talaat Fouad Qassem, whose *nom de guerre* is "Abou Ta-lal al-Qassemi," is 38 years old. Born in Minieh in Upper Egypt, he par-ticipated, at that city's university, in the early stages of the creation of the Gama'a Islamiya, before enrolling in their armed branch at the end of the 1970's. Eleventh on the list of Sadat's assassins, he was con-demned to seven years of forced labor but was given a remanded sen-tence, like 190 of his fellow-prisoners. Arrested again, he managed to flee to Sudan, from which he made his way to Afghanistan in order to join the mujaheddin of the "holy war." After the Soviet army's with-drawal, he settled in Peshawar with other chiefs of the Gama'a, includ-ing Mohamed Chawki Islambouli, Moustafa Hamzeh and Moustafa Nouara. Director of the review *Mourabitoun*, official organ of Gama'a, he traveled in several European countries where he gave talks and col-lected money for "the cause." In 1992, he was invited by friends to Den-mark, where he decided to settle. Condemned to death *in absentia* in Egypt, he asked for and obtained political refugee status in 1993.

To the Croatian police who questioned him, Talaat Fouad Qassem explained why he was in transit in Zagreb. His real destination was Sarajevo, where he was to meet with keys members of the Bosnian re-sistance in order to write a book on Serb aggression against the Mus-lims of the Balkans. After two days in police custody, then a judgment for "violation of the law on stays from abroad in Croatia," he was ex-pelled to an unspecified country. That is the official Croatian version. Then his trail was lost, although several European Islamic associations published official statements demanding the liberation of the Islamist leader.

Gama'a Islamiya, which had threatened Croatia with reprisals for arresting their "official spokesman," affirmed on October 21 from Cairo that they had fulfilled their threats against Zagreb the day before by blowing up a car in the coastal city of Rijeka: one killed, 29 wounded. In the same press release, Gama'a threatened to continue their reprisals. For its part, in the bulletin published by the Mujaheddin in Switzer-land, the Egyptian organization Islamic Jihad claimed that "Talaat Fouad Qassem was extradited by Croatia to Egypt and its apostate re-gime. He has already arrived in Cairo, where he is undergoing cruel torture in the buildings of the state security services." Croatia's ambassador to Cairo responded that the Jihad's assertions were "devoid of any basis, for two reasons. The first is that there was no Egyptian request for extradition. And the second is that since September 14, this Islamist was not in Croatia anymore and thus Zagreb could not extradite him."

In Copenhagen, the Qassem family lawyer claims to have asked the Danish Ministry of the Foreign Affairs send the Croatian authorities a request for information on Talaat. In addition, Claus Bergsoee, Esq., explained to the Agence France Presse that he wondered whether his customer was not rather in the hands of the Croatian security services. "My impression," he added, "is that the security forces in a country that is at war have far more power than in other countries." Lastly, on September 16, two days after the declared expulsion of Qassem, the Egyptian Minister for the Interior, Hassan al-Alfi, affirmed that "the countries that allowed terrorists to enter onto their territory have now understood the danger and are seeking to coordinate their action with other countries." The same day, the daily newspaper *al-Ahram*, close to those in power, reported that "contacts have been intensified with a certain number of countries to obtain the extradition of terrorists. . . and they have shown positive results."

While the disappearance of Talaat Fouad Qassem has still not been explained, it is known — according to the Egyptian special services — that he went to Switzerland fifteen days before his disappearance in Zagreb (and two months before the diplomat was assassinated). Accompanied by a compatriot residing in Germany, Mohamed Mehdi Akef, he is supposed to have been charged by the Gama'a military command with recovering some of the Muslim Brothers' funds that were being managed in Switzerland. But the discussion with the local representatives of the Brotherhood having failed to produce their intended result, the two men then are said to have offered very serious threats against the leaders of the Brothers in Switzerland, in particular against those who had entered into discussion with the Egyptian authorities to negotiate their return to that country. What was at stake in this negotiation, essentially, was the guarantee that funds managed in Switzerland would absolutely remain in Europe in order not to directly finance the armed struggle in Egypt. The "Case Officer" charged with securing this guarantee: the commercial attaché of the Egyptian

U.N. Mission in Geneva, Alaa el-Din Nazmi.

And why him? It's logical, a source close to the investigation would answer. Since he attended the mosque assiduously, he was quickly located and contacted by the Muslim Brothers, who put the matter in his hands. After having received a green light from his higher-ups, Alaa el-Din Nazmi thus established relations with the Brothers' bank in order to obtain guarantees attesting that the several million dollars would be dedicated to financing Islamic associations in Europe, and not to the armed struggle against the Egyptian regime. The assassination of the diplomat would thus fulfill two motives: mainly, to express a firm and clear rejection of this deal, but also to avenge the disappearance of Talaat Fouad Qassem, kingpin of the "Arab Afghans" in Europe.

The assassination of a diplomat in Switzerland to recover funds and to avenge the disappearance of "a very special envoy" in Bosnia; a proliferation of incidents all over, not only in Croatia or Pakistan, but in France and Saudi Arabia. This sequence of related events illustrates a new strategy of the armed Islamist groups, and a redistribution of tasks. Initially, this work of restructuring was mainly carried out by the military leaders of Gama'a Islamiya and of the Jihad, who thus sought to focus the war effort of most of the "Afghan" networks on Egyptian objectives. This orientation had more to do with the origins of the most enterprising actors than with the emblematic situation of Egypt.

Egypt's situation rests on three pillars. First, from Cairo (the historical birthplace of the Islamist ideology), the fraternity of the Muslim Brothers coordinates its international representation in various countries and remains, for this reason, the "home office" of most of the contemporary Islamist structures. Second: starting with the death of Nasser, the Egyptian authorities themselves supported an increasing Islamization of society and contributed to making their country the "weak link" of the regimes despised by the Islamists. Lastly, the third pillar: al-Azhar, the venerable and prestigious university whose word is law for the whole of the Sunni world, continues to legitimate, more or less openly, the theological-political tribulations of the Islamists. In any case, many Egyptian observers reproach al-Azhar for not taking full advantage of its prestige and its influence to condemn clearly and firmly Islamist terrorism every time it is expressed in Egypt or elsewhere in the world.

"This focus on Egypt," notes Antoine Jalkh in *Arabies*[1], "corresponds to what a leader of the Egyptian group al-Jihad wrote in 1987, under the pseudonym of Aboul Fida, on 'the geography of confrontation.' This text posits the importance of Egypt for 'Islamic change,' and insists that this country 'must become the target of all the combatants of the Islamist movement in the world.'" The extent and the promptness of the reactions to Talaat Fouad Qassem's disappearance must be put in this perspective, but they are also explained by the central role that he played in the organization of the "Afghans'" international networks, especially in Bosnia-Herzegovina.

**Bosnia.** Whereas the Serb army was built from the preexistent structures of the ex-Yugoslav army, the Bosnian army and the Croatian forces of the HVO could only count on the local infrastructures of the police force and on external support. Before they had any deliveries of American weapons, these young armies were entirely dependent on humanitarian organizations and support from the diaspora. The Serb territorial conquests of 1992 and a systematic application of ethnic purification led to the formation, around Sarajevo, the besieged capital, of the Muslim enclaves of Bihac (western Bosnia), Zepa, Gorazde and Srebrenica (eastern Bosnia). Moreover, the Croat-Muslim confrontations of 1993 led to the encirclement of Mostar-East and the pockets of Zenica ( in central Bosnia) and Tuzla (northeastern Bosnia).

The isolation of the Bosnian Muslims combined with the rhetoric of an international community that was impotent — because it was fundamentally indifferent to the fate of the Muslims — gave rise in 1992 to rather spectacular initiatives. Since then, we are witnessing a repetition of the campaign of solidarity in favor of Afghanistan that developed starting in the early 1980's. Taking advantage of the "Afghans'" skills, American benevolence and Saudi money, new actors are stepping up operations. "Islamic religious organizations also organize convoys, which are not humanitarian convoys," explain Aline Angoustres and Valerie Pascal, "especially from Germany, where these organizations depend on other Islamist networks, notably that of the Turkish Party of Prosperity (Refah). These organizations also take up collections via the religious tax. In 1992, the Union of Islamic Organizations in France (related to the Muslim Brothers) probably collected nearly $150,000 in

France. *Secours Islamique* (Islamic Relief) seems to be involved in weapons deals with Bosnia, and an Italian journalist looking into the connections, in this arena, between Bosnia, Algeria and Somalia was arrested in Sarajevo."[2]

As for the "holy war" against the Soviets, the recruitment of Arab volunteers goes through many stages, above all the Muslim Brothers and the charitable organizations of many countries in the Arab-Muslim world. Quite naturally, the "Afghans," who already have their military and paramilitary structures, find Bosnia to be a new outlet and also a favorable laboratory for redeploying their various activities, in particular toward the Maghreb and the European countries.

In 1990, Talaat Fouad Qassem was designated by his peers — all veterans of Afghanistan — to head up the planning of the "Bosnian network." This was to be based mainly on three relationships: London, Peshawar and Sarajevo. He often shuttled between his Danish refuge and the districts north of the British capital where many Egyptian refugees (as well as the leaders of the Algerian Community in Britain) have settled. Helped by an ex-pilot from the Algerian rout — expelled from France — Kamareddin Kherban, and by another member of the ACB, Boudjemaa Bounoua, Qassem would come to centralize for all Europe the requests for volunteers ready to join the "Afghan" camps of Bosnia. Thus, some two thousand "Europeans" were distributed between the camps near Zenica and those around the principal antenna of Tuzla, placed under the direct responsibility of Kherbane. These very special induction facilities work under the cover of nongovernmental organizations (NGO's) and of Islamic humanitarian associations. Their financial needs and their logistics are covered by the international branch of the Muslim Brothers.

And this is the intermediary that provides training courses on the handling of weapons and explosives for young people in the French suburbs. The principal authors of the waves of terror that flowed through Paris and the Lyons area during the summer of 1995, Kelkal, Ben Saïd and Ali Touchent, came from there. The French investigation established beyond a doubt that the GIA network had help and support from the Egyptian "Afghans." Abou Farès (called Rashid Ramda), indicted in London as a leader and financier of the commando, traveled through Sarajevo and Peshawar, as did Karim Koussa. One of the perpetrators of the Hotel Atlas-Asni shooting (Morocco, 1994) also came from the same "school." Indeed, in addition to offering a traditional military education for men destined, in the short run, for the various Balkan fronts, the instructors train volunteers in various techniques of urban guerrilla warfare, including car-bomb attacks and the preparation of various explosive devices. These "lectures" are given in Bosnia, and are filmed; the video cassettes are shown at many of the "Islamic Arts Centers" and mosques in Europe.

The year 1995 was crucial. The four attacks claimed by Gama'a Islamiya indicated that the Egyptian "Afghans" now held the military command of the old networks that emerged from the "holy war." Between their historical Afghan-Pakistani sanctuaries and their outposts in Europe, they have a hub in the Balkans that helps the Bosnian brothers by implementing the traditional techniques used during the "holy war." But the "Bosnian laboratory" has three main objectives: to reconstitute the Egyptian networks (which were decimated by the successive waves of repression); to increase support for the networks of GIA operatives in Algeria and France, and finally to coordinate better with the Saudi brothers who, upon their return to that country, are preparing to play a major role in determining the succession of King Fahd.

**Afghanistan.** After having fought the Soviets between 1979 and 1989, the Arab "Afghans" (some 10,000 volunteers) dispersed; then were brought together again and put to the service of other "holy wars" carried out in other latitudes. Whatever their tribulations, all bear the mark and the allegiance forged by this now legendary epic. The "Afghan legend" has become the basis of a coherent imaginary community: with the halo of his victory against the Soviets, the figure of the Afghan now embodies military courage, religious purity and the spirit of sacrifice throughout the world.

By claiming the assassination of the Egyptian diplomat, "Gama'a International Justice" proclaimed the existence of the "battalion of the martyr Abdallah Azem." We never pay sufficient attention to the words used in connection with claims of terrorist attacks. When they are authenticated, they often give information concerning the motive, and the silent partner(s) behind the operation. In fact, this one clearly indicated its affiliation with the "Afghan legend."

The Soviet army invaded Afghanistan on December 27, 1979. The five mechanized divisions led by General Moussa Ivanov, supported by an airlift to Kabul that began two days earlier, thus went to the aid of the only Communist power to have been declared anywhere in the Arab-Muslim world — a power resulting from a coup d'état that had occurred one year before. A month later, an "Islamic Alliance of Resistance" was created on the joint initiative of Pakistan and Saudi Arabia. Early in 1980, Abdallah Azem, a 28-year-old Palestinian, a member the international branch the Muslim Brothers bearing an Egyptian passport, founded "The Office of Islamic Services" in Peshawar, the first organization for enrolling, inducting and assigning Arab volunteers, the future Afghan "mujaheddin."

He worked with the four organizations that share the Muslim Brothers' ideology: "Hezb-i-islami," which proclaims a radical form of Islamism and is directed by its founder Gulbuddin Hekmatyar; "Hezb-i-islami, the Khales division," which derived from a scission of Hekmatyar's party (its chief, Yunus Khales, preaches a less radical and more traditionalist Islam); "Jamaat-i-islami," the principal political-military resistance organization of the future president Burhanuddin Rabbani; and "Ittihad-i-islami," which was founded at the instigation of Saudi Arabia by Abdul Rasul Sayyaf and which favors a form of Islam that is very strict on questions of conduct, in particular, women's place in society. With a visceral hatred for the Shiites, Sayyaf also seeks to be the champion of "a crusade against the West." A historian of the Afghanistan War, Assem Akram calls these four movements the "*ikhwahabis*," i. e. influenced by the ideology of the Muslim Brothers (*ikhwanism*) and by *wahhabism* (the conservative doctrines of the Saudi monarchy), all fighting for the installation of an "Islamic revolution" in Afghanistan.

"The relations were mutually advantageous," he writes. "In exchange for taking in the Arabs, the Afghan parties received abundant financial support from the *ikhwahabi* groups and their sympathizers around the Gulf. Moreover, they took advantage of their networks to establish politically and financially profitable relations with the governments of a number of these countries, where they were able to set up representative offices. Lastly, these Arabs helped the four *ikhwahabi* parties to publish Arabic journals on the Jihad in Afghanistan, to bring themselves to the attention of a broader audience and to take advantage of the financial repercussions of a skillful propaganda campaign."[3]

This preoccupation with propaganda is not unilateral, for the "Arabs" who came to fight in Afghanistan, particularly partisans of the

Muslim Brothers (*ikhwan*) and the *wahhabis*, also pursued religious and political goals such as challenging Sufism, which was one of the bases of Afghan society. The military engagement overlapped with a mission for religious standardization, in the name of the correct interpretation of Sunna (the tradition of the Prophet), of which the Muslim Brothers and the *wahhabis* claim to be the only agents. For this reason, Abdallah Azem embodied not only the figure of the precursor and the mastermind of Arab-Muslim solidarity, but also that of political cop of the *Jihad News*. On his way to becoming its uncontested chief, he would be assassinated by Mossad in November 1989.

For the use of future recruits, his political testament is outlined in a propaganda booklet entitled *The Defense of Islamic Countries as an Inherent Duty*. Abdallah Azem gives his theological justification for participating in the holy war as one of the fundamental duties of every good Muslim, like the five daily prayers and the pilgrimage to Mecca. And this "prime duty," which applies to each member of the Oumma, does not relate to Afghanistan alone, in fact, but to every part of "Dar al-Islam," that is, every region where the Word of the Prophet holds sway. The booklet then expounds a theory of "the Circles of Proximity," which Assem Akram summarizes as follows. "If a Muslim People or state cannot manage to overcome its enemies alone, then the neighboring country, or the nearest Muslim state, is obligated to come to its aid and join the Jihad. If this coalition is still insufficient to vanquish the enemy, then other Muslims coming from more remote states are obligated to lend a hand to the mujaheddin. And the circle will grow this way until it includes all the Muslim world, if necessary."

From this standpoint, the various operations carried out in Afghanistan have no finality but are only a stage on the way toward liberating all of the Muslim countries, first and foremost, of course, Palestine and Jerusalem. But the same obligation to join in the war is also applied to the "false" Muslim countries, directed by infidel and shameful governments; at the top of this list are Egypt and Algeria. Next come Tunisia, Morocco, Libya, Syria and Jordan, plus the new states of Central Asia, Africa and the large Muslim countries of the Far East. As a breviary of the "Afghans," as a manifesto of the holy war, and as a theological-strategic treatise, *The Defense of Islamic Countries as an Inherent Duty* is a key text of contemporary Islamist ideology. Not only is the military engagement in Afghanistan described there as just one stage of a Jihad that should not stop until the final liberation, but this engagement must aim for the advent of the only theological-political order possible, in conformity with the strict application of the *Sharia*, according to the interpretation of the Muslim Brothers and the *wahhabis*.

"The infinite diversity of Islam definitely has a hard life," Olivier Roy often points out. Indeed, from a strictly religious point of view, Azem's proselytism was not much of a success, and did not really fit in with the specific characteristics of Afghan society. On the other hand, it galvanized most of the "Arabs," even those who had spent only a short time in the Afghan underground. But the majority of them would go back home religiously and politically "reformed," and imparting the same categorical imperative: to continue the holy war. Back home, the image of the "Afghan legend," as well as the various fraternities of former mujaheddin (maintained and financed by the World Islamic League, al-Rabita al-Islamiya al-alamiya), contributed to the creation of the "Afghans." They are found in Bosnia, Sudan, Yemen, Somalia and Kosovo, and in the seedbeds of most armed groups in Egypt and Algeria, South Africa, Zanzibar and the Philippines.

For a long time, Afghanistan stood out as one of the priorities of the World Islamic League. Bordering on Pakistan (an ally of Riyadh), this country is one of the access keys to Central Asia. Stepping up its activity to contain the Shiite influence following the Iranian revolution (which could have enabled Iran to contest Saudi Arabia's Islamic hegemony), the League made the holy act of war "against the atheistic Communist invader" its principal propaganda point.

The World Islamic League (Rabita), created in Mecca in 1962 by the crown prince of that time — Fayçal Bin Abdelaziz — to counter Nasserism and other incarnations of secular Arab nationalism, now has the vocation of defending Islamic interests throughout the world. Directed from Mecca by a General Secretary — who is always Saudi and who enjoys diplomatic status — Rabita is the most powerful tool of Saudi domination over the Islamic communities of the world. An extremely tightly structured administration, it designates an executive council of 53 members representing the ensemble of the Islamic countries. Meeting once a year, this executive council appoints regional Islamic supervisors for the five continents. The council assigns various objectives to them, intended as much to expand Islam in general as to control the Islamic institutions (especially in non-Muslim countries).

For this reason, Rabita subsidizes numerous social organizations.

The key figure in this singular administration is none other than Prince Turki ibn Fayçal, son of the founder of Rabita, and chief of the Saudi secret service. With great discretion and efficiency, he has established close relations with the four principal "*ikhwahhabi*" groups. By taking control of Abdallah Azem's organization, the special services gained control of the Arab volunteers before initiating their own direct ties. With assistance from their Pakistani homologues in the Inter Service Intelligence (ISI), they also direct the logistics and the provisioning of the camps, in Peshawar as well as in the Afghan underground, and the routing and distribution of weapons (according to very selective ethnic-religious criteria).

Regarded as the most effective information service in the Third World, the ISI is the principal subcontractor of Saudi and American aid that Islamabad forwards, above all, to the most radical Islamist factions. Such favored treatment is explained only by a common theological-political radicalness. The functionaries of the ISI and those of the Pakistani army are mainly Pashtuns, like their Afghan protégés. Long before the Soviet intervention, this family preference encouraged by Saudi Arabia was a boon for Zbigniew Brzezinski, President Jimmy Carter's security adviser. Convinced that he should rely on the best bridgehead to counter the Soviets, he persuaded the American administration to allow the ISI and Saudi Arabia to coordinate the assistance to the various Afghan parties. The Reagan administration expanded the operation.

Chief of the Afghan Office of ISI from 1983 to 1987, brigadier general Mohammad Yousaf recounts his first meeting with the head of the CIA, William Casey, at the Inter Service Intelligence headquarters in Islamabad, in early 1984. "I watched Casey closely. Sometimes he seemed half asleep during the analysts' discussions, but as soon as an important subject was broached, he immediately became very alert. He had a quick mind, with a bold and merciless approach towards the Soviets. In fact, like many people in the CIA he considered Afghanistan to be the place where America could be avenged for its defeat in Vietnam. His often-repeated point of view was that the Soviets should pay with a lot of blood for their support of the North Vietnamese. 'Those bastards have to pay,' would be a good summary of his philosophy for the war, and no means of achieving that was repugnant to him."[4] Every time, he was fully satisfied when he was making his rounds, and Casey almost always obtained budget increases for his dear "freedom fighters."

Following his visit in June 1985, the CIA's financing of the Afghan mujaheddin was doubled, attests a report from Congress which records an amount of $285 million. "For each dollar provided by the United States, another dollar was added by Saudi Arabia," General Yousaf adds. "The funds, which rose to several hundred million dollars per annum, were transferred by the CIA through separate accounts under control of the ISI in Pakistan. These accounts were completely separate from those that were used for arms purchases. Nevertheless, it was essential for the war effort." This evolution not only made Pakistan the principal sanctuary of the American crusade against Communism, it unilaterally gave precedence to the "cousins" of Islamabad, and their Arab "Afghans."

The most spectacular consequence of this subcontracting occurred during 1986, when the Pentagon's strategists decided to deliver the famous Stinger ground-to-air missiles to the Pakistani special services. The latest breakthrough in American weapons production, this terrifying weapon, according to the same strategists' recommendations, was to equip American troops exclusively and those of their allies within NATO. Weighing about 35 lbs, the machine can easily be use by a team of two men: the gunner, who aims and shoots the weapon by supporting it against his shoulder, and the observer, who is responsible for aerial observation, radio contact, and management of the shooting operation. This light weapon goes by the rule of "fire and forget." It is equipped with a very powerful homing device that reacts to the infrared rays of the target and follows them autonomously. The homing head is so sensitive that it makes it possible to fight planes and helicopters flying at low altitude in all firing configurations: approach, turn, retreat, etc..

Certainly, introducing this small wonder to the Afghan scene immediately reversed the balance of forces by paralyzing aviation, the preferred tactic of the Soviet army. Thanks to the Stinger, dozens of Russian helicopters and planes were shot down in a few months. Trained by American instructors, Pakistani officers in their turn trained their mujaheddin friends to handle the missile. A thousand specimens were thus distributed among the Afghan underground. After the Soviet withdrawal in 1989, the local arms dealers fought for these ballistics gems, bidding up to $150,000 dollars a piece. In the early 1990's, the same Pentagon experts would break into a cold sweat when examples turned up in North Korea, Qatar, and the GIA underground. The Pakistani intelligence services exonerated themselves, and blamed Iran. They claimed to have lost possession of the magical weapons after a series of shootouts with factions ruled by Tehran.

According to a CIA report, cited in the American press, several hundred Stingers delivered to Afghanistan earlier were still operational. The threat was so grave that the U.S. set up a vast program to recover the stray missiles. According to the heads of this operation, quoted by *The Washington Post*, "the buy-back program launched by the CIA has proven to be disastrous," in spite of a big budget — $65 million (that is to say, twice the real cost of the equipment). The attempt was fruitless and, according to same sources, the buy-back program stimulated demand so much that it simply raised the prices.

If the Americans responsible for fighting terrorism today are biting their fingernails, the decision-makers of the time (who gave a green light to these deliveries) do not seem troubled by any doubt, at least if one judges by Zbigniew Brzezinski. "Which is more important from the perspective of world history? The Taleban, or the fall of the Soviet empire? A bunch of excited Islamists or the liberation of Central Europe and the end of the Cold War?"[5] In accord with William Casey's "philosophy of war," this judgment offers a curious summary of world history, entirely conditioned by the desire for payback for Vietnam, and at any price.

This policy of a "kick in the ass" not only encouraged the proliferation of Islamist terror, it shook the geopolitical reality of the whole area. Unable to wage this guerrilla war strategically, and challenged by Moscow's assertion that it was promulgating an indirect East-West conflict, Washington gave over to the ISI full responsibility for the operations. In addition to the Stinger affair, this war by proxy had two other major consequences. Having become a state within a state, the ISI supplanted more and more the Pakistani Ministries of Defense and Foreign Affairs. Worse yet, ISI, powerful in its increasing autonomy, took advantage of its position to develop the Pakistani nuclear program. Conducted in overt opposition to the American declared philosophy of non-proliferation, this initiative would lead to the Indian nuclear tests and the Pakistani counter-tests in spring 1998.

And the fate of the Afghan people in all this mess? The Soviets went home, and the difficult unanimity of the Afghan resistance broke into splinters. A civil war ensued that was quite as lethal as the preceding one. The second Gulf War had not settled anything when the Pashtuns, protected by the ISI, chose Saddam Hussein. Obsessed with achieving ethnic homogeneity on its southern flank, Islamabad enrolled battalions of students, also Pashtuns, from the Koran schools. Riyadh and Washington played their parts. With their fear of women and other reactionary obsessions, the Taleban made their explosive entry onto the Afghan stage at the very moment when Central Asia was devoting itself to a new "great game." A century after the Russo-British confrontation, maneuvering for control of petroleum reserves as great as those in the Middle East, history takes on a feeling of *déja vu*. Some of the Arab "Afghans" went into the Taleban, others left and returned to their own countries to put into practice the teaching of Abdallah Azem: pursuit of the "holy war."

**Khartoum.** On the route used by the Afghan underground, the Khartoum way-station works in both directions, outbound and returning. Today still, it guarantees a safe haven to the former and the newer Afghans. Since the camps were started in the suburbs of Khartoum, and through the end of the Afghanistan War, the Islamist networks in eastern African have grown tremendously. And the myth of an Islamist *Internationale* is certainly derived from Sudanese leaders' efforts the to build one. Khartoum hosted the largest world gathering of Islamist organizations ever seen, attempting to forge a joint organization. While this attempt at unification was obviously not initiated by the United States (unlike what happened in Afghanistan), the "Afghans" trained by the CIA did play a crucial role there.

Fomented by the "military-Islamist" team directed by General Omar el-Béchir, the coup d'état of June 30, 1989, which overthrew the government of Sadeq el-Mahdi, was largely inspired by Dr. Hassan el-Tourabi, chief of the Islamic National Front (FNI). Considered by foreign ministries to be "a pope" of Islamism, Tourabi is the true inspiration and master of the new Islamic state. In this context, shortly after the second Gulf War, Hassan el-Tourabi took the initiative to bring together the Islamist delegations of about fifty countries of Africa, Asia and Europe in order to organize a response to a "West that is increasingly arrogant and scornful towards Islam."

Thus, the first "Arab and Islamic Popular Congress" (CPAI), was held in Khartoum from April 25 to 28, 1991. It brought together Arab representatives with those of Afghanistan, Pakistan, the Philippines, Malaysia, Algeria and Albania. Observers immediately saw this *internationale* involving three continents of Islamism as an attempt to organize a kind of Comintern. The structure of the new organization reinforced this interpretation: a permanent council of 50 delegates — from the 50 countries represented — to meet every three years, associated with a general secretariat of 15 leaders in charge of the implementation of the objectives laid down by the council.

By acclamation, Hassan el-Tourabi was elected General Secretary of the new organization; its headquarters, naturally, was to be housed in Khartoum. The invited Western news services echoed the new General Secretary's general declaration of policy. "This congress is the first time we have pulled ourselves together after the crisis of the Gulf. It has brought together representatives of the Eastern and Western sides of the *Oumma*, those who speak Arabic and those who speak other languages. It is not an official banquet to which people are invited under the aegis of the sultan, neither is it a coterie for circumscribed theoretical debates. But it is the determination to defy the tyrannical West."

A graduate of the University of London and Doctor in Law from the Sorbonne, Tourabi is an old political fox with many years' service. Even though his own actions are much more pragmatic, he knew by experience that in "the complicated East," it would be necessary to take into account not only the Shiite-Sunni confrontation but the fundamentally schismatic nature of the Islamist factions that were listening to him. He also knew that, taken as a whole, the theme of a monolithic West is the only common denominator for the range of Islamist components represented. Such a common denominator had been missing until now. Anxious to embody the new spirit of world Islamism, Tourabi identified himself with his historical model: Hassan al-Banna, founder of the Muslim Brothers. Like him, by elevating the West to the lead role of the Great Other, Tourabi took up the ideology of his peers in the Egyptian Brotherhood, even if he had not always entertained the best relations with its international branch.

The proclamation of his "anti-Western party" was articulated around five main points:

1) Any future emancipation from the Western yoke starts with God, "God who is greater than the West;" and it is around him that the Muslims of all the countries must unite. "The only God is God, for however powerful the West may be, God will remain the greatest." Denying this reprehensible West the right to embody the whole world, Tourabi reversed the proposition and postulated that "the Muslims are the conscience of the world;" that "their liberation conditions the liberty of the world."

2) In response to the planet-wide decadence driven by "an absolute and tyrannical force of materialism," only the Islamic religion remains — the "only true religion," Tourabi explained, because "on our premises the divine law still persists to govern the action of the state, while organizing the relations between individuals." This is the quintessence of Hassan al-Banna's teachings, a fusion of the religious and the political.

3) Carefully constructing a unifying ecumenism, Tourabi's discourse was addressed as well to the Sufis, the *wahhabis*, the traditionalists and the modernists. This sense of openness was not directed at political pluralism in the sense of an acceptance of the existence of various political forms, in particular secularity, but at organizational pluralism, "provided that it is not weakened and that it continues to be governed by the unity of the *Shura*" [*ed. note: shura* may indicate a council of state, advisers to the sovereign, or a parliament; it conveys the sense of the Koranic injunction for believers to conduct their affairs "by mutual consultation"]. Pluralism was also intended on the international level, but without interfering in the internal concerns of the members.

4) Strategically and politically most important, the fourth imperative relates to nationalism, the historical bullet of the Islamist ideology. "The surest means to break the barriers between the Islamist movements and the nationalist and patriotic formations," Tourabi insisted, "is to put an end to the Byzantine discussions on nationalism and Islam." There is no contradiction, therefore, between the *Oumma* and the national liberation movements.

5) As a corollary, the fifth directive is a new call to gather all the Muslims of the world. The method: to wipe clean the slate, so that memory of the past no longer represents the *Oumma's* greatest obstacle to progress. "This history of past divisions is, today, the principal barrier to our rebirth," Tourabi noted again.

To these five points a corollary was added that relates to an abso-lutely crucial point of methodology. It dictates the strategy of Islamist militants immersed in the West. This additional loan from the ideology of the Muslim Brothers is based as much on Jesuitical acculturation as on Sun Tzu's teachings on war: without ever giving up anything funda-mental, to avoid direct confrontation and to display accommodating attitudes; to transmit a positive message founded on the primacy of justice. "It is more a question of fighting against injustice by upholding the law," recommended the General Secretary of the congress, "and of moving ahead the dialogue in our interaction with the world. It is even possible to work with the West, if it seeks cooperation founded on something very different from the current system (which is completely iniquitous)." Rather than sinking into breakdowns and "isolating our-selves in times of trouble, which does not correspond to the needs of today," Tourabi invited the members of his congress to use the most modern methods of confrontation and to demonstrate adaptability, in particular in "the current political fight, which requires the use of stratagems more than of force." Tourabi recommended, finally, a boy-cott of "the traditional organizations, who have been unable to encom-pass and mobilize the Arab and Islamic society."

Along with the Algerian representatives of the Islamic Salvation Front (FIS), the Palestinian Hamas, the An-Nahda movements of Tuni-sia, the Egyptian commanders of Gama'a Islamiya, and Syrian, Bosnian and Pakistani delegations, there were key individuals such as Gulbud-din Hekmatyar, the chief of the "Afghan" Hezb-i-islami. Nevertheless, their presence and the convergence of views did not automatically indi-cate that their political and military activities would be coordinated.

Besides, Dr. Tourabi had other more immediate concerns with the civil war that since 1983 had set the Sudanese governmental forces against the guerrillas of the South, who were for the most part Chris-tians or animists. In recent years, the regional expansion of the conflict (which has drawn in increased support from the neighboring Ethiopia and Uganda) has reinforced the fear of generally being surrounded and hemmed in by the West. The big American companies calculate that Sudan holds sizable oil reserves — more than 20 billion barrels — even though the current production of petroleum is ridiculously low. In the short run, this configuration of isolation, added to a promising mineral wealth, is all the more certain to activate terrorist connections such as the Arab and Islamic Popular Congress. Thus the Sudanese orchestra sets the tempo, but more in relation to the regional music than to a vague international partition.

Far from bringing about the establishment of new Islamic states or hegemonic Islamic societies, a preliminary assessment of the results of Tourabi's CPAI indicates that Olivier Roy was right when he suggested the failure of political Islam. "It's more a cultural influence than political action that is communicated via international networks," he writes. "These networks are periodically devastated by the conflicts that set the Middle East states against each other, as the second Gulf War demonstrated: Muslim brothers, *wahhabis* and Pakistanis aligned themselves at that time according to the positions of their respective countries. The national dimension still dominates. Local organizations are shaped, above all, by the national policy; the supranational institutions are financial and distribution networks rather than command and control organizations."[6]

Indeed, the money trail makes it possible to track down the true underwriters of Islamist terrorism. The *Internationale* of the financiers is definitely more at issue than that of ideologists and planters of bombs.

The Sudanese state bodies and economic circuits are heavily populated with militants, particularly those of the FNI. Under protection of the great tribal "families" and with easy access to a rich clientele and networks of influence, fortunes have been built quickly, as the real estate boom and the number of Mercedes that dart through the capital testify. Now there is a cadre of Islamist businessmen who have good relations in the new administration and within the government and the army. In Khartoum, as elsewhere, Islamism often means mixing business and politics, as those new to power openly give preference to their own people when it comes to contracts, markets and assistance of all kinds. Resolutely engaged in liberalizing the economy, the Islamic power has launched a vast program of privatization that has especially benefited this news caste of Islamist businessmen — a development that has some bearing on the financing of the Islamist organizations and their terrorist activities.

How Tourabi's Islamic National Front is financed provides more insight into the internationalization of Islamism than does any report from the meetings of the Arab and Islamic Popular Congress. Nerve center of the holy war, its various sources of financing thus bring us back to the associations between former and new "Afghans." "The Sudanese Islamists found flexible institutional forms to collect the money and to mobilize forces," explains Roland Marchal. "By disconnecting the political game from the financial game, the FNI also succeeded in getting beyond the first circle of sympathizers and assuring itself, before and after the Gulf War, of support (half-naive, half-calculated) from institutions like the Kuwaiti Funds of the *Zakat* [the religious tax]. These networks were also instrumental in the development of Islamist organizations in the host countries. They made it possible to identify the most religious people and those who were most disposed to get involved in local political activity. The Sudanese played so direct a role in developing the al-Islah movement in Yemen and the fundamentalist cliques in the Gulf states that it led to incidents with certain states."[7]

Another source of revenue is the currency exchange market, which is particularly intense because of the significant number of migrant workers from Sudan. The Sudanese Islamists, because they inspired confidence, were able to become the middlemen who collect the wages earned by their compatriots in the Gulf countries and transfer them to their families in Sudanese pounds, at a preferential rate very close to the parallel market. The Islamic banking structure guaranteed other contributions, in particular through the intermediary of the large Saudi banks Baraka, Tadamon, Faysal and Dar al-Mal al-Islami (DMI), where Tourabi directed the office of Islamic oversight. The banks' presence in Khartoum makes it possible to attract foreign investors and to create many joint ventures. These activities support the emergence of that circle of Islamist businesses that we have already observed were among the principal beneficiaries of the coup d'état of June 1989.

Much money is also invested in Islamist NGO's, which have become an economic sector on their own. Independent of their functions of training and regulating youth, these actors in the Sudanese economic and social life take advantage of their tax exempt status and their abundant cheap labor to specialize in import-export trade. Lastly, the close relations maintained with the various factions of Afghan resistance have made it possible to develop major channels for recycling money from drugs.

According to the United Nations International Program for Drug Control, Sudan has become one of the main hubs for laundering the considerable profits derived from selling opium. Afghanistan is the greatest producer in the world. In accordance with the structural logic of organized crime, parallel to these money-laundering systems there is a burgeoning trade in light weapons supplying the various markets of eastern Africa and particularly Somalia and Yemen. These theological-racketeering links with "happy Arabia" are quite convenient, since the Islah party activists (a Yemeni version of the Muslim Brothers that participates in the governmental coalition of Sanaâ) are, for the most part, former fellow travelers of the Sudanese Islamic National Front (FNI). At the extreme southern edge of the Arabian Peninsula, the Yemeni Islamists also shelter and employ "Arab" Afghans.

**Yemen.** Bounded by the Indian Ocean and cut off from Africa by the Red Sea, Rub al-Khali, the hottest desert in the world, extends toward the valley of Hadramaut, backdrop of the incense road. To the north, fortified villages cling to the sides of the mountains that elevate the old capital of the Sabaean empire to an altitude of 7600 feet. Since deepest antiquity, Sanaâ and its high houses have not moved. Legend claims that it was the first city built after the flood; the generous and turbulent traditions of hospitality of tribes consuming qât, the indispensable euphoria-producing plant, add to the legend. Revisited since the *Voyage de l'Arabie Heureuse par l'Ocean oriental et le détroit de la mer rouge* (by Jean of Rocque, 1716), the vision of "Happy Araby" haunts the writings of Rimbaud, Henri de Monfreid, Joseph Kessel, Paul Nizan, and Malraux when he was seeking the Queen of Sheba.

With its 14 million inhabitants, expanding at a rate of more than 3% per year, Yemen is the home of the greatest population on the Arabian Peninsula. In the early 1990's, North Yemen (the Arab Republic of Yemen, supported by the West) was unified with Southern Yemen (the Popular Democratic Republic of Yemen, allied with the USSR). The new republic was proclaimed on May 22, 1990. The first "Afghans" arrived in the context of this unification. Some 300 Egyptians, Jordanians and Libyans came from the Peshawar camps where they had followed the military-religious teachings of Abdallah Azem. One year later they were joined by two contingents, Algerian and Syrian, of several hundred men.

Welcomed as heroes by the ideologist of the Islah party (Sheik Abdel Majid al-Zandani) and by colonel al-Ahmar (commander of the

Yemeni second armored division, and, more important, half-brother of President Ali Abdallah Saleh), they were assigned to units quartered in the northern mountains, around the town of Saada. According to the Egyptian information service, these "Afghans" were then divided into three special brigades. One, specializing in the techniques of urban guerrilla warfare, mainly was made up of the future militants of the Algerian Armed Islamic Groups (GIA), members of Gama'a Egyptian, and Saudi and Libyan activists. The second was created especially for handling explosives used in the preparation of car bombs, attacks on barracks, and time bombs. Individual and personalized assassinations were the specialty of the third brigade, which was for the "internationalists" among the "Afghans," who could be engaged in any theater of operation.

Before being permanently assigned, the "Afghans" were welcomed and stayed in a transit camp close to the port of Hodeida, on the Red Sea. That is the gate that opens on the northern part of the country. Consequently, it is no surprise that in spring 1994, most of the 2000-odd "Afghans" who were taking refuge in Yemen were taken in hand by officers from the Sanhan tribe (that of President Saleh), who belonged the Hashids, one of the three great federations (groups of tribes) in the North. In the South, the Egyptian services located two "Afghan" camps, one in the Hadramaut Valley and the other on the mountain, al-Mahrhashiqa. Those camps were dismantled on the initiative of the leaders of the Yemeni Socialist Party, which had insisted that these "foreign combatants" suspend all activity in the South of the country. Those expelled would find refuge among the Hashids in the North. This different treatment crystallized and presaged a new confrontation between the "two Yemens."

Hostilities opened on May 5, 1994 with a morning air raid by the South, on Sanaâ. The northern units crossed the old frontier line, advanced toward Aden and engaged in the valley of Hadramaut in order to eradicate the socialist opposition that, according to President Ali Abdallah Saleh, "threatens the unity of the country, disputes the supremacy of the regime and paralyses political life." Various military sources established that several groups of "Afghans" had joined forces with the northern Hashid militia and the first mechanized division, against the brigades of Southerners. Several hundred "Afghans" were also engaged in the provinces of Abyan, Shabwa and Lahej to liberate

Northern troops that had been surrounded by the Southerners. In spite of this "Afghan" support, and taking into account their inferior manpower, it was only around July 7, 1994 that the government forces managed to bring both sides together. Thus the entire national territory was reunited once again by arms. The losses, mostly military, amounted to 5,000 dead and 6,000 to 7,000 wounded. The infrastructure of "Happy Araby" was relatively spared, with the notable exception of Aden (which was plundered).

One of the masterminds behind this reconquest was none other than the principal guardian of the "Afghans," Sheik Abdallah Bin Hussein al-Ahmar, chief of the al-Islah party, the Yemeni Gathering for Reform. Approximately 60 years old, he is the very powerful chieftain of the Hashid confederation and thus holds great authority over the northern half of the country. A member of the international branch of the Muslim Brothers, this prototypical feudal lord has always enjoyed political and financial support from Saudi Arabia, as well as from one of his close friends, Osama bin Laden (himself of Yemeni origin). During a conversation with a Sudanese military attaché on mission in Aden, bin Laden explained the reasons for his engagement with the northerners and told how "his" Afghans killed 158 leaders of the Yemeni Socialist Party between 1990 and 1994. During this same period, bin Laden was constantly preaching in the mosques of Sanaâ, Abyan and Chabwa, where he launched "*fatwas*" against "the heretic Communists, principal enemy of the Muslims and the reunification of Yemen."

Once peace was restored, the Yemeni president knew he could not allow himself a head-on confrontation with the power of the Islah (which could raise, overnight, tens of thousands of men-at-arms); he chose to resign himself to governing the country in association with them. This association was closely monitored, for the president of the Yemeni Republic understood perfectly well that, in accordance with the ideology of the Muslim Brothers, the Islah's final objective is to introduce an Islamic state to Yemen. "Saleh did not fall with the last rain," explains a European diplomat stationed in Sanaâ. "He allowed the Islah, which is his obligatory partner in government, to establish itself in the South and replace the urban social framework of the mass organizations of the Yemeni Socialist Party, heirs of the Soviet model. But in parallel he was negotiating with the Socialists and planning to restore to them some of their patrimony and their resources, before reinstating them in the governing coalition as a bulwark against an ever more invasive Islamist presence."

In the wake of the Islah, the "Afghans" also infiltrated the South of the country and became very active in the currency trade by creating many import-export companies with the support of Sudanese Islamist businessmen. They did not establish themselves there without strife, because in addition to their dominant position in business the "Afghans" also want to dominate local religious practices. This will to establish hegemony over commerce in merchandise and in souls came to dominate the scene in various ways. . . and sounded the trumpet for the advance.

On September 29, 1995, a group of Egyptian and Libyan Afghans led by an Algerian militant, Adam Abdel Rahman, directed a punitive expedition against a beauty salon in the town of Dhaleh, 50 miles from Aden. The confrontation degenerated into a battle with a squadron of the 35th Yemeni military brigade. The official tally by the Ministry of the Interior declared three dead (including two police officers) and five wounded. This "battle" followed upon incidents at the beginning of September in Aden between police officers and activists of the Yemeni Jihad, the armed militia of the Islah party.

These confrontations, the first since the end of the civil war between the Northerners and Southerners, had caused the death of seven people including four police officers, as well as ten civil casualties. The conflicts had erupted after the Islamists destroyed a *marabout* (shrine) covering the tomb of a local saint. The Islamists considered the existence of this mausoleum to be contrary to the practice of the "true religion." Since then, the "Afghans" have been implicated in a series of similar acts of violence, in particular an attack in the province of Ibb (in the south of Sanaâ) made against a local leader of the General Popular Congress (CPG), the party of President Saleh. These repeated events ended up souring relations between the CPG and the Islah party, several of whose militants were implicated in the acts of violence ascribed to the "Afghans." "From now on, the Yemeni government is going to smother in the womb any inclination toward religious extremism, whoever the authors may be," warned the Interior Minister, Colonel Hussein Arab. The minister also denounced "the radical movements revolving around 'al-Islah' which are financed by Saudi Arabia, and which dispute the authority of the regime."

As a consequence of the battle of Dhaleh, the Yemeni officer deal-ing with the "Afghans" from the North, Jamal al-Nahdi, had to disman-tle the three camps in the vicinity of Saada. The Egyptians Moustapha Hamza, Rifahi Ahmed Taha and Tharouat Salah, like 123 other Egyp-tian "Afghans," accompanied by "the Sudanese" of the al-Aroussa camp, also had to leave the environs of Sanaâ. Several dozen Libyans were expelled from the universities of Hadramaut, where they had enjoyed student status; the university in Sayun, in particular, was regarded as one of the most important "Afghan" induction facilities in the south of the country.

In this "open war" against "religious extremism," the Yemeni gov-ernment proceeded to expel from the country several hundred "Arab Islamists of the Yemeni Jihad and Afghanistan veterans," at the end of 1995, according to a declaration in the *Yemen Times* by General Yahia al-Moutawakkei (adviser to the President for security matters). In 1997, several dozen other "Afghans" were again officially expelled, after the Interior Minister's revelations on "the dismantling of a terrorist net-work led by a naturalized Syrian of Spanish origin" and condemned by a court in Aden for a terrorist attack and for criminal conspiracy against the security of the state.

The Yemeni government has little enough room for maneuver; and the religious factions are also circumscribed. . . Although he is encour-aged by international pressure, President Saleh's determination to fight against Islamist subversion cannot fly in the face of the powerful Islah party. In a regional context where relations with the neighboring Saudis are deteriorating, the president wants to avoid seeming to be the enemy of the religious who participate in his governmental coalition — a coalition upon that rests the fragile consensus of the great tribal fed-erations. "But the Islamists of the Islah can hardly allow themselves to be overrun by groups that are more radical than they themselves," ex-plains an Arab diplomat stationed in Sanaâ. "In other words, the 'Afghans' have become awkward for everyone," and officially undesir-able.

In his new headquarters of Dhira al-Hindukush, deep in the mountains of Khorassan, Osama bin Laden took refuge. At his side were Sheik Abdel Majid al-Zandani, now chief of the armed militia of the Islah, and two emissaries of the international branch of the Muslim Brothers. Their objective was to re-deploy the whole of the Afghan "apparatus" between Yemen and . . . Somalia. With Islah and the Yemeni president wrestling for control, new camps were equipped in the depths of the valleys of al-Maraqcheh, Libin and the areas of Lahejj and Saada. Since the Popular Congress had not been able to regain control of the province of Abyan, that is where Tareq al-Fahdli's "Afghan" groups moved. Since the airport of Sanaâ is now under too much surveillance, the new preferred access route is the port of Aden, which is far more porous due to its two-pronged sea traffic: to the Red Sea and the Indian Ocean. Some 5,000 passports are stolen every year from the main registration office in Sanaâ.

The so-called expulsion at the end 1995 and during the following year dispersed approximately 400 "Afghans," accompanied by a few dozen Yemenis; it was not, as the Yemeni government claimed, "the result of a total war against the religious extremists" but the planned "Afghan" redeployment between the Horn of Africa and the Arabian Peninsula. These departures were conducted, with weapons and baggage, under the responsibility of bin Laden himself, of the Islah, the international branch of the Muslim Brothers, and of Mokbel al-Wadihi (director of the Yemeni Jihad). Aboard "*zarugs*" (those narrow boats with the characteristic steeply-slanted masts, the legendary sailing ships of pearl fishermen that one may see in the straits of Bab el-Mandab) successive loads were sent out in broad daylight and with great public fanfare for the Somali coast, the Afghans' second base on the Red Sea.

Entirely sponsored by the Saudi financier, this redeployment between Yemen and Somalia was nearly complete by the end 1997. It met two objectives: to permanently install the "Afghans" in the mountains of Yemen, where the introduction of an Islamic state was within reach, and even more so, to bring together the new "Afghans," partisans of the Taleban, and the "Hezb-i-islami" party of Gulbuddin Hekmatyar, which was at war against the Taleban. That was bin Laden's great dream: to forge a reconciliation between his new Taleban friends and his "Afghans," most of whom were still part of Hekmatyar's forces. Using the redeployment sanctuaries in the Yemeni mountains, the Somali station took care of setting up "secondary camps" from which the old and the new "Afghans" could expand, not only in eastern Africa, but also in the countries of the Gulf.

**Somalia.** Somalia has been part of bin Laden's plans for a long time. It serves as the intermediate stopping place between the Yemeni camps, the Sudanese bases and his Afghan palace of Kandahar. This installation was duly negotiated with the Somali Islamic Union (SIU) under Sheik Ali Warsama and the forces of warlord Mohammad Farah Aydid, directed by his son, Hussein. The SIU was thus committed to supporting the Aydid clan against the opposing clan of Ali Mahdi, in a new civil war adventure marked by outrageous violence. This was a fight to the death for the power that had been in place since the Somali dictator Siad Barré fell on January 29, 1991. In return, the Aydid clan gave the Somali Islamists *carte blanche* to manage the mosques in their zones of control. With their Afghan "allies," the Islamists could thus accommodate their sister "nongovernmental organizations" and make their business flourish, especially the juicy trade of qât, which is consumed by all and sundry in Yemen. In addition to dealing in cars, the Islamists also own most of the retail trade, starting with the ports which they control.

The old "Aromatic coast" — incense and cardamom — was the only country of Black Africa with the same ethnic background, sharing the same Somali language and Sunni Islam, at the extreme tip of the Horn, that strategic piece of land that constitutes the natural bridge between the African continent and the Arab world. Who remembers today the children with outrageously inflated bellies whose photos were shown every day on CNN? "God's work," George Bush exclaimed, to justify the American intervention. And that is undoubtedly the feeling that the American soldiers shared on December 9, 1992, when they disembarked in the Bay of Mogadishu in front of every TV news team on the planet.

Caught up in the euphoria of "the new international order," the new-found unity of purpose between the U.N. and the all-powerful United States was heavily covered by the media. This intervention in Somalia, which ended in the military-humanitarian operation of December 1992, was to inaugurate a new means of settling conflicts. For the first time in its history, the United Nations faced one of the major challenges of the post-Cold War period: the implosion of the structures of state and the absence of any government in a country given over to famine and at the mercy of warlords who were oblivious to the elementary needs of their people. Fifteen months later, in April 1994, the

American armada departed, without glory, carrying in its hydroplanes and its combat helicopters 44 "boys" in body bags, victims of the "first humanitarian war" in the history of the world.

With the American Rangers gone, the television teams packed their bags, too. Except for some sudden convulsions when a Western humanitarian worker is taken hostage, Somalia has sunk back into the quiet image of the "country of Aromatics." "The people of God" no longer exist and the fratricidal fights of the warlords have once again become the primary economic activity in this forgotten land. Today in Somalia, the wild state has returned in full force, and all forms of trafficking has resumed, every form of slavery and profiteering. Why, then, should we be astonished that the "Afghans" make it one of their new hunting grounds? Service in Mogadishu was compared to Beirut; for the current decay of the Somali capital directly evokes Beirut as it was during the Lebanese civil war: the natural environment of international terrorism.

Around the airport, in the southern districts of Mogadishu, Moustapha Hamza, Mohamed Rifai Taha, Tharout Salah and their Egyptian "Afghans" established their headquarters. With their Yemeni assistants, approximately 400 "Afghans" currently work with the "united Somali coalition," that groups together the various militia under the orders of Hussein Aydid. Their food is flown in once a week from Sudan. The chief regional alliance has been made with the Eritrean Islamic Jihad party. Bin Laden calculates that they have to rely on unknown groups within the foreign information services to prepare "operations" in the Gulf states.

Other agreements have been made with more local organizations, like the Somali party al-Itihad (whose activists were trained by the Egyptian "Afghans"). This movement set off a bomb on February 12, 1997, in a hotel in Harar (eastern Ethiopia), that killed two and wounded seven. Three other Ethiopian hotels were targeted by the same movement during the previous year. In October 1997, more "cadres" of the Arab "Afghans," coming from the Balkans and Afghanistan, were settled in Mogadishu. They populate the local offices of 27 import-export companies whose main offices are registered in Ta'ez, Abyan, Chabwa and Saada in Yemen; their capital is estimated between $20 and 25 million.

Parallel to the traditional military and paramilitary activities of the "Afghans," who are locked into becoming their hosts' mercenaries, the same economic shifts are taking place in Somalia as those that have begun in Sudan and Yemen. The "Afghans" are looking to make fast money by joining forces with pre-existing local criminal networks. Very much in the know at the hotel al-Sahafy, an important link in Aydid's business nebula, an Italian businessman explains with great animation how, for years, Somalia has helped to launder the funds of certain Italian political parties. The Aydid clan in particular was used as a link in the recycling of the Italian Socialist Party's funds, until a fatal quarrel intervened with Pilitteri who was, at the time, treasurer of the PSI and Mayor of Milan, the source of spicy legal incidents that would gain new impetus before the Italian courts.

For their part, the Italian Christian Democrats and their financial structures turned instead to the Libyan special services to prime their "money pumps." However, since Tripoli recognized the Aydid clan as the only legitimate Somali authority, and opened an embassy in Mogadishu, several observers have noted the return of certain financial activities to Somalia. Annoyed with the financiers of the PSI, it is probable that the Aydid clan, anxious not to lose the Italian recycling business to their competitor Ali Mahdi (who was also a "specialist" in Italian finance), decided to put its know-how to the service of the Christian democrats.

A permanent representative of the Aydid clan is housed in Rome at the headquarters of a company which is also the seat of the Italy-Somalia Chamber of Commerce. In 1996, the treasurer of this organization disappeared; he found it easy to cover his tracks. But, according to several well-informed sources, this Chamber of Commerce worked particularly closely with several European companies belonging to the bin Laden group.

The Afghan phenomenon cannot be reduced to the map of its successive sanctuaries, to the personality of its known religious leaders and its soldiers, nor to the chronology of the attacks that carry its imprimatur. Nevertheless, through its networks, the same three components are always at work. The first and most obvious bears the theological-political hallmarks of the movement's birth during the "holy war of Afghanistan," namely, a fusion of the ideology of the Muslim Brothers with *wahhabism*. The chief draftsmen of this "fusion" were Prince Turki (head of the Saudi intelligence services), Abdallah Azem, who claims to follow Aboul Nasr (director of the Egyptian Muslim Brothers), and the ISI (the secret service of the Pakistani army). And this vast political-religious construction project could never have gotten off the ground without the logistical and financial support of a fourth partner, the CIA.

This ideological-military construct is developing in tandem with the expansion of rackets, a cross between trade and political favoritism; this, too, is encouraged by the American services, which are especially keen to avoid dipping into their own budgets. This second dimension involves, once again, the Muslim Brothers and the various Saudi financial instruments. The diversification of these instruments often leads into other criminal financial structures, gradually merging with a clearly mafioso sector and with "gray" markets that are harder to define.

Lastly, one man and his many financial companies are found at every level of the edifice: Osama bin Laden and his family company, the "bin Laden Organization." Successively a financier, a war lord, a political leader and a preacher, bin Laden is a pure product of the American intelligence services. He currently lives between Somalia and Yemen, but also in London and in Kandahar, Afghanistan, where he is protected by his friends — the Taleban and the Pakistanis. Where does he get his immense resources? For whom is he working today? Has he really broken off with his former bosses?

Footnotes

1. February 1996.
2. "Diasporas et le financement des conflits," in *Economies des guerres civiles*, Hachette, 1996.
3. Assem Akram, *Histoire de la guerre d'Afghanistan*, Balland, 1996.
4. *Afghanistan — L'Ours piégé*, Alérion Editions, 1996.
5. Remarks recorded by Vincent Jauvert, *Le Nouvel Observateur*, No. 1732, January 1998.
6. Olivier Roy, *L'Echec de l'islam politique*, Le Seuil, 1992.
7. *Eléments d'une sociologie du Front nationali slamique soudanais*, Etudes du Ceri, September 1995.

Chapter VI

OSAMA BIN LADEN, OUR MAN IN KANDAHAR

> "We've done a good job on questions of competitive-
> ness, where other countries are using, illegally or in-
> elegantly, methods that put us at a disadvantage. We
> will continue on this course, even if governments or
> companies band together to handicap another gov-
> ernment or another company in a trade agreement. I
> do not see us engaging in what you would call indus-
> trial espionage."
>
> Richard Kerr, Deputy Director of the CIA

Who is this man with the enigmatic smile? Abruptly elevated to
the rank of "planetary public enemy number one," the federal court of
New York has issued an international warrant for his arrest. This 43
year old Saudi, a veteran of the first Afghanistan war, is the son of a billionaire and is a billionaire himself. Leading an army of 7,000 men and
an international financial empire, he is more powerful than a head of
state. He invented a form of terrorism that is privatized and practically
quoted on the stock exchange. For him, it all began in Afghanistan,
with the "holy war" against the Red Army. First, he was a recruiter of
"Arab volunteers," then a front-line soldier. At that time he sealed a
secret agreement with the CIA. This "public enemy number one" enjoys
the protection of the American agency, and has close relations with the
Saudi special services as well. Their chief, Prince Turki Ibn Fayçal, continues to "handle" Osama bin Laden, despite his having been deprived
of Saudi nationality in 1994. The billionaire also maintains close relations with his family, even if he had to wage a war for control of the bin
Laden financial empire. After several sojourns in Sudan and Yemen, he
is back in Afghanistan. He took refuge with his Taleban friends, from
whom he acquired control of a whole province producing opium. This
"man who wanted to be king" has thrown all his weight into the process of arranging the succession to the throne of Saudi Arabia. Is he still

the CIA's joker in the game for the future of the monarchy, which is a matter of such great concern to the United States?

London, April 28, 1998.

"I'll repeat, Osama bin Laden is very important to the life of our organization. He is also a great friend.

"He is member of our Consultative Assembly. In this capacity, he makes recommendations.

"We speak together fairly often . . . He participates directly and indirectly.

"He has been an important figure for several years.

"He personally participated in the holy war of Afghanistan for a long time.

"Today, he has become a sort of international figure."

This is Khaled al-Fawwaz speaking, spokesman of the ARC (Advice and Reformation Committee[1]), an association that the British and French intelligence services consider to be bin Laden's London antenna. This organization regularly publishes press announcements through which the Saudi financier gives his point of view on the events of the day and on the state of the "international holy war."

For the occasion, the spokesman was dressed in the traditional abaya of the sheiks of Hedjaz. Wearing the red and white checked keffieh encircled by the aghal, the black cord that serves as a head-band, he weighed each word calmly, almost meditatively, welcoming us in the name of Allah, the powerful and the merciful.

Night was falling on the districts north of London. Cancelled and then postponed on several occasions, the appointment was finally kept at the association's premises, more precisely at al-Fawwaz's own premises, in a small house that was in no way distinguished from any of the others in Wembley. Our host had just finished the fourth prayer of the day, and from the start, the conversation took a rather particular direction. Always beginning his speech by evoking the name of Allah, the powerful and the merciful, our interlocutor successively turned aside all of our questions in order to continue a reflection that seemed to be connected with an internal monologue.

"If you, you have a brother, for example in Bosnia, in Chechnya, Sudan, or anywhere else in the world, and if he has problems . . . naturally, you do all you can to help him by giving him food; and if you have a little power, you can help him with weapons, and even by raising an army to send to his aid. That is how we Muslims reason!

"We believe that we form only one body, and that each one of its parts is absolutely indebted to all the others. Unfortunately, this attitude is still in the extreme minority, because not all the States that call themselves Islamic truly are, except the Taleban, who are on the path of the true religion . . . They are about the only ones, today! Under such conditions, it is absolutely natural that private individuals and associations that have the means to do so should make up for the general negligence.

"London is our association's headquarters. This city is the nexus between America, the Old Continent and the Arab countries. The use of the same language is a great advantage and the authorities are very tolerant, as long as one does not interfere in questions of internal politics."

Beyond certain general considerations on democracy, the "most hypocritical system invented by men," we learned nothing more, neither about the way of life of Osama bin Laden, nor about the bin Laden Organization as a financial group.

In February 1996, Fayza Sa'd interviewed bin Laden for the weekly magazine *al-Watan-al-Arabi*, published in London. Partially recapitulated in the Egyptian weekly magazine *Rhoz al-Yussef*,[2] this interview was held at Khaled al-Fawwaz's, in Wembley. The Islamist bulletin *Yemeni al-Haq*[2] (*The Truth*) reprinted extracts calling for an "international holy war." According to several authorized sources, Osama bin Laden traveled many times to the British capital between 1995 and 1996, on his private jet.

At the heart of the Afghan "apparatus," Osama bin Laden is considered today to be the kingpin in all the attacks that bear the mark of the "Afghans." He is not only their "banker," but also a respected war chieftain who participates in developing the movement's strategy. Parallel to his military tasks — and indissociably related to this role — his role as a preacher gives him the opportunity to legitimate his political convictions.

Osama bin Laden was born in the Mecca in 1956, of a mother of Syrian origin, Aalia Aaziz Ghanem, and a father from a great family from Hadramaut (an area in South Yemeni). He has about fifty sisters and brothers. In the 1940's, the family settled in Jeddah, in Saudi Arabia. An influential religious sheik, his father became a close friend of the Saudi royal family and created one of the largest home-building and public works enterprises in the Middle East. In addition to major highway and infrastructure projects, King Fahd entrusted to him the expansion of the mosques of Mecca and Medina. Saudi subsidies intended for the construction of mosques in many Arab-Muslim countries ensure the bin Laden Group of entrée in many markets. But it was mainly princely Saudi Arabia and its orders that ensured the family company's rise to power.

Destined for an important role within the group, young Osama studied civil engineering. In 1979, he graduated from the university of King Abdul Aziz of Jeddah. Most of his innumerable relations with the sons of families from the Gulf date back to this period. At that time, his fellow students described Osama as "deeply religious" but "full of himself." Today, he has six wives, including a Syrian, a Sudanese and an Afghan. Holding a Sudanese diplomatic passport under a borrowed name, he also has identity papers from Lebanon and a passport from a European country. Once he had his diploma in his pocket, he saw little appeal in his well-charted future as a builder of mosques. He seized upon the outbreak of the war in Afghanistan to escape this destiny as a building contractor.

This shift of focus was met with paternal outrage. Osama extracted himself from the family fold and holed up in Istanbul, where he had student friends. There, he became acquainted with several wealthy Iranian traders who had left their country during the war with Iraq. These businessmen hoped to find some outlet in the Gulf, through Osama, and he reckoned that such contacts might be useful for the family company. This filial reflex reconciled him with his father and with his brothers (who understand better his need for new horizons). Around this time, under circumstances that remain unclear, he established ties with the CIA. The American intelligence center had chosen Istanbul as a way-station for the volunteers it was recruiting for the Afghan underground.

Initially, Osama provided them with food aid and medicine. From the very start, Saudi Arabia was also a donor to this holy war effort, particularly in terms of armaments (which the Americans could not provide directly). In partnership with the CIA, the Saudis collected the funds necessary to purchase the weapons (which they obtained on the Chinese market). Such a partnership clearly made it possible to exonerate the United States, accused by the USSR of encouraging an East-West confrontation. This traffic was carried out with the agreement of the family, which was operating in unison with Saudi royal policy; very quickly, Osama bin Laden became the essential intermediary. The bin Laden Group went as far as to make available several of its workmen, who also headed off to the holy war.

In 1980, Osama bin Laden — alias Abou Abdallah — set off for Afghanistan himself with a contingent of volunteers. He would remain there almost until the Russians' departure. Arriving via Peshawar, bin Laden was soon in touch with Abdallah Azem's "Office of Islamic Services," the primary organization responsible for the enrollment, induction and assignment of Arab volunteers. Together with the resident CIA chief in Peshawar, he founded "Bayt al-Ansar" (the house of partisans), reorganized the "Arab connection" and set up sixteen training camps on the Pakistan-Afghan border.

His experience with weaponry and with transport naturally led him to take responsibility for the military material shipped across this border. Very quickly, Osama lost patience with this relatively technical work; he took on an increasingly dominant role in the distribution of weapons to the various resistance factions, an eminently political task. While continuing to fulfill his responsibilities for logistics (which he delegated to managers from the family company), he became more engaged within the party of Gulbuddin Hekmatyar, who was preaching the most radical Islamism.

Fascinated by Hekmatyar's charisma and having become his friend, bin Laden got his real political-religious education at the side of this Pashtun chief (who was protected by the ISI, the Pakistani army information services). His baptism by fire engendered admiration. His actions at the front, with his cane and his Koran, brought him celebrity well beyond Peshawar, especially since he was congratulated and encouraged by Prince Turki himself. From 1982 to 1989, during the most intense phase of the war, Osama bin Laden was devoted entirely to the armed struggle against the Russian occupiers. February 13, 1989 marked the end of the Soviet troops' evacuation of Afghanistan, but Najibullah's Communist regime remained in place.

During this period of active mobilization he became acquainted with a group of three Sudanese; one of them, al-Tâher (an engineer like him), is the pure product of the "Arab connection"; al-Tâher became his inseparable lieutenant. The two men were never parted again. The death of their comrade-in-arms, the famous Sheik Abdallah Azem, was killed in a bomb attack in Peshawar by the Mossad; this signaled a change of climate. Through his regular contacts with the local CIA outpost, bin Laden felt a growing contradiction between the absolute confidence of his local contact officers and the official declarations of the State Department, which led him to fear an interruption of American support. Visualizing an Afghanistan without the Red Army, the American sorcerer's apprentice was coming to his senses. . . the State Department was starting to realize the consequences of its unconditional support for the most radical Islamist factions of the Afghan resistance.

"The Americans saw a fundamentalist Islamic government in Kabul. They saw leaders like Khales, Sayyaf, Rabbani and especially Hekmatyar establishing an Iranian type of religious dictatorship, which would make Kabul as anti-American as Tehran. Because of that, the United States sought with increasing intensity to break the hegemony of the party bosses. They wanted to exploit the disagreements between the parties and their commanders."[4] Indeed, the fever of the "holy war" was diminishing. Each faction of the resistance was jockeying for power. In Peshawar, the atmosphere became very volatile.

Bin Laden and al-Tâher understood that it was time to organize a retreat scenario. Several authoritative sources concur that such a plan was carefully studied in Peshawar, with the local leaders of the CIA. Several secret meetings were held at the end of 1991, at Green's Hotel, under the authority of Prince Turki himself. The American and Saudi services shared the same analysis: there could be no question of giving up their "Arab" Afghans, no question of selling off the assets of such a profitable collaboration, no question of breaking the fabulous instrument that the "Afghans" had become, just because of a momentary diplomatic reversal — a traditional dilemma between the men on the ground and the "technocrats of Washington," who were susceptible to all forms of weakness, if not treason.

The exact substance of the agreement made between bin Laden, the CIA and the Saudi special services is not known. The American agency wanted to preserve its access points in Afghanistan, which had become the vital route to Central Asia where the great oil companies were preparing the energy *eldorado* for the coming millennium. A major difference of opinion on the new regional configuration and the part that the "Afghans" could play there then set the CIA and the American State Department against each other. The "vital stake for the Americans, as for the Saudis," explains an Iranian diplomat who was stationed in Kabul, "is to preserve at all costs the association between bin Laden and Hekmatyar, blessed by Pakistan, a triangular alliance that should enable them to impose their will on the future of this tormented area."

Osama bin Laden would have to oversee the purchase and deliveries of weapons to Hekmatyar's troops, which were organized mainly from Sudan. With the assistance of his faithful Sudanese lieutenant al-Tâher, bin Laden naturally moved to Khartoum. He was starting a new life. The legend of the "Afghans" began to take on its true dimension.

Osama bin Laden had already visited Sudan in 1990, where he met Dr. Hassan el-Tourabi and joined the Islamic National Front. But he really settled in, in the Khartoum suburb of Omdurman, in 1992. Together with weapons deliveries, he would manage an opium supply chain that was established before he departed for Afghanistan with Gulbuddin Hekmatyar (who ruled over the province of Helmand, the "poppy garden" of the country).

This drug trade brought him an enormous amount of money. Meanwhile, his Sudanese lieutenant was developing the importation of vehicles and machine tools from Germany. Always with family support, Osama extended large loans to the Islamic regime. In exchange, the bin Laden Group launched great infrastructure construction projects (highways, bridges and airports, and several luxury residences). Business was going gangbusters. With the treasurers of the FNI, bin Laden founded the al-Chamâl Bank in Khartoum. At that time, his fortune was already estimated at several billion dollars.

In April 1992, Najibullah's resignation signaled the end of the regime in Kabul. The fall of the Communist power also broke up the unity of the Afghan resistance. Under pressure from the U.S. State Department, the Saudi authorities announced their decision to "officially" suspend their assistance to the Arabic "Afghans" — a decision without much consequence, since their support had already been effectively replaced long since by the bin Laden "subsidies." A fratricidal war between the former comrades-in-arms soon erupted between Gulbuddin Hekmatyar (the chief of "Hezb-i-islami"), and the Rabbani-Massoud coalition. On orders from bin Laden, the "Afghans" engaged in the civil war as part of Hekmatyar's extremist militia. There was continuous shuttling between Peshawar and several agricultural areas around Khartoum, as well as other camps near the town of Lobiod, where Egyptian, Jordanian and Tunisian combatants were trained.

These "Afghans" not only reinforced Hekmatyar's militia engaged around Kabul, but also swelled the ranks of the popular militia of Hassan el-Tourabi in Sudan. Other "Afghans" chose to return to their countries of origin. At the fringes of the banned Islamic Salvation Front, the Algerian "Afghans" provided the foundations of the first "Armed Islamic Groups"(GIA). In Algiers, their favorite mosque was renamed Kabul, and one their first "martyrs" was renamed Mourad al-Afghani. Other fighters joined the Egyptian Gama'a, and the clandestine organization of the Muslim Brothers in Syria and Libya. In several Arab countries, the "Afghan legend" entailed a radicalization of the opposition. The "Afghans" were recruiting among the victims of the economic liberalization that was underway; in addition, their Islamic-egalitarian rhetoric was used "to clean up" and integrate the local hoodlums into the circuits of larger businesses.

These various forms of Islamic-racketeering inveiglement were then reconfigured into so many different companies and nongovernmental organizations related to the "Sudanese orchestra" directed by Osama bin Laden. Then he financed 23 training camps, in the interests of which he often returned to Afghanistan. On each of his visits, bin Laden met with the CIA experts. He also maintained contact with Islamabad and in fact served as one of the leaders in the "Board of Appeals" (Lajnat al-Daawa), a coalition of Islamist factions controlled by the Pakistani services. This is the period that made him famous as the "Banker of the Jihad."

This notoriety finally disturbed even the Saudi authorities, who symbolically stripped him of his nationality in 1994. In a press release dated April 6, the Saudi Ministry of the Interior indicated that this decision was made due to bin Laden's "irresponsible dealings," which were "in obvious contradiction with the interests of the kingdom and which harm its relations with its brother countries." The text concludes that the financier "did not heed the warnings that were transmitted to him on more than one occasion." On American orders, Riyadh issued a series of declarations giving assurances that ties had been cut, including with his family, which is supposed to have disowned him.

During his annual pilgrimage to Mecca, the head of the Sudanese state promised King Fahd of Arabia to expel Osama bin Laden, since he had become too conspicuous. Subjected to strong Egyptian pressure and to economic sanctions adopted by the U.N. Security Council, Sudan too had to give some symbolic pledges of goodwill in order to burnish its reputation (which was somewhat tarnished by bin Laden's terrorist orchestra).

The same as when they handed over the terrorist Carlos to France, the Sudanese authorities even proposed to turn bin Laden over to Saudi Arabia in order to accelerate normalization between the two countries. But the Saudi services under Prince Turki were against it. . . In May 1996, bin Laden left for Dubaï before a stopover in Pakistan — for a tête-à-tête with the ISI — and then, finally, made his way to Jalalabad in Afghanistan, headquarters of his friend Gulbuddin Hekmatyar.

As soon as he had arrived, and to prove that he had, indeed, left Sudan, bin Laden obligingly gave an interview via CNN. He stated, on the American TV station, that he had "declared a holy war on the government of the United States because it is unjust, criminal and tyrannical." These agreeable remarks seemed to lack something in candor. In several foreign offices, experts on Arab affairs remembered the discretion of the "Banker of the Jihad" during the Gulf War. During that conflict, which once more divided the Arab world, very few joined Yasser Arafat in his recriminations against the new imperialist aggression against the Muslims. Hekmatyar clearly took the part of Saddam Hussein, which upset his Pakistani guardians who had rejoined with the Western coalition. But Osama bin Laden had kept quiet.

There was another disconcerting element: although stripped of his Saudi nationality, bin Laden was still in regular contact with the all-powerful Prince Turki. In addition, the Bin Laden Group still enjoyed a steady stream of orders from the Saudi government, orders that were placed directly by King Fahd and the royal palace without being endorsed by the Finance Ministry, and were always paid in full on the spot. Such a practice is so unusual in that country that it ended up becoming the talk of the town in the business circles of the Gulf. In addition, several sources agree, Osama was not estranged from his family, contrary to the claims of the Saudi authorities.

Lastly, his two sons Saad and Abdurahman still occupy bin Laden's villa in al-Manchieh, the residential district of Khartoum. He seems to be remarkably well-integrated in normal life, for a "most wanted" sought by the police forces of the whole world. And Osama bin Laden returned to Khartoum in August 1996, with a green light from the Sudanese authorities.

This return can no doubt be explained by the progress of the Taleban offensive that captured Kabul on September 26. To signify a final break with the old order, they hanged the former Communist president Najibullah, and his brother Chahpour Ahmadzay. Even though the order founded by the Taleban soon turned out to be deliri-ous, it was immediately recognized by Saudi Arabia, Pakistan and the United Arab Emirates. The U.S. State Department reckoned, for its part, that the "recent events that have occurred in Afghanistan are heading in the right direction for a return to stability in the area."

Bin Laden was wary of the young students trained in the me-dressehs (Koran schools). But they ended up extending their influence over two thirds of the country, including the poppy-producing areas. Osama bin Laden thus temporarily lost control of the Afghan opium route, as the Taleban had no intention of giving up this windfall. Soon, through the essential intermediary of the Pakistani services, they would submit some interesting proposals to the indispensable "Banker of the Jihad."

While he waited, the Saudi financier flew to London to the head-quarters of his association, the "Advice and Reformation Committee." According to several Arab diplomatic sources, this trip (which was not his first to the British capital) was clearly under the protection of the British authorities.

Regarded as the world capital of Islamism, where nearly all the groups have a toehold, London and its City are also home to the Saudi banks and to large Arab-language newspapers. Every Saturday morn-ing, calls for a planetary holy war and the global introduction of Sharia resound in Trafalgar Square. In this open air market of Jihads, one meets militants of the ACB (Algerian Community in Britain) as well as the Philippine Moros and Chinese Uighurs.

Under the placid monitoring of the bobbies, the enemy is clearly identified: the West, and democracy. Each faction competes to make its stand remarkable, and the speakers follow one another under Nelson's column, whose pedestal bears an immense banner inscribed, "God is Greatest."

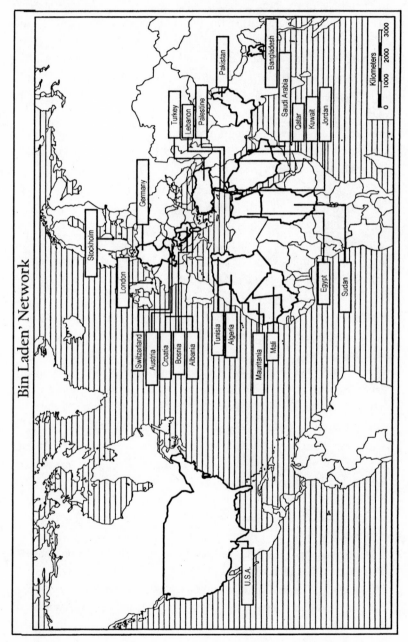

The leader of the Saudi opposition, Mohamed al-Masaari is one of the most popular speakers at these gatherings. This former friend of Osama bin Laden does not consider the Saudi financing of Islamism to be any secret. After the demonstration, he invited us over to his place, in Wembley, in the same neighborhood as that of bin Laden's spokesman. Masaari explained that the financing tapered off after the Gulf War, except for the largest organizations. In fact, the financial ties are ongoing with the Pakistani, Indian and Bangladeshi Islamist organizations, as well as with the Muslim Brothers of Egypt.

Married to an American, this former judge and General Secretary of the Council of Grievances under King Fayçal is a graduate of the universities of Riyadh and Cologne. His fast and flowery discourse is as formidable as the meditative withdrawal of bin Laden's spokesman, about whom he refused to speak openly.

When we were taking our leave, Masaari very ironically advised us to go to Jeddah. "It is there," he concluded, "that the answers to your questions lie, because that is where the head office of the bin Laden Organization (the family company) is." As we verified in the commercial and financial circles with close ties to the Middle East, the group is regarded as an quasi-appendix of the Saudi royal house.

Very little information is publicly available on the activities of the bin Laden Organization. Except for a luxurious brochure that gives a general presentation of its various services, the group does not publish an annual report. A Lebanese banker, very anxious to preserve his anonymity, indicated to us that the group has a large subsidiary company, Saudi Investment Co. (Sico), whose head office is in Geneva but which has branches in the other European countries, the United States, the Arab countries, and in several tax havens including the Bahamas.

Created in May 1980 in Switzerland, Sico (whose stated activities are "wealth management and investment services") is directed by Yaslem bin Laden, brother of Bakr bin Laden, the patriarch of the family. Its board of directors includes in particular a Swiss business lawyer, Baudoin Dunand, Esq., who also worked for the big Lebanese group William Kazan. A memo from a European intelligence agency specifies that since 1984 this lawyer has created for Sico numerous offshore companies in tax havens. Frank Warren also sits on the board; he is President of an American sporting goods company and a shipping company, Proteus; along with a Swede, Kjell Carlsson, and two Swiss,

Bruno Wyss and Béatrice Dufour — ex-sister-in-law of Yaslem bin Laden, who divorced Carmen Dufour in May 1997.

Two other branches of the bin Laden empire developed as holding companies. The first, Falken Ltd, is based in the Cayman Islands, and the second, also baptized Sico, is registered in Curaçao. Falken Ltd controls Sico-London, which was founded in 1984 and is directed by Béatrice Dufour, and Sico-Great-Britain, created in 1985, under the direction of Baudoin Dunand, Esq.. Sico-Curaçao, whose director is Yaslem bin Laden, is a player on the real estate market worldwide. The board also comprises Saleh bin Laden, Béatrice Dufour and an American real estate developer, Charles Tickle.

The bin Laden empire invested in a private airline that offered services between Great Britain, Switzerland and Saudi Arabia. It employed 175 pilots and had about fifty pieces of equipment between 1995 and 1997. At that time, its two principal shareholders were a Swiss businessman and Yaslem bin Laden, the president of Sico.

While there is nothing criminal in such an organizational chart, in itself, this is still an exemplary outline of the complexity of the ensembles of shell companies that can be used to disguise what the experts call the "legal financing" of terrorism, a sort of "reverse laundering" that takes full advantage of all the banking industry's secrecy. Here, clean money becomes criminal as it flows through legal companies and "investments," leaving no hint to suggest that it might later be diverted. It is hard, then, to identify the chinks whereby this money might, nevertheless, leak out to become criminal. For example, the Thai intelligence agency affirms that bin Laden's brother-in-law, Mohamed Jamel Khalife, regional manager of the International Islamic Relief Organization (IIRO), is used as a screen for the financing of several Philippine Islamist organizations. Activists from these groups show up in the training camps in Pakistan and in Afghanistan, and at the Islamic international university of Islamabad (which is known to be used as a cover for students eager to acquire a paramilitary education).

The zones of porosity are hard to identify precisely. Without leaving a paper trail, the funds are transferred directly into liquidities, and the actors are seldom caught with their hands in the bag. "That is the trouble with money," explains George Kardouche, the president of the Association of Arab Bankers in London. "If an honorable company decides to invest in another company, which gives funds to such and such humanitarian organization or charitable association, which itself may transfer the funds to extremist groups, there is nothing you can do about it. Money is like water, it seeks level ground, therefore it runs wherever it can. . ."

The same viewpoint can be heard in the Geneva business district, where the bin Laden Organization enjoys a solid banking reputation, just like Sico, an honorable and above-board organization installed in a patrician house in the center of the city of Calvin. While he does not spend most of his time among the financiers and business lawyers of Geneva, its boss, Yaslem bin Laden, fuels conversations — not only because he continues to maintain contact with his famous brother, but especially because of the war that raged at the top of the bin Laden empire.

"In concert with Osama," relates a businessman who hails from one of the Gulf states, "Yaslem bin Laden is suspected by his own family of instigating the death of his elder brother Salem Mohamed bin Laden. The latter perished in a mysterious explosion of his private jet during takeoff at the airport of Riyadh in 1988. The cause of the explosion was never explained, and the Saudi police force abruptly marked the case as classified. In Riyadh, it is considered that this attack made it possible for Yaslem to be propelled to the head of Sico, at the very moment when it was building offshore companies specialized in the traffic of weapons bound for Afghanistan."

Other sources confirm this account and the frequent meetings between Osama and several of his brothers, in Khartoum and Yemen, starting in 1990. It is, indeed, by tracking the parallel traffic in arms and drugs that one inevitably finds traces of the "Banker of the Jihad."

In September 1996, the office in charge of counter-terrorism at the U.S. State Department said it had no more news of Osama bin Laden, who had been seen successively in Yemen, Sudan and in Jalalabad, Afghanistan — where it is unlikely, according to the State Department again, that he would seek to be reinstalled. The same sources mentioned that it is difficult to know how the relations between the Taleban and the "Afghans" would evolve.

However, at that very time, the CIA knew perfectly that bin Laden was back in Afghanistan to reopen the opium road. At the start of their offensive, the new Masters of Kabul began by closing several camps of the "Afghans" who had taken up weapons against them. The

State Department had urgently asked the Taleban to close these camps, but they responded, (as they did with regard to opium) that Islam does not tolerate terrorism. However, shortly thereafter, several diplomatic sources insist that the drug traffic had increased to a troubling degree in the zones under their control. To reopen the opium roads, Osama bin Laden had to break with his friend Gulbuddin Hekmatyar and join the dissidents of the party Hezb-i-islami, the factions of Yunus Khales, allied with the Taleban. It was under their protection that he could re-commence his lucrative trade. Bin Laden applied the same recipe that had succeeded so well upon his arrival in Afghanistan, and put the financial power of his group at the service of the new Masters of Kabul, who were in need.

In September 1997, the "Banker of the Jihad" once again ruled over the regions that devoted most of their arable land to poppy cultivation. King of opium, bin Laden wanted to become king, period, and he sought — with the help of the Taleban — to gain direct and complete control of these provinces of northern Afghanistan. He sought to found a political party there and to have regular air time on the government-run radio of Kabul, in order to invite Arabs to join him in Afghanistan, to join the international cause of the Jihad. Several foreign military attachés have since confirmed the participation of "Afghans," faithful to bin Laden, in the war waged by the Taleban.

Being prudent, the Taleban were not eager to concede too much autonomy to this providential ally who might grow too large; they preferred to see him settle in the town of Kandahar, in the south of the country. If he could not become king, Osama bin Laden would at least have his palace. Right in the center of the city, he had an imposing villa built, luxurious and impressive, the image of power. As he had done in Khartoum, he established, near the airport of Kandahar, several training camps for his "Afghans"; he never likes to be far away from them.

Being on the best of terms with Mohammad Omar, the mullah who was chief of the Taleban, he sought to supplant the Saudi services that were financing the Taleban's military operations in the north of the country. Bin Laden took it upon himself to establish, for example, an airlift linking Kabul and Qunduz, the largest airborne operation since the Russian occupation.

Deprived of his Saudi nationality, Osama bin Laden is officially *persona non grata* in Riyadh. How can it be that the Taleban regime receives Saudi aid, while at the same time it shelters bin Laden, described by the worldwide press as a declared enemy of the monarchy? The question began to pose a problem for the Taleban, just as it did for their Saudi and Pakistani supporters.

The Kabul representative of the Pakistani army information services (ISI), Colonel Afridi, did not hide his embarrassment from several diplomats as he claimed to be doing everything within his power to "maintain surveillance over [this cumbersome guest] and to prevent him from doing any harm." The official authorities evinced the same embarrassment when the Taleban vice-minister for Foreign Affairs, Mr. Stanikzai was directly challenged by several chancelleries. His response was that Osama bin Laden returned to Afghanistan during the summer of 1996, and thus he passed responsibility for his presence to the preceding government of Rabbani-Massoud. The rest of the remarks deserve to be reported in detail:

"The Taleban government was not trying to dissimulate his presence from Saudi Arabia and the United States. Bin Laden being undesirable in his own country, he may remain in Afghanistan indefinitely — enjoying the status of a guest — as long as he commits no reprehensible act.

"He It currently resides at Kandahar, where he lives under the permanent surveillance of the Afghan authorities. We preferred to have him leave Jalalabad, from whence he would have been able to conduct various operations in Pakistan and in the tribal zones. In Kandahar, he is to some extent neutralized.

"We have made a firm commitment to the U.S. authorities represented in Kabul to take all necessary measures if we learn that bin Laden is preparing any terrorist activity whatsoever.

"In the long run, bin Laden's presence on our territory may be beneficial, for we hope soon to create the conditions for his reconciliation with the Saudi authorities."

He did not discuss what was meant by "reprehensible act," and neither did the Taleban's vice-minister clarify any further the financial aspects of the "guest status" that bin Laden enjoyed in Kandahar, nor the conditions of his resumption of activities tied to the opium trade. Clearly, these two aspects had been the object of an understanding, if not a deal, with the Taleban.

Lastly, bin Laden did indeed return to Afghanistan during the summer of 1996, before the end of the Rabbani-Massoud government. But he arrived from Jalalabad on board a Hercules C130, a Pakistani military plane, before reaching the valley of Kounar, a "neutral area" that was, at that time, outside the control of Rabbani's and Massoud's troops.

Except for the fact that, at every step, Osama bin Laden renewed contact with his CIA keepers, the last point of the Taleban's vice-minister's explanations has the merit of fixing the "bin Laden mystery" in its most relevant context and of thus lifting the veil obscuring the American services' unconditional support of bin Laden. In seeking to create the "conditions for a reconciliation between bin Laden and the Saudi authorities," the Taleban indicate that they are fully aware of the central role that they could play in the contentious succession of King Fahd of Arabia.

For several years, Saudi Arabia has been under examination in "confidential proceedings" — known as Procedure 1503 — by the U.N. Commission on Human Rights. Through the intermediary of Prince Turki (in charge of relations with international organizations) the Saudi authorities managed to have this "regimen of discreet monitoring" eliminated. The property of just one family, this country (which decapitates some two hundred individuals per annum, and which confines women to second-class status and foreign workers to a regimen of forced labor) earned its name as a "protected dictatorship."[5] Directed by an obscurantist gerontocracy, the regime is however confronted with opposition forces that are becoming more organized, to such an extent that today comparisons are burgeoning between this feudal petro-monarchy and the last shah of Iran in 1979.

Although the succession to the head of the Saudi monarchy is resolved through dynastic considerations, the competition between clans and tribes is extremely keen. And Washington is pondering the blackest scenarios regarding the future stability of this monarchy that has always experienced the most unstable periods of interregnum. In this context of stubborn personal and political rivalry, Osama bin Laden has become a trump, the card that the CIA has been playing since King Fahd *de facto* left the regency of the kingdom to his half-brother Abdallah in November 1995, following a cerebral embolism.

Officially, however, the succession is regulated like sheet music:

upon the death of King Fahd, who is 78 years old, his half-brother Prince Abdallah (75 years) should accede to the throne. Abdallah is the son of King Abdulaziz and a princess from the powerful tribal confederation of Chammar, with branches in Iraq, Syria and Jordan. Since 1963, he has overseen the command of the National Guard (a Praetorian force of the regimen made up of 40,000 Bedouins). More austere than his half-brothers of the Sudeiri clan (Fahd, Sultan, Nayef, Salman and Turki), the prince enjoys the respect of the religious circles and of the tribes, with whom he maintains close relations. Striving to manage the State's finances with rigor, he has reoriented the kingdom's budget gradually toward educational and social infrastructures, to the detriment of the great arms programs.

Without being opposed in principle to the pro-American orientation of Saudi diplomacy, he has worked toward a rebalancing the Arab-Muslim world by supporting a rapprochement with Iran, a strengthening of relations with Syria and a détente with Iraq. Prince Abdallah has made his mark on the administration of the kingdom by seeking to loosen the American vice grip. He thus lacks the confidence of the United States, which continues to prefer the very powerful Prince Sultan (74 years), second in the line of succession. A son of King Abdelaziz and the Princess Hassa al-Sudeiri, Prince Sultan is now chief of the Sudeiri clan, which is called the "clan of the seven," the seven sons of the founder of the monarchy.

This rift is not only tribal; it concerns very divergent political-economic choices. As Abdallah is regarded as the architect of a "Saudization" program, so his rival Sultan is seen as Washington's man. "His pronounced taste for money and luxury has earned him criticism from the religious circles as well as a poor image in public opinion," wrote Jean-Michel Foulquier. "His reputation of being corrupt sticks to his skin like a tunic from Nessus." Prince Sultan is, however, supposed to become crown prince in his turn, when Abdallah is king. He should not then retain his post as Defense Minister which he has occupied since 1962. Prince Abdallah, whose precedence he does not dispute, already leaves him only a carefully measured share of the real power.

This loss of apparent influence, however, is largely compensated by the solidarity of the Sudeiri clan. Thus, Sultan can count on the unfailing support of Princes Nayef, Minister for the Interior, Salman, governor of Riyadh and administrator of the *zakat* (the religious tax), and Turki, the clan's strongman. "Head of the international intelligence services since 1977, Turki is the principal special adviser to the royal house since 1968," explains Simon Henderson. "It is he who personally manages the very close relations with the representatives of the CIA and the British Intelligence Service, who are stationed Riyadh under diplomatic cover. He is always described as 'very brilliant,' which should be taken with a grain of salt, since that qualifier is much too often used by Westerners to describe members of the royal family."[6] Still, for years he has been the man of all work for the regime in general, and of the Sudeiri clan in particular.

According to the United States embassy in Riyadh, Prince Turki is one of the vital wheels of the complex mechanism that is the process of succession. Nothing escapes him, especially not the Saudi opposition's demonstrations abroad and internally. Responsible from Day One for the Saudi engagement in Afghanistan, "From the start, it was he who assumed the role of contact officer for Osama bin Laden," confirms a European military attaché posted in the Gulf for many years. In this sense, Prince Turki always maintained high-level control over the recruitment and the engagement of the "Arab" Afghans, commanded on the ground by Osama bin Laden. This military supervision was carried out through the military-business complex of the bin Laden Organization.

Contrary to its recurring denials, the bin Laden family never cut its ties with Osama, the prodigal son. In spite of his loss of Saudi nationality — which was announced in response to international requirements — Osama always relied on the family group to conclude the training and the many relocations of his "Afghan" mercenaries.

These successive redeployments were always carried out at the instigation of Turki and in connection with his CIA contacts. Among his many activities, the chief of the Saudi secret service, endowed with a power that cuts across many fields, politically supervises the allocation of State contracts and always gives preference to the bin Laden Group and ensures it the best terms of payment. This meticulous care partly explains the financial power of the "Banker of the Jihad." And the drug traffic would add a considerable supplement to the fortune of Osama bin Laden, estimated today at $3 billion.

On a strictly military level, the last redeployment of the "Afghans," conducted in the north of Yemen, signifies less the risk of a recrudescence of terrorist attacks than the emergence of a potential means of pressure to be directed against Prince Abdallah and his National Guard. Various qualified observers estimate that by the end of 1998 Osama bin Laden had three thousand "Afghans" in his camps in the north of Yemen. Half of this trained and seasoned army would be made up of Yemeni recruits, plus approximately six hundred Saudis, with the remainder being Egyptian, Tunisian, Libyan, Eritrean and Somali "Afghans."

A highly threatening political lever, poised at the very borders of the Saudi kingdom, this company of mercenaries can be mobilized very quickly. "In the context of a succession that has yet to be concluded and that could, at any moment, degenerate into open war between the National Guard and the Sudeiri clan," our military attaché adds, "this force constitutes a 'wild card' of the greatest importance for the future of American supremacy, not only in terms of access to the Saudi oil wells, but the whole area." As in Afghanistan (1979-1989), Yemen (1994) and Bosnia (since 1995), bin Laden's "Afghans" could wage a new war in the context of the succession to the throne of the Saudi monarchy.

Still today Prince Turki, the constrained friend of the CIA, and his secret service make abundant use of Osama bin Laden's networks, whereas the federal court of New York has issued an international warrant for his arrest. . . Taking into account the close ties between the United States and Saudi Arabia, it is inconceivable that bin Laden remains beyond reach! Bin Laden's networks, with all their many branches, also enjoy the active support of the Muslim Brothers. The powerful religious fraternity never refused to put its military and financial logistics at the disposal of the Saudi billionaire. Islamist activists still have to pass through the fraternity of the Muslim Brothers, the richest and most highly structured organization in the Sunni world.

## Footnotes

1. In Arabic, *al-Nassiha wal-Islah*, that is, the Committee for reform and advice.

2. No. 3549 of June 17, 1996.

3. No. 260 of June 30, 1996.

4. Mohammad Yousaf & Mark Adkin, *Afghanistan — L'Ours piégé*, Alérion Editions, 1996.

5. Jean-Michel Foulquier, *Arabie Saoudite — La Dictature protégé*, Albin Michel, 1995.

6. *After King Fahd — Succession in Saudi Arabia*, Washington Institute for Near East Policy, 1994.

Chapter VII

THE MUSLIM BROTHERS' HOLY (AND FINANCIAL) WAR

> "These 'Islamist' clerics may be seen as factors in the destabilization and the de-legitimization of the political power on two levels. First of all, because they have been able to turn themselves into private quasi-monopolies in key sectors of the economy. . . . Then, by the very manipulation of the religious reference, President Mubarak's regime associates them more and more with the success of Islamism."
>
> Michel Galloux

Who are the Muslim Brothers and what do they want? Their doctrines are organized around the central tenet of the fusion of religion and politics, the essence of the Islamist ideology. The history of the Fraternity makes the Brothers' concept of the Islamic State clear: a theocratic State of fascistic inspiration. Pursuing this goal, their methods alternate between reformism and terrorism, collaboration and confrontation with the Egyptian government. Starting in 1954, then in 1965, Nasser tried to decapitate the Fraternity. Sadat chose a subtler approach and tried to integrate the Islamists into the political game, before he was assassinated by radicals. Today, the fraternity of the Muslim Brothers has become more or less clandestine.

Seized by the demon of business, its new chief, the guide Mashhur, has chosen to increase the organization's economic and financial influence. The Muslim Brothers' bank has invested in several economic sectors, which helps it finance the propagation of Islam. Several leaders of the international organization of the Brothers sit on the bank's board of directors. Some of them were fellow travelers of the Nazis, and are still trying today to resuscitate the old alliance of Islamism and the swastika. The Brothers' bank maintains relations with many Islamist organizations.

Its clandestine branch recently lost track of $25 million. An internal investigation brought to light a web of connections, financial companies and humanitarian organizations through which the Brothers' funds are channeled. The European organizations of the Fraternity also receive some of this aid. With the support of the "Saudi godfather," the indispensable backer, the heirs of the organization's founder are looking to take control of the Muslim communities of Europe.

After the Luxor massacre, Egypt stopped in its tracks as though trapped in a sandstorm. A heavy silence enveloped the historical sites of the Nile valley. The banks of the great river bristled with the naked masts of beached *felouques*, like so many desiccated beetles. Cairo, used to laughing off setbacks, was stunned. Even the supple dance of the traffic cops, who normally direct an uninterrupted flow of vehicles, became leaden. On Midan el-Tahir, the conversations at the coffee houses were muted.

The free tonalities of the Cairo press were replaced with official bulletins from the new Minister for the Interior. Foreign correspondents in particular were targeted and the president's press office systematically canceled all authorization for reporting on anything that touched from near or far on security questions. Nabil Osman surveyed his office, repeating that he did not want to hear any more talk about "terrorism." Famous in all the editorial offices for his quiet megalomania, Osman dictated the only possible interpretation of the president's line of thinking. When I interviewed him, at his insistence, he returned time and again to the same idea. "You have only to investigate on your own territory, in Europe; there is the real origin of the criminal violence that regularly bleeds Egypt." I had hardly left his office when I noticed I was being followed by policemen in plain clothes who tailed me until the time was approaching for my appointment with the most accessible man in Cairo. Fortunately, the Marriott Hotel in Ghezira has several entrances, and a pedestrian can easily slip out, without being noticed, to the beautiful shaded streets of Zamalek. It is in the old embassy district that Muhammad Saïd al-Ashmawy lives.

For years now, the former president of the High Court of Justice of Cairo has denounced the political Islamism that threatens Islam.[1] His books and articles continue to earn him death threats on a regular basis. Round the clock, two armed guards protect the stairwell of his building. A recluse in the midst of the innumerable curios piled up in his apartment, reminding him of past voyages that he recalls with nostalgia, the solitary former magistrate pursues the mission he has assumed: to fight, by pen, the religious fanaticism that is destroying the religion of Islam. "Make a clear distinction between political Islam and authentic Islam," he begins by explaining to every one of his visitors. "Political Islam can be defined as an ideology, like Fascism or Nazism. The principal slogans of this ideology are: 'Sovereignty belongs only to God; he is the sole judge and legislator, and anyone who says or thinks otherwise is an infidel;' 'We must govern by the divine Law, by that and that alone; none of its provisions can be amended, suspended or regarded as relative or obsolete; if the texts are obscure, one must refer to the *ulemas* who alone can interpret them and pronounce *fatwâs* and judgments,' 'contemporary society is pagan, it must be wiped away entirely,' 'There are only two parties: the party of God (hizb Allah), in other words the leaders of political Islam and their followers, and the party of Satan (all their adversaries); the former must carry out the jihâd and the holy war everywhere, without quarter nor mercy, until the government of God is established.' . . . This ideology is destroying authentic Islam, and endangers the values of the Muslims and the principal values of humanity. More specifically, I want to say that this ideology that claims to monopolize Islam, has, in fact, made it into a business. Moreover, the principal Islamist leaders are racketeers. These ideologists have neither values nor scruples; they regard Islam as a business, and nothing more. Through this 'business,' they can override any principle and do what they want, in their own interests, in the name of Islam. Furthermore they have created, and continue to create, many financial and commercial associations and companies. Currently, they have built an 'politicization infrastructure' for Islam; a politicization that started in Egypt with the fraternity of the Muslim Brothers. We, the Egyptians, are particularly responsible for this development that we nourished and encouraged. In the early 1970's, dismissing the pro-Nasser Socialists made room for the Islamist groups that cozied-up to those in power. Certain members of the fraternity of the Brothers, who were close to the Raïs, persuaded him to let them act in the name of their alleged common interest, but in fact for their own benefit. Then we saw the Muslim Brothers coming back from Saudi Arabia and other Arab countries (where they had emigrated under Nasser), and working their way into politics, trade and finance, while cultivating close connections with their former guardians, particularly the Saudis. The pol-

icy of economic openness, especially the establishment of allegedly Islamic banks, and the massive emigration of Egyptians to the Arab oil-
producing countries also supported this trend. Ultimately, this new
pan-Islamism found that Egypt offered a very propitious climate for
achieving its objectives, which were often contrary to the interests of
Egypt itself. They made their way through the intermediaries of the
financial institutions and the nation's media, as well as by the means of
certain *ulemas* who were richly compensated by the Islamic banks
where they were selected to serve as advisers, or by the states who
called upon their services." Muhammad Saïd al-Ashmawy continued:
"All my research always brings me back to the same point: at the beginning of this process of the perversion of Islam are the Muslim Brothers,
an extreme Right cult."

An extreme Right cult? "The history of the Muslim Brothers is
infused and fascinated by fascistic ideology," Saïd al-Ashmawy adds.
"Their doctrines, their total (if not totalitarian) way of life, takes as a
starting point the same obsession with a perfect city on earth, in conformity with the celestial city whose organization and distribution of
powers they can discern through the lens of their fantastical reading of
the Koran."

This "Fascistic affiliation" would crop up in the analyses of several
of our interlocutors, in particular that of the journalist Eric Rouleau
who is a specialist in the Middle East, Former French ambassador to
Tunisia and Turkey, he recalls that several thousand Muslim Brothers
were arrested in 1965 after a plot against the Nasser regime was discovered. "Before the war with Israel in June 1967," he specifies, "Nasser
had decided to release the political prisoners. But only about thirty
Communists benefited from this measure. As for the Muslim Brothers,
Nasser supposedly told his advisors: 'No, they are not patriots, they will
stab us in the back at the first opportunity.' When they learned, in
their prisons, of Nasser's resignation, the militants from this far Right
organization let out a burst of indescribable joy, they were so pleased
with the defeat of the Raïs."

Since 1956, the fraternity of the Muslim Brothers regularly received aid from the CIA. That year, Nasser broke with the United
States when John Foster Dulles, Secretary of State for foreign affairs
under the Eisenhower administration, scuttled the agreement to give
the Raïs American funding for the construction of the Aswan High

Dam. This decision impelled Nasser to nationalize the Suez Canal; it was the first step in his rapprochement with the Soviet camp.

The history of the Fraternity also shows how the Brothers used assassinations in politics. From the 1970's, their partisans were prevalent in the "Islamic fraternities" (Gamaat al-islamiya), including the one that would claim the Luxor massacre, November 17, 1997. From the Afghanistan War to the "Afghans" of the CIA, the Taleban to the "new Islamist terrorisms," the fraternity of the Muslim Brothers remains the essential linchpin in the Islamist ideology.

Right from the start, the Fraternity set itself the supreme objective of introducing an Islamic state in Egypt. Its emblem is a Koran crossed by a sword. The theoretical reformism displayed by some of its ideologists has not prevented it from resorting to violence and terrorism. "The reformer who is satisfied with giving advice and guidance, neglecting government and action, will fail," wrote Hassan al-Banna; he never precisely described the methods of his concept of political action, and he never clearly answered the question of political violence, although he regularly issued specific condemnations of armed struggle.

In the 1940's, the Muslim Brothers set up a clandestine armed branch that still exists today. In less than twenty years, the Fraternity established itself solidly in Sudan, Palestine, Jordan, Lebanon, Syria, Algeria, in the Gulf and other countries around the Arab-Muslim world, as well as within the Muslim communities of Europe. Still the home base of most Islamists today, the fraternity of the Muslim Brothers is an essential part of the political history of contemporary Egypt.[2]

A component of socio-economic entities that date back to the 15th century, religious fraternities have always played an important role in the history of Egypt. Adapting perfectly to the kinship systems that structured rural communities and to the incorporation of trades in the cities, they continued to dominate Egyptian society in spite of the secularization of public services undertaken under Méhémet-Ali (1804-1849). Their administrative and political channels survived parallel to all the attempted reforms. The efforts to create a lay society, continued by King Farouk, never reached deeply into the society nor really shook the power of the chiefs of the religious fraternities. It is thus not surprising that the fraternity of the Muslim Brothers gathered a large following since its creation on April 11, 1929 by Hassan al-Banna, a 22 year old teacher.

Right from the start, the Fraternity benefited not only from a historical memory that favored its rapid expansion, but it arose at a propitious moment during a confrontation between partisans and adversaries of the revival of Islam. This debate reached its apogee with the publication of Sheik Ali Abdel Razzak's book, *Islam and the Origins of Power*, which resolutely promoted the separation of the State and the religion. The work was burned in public, and book-burnings were followed by proclamations that stoked the fires of tradition. The British occupation also encouraged this movement. Lastly, the emergence and the rise to power of Fascism, hostile to French and British colonialism, gave rise to many analogies with corporatist propaganda and the methods of mobilization of Mussolini's gangs.

Denouncing philosophy and the social sciences as practices contrary to the teachings of the Koran, Hassan al-Banna founded the essentials of his message on the condemnation of the principle of separation of the State and religion, and set the establishment of a theocratic State as his movement's goal. He also preached the re-establishment of the caliphate as the only framework that could be effective in uniting all the believers, and promoted the dissolution of political parties which, according to him, divide the Muslims. Reducing Western civilization to colonialism, Hassan al-Banna summarizes his movement's ideology thus: "Islam is doctrine, divine worship, the fatherland, the nation, religion, spirituality, the Koran and the sword."

Hassan al-Banna's son, who lives in Cairo today, prepared for me a selection of photographs dating from the creation of the Fraternity. In most of them, the founder poses in suit and tie, his famous fez on his head. Seif al-Islam explained that his father intended to express via his vestimentary choices (and those of his companions) the alliance of tradition and modernity. "Hassan al-Banna," he says, "understood very well that Islam governs not only the relations between man and God, but all aspects of political, economic, social and cultural life. He understood Islam as it was originally, i.e. as a total way of life."

In 1933 Hassan al-Banna, a teacher in Ismaïlia, was nominated to Cairo where the organization's headquarters were established. He took the title of "supreme guide" and worked toward the development of a political, economic and social program. On the basis of his interpretation of the fundamental texts of Islam, the Fraternity adopted a program in 1939 whose principal political objective is to have a constitution adopted that would arise directly from the Koran. "The Islam in which the Muslim Brothers believe views political power as one of its pillars," indicates Hassan al-Banna. "Correct application is as important as the orientation of principle. The Prophet made political power one of the roots of Islam. And in our books of Muslim law, political power is counted among the articles of the dogma and the roots of the law, and not as an element of the development of jurisprudence, as one of the branches of the legal structure. For Islam is at the same time injunction and execution, just as it is both legislation and teaching, the law and the court, not one without the other."[3] Koranic law (*sharia*) guarantees the source of public and private rights. The government must be "moralized" by fighting against corruption, the "holy war" (jihad) must be restored, and nationalism must be identified with pan-Islamism as a function of Islam and the State being identified with each other in totality.

Taking Italy's choices under Mussolini for inspiration, the economic program set three priorities: the instigation of a land reform, the prohibition of usury and the termination of income tax (which was replaced by the religious tax, the *zakat*). The social policy foresaw a new law on labor, founded on corporations. This economic program would more directly reveal its relationship to totalitarian ideologies a few years later, with the works of Mohamed Ghazali, *Islam and Economic Questions*, of Sayed Qotb, *Social Justice in Islam*, and of al-Bahi Lotfi, *Islam: Neither Communism nor Capitalism*. The populist content of such writings corresponds to the social profile of most of the followers, who were recruited from the better-off rural populace and the urban middle class. The Brothers denounced the profiteers and those who were starving the people. Mohamed Ghazali recommended "an economic regimen similar to that which existed in nazi Germany and fascist Italy."

The moral code is also an important component in this program, which is intended to create the "new Muslim man." It is founded on the strict observance of the rules of Islam, the punishment of any transgression, and on a teaching strictly in conformity to the precepts of Islam. Women's role in society is examined closely. The notion of the equality of the sexes is inherently negated by the concept of the supremacy of male social responsibilities. Justified by a literal interpretation of the Koran, the "natural" place of the woman is in the home. Repudiation and polygamy are legitimated by the same reading.

In 1939, the Fraternity held its fifth general meeting. It celebrated its tenth anniversary and placed its focus on the practical means for disseminating its program. To gain greater access to the middle class, which provided the bulk of their clientele, the Brothers opened a series of offices in the larger cities and rural areas. Teaching (both Koranic and technical classes with a solid religious basis) constituted a second set of priorities. Evening courses were provided, to ensure access for workers. Health issues were also addressed, and a series of clinics was opened, primarily in urban settings. This matrix of civil society was supplemented by sports clubs and religious organizations.

In accordance with its program, the third pillar on which the Brothers intended to build their influence supports the economic activities of the traditional religious fraternities founded on the corporations of trades. In line with the interests of its customers, the Fraternity developed a major sector for small industrial and commercial companies. In *Fiches du monde arabe (Files on the Arab World)*, Lucien Georges cites, among others, the "Islamic Transactions Company," specializing in transport; the "Islamic Press Society," which puts out various newspapers and publications; the "Muslim Brothers' Company for Spinning and Weaving," a kind of cooperative belonging to its employees; and the "Engineering Trade and Labor Company," which associated several companies in the vicinity of Alexandria.

By the end of the 1930's, the Fraternity claimed some 500,000 members. Up until the Second World War, it strove to develop its economic sector, to refine its ideological concepts, to train its representatives, and to improve its organization and its techniques of social penetration.

In 1936, during the Arab revolt in Palestine, the Fraternity made its first incursion into the political arena. The Muslim Brothers tried out their pan-Islamic slogans against British colonialism while proclaiming their support for the mufti of Jerusalem. And King Farouk was not opposed to this activism, since it seemed likely to bar further progress to the Egyptian left and the Wafd nationalists who had always claimed to be the sole incarnation of the Egyptian nation. "While the seeds of a later conflict with nationalism already existed in the opposition between popular legitimacy and divine legitimacy," Henry Laurens observes, "it would be anachronistic to set in the 1930's a showdown that really only started in the 1950's, when nationalism and Islamism had each selected in their own way the revolutionary path."[4]

Nevertheless, Hassan al-Banna took advantage of this favorable climate to expand his movement's room for maneuver and to have a decree adopted punishing adultery and prohibiting the drinking of alcoholic beverages. But these instances of collaboration with the Egyptian government remained exceptional and, in 1942, the Fraternity clandestinely established its military branch. This came to light in a spectacular way with the assassination, while the Parliament was in full session on February 24, 1945, of Prime Minister Ahmad Maher (he had just declared war on the Axis powers). The Brothers would also finance the assassination of Minister Amin Osman Pasha, on January 5, 1946, for the crime of anglophilia, and, the same year, that of the chief of the police force, Sélim Zaki Pasha.

In 1947, the Muslim Brothers fought in the first rows in the war in Palestine. One year later, in Egypt once again, the Fraternity's armed branch did not put down its weapons but engaged in a direct confrontation with the ruling power, following the dismantling of one of its training camps at Mokattam in the Cairo suburbs. Another political assassination followed, in March 1948, this time killing judge Ahmad Khazindar, who had just condemned one of the Brothers for his participation in an armed attack. The Fraternity, suspected of preparing a coup d'état, was dissolved at the king's orders on December 6, 1948. Twenty-two days later the Brothers responded by assassinating the Prime Minister Nokrachy Pasha. An immediate crackdown was intended to break up the organization. Some 4,000 members of the Fraternity were arrested and the "supreme guide" was assassinated on February 13, 1949, under circumstances that remain obscure.

The military branch was temporarily shaken. The new guide, Hassan Hodeibi, a counselor at the Court of Appeals, lacked the authority of Hassan al-Banna. He was overwhelmed by the rest of the movement, which formulated impromptu armed groups to wage guerrilla warfare against the British; they set the banks of the Suez Canal ablaze at the end of 1951 and throughout the following year. The Muslim Brothers played a prominent role in the riots and attacks in Cairo, Alexandria, Ismaïlia, Port-Saïd and the canal; these events led to the revolution of July 23, 1952 and the abdication of King Farouk. At 7:00 AM, Sadat got on the radio to announce the coup d'état to the Egyptian people. The "free Officers" seized power. They were practically un-heard-of. Nasser, founder of the committee of the "free Officers" and the dominant voice in the left wing of the organization, was already opposing those of his companions who were closest to Hassan al-Banna.

Since 1940, the Muslim Brothers had had clandestine contact with the soldiers who went on to become the "free Officers." At the time, the group designated Anwar al-Sadat to approach Hassan al-Banna to come up with a common political platform. The two men met regularly until 1942, nevertheless without leading to an agreement; the soldiers sus-pected Banna of playing a double game with the royal government. Af-ter Banna's assassination, contacts were established again during the riots at the end of 1951. "Several members of the Revolution Command Council (RCC) — Anwar al-Sadat, Hussein Chaféi, Abdel Latif Bagh-dadi and Gamal Salem — are considered to have had solid ties with the Fraternity," notes Lucien Georges; "Rashad Mehanna, known to be sympathetic to the Muslim Brothers, was appointed to the Regency Council." The Muslim Brothers entered into negotiations with the RCC, seeking to have an Islamic State established and the program of 1939 applied, in exchange for the support they had provided. The "free Officers" rejected the offer but increased the concessions to the Frater-nity, whose profound influence in the country they feared.

In spite of these efforts at cohabitation, the new guide opposed the creation of the single party promoted by the soldiers, the "Gathering for Liberation." The Fraternity was divided into three fac-tions. One, with Sayed Qotb, favored unleashing an armed conflict to seize power unilaterally; one preferred to establish an alliance with the leftist groups; and the "reformists," who traditionally chose to frame the society in civil terms but would oblige the regime to make a gradual but ever more thorough move toward Islamization. Perfectly well aware of the divisions that were weakening the Fraternity, Nasser thought that the moment was right to get rid of these inassimilable reli-gious activists. On the pretext of infiltrating the army in preparation for a coup d'état, the RCC announced the dissolution of the Fraternity. However, on July 8, 1954, after wrestling with Nasser, the president of the Egyptian Republic, Mohamad Néguib, succeeded in breaking the prohibition.

A new showdown set Nasser against the Fraternity, which was

challenging the agreement on the British withdrawal from the Suez Canal. The Brothers considered the treaty to be inadequate, as it envisaged a redeployment of the British forces in the event of war; the Brotherhood formed a "unified front" with the Left. In an open letter, Guide Hodeibi demanded Nasser to reject the agreement. Nevertheless, the Anglo-Egyptian treaty was signed on October 18, 1954 and the guide was arrested. Eight days later in Alexandria, a Brother fired eight shots at Nasser, who emerged unscathed. On October 29, the Fraternity was dissolved, this time officially.

On November 14, President Néguib was relieved of his duties, particularly because of the relations which he entertained with the Muslim Brothers. Nasser acceded to the head of the Egyptian state and launched a crackdown to finish off the Fraternity once and for all. On December 8, 1954, six of its leaders were executed, Guide Hodeibi was sentenced to forced labor for life, some 800 militants were sentenced to several years of detention, while thousands of others were imprisoned without sentencing. The leaders who escaped arrest went into exile.

For the Brothers, the crossing of the desert would take ten years, until the proclamation of a general amnesty in their favor. In 1964, Nasser attempted to rehabilitate the Brothers in order to counter the growing influence of the Communists, who had also been released recently. The majority of the Brothers, indeed, were rehabilitated and took the opportunity to reconstitute their network. They re-established their strategy of taking over the social framework. It was during this period that the first financial and logistic aid came from the CIA, who bet on the Fraternity to destabilize the Raïs (who had just chosen the Soviet camp). And, the reconstituted military branch still hoped to overthrow Nasser. In January 1965, it started preparations for a new showdown. From Moscow, August 29, 1965, Nasser announced the discovery of a new plot fomented by the Muslim Brothers but thwarted by the security services. A second massive repression was then launched against the Fraternity.

Thousands of militants were imprisoned again and three of the historical leaders (Sayed Qotb, Yussef Hawash and Abdel Fattah Ismaïl) were hanged. An investigation that received tremendous media coverage revealed that the Fraternity's armed branch had succeeded in penetrating the vital corps of the police force and the army. During a trial, which also had great repercussions, foreign complicities were blamed.

For the first time, Saudi Arabia was accused by name of encouraging and financing the Muslim Brothers. The leader of the Fraternity's international organization, Saïd Ramadan, son-in-law of Hassan al-Banna, was condemned *in absentia* to forced labor for life. Having escaped via Saudi Arabia and Pakistan, he settled in Munich, then in Switzerland, where he manages the movement's funds. Forced into clandestine activity for another five years, the organization re-emerged from its ashes only upon Nasser's death and Sadat's arrival on October 15, 1970.

The accession of Anwar al-Sadat to the presidency of the Egyptian Republic supported the political re-entry of the Fraternity, whose many activities were once again permitted. Nasser's successor, who wanted to put an end to the partnership between Egypt and the USSR, counted on the Brothers to counterbalance the weight of the pro-Soviet faction of the regime. Moreover, his concept of a "new society based on faith and science" established Islam as the "primary source of inspiration for the constitution and the laws." In its October 21, 1971 edition, the very official *al-Ahram* announced that the "supreme guide" Hassan Hodeibi and many Brothers were coming back, returning from exile. But less than a year later, serious incidents broke out between the armed wing of the Fraternity and members of the Copt minority. Sadat then addressed a severe warning to the Brothers, which obliged them to retreat to semi-clandestinity.

The Fraternity officially made its come-back on March 14, 1976 when the Arab Socialist Union (the single party) was authorized to establish "tribunals" in anticipation of the establishment of a multi-party system. The new system was officially adopted on November 11. This being the case, the Fraternity intended to refound itself through the creation of a legal political party. Sheik Omar Telmessani, considered to be the "supreme guide" since Hodeibi's death in 1973, favored active collaboration with the regime in order to obtain the exemption necessary to form a political party that would be legally recognized by the authorities. A second faction, led by Saïd Ramadan from his exile in Switzerland, wanted the Fraternity to have a share in power, with a common program of Islamic action. At the time, this faction still enjoyed the political and financial support of the oil states of the Arabian peninsula.

Given the Brothers' lack of unity, Sadat did not go after them. They adopted an openly critical attitude against him after he visited Jerusalem on December 19, 1977. At this tension was building, the Fraternity was working to recover the ground it had lost among the students, who condemned its reformism and its attempts at collaboration with the regime. The Muslim Brothers infiltrated the Islamic fraternities (Gamaat al-islamiya) that had been created in the universities on Sadat's initiative. Indeed, the Brothers had to be careful not to be overtaken by Islamist groups of any kind, lest they jeopardize their declared ideological hegemony over the Islamic movement as a whole.

The Fraternity joined forces for the first time with the Egyptian left in its savage opposition to the rapprochement with Israel preached by Sadat. It adopted an attitude of open hostility from the moment the Camp David accords were signed on September 17, 1978. It denounced the Israeli-Egyptian peace treaty of March 26, 1979 and during the summer of the same year waged a campaign against the normalization of relations between the two countries. Its preachers called for the army to prepare for the "holy war" and demanded that all negotiations with Israel be terminated. Sadat responded by seizing the Brothers' newspapers, by prohibiting political activity in the universities and, on August 29, 1979, by publicly accusing Omar Telmessani and his companions of being a threat to state security.

The Fraternity continued to harden its positions, calling for the immediate cessation of any discussion of autonomy for Gaza and the West Bank, the expulsion of the Israeli diplomatic representation in Cairo, and the collective resignation of the Parliament and the government during Israeli President Itzhak Navon's visit to Egypt on November 9, 1980. Lastly, the Brothers fulminated a press campaign against the Israeli Prime Minister Menahem Begin's visit to Cairo, August 28, 1981. Their newspapers were confiscated again, but Sadat hesitated to destroy an organization that he still thought might be of use against his real enemy, the Egyptian left. Still, he could not avoid taking a tougher tone following the new denominational incidents that caused bloodshed in Upper Egypt from June to September 1981. Sheik Omar Telmessani was sent to prison, with several preachers from the Fraternity.

The assassination of President Sadat on October 6, 1981, by a commando proclaiming Islamist ideology, has been implicitly attributed to the Muslim Brothers. Since they had based their historical legitimacy on the hegemonic control that they still claimed to exert over the entire Islamist movement, the Brothers had difficulty denying any ties with the assassins. Once again, the saber cut across the Koran in their emblem. Although the material implication of the Fraternity could not be proven during the trial, the international public considered them to be behind the assassination. This was a problematic responsibility for the movement which, ever since then, has protested its dedication to "peaceful reformism." Nonetheless, the specter of Sadat still tarnishes the image of the Muslim Brothers and their semi-clandestine existence.

The history of the Muslim Brothers shows that they do not hesitate to use murder as a political tool. The Fraternity chooses violence and legal action by turn. Its leaders have practiced double talk so often that they are called "the Jesuits of Islam." Consequently, it is no surprise that their activities and declarations engender suspicion, mistrust and confusion. Today, the ambiguity is no less. Mustapha Mashhur, the new guide who succeeded Aboul Nasr (deceased in 1996 at the age of 83), is the perfect incarnation of this ambivalence. Whereas Telmessani was a media figure and Aboul Nasr a historical character without real power, Mashhur has been the strongman of the organization for two decades already. A former Muslim brother, one of his early colleagues from the Faculty of Science at Cairo says that Mashhur and the other military leaders still hold the power within the Fraternity: "We joined the organization at the same time, in 1943. After being imprisoned three times in 1948, in 1954 and 1965, Mustapha Mashhur was promoted. When the Brothers were released from prison at the beginning of Anwar al-Sadat's presidency, the military branch created in the 1940's reconstituted itself under the name of the 'Special Order'. Consequently, this armed group has run the Egyptian and international branches of the organization. Mashhur was one of the heads of the special Order and so it is absolutely natural that he is the new 'Supreme Guide' today. Strangely, he left Egypt just a few days before the assassination of Sadat."

Mashhur returned to Egypt only in 1986, and from that time on, he devoted himself entirely to making the international organization of the Brothers in the service of the Arab volunteers for Afghanistan. "At the time, he saw that holy war as heralding the creation of a future Islamic state in Afghanistan," adds his former counterpart. "At the time, the Fraternity saw that country as the first site for the re-founding of the

Caliphate, the only political structure likely to unite all the Muslims one day." Today, Mashhur is 77 years old. The Egyptian special services, which never lose sight of him, believe that he is still as radical as ever, and that he still runs the Special Order; and that organization still maintains contacts with the armed groups currently operating in Egypt, that is Gama'a and Jihad.

"Having taken over the secret organization of the Brothers, Mashhur also, *ipso facto*, took over the international branch of the Fraternity," confirms Rifaat Saïd. Saïd is a Deputy, and he chairs the Gathering, the principal opposition party in the Egyptian Assembly. It is made up of former Communists and has five deputies. Saïd is one of the Egyptian politicians most threatened by the Islamists. He has miraculously escaped two attempted murders attributed to the latter. Since then, his travel plans and movements are kept secret and he always keeps a nine millimeter gun in his belt, even during our conversation at his office in the Assembly. During his entire political life, he has been in direct confrontation with the Fraternity. "Obviously, taking control gave Mashhur and his friends access to the financial resources," he adds, going on at some length about the economic, commercial and banking empire of the Fraternity. According to him, this is the Fraternity's most powerful sector today. Behind the window-dressing of small businesses and the social objectives of the societies, several billion dollars are circulating, according to the best-informed experts. The Brothers' money — the central nerve of the "holy war," the central nerve of their influence — is the true source of their secret power.

Obviously, one runs into a wall of silence and fear as soon as one evinces too much interest in the Fraternity's economic and financial activities. However, since the late 1920's, it has run a parallel economy. In Cairo, its five supermarkets bearing the sign *al-Tawhid* ("unity") are well-known, as are certain butcher shops and car showrooms. But these establishments represent only the visible layer of an economy that is far more ramified. Nothing official, of course, just some modest shops, a constellation of small businesses: butchers, spinning mills, drapers, fabric dying and small currency exchange offices, so many tradesmen who will never acknowledge their links with the Fraternity but whose profits flow into the Islamic banks and capital investment companies that, for their part, operated in broad daylight in the 1980's.

Thanks to the liberalization of the banking sector, these companies have come out of the shadows to some extent, to take advantage of the various tax and financial benefits made possible by the new legislation, but also openly to defy the legitimacy of the Egyptian State. "Believing that this would help defuse the Islamists' demands for the application of the *sharia* and for the Islamization of the society, presidents Sadat and Mubarak themselves supported the emergence and the growth of an 'Islamic world of finance' since end of the 1970's," adds Saïd. "This specific economic area gradually has been transformed into a forum for disputing the Egyptian economic and political order."

Through "legalistic" economic and financial practices, the Muslim Brothers and their other Islamic partners in finance work to crack the two pillars of the legitimacy of the State, that is, the neutrality of its banking structure and the sovereignty of the decisions it takes in the context of the national economy.

Under Mashhur's guidance, the Fraternity's economic apparatus pursues the same goal as the military apparatus: the obligatory reunification of the Muslim community. In this economic view, the believers will no longer be brought together by overtly political or insurrectionary means, but by means of the none-too-easily controlled financial transactions. Since religion is not to be separated from the economy, the various financial practices will have to conform with Islamic law in order to constitute an economically autonomous system of exchanges. Islamic finance: the extension of the "holy war" by other means...

While they are particularly involved in this new theological-financial strategy, the Muslim Brothers do not have a monopoly on it, and they benefit from the transnational financial tools of the Gulf countries working on a planet-wide scale. The "pan-Islamic propaganda of the great Saudi banks, like that of the International Association of Islamic Banks chaired by Prince Muhammad Fayçal, makes much of the necessity to unify the Muslim community through finance, and in this respect it is significant," explains Michel Galloux, a researcher at the Center for Economic, Legal and Social Studies and Documentation of Cairo (Cedej). "The ways in which the practices are implemented can also pose a problem, whether it's a matter of these banks preferring to address themselves to foreign colleagues rather than to the Central Bank for refinancing and for investments abroad, or their tendency to prefer (non-Egyptian) Muslim shareholders rather than public institutions that are 'non-religious', when new issues of capital are coming up. Lastly, their resistance is also expressed with respect to banking regulations, often considered to be unsuited to their ways of operating and, there again, it seems that one might interpret such claims as an implicit criticism of the national banking order."[5]

Besides financing his international organization and that of other "friendly" movements, the Muslim Brothers' financial strategy clearly fits in with the national framework of a program to destabilize the Egyptian state and its policy of economic liberalization. These days, the financial weapon used by the Saudi, Osama bin Laden, the "Banker of the Jihad," and by the big Saudi banks as well, has increased the impact of contemporary Islamist groups considerably. We will see later on how this strategy, developed through transnational currency flows, tends more and more to produce major geopolitical effects.

For the moment, let us follow the trail of the financial actors of the Muslim Brothers, in particular the "Islamic Capital Investment Companies" that place themselves more or less directly in the service of the Islamist ideology and whose financial arm they constitute, to some extent. The best-known, al-Sharîf, built up a center for financial transactions in Cairo whose turnover is something over $1 billion. In 1986, after having acquired one third of the capital of the International Islamic Bank for Development (BIID), al-Sharîf tried in vain to take control of its board of directors. In 1994 alone, it distributed some $760 million to a whole series of arts centers, charitable associations and Islamic research institutes.

"The case of al-Sharîf is probably not the only one that suggests the existence of a possible link between the 'Islamic Capital Investment Companies' and Islamism," continues Michel Galloux. "The company Talia al-Imân, also founded by a Muslim Brother from Assiout, made donations to the Student Union of the University of Assiout, which is controlled by the Islamist faction. These funds were used to finance housing costs, the distribution of propaganda and political leaflets and, more generally, for extending the Islamist base among the students. And in addition, it was often said —although it was never possible to support the charge — that these companies financed the purchase of weapons for the Muslim Brothers, that the latter put pressure on the Egyptian expatriates in Saudi Arabia so that they would entrust their funds to them, that the land bought by al-Sharîf might be used for training camps for members of the organization, and that these companies had financed Islamist candidates in the 1987 elections."

Several of these "companies" were blamed, by name, in the debates that went on within the Assembly of the People during spring 1992. Criticism of the deputies related not only to their acknowledged Islamist sympathies, but also to the monopolies that they manage to forge in many key sectors of the national economy, especially that of wholesale distribution.

Lastly, just how Islamic are the financial structures (supposedly founded on the prohibition of usury or *ribâ*) has been contested strongly by the deputies from the National Democratic Party. One of them specifically stated, "We want to tell those people who have created Islamic banks — and who claim that the national banks must be avoided because they practice *ribâ* — that their institutions are political banks, external to the nation, and in fact they work with *ribâ* but under another name. Thus, there is a bank, based in the Bahamas, that is not only economic but political and uses slogans; the government was informed about it and unfortunately we did not pay sufficient attention to it; it takes all the money from its investors in Egypt and transfers it to the Bahamas. So, what is *halâl* or 'licit' and what is *harâm* or 'illicit'? We . . . say to these people, who are taking Muslims' money to put it in banks that are political in character, that piety is in the heart and not in the islands of the Bahamas."[6]

This bank was not cited by chance. In Near-Eastern financial circles, A.T. is regarded as the Fraternity's bank. For years, Abdelkader Shoheib, deputy editor-in-chief of the weekly magazine *al-Mussawar*, has been investigating this bank and its activities. "Initially, A.T. Bank was conceived as the central economic instrument of the Muslim Brothers, in particular of the international branch; it used to be directed by Yussef Nada, one of the Brotherhood's Egyptian activists who had to flee Egypt after Nasser came to power," he says. He adds that "This bank was founded on the collecting of funds and bank deposits from small investors, intended to finance real estate projects or import-export transactions, deals that in themselves were intended to provide financial support to more radical Islamist groups operating in various countries."

"Islam does not distinguish between religion, politics and economics. Islam embraces the religious, the political, the whole of economic-social life, faith and the doctrines. And we, although we are not a political party but a movement calling for the advent of Islam in all its political, institutional and legislative components, we assert this totality by all possible legal means, without transgressing the laws," the guide Mustapha Mashhur explained to me.

I ask him whether he knows the founders and the current leaders of A.T. bank. "The heads of the bank are our brothers Yussef Nada and Khaled Himmat. They created this bank, not in the name of the Fraternity, but to make it an Islamic bank, for there are many Muslims in Egypt and in the world who wish to invest their money licitly, in accordance with the faith. Ordinary banks work according to illicit methods, because they practice usury and interest. The founders and shareholders of A.T. want to help the Muslims to use their money in licitly, i.e. without interest, as the Prophet asks us to do."

An advisor who insisted on anonymity would later provide me with a confidential list of the founders of the bank and the first shareholders. I thus learned that the president of A.T.'s office of religious control is Dr. Yussef al-Qardawi. Regarded as the theorist behind Islamic international finance, he is famous throughout the Arab world for the radical sermons which he gives regularly on the national television of Qatar, where he is living in exile. This confidential list also mentions several eminent personalities of the Tunisian and Syrian Muslim Brothers, as well as leaders of the international organization of the Fraternity.

On the basis of information from several Near-Eastern financial experts, recapitulated by information from the Egyptian services, it appears that A.T. is indeed the bank of the Muslim Brothers. The legal authorities of Cairo banned it in 1988. A.T. thus moved its registered location to the Bahamas, where it was represented by the BSI (Banca della Svizzera Italiana, today absorbed into the Society of Swiss Banks — SBS). In Nassau, the BSI also covers the big Saudi bank Dar al-Mal al-Islami (DMI). The business lawyer in charge of the three banks is none other than Arthur Hanna, former Vice-Prime Minister of the Bahamas. He had to resign following a corruption scandal. While establishing its headquarters in a tax haven, the Brothers' bank opened a branch, A.T. Management Organization SA, in Italian Switzerland, in Lugano. Lugano, a discreet frontier banking locale, is a stone's throw from Milan, a major financial center, and above all the Islamist groups' entry point to Europe.

A.T. Management Organization SA appeared for the first time as a corporation under Swiss law, registered on August 9, 1988. Its capital was relatively modest, just 100,000 Swiss francs. Its declared activities, "administrative services, accountancy and business consultation," also cover estate management and securities, real estate, industrial, financial and commercial investments. In addition, the society engaged to promote the development of business connections between Islamic and Western financial partners. Recorded on September 8, 1997, an increase fixed its new capital at 225,000 Swiss francs. As the editor of *al-Mussawar* had indicated, the board of directors is chaired by an Egyptian, Mr. Yussef Nada.

A.T. is situated on the top floor of a small glass building, right in the center of Lugano, in the banking district, a district where overly-curious journalists are immediately denounced to the police who then conduct American-style identity checks in the middle of the street. . . In Lugano, bank secrecy is no laughing matter. Several times we tried to meet Mr. Nada, who eventually responded by mail, "We allow neither you nor any other journalist, nor publication, to speak about us — positively or negatively — without our written permission." Signed, Yussef Nada.

The man is, however, interesting in more ways than one. He holds Tunisian and Italian passports, and he runs an office of "consulting advice" in the Italian enclave of Campione — near to Lugano — where he lives. He has an Italian diploma in engineering; and he is very well introduced into the financial and political circles of the Peninsula where he has many influential friends. On October 18, 1992, in Rimini, Mr. Nino Adolfo Cristofori (the president of the International Research Committee of the Pio Manzu Center), gave him the medal of the government of the Italian Republic in recognition of "sixty years of development of the financial, economic and political relations between Europe and the Islamic countries"!

In private, he had declared his solidarity with the Egyptian Muslim Brothers and the Algerian Islamists who "are just now completing their war of decolonization." But Yussef Nada is even better-known to the Egyptian services, who have evidence of his membership in the armed branch of the fraternity of the Muslim Brothers in the 1940's. At that time, according to the same sources, he was working for the Ab-

wehr under Admiral Canaris and took part in a plot against King Farouk. This was not the first time that the path of the Muslim Brothers
crossed that of the servants of the Third Reich.

The founder of the Fraternity himself, Hassan al-Banna, served as
an intermediary between those who went on to become the "free officers" (in particular Anwar al-Sadat) and the agents of Nazi Germany.
"The missions assigned to the Abwehr from this point forward began to
go beyond simple military information," write Roger Faligot and Rémi
Kauffer. "The agents of Canaris would try to engage men of power in
the great German plan, along with clandestine nationalists, ethnic
groups with separatist aspirations, whole regions ready to rise up
against the two empires that really counted, the French and the British."[7] In 1954, Yussef Nada would also be implicated in the preparation
of the failed plot against Nasser, before he fled to Germany, and finally
to Italy.

Another member of the A.T. board of directors links the history of
the bank to that of the complex bonds woven between Islamism and
the swastika. Very well-known in the Swiss and European Islamic
landscape, A. H. is a character who is as bizarre as he is colorful. To
prepare for the interview that he granted us in order to "correct the
false ideas which sully Islam," this character sent a *curriculum vitae* entitled, "In the name of Allah, the lenient, the merciful one." Born in
Freiburg, Switzerland, in 1927 to Protestant parents, and given the fore-
names A., F. and A., he was a journalist for a many years, a parliamentary correspondent accredited to the Federal Palace in Bern for the
Swiss social democratic press.

Since 1981, he worked exclusively for Ringier, the largest Swiss
press group. In 1989, he was fired for having publicly supported the
*fatwa* condemning Salman Rushdie for his book *Satanic Verses*. "I fully
support the death sentence pronounced against Rushdie, for there can
be no other penalty for blasphemy uttered out of personal interest and
for the sake of profit," he declared on Swiss television.

In 1994, his revisionist standpoint got him expelled from the
Swiss socialist party of which he had been a member since 1952. H.
readily explains how the "good Protestant and pro-Israeli Swiss" that
he had been was "suddenly re-awakened by discovering Islam during
the Algerian war." In 1961, he made his "*shehada*," his profession of Islamic faith, at the Muslim Brothers' Islamic Center in Geneva, an edu-

cation that he would supplement at the al-Azhar University in February 1962.

Upon his return to Cairo, he married the secretary of the Egyptian ambassador in Bern, and with her he has two sons, S. and A., who have become active Islamist militants in Europe. Twice, in 1963 and 1965, in the Egyptian capital, he met Johannes von Leers, the former right-hand man of Dr. Goebbels, who "opened his eyes to the real meaning of the great adventure of the Third Reich." Now proclaiming a "moderated revisionism," he acknowledges that there was indeed genocide but refuses to accept the "distorted interpretation" given by the "Americans, the Russians and the Israelis."

In tandem with this growing fascination for the "architects of the new order," he took up various Arab causes one after another. The walls of his office, like some kind of Ali Baba cave of revisionism, are covered with portraits that symbolize this "convergence of the revival between Islam and the Christian West." The place of honor is given to Chancellor Hitler, the "man who upset the world the most and made his mark on universal history."

A second photograph, in which Hitler is talking with Himmler, hangs next to those of Necmettin Erbakan and Jean-Marie Le Pen. Erbakan, head of the Turkish Islamist party, Refah, turned to A. for an introduction to the chief of the French party of the far Right. Exiting from the meeting (which took place in September 1995), H.'s two friends supposedly stated that they "share the same view of the world" and expressed "their common desire to work together to remove the last racist obstacles that still prevent the union of the Islamist movement with the national right of Europe."

Lastly, above the desk is displayed a poster of the imam Khomeini; the meeting "changed my life," H. says, with stars in his eyes. For years, after the Federal Palace in Bern, A. H. published a European press review for the Iranian leaders, then for the Turkish Refah. Since the former lacked financial means, A. H. chose to put his efforts to the service of the latter. An outpost of the Turkish Muslim Brothers, Refah thus became A. H.'s principal employer; and it was through the intermediary of the Turkish Islamist party that this former parliamentary correspondent became a shareholder in the bank A.T.

"I joined the board of directors of A.T. for the simple reason that its founders needed Swiss guarantors," A. H. explains. "I got information from friends who are well-placed in Swiss banking circles. One gave me a 'green light,' he said that everything was in order, the bank of the Muslim Brothers is clean because it finances only development plans in Africa and in the Arab countries: agricultural, real estate, medical and educational projects. A.T. is based in Switzerland, for this small country is a major money market, a place that is not compromised with Mossad, nor with anybody else! When you put your dough in Switzerland, the world doesn't know anything about it. If you make payments Hamas or to FIS, the enemy does not know anything! The enemy cannot learn anything! That is what creates confidence in Swiss banks. As for the money, I cannot give details — except for Saudi Arabia, because that will change the bad perception people have of this country. Of course, the government is under American surveillance, but the kingdom has the advantage of being a feudal State that leaves the great families total freedom to manage their oil funds as they wish. That's great! And today, the Saudis are very active, but the details of their funds that come to the bank are a matter of bank secrecy."

But A. H., who acknowledges he is "not a specialist, nor do I know how to read a budget," prefers to turn the conversation back to the great intention of his life as an indefatigable lecturer and propagandist of political Islam, to wit, what he calls the "great reunification," that of Islam and the Christian West. A member of the group "Avalon," which claims to be based on the "great Celtic tradition," at every solstice he meets under the moon, amidst great trees, with a few hundred European druids with whom he is preparing the "end of our decline." With the group "Thule" — a secret society particularly popular in the German administration and the political class — he works for the restoration of "greater Germany." The Thule group's ties with Islam go back many years, in particular through the theories of Haushoffer, Horbiger and René Guénon. In the wake of Ahnenerbe, the Nazi society for esoteric studies, bonds were woven between Islam and the neo-Nazi far Right.[8] With the French hard-right Club de l'Horloge, the bank shareholder strives to make contact with "all true European and American nationalists." Recently, he went to Chicago for a discreet congress that brought together the "authentic Right and the fighters for Islam," and he says that "major decisions were taken . . . the reunification is under way."

During his many tribulations, A. H. became acquainted with the neo-Nazi banker François Genoud, whose path in life presents a singular summary of the interconnections, the specific alliances that have been tied and untied between Islam and the swastika. Pierre Péan, who thoroughly studied the parallel lives of this enigmatic destiny, interviewed A. H. at length. A. H. explained to him that he is sympathetic to François Genoud because "everyone jumps on him."[9]

Still referring to the neo-Nazi banker, A. H. told Péan, "I never asked him any questions, but I noted that, in circles as different as the German Right, the Islamic movements of Asia, the Palestinians, and in the Maghreb, people speak of him with great respect. Everyone told me: he helped us. I have the impression that he played an important, though discreet role. . . . It was I who introduced him to the Iranians. I said to them: 'He is a friend, you can trust him.' Here, in Switzerland, he was very active in opposing the antiracist law inspired by the Zionists who wanted to criminalize 'revisionism'. Genoud was with us. Officially we lost, but by such a small margin that the law is not applied."

A. H. is proud to be Swiss. "I often say to my friends at the bank that they are lucky to be in Switzerland, because it is a country (perhaps the only one in Europe, along with Great Britain) where they can express and practice Islam and defend their convictions, without worrying as one does, particularly in France, that fundamentalist lay republic." Snow started to fall in this suburb of Bern. A. H. was about to make his fourth prayer for the day. Accompanying us back to the door of his small house, he once more praised the Muslim Brothers. "Before them, Islam had degenerated into a purely religious thing. Now, and mainly thanks to them, it is more. We are winning."

In November 1997, the Italian newspaper *Corriere della Serra* pointed a finger at A. T. again, in the context of an incident that hit hard on the Muslim Brothers of Gaza and the West Bank. "Hamas Loses Half Its Finances — Treasure and Terrorism, 50 Billion Lire ($28 million) Disappeared," was the headline on the Milanese daily. It confirmed the financial aid that the bank of the Muslim Brothers granted to Palestinian Hamas, as well as to several Egyptian, Algerian and Tunisian Islamist organizations.

The chiefs of Hamas of Gaza and the West Bank were absolutely furious when they discovered, in spring 1997, that half of their annual budget had gone up in smoke, probably diverted by not very scrupulous intermediaries. Each year, the movement receives approximately $50 million, all sums collected from charitable societies, generous donors and sympathizers of the Islamist cause worldwide. "These financial flows," the author of the investigation, Guido Olimpio, explained to us, "follow a triangular circuit whose first pole is the various donors who direct the funds toward bank A.T. (the second pole in the circuit). A. T. distributes this money between various shell organizations in Gaza, including the corporations of Ramallah, as well as data-processing agencies and the Arab Press Offices based in London, which constitute the third partner."

Thus, Hamas, which seeks to supplant the PLO by the base, can continue to use the various tools for penetrating society (schools, asylums, hospitals and sports clubs). The organization also runs marriage bureaus, and thus takes charge of the financial aspect of its troops' marriages. But it is the armed struggle that costs the most. There is the cost not only of weapons and the maintenance of the training camps, but also of guaranteeing to the families of martyrs a "pension," on which their existence depends from now on. The least decline in funds thus has dramatic political consequences for Hamas, whose money is today the real power in the Palestinian autonomous territories, which are gradually getting away from the legal authority of Yasser Arafat.

In spring 1997, the chiefs of Hamas opened an internal investigation to try to recover that half of their last budget, which had mysteriously vaporized. They dispatched an emissary, Hamdan Youssra, to the president of the International Committee of Hamas, Imadal Rami, who lives in Istanbul. Youssra showed his interlocutor his orders to conduct a financial audit of al-Quds Press and Interpal, two Palestinian agencies based in London. They centralize the bulk of the funds collected in Europe, which are placed in accounts with the bank A.T. (which is "considered to be the financial heart of the Islamist economic apparatus") with "the remainder of the money coming from the United States, the Middle East or the Gulf states," adds Guido Olimpio.

Youssra's internal investigation cast suspicion on the London leaders of Interpal. The latter apparently had acquired, during the last three years, sumptuous villas in Spain, South America and the Far East. Three men in particular were in the spotlight: Abu Daya, president of Interpal; its director Issam Yussef; and the treasurer, Jihad Kandil. A fourth man, al-Hafez Ajaj (a specialist in investments in tax shelters and especially well-connected on the Latin-American markets) was responsible for identifying good deals. Youssra would center his investigations on al-Quds Press.

This "press agency" was used as a cover for the main office of Hamas in Europe. In fact, the agency specialized in supplying weapons and obtaining information. Charged with maintaining relations with friendly organizations, al-Quds Press was particularly active in Beirut, which became one of the principal geographical terminals for Saudi financial assistance to Islamist groups. The Palestinian agency also, apparently, handled funds for other Islamist groups.

The chiefs of Hamas in Gaza thus accused the al-Quds administrators in Beirut of keeping two sets of books, with the help of A.T. "This bank is the financial engine of the Islamist movement because it has worldwide investment capability and mobility of funds," explains a Palestinian financier. "It would cash in funds directly, or via its subsidiaries, and then transfer of the funds to Gaza, after they had passed through the Bahamas. Moreover, the head office in Nassau directly managed Hamas' biggest portfolio."

Al-Quds Press and Interpal are also partners of Beit Almah, a center for commercial activities in Ramallah. Its number-two man, Salah Kamil Herzalla, an expert in currency exchange deals, has a personal account at Arab Bank of Kensington in London. This agency, where Interpal has several accounts, regularly recorded large transfers coming from A.T. After being presented to Sheik Yassine himself — the supreme chief of Hamas — the conclusions of Youssra's investigation were semi-officially distributed in various Near-Eastern financial circles. The data that it revealed were too precise to remain unanswered and, this time, the president of A.T. was obliged to depart from his customary habit of discretion. Yussef Nada chose to counter-attack in the daily newspaper al-Hayat.

In the December 5, 1997 edition, Nada declared that A.T. "is not the bank of the Muslim Brothers, nor does it finance Hamas, nor any other political organization." Nada did not deny that the bank entertained relations with the Muslim Brothers, nor that his personal sympathies were with the "moderate Islamist movements," but he defined his bank as a purely economic institution functioning according to the Islamic methods of finance. "Certain shareholders are members of the Fraternity," he explained, "but their number does not exceed 8% of the ·

1,500 shareholders who represent twenty-two nationalities." *Al-Hayat* recalled that the capital of the bank officially declared in the Bahamas went up to $229 million in 1997. "Since our creation in 1987," continued Nada, "we have realized great enough profits to be able to give our shareholders annual returns of 9%. I would not have been able to achieve such a result if A.T. were the Muslim Brothers' bank."

Since the beginning of its activities, Yussef Nada explained, "A.T. placed all its transactions under the control of Sheik Yussef al-Qardawi. Admittedly, he is one of the known leaders of the Brothers, but he only checks to see that our transactions conform with the Islamic rules of finance, rules based on partnership in profits." The *al-Hayat* article concluded with the expertise of Mohamed al-Karry, a Saudi economist, professor of Islamic economics, and a consultant to several Saudi banks: "A.T. is one of the most prudent Islamic banks with regard to its financial transactions and their conformity with the principles of Islamic conduct." While Nada's explanation is firmly based on his argument that A. T. bank conforms to Islamic practices, it does not add much to anyone's understanding of the real nature of its activities.

At *al-Hayat's* editorial offices in London, the (Lebanese) director Khairallah Khairallah, cannot infringe the rules of hospitality, but receives me with some reluctance. Small of stature, snappy in spirit and with a gaze that is always sharp, he becomes very nervous as soon as the question of A.T. and the Saudi financing of Islamist groups is broached. "These people are very dangerous," he kept repeating, "the rich Saudi families have always helped the Muslim Brothers. Most of them open bank accounts, here in London or elsewhere, and then begin to finance a benevolent committee to build a mosque in Algeria, Egypt or Turkey. Money is forwarded by the account but never arrives at the mosque. Nobody can keep the great Saudi families from doing it. It is unverifiable, therefore the newspaper does not waste its time in addressing these questions."

The director reminds me that the editorial office of its newspaper was the victim of several letter bombs, "attacks probably related to the people about whom you are speaking," he says, accompanying me back to the security gate that controls access to the building. This daily, the largest Arab newspaper, belongs to a member of the Saudi royal family, Khaled Ben Sultan. In addition to *al-Hayat*, the princes and their close relations control the all the major Arab-language news outlets, such as the agency called United Press International, and MBC, a satellite television network broadcasting from London.

My strange visit to the *al-Hayat* offices did not bring me luck. Without wishing to claim a direct link of cause and effect between that visit and the course of my continued investigation, the fact is that after my London tribulations the doors would close hermetically, one after another. For several months, the trail from A.T. led to a succession of holding companies and shell companies in various tax havens, and I kept losing my way in a maze of more or less unverifiable financial connections. Many times, my approaches were met with dissuasive threats from lawyers, firmly expressed in rather clear terms.

My only satisfaction was that the commercial attachés of two European embassies, in Khartoum and in Cairo, formally assured me that A.T. had indeed been identified as a financial relay for Algeria, as well as Tunisia, especially for the An-Nahda movement since the beginning of the 1990's. In 1994, in several Near-Eastern capitals, the bank guaranteed various transactions on behalf of "Gama'a islamiya" of Lebanon. It effected several fund transfers to the profit of a chief of this organization, the Lebanese Fayçal Maoulaoui, former leader of the "Union of Islamic Organizations of France" (UOIF), the Muslim Brothers' organization in France. The transfers intended for Maoulaoui were executed by the intermediary of an account opened through the agency of Paribas in Lugano.

In addition to this France-Tunisian financing, the maze of subsidiary companies and banking partners converged on three axes: an Algerian connection that led to the Muslim Brothers of the ex-Hamas of Mahfoud Nahnah; a Milanese branch directed by a Kuwaiti Brother, Nasreddin Ahmed Idris; and finally, a group of humanitarian organizations led by a Syrian Brother, Khaldoun Dia Eddine, which led to the Balkans.

**The Algerian connection** was particularly active after the end of 1991, following the disruption of the electoral process. The Islamists of FIS went underground. The Algerian Muslim Brothers, for their part, chose to fill the political vacuum that had been left, by setting up a political apparatus to work with the Algerian power in re-starting the political process. Then it was up to Mahfoud Nahnah and his partisans to recapture the Islamic vote and thus to supplant FIS, certain of whose members were involved in the armed conflict. To punish FIS, which had chosen the Iraqi camp during the Gulf War, Saudi Arabia supported the option of the Algerian Muslim Brothers. The large Saudi banks, who sought to get out of the spotlight on the Algerian stage, participated via subcontractors, including the bank A.T.

After long months of difficult negotiations, the former manager of a big Saudi bank that worked closely with A.T. agreed to talk to me, on the condition, of course, that I guarantee him the strictest anonymity. During the interview that was held in a large hotel in Zurich, the former partner of A.T. formally confirmed that it is the "principal financial tool of the Brothers, particularly of the international organization of the Fraternity which is now directed from Lugano and Milan." A.T., my advisor told me, is an assiduous partner of the Saudi bank DMI (Dar al-Mal al-Islami), and "this partnership helps to explain A.T.'s financial relations with the Muslim Brothers of Tunisia and Sudan," he added, "but most of the financial activities related to political support have most recently been concentrated on financing election campaigns for the Algerian Brothers."

Indeed, in Algeria, the Fraternity has a solid bridgehead with Mahfoud Nahnah, who heads the Movement of the Society for Peace (MSP), formerly the Movement for an Islamic Society, the Algerian Hamas. Number three in the Muslim Brothers' international organization — and faithful to the fraternity's strategy of immersion — Nahnah seeks to found an Islamic order in Algeria via the ballot boxes. In October 1994, Nahnah traveled in great secrecy to Lugano, where he met the leaders of A.T., who promised to continue their payments to the Algerian Brothers.

When I questioned him about the exact nature of his personal and financial relations with the president of the bank, Mahfoud Nahnah observed a long silence before answering. "Listen, I know a lot of people. Basically, I went to Switzerland where I met with the leaders of bank A.T.; but I also met other people involved in political activities. . ." The Algerian authorities are perfectly aware of what is going on, and they close their eyes so as not to upset Saudi Arabia.

**The Milanese connection** originates in the Bahamas. Since leaving its first head office in Nassau, A.T. established itself at NIGH (Nasreddin International Group Holdings) —10, Dewaux Street in Nassau.

The NIGH holding company deserves close attention. Yussef Nada's assistant Ali Ghaleb Himmat works there. The Bank of Gothard is NIGH's bank, through account CC/B No. 313656, through the agency of Chiasso, in the name of a Charity Foundation. The Bank of Gothard also appears, in a confidential report on A.T.'s activity, under the heading of business connections. The bank manager at Gothard, Claudio Generale, told me however that he does not knows either A.T. or its director, much less the holding company NIGH.

The president and creator of NIGH, Nasreddin Ahmed Idris, who also appears on the list of the first shareholders in A.T., is honorary consul of Kuwaït in Milan. Living in Italy, Switzerland and Morocco, this businessman directs a multitude of financial companies, most of which end up leading again to the nebula of A.T. One of them, Gulf Office (Association for Commercial, Industrial and Tourist Development between the Gulf States and Switzerland), currently dormant, had been housed in the same building as the mosque of Lugano. In 1994, the Italian judicial system had its sights on Gulf Office and conducted an inquiry into its activities in the context of the operation "clean hands."

In a chart of the Financial Brigade of Milan, the telephone coordinates of the Gulf Office are the same as those on a propaganda video for the Algerian Armed Islamic Groups (GIA) that has been sold under the table in the mosques of Europe since the end of 1994. The images were recorded after the attack on the prefect of Tissemsilt and its guards, some 80 miles south of Algiers. It was one of the first large-scale ambushes by the GIA, in January 1994. The document does not deal with the attack itself, but to the return of the Islamists to their camp; it shows their joy at having brought death to irreligious people, to have caused death in the name of Allah.

Lingering on the weapons seized during the ambush, the camera closes in on the commandos' chief who harangues his flocks. "These weapons which are here before you. . . we seized them from the impious, thanks to God! When our brothers in the true faith see this film, they will see that God is with them, and that God will help them, as he helped us, to overcome their enemies, praise God!"

In fact, Gulf Office served as a financial and material cover for the Islamic communities of Tessin and Milan, where a certain "Saad" officiates; he has free access to all the company's facilities to provide support for various Islamist groups of the Maghreb. Through his relationships with the "representatives" of the Algerian Islamic Salvation Front (FIS) and its antennas in the Lyons region, Saad saw to the importation of the video cassettes produced an agency in Kuwait-City.

But Nasreddin Ahmed Idris's real representative at the head of Gulf Office is another member of the Muslim Brothers, Khaldoun Dia Eddine, who belongs to the Syrian branch of the organization. He too was "employed" by the bank A.T., which he represented in Lugano before he took on the coordination of the activities of "Mercy International," an Islamic humanitarian organization.

**The humanitarian organizations**, Islamic nongovernmental organizations (NGO's), represent one of the other "derivative products" from A.T. bank. Mercy International is a Swiss association founded on May 13, 1989. Its charter specifies that its goals encompass "all humanitarian actions, especially in the cases of natural catastrophe and war."

Mercy International became well-known for its various charitable activities on behalf of the Bosnian Muslims, but it was also active in circumventing the embargo on weapons bound for the Bosnian army and in recruiting mercenaries and "international volunteers" for that country. Mercy International diversified its activities toward Algeria, in particular in the field of repatriating the "Afghans" to this country and providing them with funds and logistical assistance.

The official personnel chart of Mercy International indicates that the association is chaired by Jassem Muhallal el-Yassin, a resident of Kuwait. Chief of the Kuwaiti Muslim Brothers, he oversees the management of the political branch (the Islamic Constitutional Movement); the social branch (The Association for Social Reform); and the branch for external action (Solidarity Committees). He collaborates closely with the Sudanese leader Hassan el-Tourabi, to coordinate support for the Islamist movements of the Maghreb. Lastly, the director, Majid al-Rifai, who is also a Kuwaiti, is a member of the Muslim Brothers and serves as president of the Organization of the Islamic Appeal (al-da' wa al-islamiyah).

Today, Mercy International has moved its headquarters to the

United States; it declares a gross budget of $2 million. Officially, its emergency humanitarian aid programs focus on delivering food, drugs, clothing and shelter. In the Balkans, Mercy International is still active in Bosnia. Lately, its efforts have also been seen in Albania, where it has developed several hospitals and orphanages. In his offices in Tirana, one finds Khaldoun Dia Eddine who, in addition, manages one of the principal channels for weapons delivery for the Kosovo Liberation Army, with the financial and logistic support of the World Islamic League.

Continuing our exploration of the maze, my anonymous inter-locutor — the former manager of a large Saudi bank — affirmed that alongside Yussef Nada there is another Egyptian, I. S. (called "Ismaïl"), who oversees matters connected with several holding companies in which the bank is a shareholder. Director of the company "Spacetronic Salah International," an electronic products company that trades mainly with Sudan, this former member of the armed branch of the Brothers followed the same route as Yussef Nada, his alter ego.

After the slaughter at Luxor,[10] he bombarded the Swiss authorities with "top secret memos," in which he blamed the Israeli secret service that, according to him, directed the attack. Using his electronic products company as a cover, I. S. serves as a central go-between in the A.T. network, because "it is absolutely natural," he says, "for Muslims to help each other in business."

A key figure in the Muslim Brothers' economic organization, I. S. is not very willing to talk about his businesses and those of the Fraternity. He prefers to go back to the history of the Muslim Brothers, evoking the major role played by Saïd Ramadan, starting in 1954. "When the Fraternity was decimated by Nasser," he explains, "it was vital that it be reorganized abroad. From his exile in Switzerland, Saïd Ramadan started to radiate out to the Muslim communities of Europe, with many comings and goings to Saudi Arabia and the other Muslim countries. This work of 'international building' gave him a very considerable political power in the Brothers' new organizational chart. And we all remember that Switzerland always opened its door to true refugees, which we were at that time. This understanding aided the work of the Islamists very significantly, in Egypt and elsewhere."

This pivotal role in the redeployment of the Fraternity, played abroad by Saïd Ramadan, was also emphasized by Rifaat Saïd, a deputy of the Egyptian Left. "Before he settled in Europe, he made long sojourns in Saudi Arabia, with King Fayçal, then in Pakistan where he worked with lawyers on the Islamic Right. But by the end of the 1950's, he opened a new door by selling the Saudis on the idea of the 'da'wa,' i.e. the propagation of Islam, especially in Europe. Thus he proposed to them, initially, to open a center in Munich."

"Why Munich, why Germany?" I asked Rifaat Saïd. "Because there, one finds old complicities that go back to the late 1930's, when the Muslim Brothers collaborated with the agents of Nazi Germany. And furthermore, Turkish immigration to Germany had started to become an important phenomenon. By soaking up the savings of these Muslim workers Yussef Nada, like Saïd Ramadan, took advantage of an extremely favorable context and used it as a springboard for the Muslim Brothers' economic activities. For these various reasons, the Munich center quickly became very important," adds the Egyptian deputy.

During his stay in Germany, Saïd Ramadan defended his doctoral thesis in law at the University of Cologne. While we cannot analyze it here in detail, we should note nevertheless that the work is of interest on two scores: it illustrates one of the guiding principles of the Brothers' proselytism, which is to adapt the means of action to the environment in which it operates; and it spells out the exclusive approach of any comprehension of Islam: that only believers have access to the true knowledge. Entitled "Islamic Law, Its Scope and Its Equity," this very instructive text clarifies the central notion of the ideology of the Muslim Brothers, to wit, the divine need for an Islamic State. But, as the author informs us from the start, the "difficulty emanates as much from the incapacity of non-Muslim authors to understand this problem, as from the influence of Western history on many Muslim authors."

Isn't this theological-philosophical attitude, postulating both the rejection of history and the need for faith, in order to attain true knowledge, one of the oldest saws of the religious discourse? It is, in any case, one of the constant refrains of the apologetic exegesis of Saïd Ramadan, who also defends the "totalitarian" dimension of Islam. For, "all the religious ideas that mold the imagination and the contents of the human spirit, and that determine the action of the human will, are potentially or in principle totalitarian. They must seek to impose their own values and their own rules on every social activity and every institution, from the primary schools to the law and to government."[11] Having completed his thesis, Saïd Ramadan turned his attention to the future of the Munich Center, whose infrastructure would be used as a basis for the organization of similar structures in other European countries.

The Saudis advised to him to make his home in Switzerland for both financial and political reasons. After the Second World War, the petrodollars from the Gulf benefited from the discretion and efficiency of the Swiss banking world. With the Algerian War, the FLN used the French-speaking part of Switzerland as a sounding board. At the time, the "Maghreb Circus" polarized the energy of the news services, the spies and the racketeers of every type, especially since Geneva is also the hub for the financial resources of the Algerian underground. Let us mention only the incident of the treasure of the FLN, at the center of which the banker François Genoud may be found. Ramadan and the Muslim Brothers thought that they could play a part in the Algerian process as they had done in Palestine in 1947. Saïd Ramadan thus left Munich to settle in the city of Calvin.

And so, with the financial support of King Fayçal of Arabia, Saïd Ramadan established the Fraternity's political outpost for Europe in Geneva. In 1961, he founded the Islamic Center in Eaux-Vives, currently directed by one of his sons, Hani. Is this center still, today, the political tool of the Muslim Brothers? "The Muslim Brothers' message is subservience to God and fraternity among the believers. Hassan al-Banna did nothing more than provide a scrupulous interpretation of the Koran. All his doctrines are deep-rooted in the sources of Islam, so that I do not have to tell you whether or not I am part of the Muslim Brothers. The question does not make sense to me. What makes sense is whether I am part of Islam, in its authentic interpretation," answers Hani Ramadan.

Hani is the fourth son of the late Saïd Ramadan and his wife Wafa Hassan al-Banna, daughter of the founder of the fraternity of the Muslim Brothers. Born in 1959 in Geneva, Hani is Swiss by nationality. After studies in the humanities, which led to teaching positions in various private and public establishments, Hani was associated very early by his father with the propaganda activities of Center and the mosque of Eaux-Vives. Although he is a less fluent talker than his brother Tariq and has fewer ties in the intellectual and university circles, he has gained prominence nevertheless as the "theorist" of the family through his many media appearances. His letters to the editor, commentaries and other public statements defend and illustrate the "right to be different," the "debate between civilizations" and the "uncompromising dialogue with the West."[12]

His various activities have led to many "conferences" at the Islamic Center of the Eaux-Vives, where in recent years many demonstrations and open-air prayer sessions have been held for various Islamists causes, in front of the European seat of the United Nations. "The advantage of our presence in Europe," Hani Ramadan says, "is that we can take advantage of the freedom of the democratic regimes." For example on March 11, 1995, Ramadan spoke during a gathering that was officially organized by the Algerian FIS. The demonstration in fact brought together the European supporters of the Armed Islamic Groups (GIA). And the Center directed by Ramadan, which has enough meeting space for some 20 people, is also used as a hub for the European representatives of various organizations that are under surveillance by several European police forces.

Frequently invited to the Lyons area by "friendly associations", Hani Ramadan was barred from entering French territory on February 1, 1995 by the Ministry for the Interior. In a memorandum dated March 1997, the administration indicated that "Mr. Ramadan is not just a Swiss citizen teaching French in a public establishment this country. As he himself indicates, the interested party is a director of the Islamic Center of Geneva. This organization is known by the specialized police services to be a meeting place for the principal European Islamists and the point where the circuits of financing converge. Mr. Ramadan is the grandson of the founder of the fraternity of the Muslim Brothers in Egypt. Like his brother Mr. Ramadan Tariq, Mr. Ramadan Hani is thus an important figure in the European Islamist movement and entertains close relations with the Union of Islamist Organizations of France (UOIF). This association has participated in demonstrations in favor of wearing the Islamic headscarf and its sympathies extend to the Palestinian movement Hamas."

However, the two brothers have not always pulled in the same direction, in spite of Hani's declarations: "What you must absolutely understand is that Tariq and I are two sides of the same coin. We know perfectly well what we are doing and where we are going," (Hebdo, May 7, 1998). While today they publicly exhibit an inalienable complementarity, the two brothers did not always cultivate fraternal love. "In 1992, a profound disagreement set the members of the Ramadan family against each other, around the problem of the fore-seeable succession to the patriarch at the head of the Islamic Center," say one of their disillusioned former colleagues. This quarrel led Tariq to create an "autonomous Muslim cultural center" while Hani set up, inside the walls of the Islamic Center, a "Muslim cultural space" of which he seems to have been the only member. "This was considered to be harmful to the well-understood interests of the family (dominated by the mother)," adds our interlocutor, "so the estrangement did not last long, and the two brothers were reconciled in 1994."

However, in spite of their media proselytism, the Swiss context turned out not to be very favorable to the promotion of their interests. Therefore, capitalizing on various incidents linked to the wearing of the Islamic headscarf and the echoes in France of the Algerian conflict, the two brothers built a relationship with a small militant bookshop in the area of Lyon called "al-Tawhid" (the "Unity of God" ), where Hani pub-lished several doctrinal booklets for use by the young people of the Ly-ons suburbs. Taking advantage of their prestigious affiliations, the Ramadan brothers promoted al-Tawhid between Lyon and Geneva, especially in Ferney-Voltaire, through the creation of an Islamic cul-tural space and a bookshop "As-Salah."

This redeployment was also conducted via the Union of Young Muslims (UJM), explains Gilles Kepel,[13] director of research at the CNRS (the French National Center for Scholarly Research) and a spe-cialist in contemporary Islam. "After doing a great deal of groundwork in the Lyons suburbs, the UJM mainly centered its activity at the mu-nicipal level and supports a re-Islamization 'from the bottom up,' by building closer communities and strengthening the structures of daily life. Al-Tawhid was launched in June 1987, around a bookshop-library in the heart of Lyon, following the first movements toward the re-Islamization of the 'beurs' — second generation immigrants in the Rhone metropolis."

Upon the death of the patriarch, in August 1995, a remark from one European information agency indicates that "the family apparently helped themselves to a considerable sum that Saïd Ramadan was man-aging on behalf of the Muslim Brothers of Egypt. It resulted in a spec-tacular quantitative improvement of the productions and activities of the al-Tawhid bookshop of Lyon, and of As-Salah in Ferney-Voltaire (Geneva), but it seems that this appropriation opened a violent dispute between the family and the Muslim Brothers of Egypt." Beyond any ideological or militant consideration, the strategy of the Ramadan brothers apparently aims primarily to make the wealthy Saudi donors credit them with a capacity for influence and "negotiable" action within certain Swiss, French and European intellectual, media and university circles.

Not having been able, in spite of all of Tariq's contacts and Hani's doctrinal control, to make a significant dent in Switzerland where the cultural and humanitarian circles had already been solicited many times over, the Ramadan brothers retreated to the more virgin, fertile and productive field of immigrant youth in the suburbs of Lyon and Grenoble, where they could show their wealthy sponsors from the petro-monarchies more palpable successes.

"This activity was stepped up during spring 1996, as the family wished to be able to demonstrate rapid successes in order to secure solid Saudi protection and support in the face of the demands, which were being presented with increasing vehemence, by the Egyptian Brothers to recover their funds," continues the note. It would appear that the assassination of the Egyptian diplomat Ala Eddine Nazmi, in Geneva in November 1995, must be placed in the perspective in this context.[14] "Officially, the file is not classified and the investigation continues. . . . This increase in activity entailed a higher volume of poorly-controlled activism which led to Tariq being prohibited from entering French territory and cost him various prohibitions of public speech in Switzerland."

Given the need to pursue spectacular and increasing militant action for the benefit of audiences in Saudi Arabia and certain Gulf States (the sponsors of the da'wa, the propagation of Islam), Hani had to follow his younger brother on a sabbatical year in London to write his thesis. But the objective remained the same: following in the patriarch's footsteps, to develop and make use of a capacity for influencing the Muslim circles of Europe in order to cultivate donors who are always ready to finance the legitimization of Islam, which would guarantee an uncontested political stability and finally a pleasant personal life.

The American information agencies — particularly the CIA, whose familiarity with the Brothers goes back many years — still supervise the Saudi sponsorship of the Fraternity. This protection of the Muslim Brothers by the house of Saud is considered by the Pentagon's "Arab" experts to be "the essential element of a structural evolution of political Islam," a confidential memo explains.

Ultimately, who is the "supervisor" of this "structural evolution" ? In the American process of foreign affairs decision-making, who takes responsibility for supporting such and such armed faction, such and such political or religious movement, such and such criminal or terrorist organization? One can legitimately ask, is there a pilot onboard the American aircraft?

Footnotes

1. Muhammad Saïd al-Ashmawy, *L'Islamisme contre l'Islam*, La Découverte, 1989.

2. This "setting in perspective" is drawn from the *Fiches du monde Arabe*, Beirut & Nicosie, 1975-1983, and two reference works: Walid M. Abdelnasser, *The Islamic Movement in Egypt*, Kegan Paul International, London and New York, 1994; and Olivier Carré and Gérard Michaud, *Les Frères musulmans — 1928-1982*, Gallimard, 1983.

3. Cited by Olivier Carré and Gérard Michaud, *Les Frères musulmans*, op. cit.

4. Henry Laurens, *L'Orient arab — Arabisme et Islamisme de 1798 à 1945*, Armand Colin, 1993.

5. Conversation with Michel Galloux, author of *Finance islamique et pouvoir politique — Le cas de l'Egypte moderne*, university Presses of France, 1997.

6. Cited by Michel Galloux.

7. Roger Faligot and Rémi Kauffer, *Le Croissant et le croix gammé — Les secrets de l'alliance entre l'Islam et le Nazisme d'Hitler à nos jours*, Albin Michel, 1990.

8. See Louis Pauwels and Jacques Bergier, *Le Matin des magiciens — Introduction au réalisme fantastique*, Gallimard, 1960.

9. Pierre Péan, *L'Extremiste — François Genoud, d'Hitler à Carlos*, Fayard, 1996.

10. See Chapter XV: "Behind the Luxor Massacre, bin Laden's Afghans."

11. Saïd Ramadan, *Islamic Law — Its scope and equity*, P.R. Macmillan Limited, London, 1961.

12. To seriously analyze this ideological output, let's consider three examples. The first part declares the failures of secularity, and offers as a response "Islam, now the bearer of a universal civilization . . . Like it or not, Islam today challenges the West on three counts: no — to the rejection of transcendence, which reduces mankind to nothing but an animal; no — to the political and military domination of those powers for which oil is more valuable than blood; and no — finally — to the abandonment of any communal plan that would allow men to live according to the principles of a healthy morality and a fraternal commitment," (*Tribune de Genève*, September 9, 1994).

    The second postulates that the "martyrdom of Bosnia rings the death knell of the Western conscience. . . . On the other hand, Muslims today are definitively set on the path that they are constrained to follow to get respect for the most elementary justice. They will not turn to the UN, NATO or the 'international community' to ask for help. They know that lambs do not gain anything by sitting down at the wolves' table. They will derive their new strength from the wisdom of Islam, which teaches that there is a case where an apparent injustice is not unjust: when it is opposed and puts an end to a real injustice. When they come of age for fighting, they will take up arms in their turn. And if they do not have any weapons, they will throw stones in the hideous faces of the attackers and the tyrants," (*Hebdo*, July 27, 1995).

The last example of Hani Ramadan's epistolary writings sheds light on the Algerian crisis. "Not only it should be admitted that the current Algerian government has no legitimacy, but it must be stressed that it bears complete responsibility for the current situation. In whose interest is the continued violence in Algeria? The army's; it derives from this climate of terror the principle of its legitimacy. By smearing with red the face of the supposed 'fundamentalists,' it affirms that its presence is more than necessary. Even though it has been proven, since, that a great number of these odious crimes were perpetrated by soldiers disguised with beards." (*Tribune de Genève*, March 1, 1998).

13. Conversation with Gilles Kepel, author of (among other works) *A L'Ouest d'Allah*, Le Seuil, 1994.

14. See Chapter V: "The CIA's 'Afghans' and Their Networks."

Chapter VIII

IS THERE A PILOT ONBOARD THE U.S. AIRCRAFT?

> "I believe that U.S. policy must integrate elements of
> 'Wilsonianism.' Realpolitik is not enough. You have
> to have convictions. Take de Gaulle. He was an ad-
> herent of realpolitik. He was also a man of convic-
> tions. For foreign policy to succeed, it must be based
> on a certain number of moral principles; you can't do
> anything without that. Of course, then you may find
> that you have to try to inculcate them into the rest of
> the world."
>
> Henry Kissinger

"Big Brother" or a ship without a rudder? It's hard to tell, especially when one is analyzing Islamism as seen from Washington. Illus-
trating the pragmatism inspired by Anglo-Saxon virtues in the field of
international relations, an eminent adviser to the State Department today asserts "the need for an incoherent foreign policy." The same man
recognizes, off camera, that in these matters the secret service has more
power than the State Department. If you want to understand that, he
says, just look at Irangate, a typical scandal! Although a major shake-
up ensued within the U.S. secret service, that did not change a thing in
terms of the international tribulations of the world's primary power,
which continuously oscillates between improvisation with no thought
for tomorrow, and a carefully-constructed Machiavellism.

Serious troubles boiled over not a week after he took command at
his new position. Christopher Ross, the new coordinator for "counter-
terrorism" in the U.S. State Department was not at all pleased, but as
usual he would pull a fast one. Having conducted most of his career in
the Middle East, he knows how to display a judicious sense of detachment regarding the dysfunctions of his own administration, and to get
angry is "not smart," as he often repeats. Ross had just finished reading
the final proof of *Patterns of Global Terrorism*, and to say the least, the fi-

nal draft of this annual report on terrorist activity throughout the world was still far from perfect.

The new head of anti-terrorism knew all too well that once it is made public, this document is taken to pieces, then microscopically inspected in every capital of the world. A misplaced comma can be disastrous. Indeed, the report that is issued every spring allows one not only to understand the U.S. executive's view on terrorism, but it indicates too clearly (and often misleadingly, by the way, according to Ross), the contradictions and possible fluctuations in U.S. diplomacy on the matter.

The exercise of indexing "the rogue states," the bad students — accused of supporting terrorist activities — seems to him to be unsuited to the new international situation. Mr. Ross does not hide the fact that he finds the method contestable, but also that it disguises less and less well the commercial repercussions of this list of terrorist prize-winners.

The 1998 edition was made public on April 30. Unchanged since 1993, the list of defendants cites, in this order, Iran, Iraq, North Korea, Libya, Syria, Sudan, and of course, Cuba . . . This year, the thorniest case was, without question, that of Pakistan, which the State Department can hardly place on the same plane as the United States' traditional enemies.

However, independently of the support rendered by Islamabad to the Taleban and to their "Afghan" friends, it has now been established that the Pakistani services are supporting terrorism in Kashmir "in worrying proportions," as the report specifies. The State Department notes "the apparent will of the Pakistani civil authorities to do something about this." Consequently, the State Department has placed Pakistan on a kind of "watch list."

Christopher Ross was not able to correct the sophism employed by the State Department to avoid including Afghanistan on the list of culprits, to wit, that the absence of a recognized government meant in fact that there was no State, therefore it would be impossible to declare that it was a state that supported terrorism . . . In connection with Afghanistan, this year the report evokes "the important role" of Osama bin Laden and devotes two paragraphs to him, whereas he was only briefly cited in last year's report.

The bin Laden case is a problem for the State Department.

Clearly, not all of the U.S. government shares the analysis according to which "the banker of the Jihad" constitutes a major threat for U.S. interests in the world. At the Pentagon, as at the CIA, expert opinion is divided over this former fighter in Afghanistan, and any question regarding the Afghanistan veterans' potential to cause trouble is treated very circumspectly.

While taking a pluralistic approach to issues analysis is method that is well-entrenched in the State Department's culture, it normally stops at the point of decision-making, especially in security matters. In the event of disagreement with the National Security Council (NSC), the Defense Department, the CIA or the FBI, the President has the last word. According to Madeleine Albright, Secretary of State, "No matter what the Secretary of State, the National Security Advisor or the Secretary of Defense might say, at the end of the day it is the President who whose vote counts most in foreign policy."[1]

But the legislative power also has a decisive influence. The U.S. Constitution allots to Congress the determining powers in foreign policy.[2]

With the decision-making power split into so many strata, each superimposing its own competing motives onto the issues, U.S. international policy takes on the form of a multi-layered baklava pastry. In this configuration, the intelligence services (including the CIA) play a central role. Many times over, the central information agency has deliberately pursued its own interests by carrying out its own policy, regardless of any influence from the presidency and the Congress. One of the most disconcerting episodes in this history erupted with the "Irangate" affair,[3] and the trauma it caused would influence the U.S. government for a long time. Its consequences are still shaping recent evolutions in international policy. The scandal is emblematic of the history of U.S. government, because it illustrates a collapse of the "baklava" structure due to an instance of the CIA's unilateral action vis-à-vis the executive power. Irangate marked a profound rupture. Now we have two eras, pre- and post-Irangate.

Irangate/Contragate inaugurated a new form of "privatization" of U.S. foreign policy, carried out via the intermediary of businessmen linked to the services in question. Mixing with private actors of various origins, especially Iranian, Israeli and Saudi, this affair also implicated Israeli government officials and capital of Saudi State. These three partners, the U.S. and Israeli services, and Saudi money, keep coming up even today in the uninterrupted history of the manipulation of Islamist movements. But, obviously, the lessons of Irangate have considerable impact.

Faithful to its pragmatic spirit and swearing that this would never happen again, the U.S. government took measures. There is little chance today of any "Bin-Laden-gate" or any other equivalent scandal exploding on the scene. Simultaneously inventing more modern mechanisms of "privatizing" its international policy and making it more respectful of the Constitution, the U.S. executive power set its house in order with a well-publicized clean-up of the secret service. Here is a scene that occurred on September 17, 1997 on the lawns of the Agency in Langley, Virginia. In the most agreeable tones, the press attachés requested that the cameramen focus only on the official platform where President Clinton had just taken his seat, surrounded by ten former heads of the CIA, and not on the learned assembly of the some 5,000 active and retired agents who had come to applaud them.

You would think it was a university graduation ceremony. In fact it was the celebration of the CIA's fiftieth birthday. Hardly recovered from Irangate, the Agency approached its anniversary in a difficult context marked by a series of new fiascoes, with the arrest in 1994 of Aldrich Ames, a double agent who caused the death of the CIA's ten best agents in Moscow, then that of Harold Nicholson, also a mole paid by the Russians, and lately several "failures" of economic espionage in France and Germany. A persistent curse seemed to hang over the CIA, which was now being closely watched by Congress (which was narrowly controlling its activities, the budget and the planning of the various international operations).

Irangate provoked a revision of the Intelligence Oversight Act; approved in 1991, this revision basically tightened up the procedures for informing Congress. Thus, it was pointed out that "clandestine operations should not be carried out in violation of the Constitution or U.S. laws." This revision also required that "clandestine operations" be authorized by the President only in written form and never retroactively. And any "significant changes" that may crop up in the course of an operation must, according to the law of 1991, be approved in the same way and communicated to Congress.

In addition, ad hoc parliamentary committees can open investigations into any question related to the various intelligence services. A special investigation was opened after Irangate, but more specific questions may be raised, such as for example the role of the special services in the war against drugs. The various agencies communicate with the Congress through the publication of summary reports and the auditing of their leaders, regularly organized by the commissions. Reports covering themes relating to, for example, "computer surveillance" or "new forms of terrorism" can be ordered up according to the needs of Congress.

Generally, the intelligence services are obliged to provide Congress any type of information that the latter requests. Concerning "the most sensitive data," the commissions, in liaison with the agencies concerned, observe ad hoc procedures intended to preserve the confidentiality of information that must remain "classified," i.e. secret. It is precisely on this mechanism that Irangate had the most impact, involving more frequent give-and-take, and more exhaustive information on "international operations," according to a former CIA analyst. "An Irangate syndrome now forces us to get authorization even for the purchase of chewing gum," he sighs, "which has significantly decreased the Agency's ability to respond."

Like most of the budgets voted on by Congress, those of the intelligence services are allotted in two phases: "authorizations," during which amounts are fixed, and "appropriations," which lead to the actual allocation of the monies appropriated. In the first phase, the commissions of the two houses of Congress establish the size of the purse after considering the agencies' proposals. The director of the CIA himself defends his requests for appropriations. The commissions also approve a draft budget for "activities related to information gathering," that is "tactical intelligence and related activities;" the budget is prepared by the committees responsible for the defense of the Union. The budget of the U.S. intelligence services has always been top-secret; however, for the first time in the history of the United States, the new director of the CIA, George Tenet, decided to proceed differently. The overall budget for 1998 reached $26.8 billion. By way of comparison, and for the same year, the budget of the French external services (DGSE) reaches a maximum of $250 million.

On top of the Irangate syndrome and its latest poor showing, the CIA has had five different directors in six years, all more or less victims of the vacillations of the White House and the political rivalries at work in Congress. On top of the scandals and incidents that punctuate its history, the CIA has always been a favorite terrain for confrontation between the presidency and the Congress. This policy confrontation (if not political confrontation) which regularly takes on the tones of a Hollywood soap opera, confirms above all the intelligence services' pre-eiminence in the field of United States foreign policy.

In addition to the executive and legislative powers, which co-exist in a permanent state of conflict, new non-institutional actors have cropped up who pursue their own interests. Doesn't the foreign policy of the world's greatest power become, under these conditions, a sham? Nobody controls the process, and the lack of control is such that one can indeed question this country's aptitude to conduct a coherent foreign policy. Does the United States still have a foreign policy?

If one sticks to the spirit and the letter of the constitutional organization of the powers, the Secretary of State Madeleine Albright is right to say that the President enjoys unquestionable primacy in defining foreign policy; but Congress, which has extended powers in this field, remains impossible to circumvent. Since the end of the Cold War (and with it, the end of the perceived need for cohesiveness vis-à-vis the Communist enemy), the U.S. Congress has felt much freer to satisfy all kinds of special economic and ethnic interests through legislation on various foreign policy questions, and it does this, often in contradiction to the declared choices of the presidency, and even in obvious violation of international law.

With the Congress dominated by the Republicans, U.S. diplomacy has gained in decibels what it has lost in consistency, especially with the all-powerful president of the Senate Foreign Affairs Commission, Jesse Helms. In Washington they say that he positions himself "to the right of Genghis Khan" and that he considers that apart from United States "the planet is nothing but a rat hole."   Representing North Carolina for twenty-five years, this Southerner who detests civil servants, Blacks, teen-mothers and foreigners has controlled the appointment of ambassadors with an iron hand.

"How can we not tremble at the thought that a man of so limited capability occupies such a central role in our diplomacy?" The New York Times deplores. In spite of Madeleine Albright's repeated attempts to charm Congress in this regard, Congress is still reluctant to pay Washington's arrears to the United Nations. And listening attentively to the fluctuations of public opinion, President Clinton does not always use his veto against laws in Congress, even when they do not in fact have the support of his administration.

Let us consider the Helms-Burton and the d'Amato-Kennedy laws, which issue universal economic sanctions against Cuba, Iran, Iraq and Libya. Indeed, constitutionally, the President can suspend the application of a law approved by Congress if he judges it contrary to the higher interests of the country, as was the case for the Dole law that proposed to transfer the embassy of the United States to Jerusalem. In fact, the need to get along with a hostile Congress hampers the President considerably, and he continues to waver as long as he can in threatening to apply these sanctions, in the face of opposition from the whole world.

Beyond Congress, "new actors," defenders of special interests, weigh more and more heavily on foreign policy decision-making. In addition to the intelligence agencies and other governmental structures — the National Security Council (NSC), the State Department, the Pentagon, the Commerce Department and the other "executive agencies," innumerable economic, ethnic and religious lobbies have grown in influence to become more and more one of the essential components of the recent evolution in U.S. foreign policy.

"Lobbying" refers to all the professionals who, at the levels of the cities, the States and the federal institutions — both Congressional and governmental — work to influence the political decisions and the legislative work in the direction of their clients' interests. In the United States, this activity has become an economic sector unto itself. In less than thirty years, the number of "lobbyists" in the capital has more than quadrupled, with 67,000 self-proclaimed professionals. Money is their primary tool of influence, the central nerve of U.S. election campaigns. After the primary elections, a presidential campaign costs approximately $200 million. You can calculate $4 to $5 million for a seat in the Senate and approximately $700,000 for the House of Representatives.

"Fundraising is an increasingly significant part of an elected official's activity, almost 50% for representatives, and this ensures their political survival," deplores an U.S. diplomat. "Half of their expenditures are invested in televised ads. Under these circumstances, it is no surprise that the lobbies with the biggest budgets manage to exert considerable influence on the people's elected officials, and consequently on the laws they vote on."

Thus, Philip Morris Co. was the biggest contributor in the 1995-1996 election campaign, with $4.2 million. Other major companies like AT&T, Seagram, RJR-Nabisco and UPS also figure among the largest electoral funders and they form part of the traditional lobbying landscape in Washington. The same holds true for the oil companies (which offer leadership positions to retiring national officials such as, for example, Henry Kissinger or James Baker), the banking association, the National Association of Realtors (the real estate industry spent $2.5 million dollars in 1995-1996), or The Motion Picture Association of America, which is in theory favorable to the Democrats.

The lobbies also carry significant electoral weight. Here one finds certain categories of the population like the pensioners, over-represented in areas like Florida; doctors and lawyers; and "special interest groups" like the associations that favor free sales of handguns, trade-union organizations in the industrial Midwest, ecological groups, anti-abortion leagues and the "Moral Revival" Clubs and other fundamentalist Christians.

On this subject, Denis Lacorne, a director of research at the CNRS (French research institute), explains that "in the early 1980's, Jerry Falwell, a particularly retrograde fundamentalist Baptist, declared that it was urgent to get into the political field to purify 'the U.S. Sodom' and to preach good conduct to counteract the depravations fed by sexual liberation . . . . He did not create his own party, but used the 'Moral Majority,' a religious lobby by which he set out to pressure the Republicans in order to use them to wage the crusade. In 1990, the Moral Majority was replaced by the 'Christian Coalition,' an ecumenical group that is open to Catholic fundamentalists and even certain orthodox Jews. The success of the Christian Coalition is amazing: in the 1996 presidential election, one out of four delegates at the republican party convention was part of it."[4]

The interest groups most engaged in questions of foreign policy are, obviously, the ethnic lobbies, such as the Cubans in Florida, the Armenians in Los Angeles and the Jewish community of New York — compared to which the U.S. Arab communities scarcely count. Because of its technical expertise, the pro-Israeli Aipac (which is always cited as an example) was used as a model by the Cuban lobby.

And, the emergence of ethnic lobbies means that members of Congress are also coming from a more diverse ethnic background, in step with what the experts call a "new immigration." Between now and 2050, "minorities" will make up almost half of the U.S. population. "This current trend makes it more difficult to form a new foreign policy consensus," notes one expert. "Given the increasing diversity of the population and the development of transnational communities that have both economic interests and political entities, it will be more difficult to define a common view of the national interest and to agree on foreign policy priorities."

Taking into account the growth of the Hispanic and Asian communities, it is considered that the United States' foreign policy in the coming decades will have to be focused more on Latin America and Asia, which play a growing part in the country's external trade.

The influence of economic, special interest, ethnic and religious lobbies may merge, conflict, compete, cancel each other out or, indeed, shape and change each other. Thus, in the matter of the gas pipeline between Turkmenistan, Iran and Turkey, the Jewish lobby, with great tact toward the U.S. oil companies who are hostile to any potential restrictions on their potential markets, deliberately chose not to react when the administration declared that the pipeline did not fall under the rubric of the economic sanctions approved by Congress.

During the wars in ex-Yugoslavia, the same Jewish lobby was among the first in line to defend the Bosnian Muslims, in unison with what is, objectively speaking, the most pro-Israeli administration in history; but it was a little too eager to use this as a means of compensating for its official relations with the Arab-Muslim world. And, to this world of precise measurements where every gram of influence is weighed like a precious spice, we must add the growing role of the non-governmental organizations (NGO's), which are frequently heard speaking in both houses of Congress and at the various government agencies.

"War is a serious matter; I am afraid that men engage themselves in it without the reflection it deserves," says Sun Tzu. Thus, it was to ponder the United States' nuclear strategy that, starting in 1945, various groups of analysts (educated in different specialties and coming from different backgrounds) were formed. Since then, these "think tanks" have proliferated and now they reflect on all questions related to security, foreign policy and economic development. The most famous is the "Rand Corporation," immortalized by Stanley Kubrick's Doctor Strangelove, who plays a mad scientist; but there are more than a thousand of them today, and their spheres of activity continue to expand, whether they focus on a particular issue or on a geographical area.[5]

An essential accessory to the principal public and private protagonists shaping U.S. foreign policy, think tanks are very different from European national university research centers. Financed by the private sector, many of them, such as the "Washington Institute for Near East Policy," work directly with the intelligence services and they work hand-in-hand at the very center of the decision-making process.

Even though in general U.S. public opinion is relatively indifferent to international issues that do not have an immediate perceptible impact on daily life, the White House is obsessed with the media effects that its decisions are likely to produce. The subjects that get the most "coverage" are the evolution of the situation in the Middle East, Cuba, the United Nations — especially its "peace-keeping operations" where the "boys" might have to be sent in. Given the traumatic memory of Vietnam, the security of U.S. soldiers and the famous "zero dead" option (which means conducting military operations without any victims) remains the public's greatest concern.

All the actors, the executive, legislative and administrative branches, and the lobbies, pay great attention to the press, which has itself become an actor in its own right. Major newspaper journalists such as William Safire and William Pfaff are feared and respected, while "CNN diplomacy" regularly imposes its own views, its choices and its morality onto the news it covers.

"Big Brother" or ship without a rudder, how should we view the process overall? The system is complex. Its often takes months, if not years, to react. The systematic search for a consensus does not inevitably focus on the most relevant national interests. On the contrary, domestic concerns end up obscuring the international questions and make it almost impossible that any "great concept" whatsoever might emerge.

"Contrary to the readily critical European press, the U.S. press obligingly passes along the administration's positions on foreign policy issues, and is therefore just a part of the external projection of America as a super power," explains a European diplomat. "It seems to be quite familiar with this concept of 'Big Brother,' the overall director, pulling all the strings from Washington."

Inherited from the Cold War, this process has not adapted to the social changes that are underway. George Bush's "new world order" was lost in the sands of the Gulf War, and the Wilsonian voluntarism of President Clinton — in particular when it comes to "preventive diplomacy" — came up short. "Democrats and Republicans both lack vision today," deplores Thomas Friedman, the foreign policy correspondent of *The New York Times*. "They have no vision on the great questions of foreign policy, be they matters of trade, NATO or China."

"We quite simply did not succeed in developing a coherent foreign policy," adds the republican senator and presidential candidate John McCain. He is one of the last visionaries on this matter to remain in the leading circles of the party.

U.S. international policy depends on domestic concerns more than ever before, and nothing seems likely to change that in the foreseeable future. Facing the prospect of increasing divisions along ethnic lines, United States foreign policy proceeds by fits and starts, with frequent changes of course. However, this "rudderless ship" policy meshes surprisingly well with the vision of the post-cold war world that informs the process.

The overwhelming certainty that they are the only winners of the Cold War places the U.S. elites in the position of the majority shareholder who wants all the dividends for himself. They are eager to see the world as unipolar and they imagine that it is reorganizing itself around the strategic, economic, financial and commercial interests of America alone. In the inevitably limited context of this view that holds that "whatever is good for the United States is necessarily so for the rest of the world," U.S. foreign policy decision makers, both public and private, no longer distinguish between "domestic" and "foreign." At the same time, their propensity to "externalize" U.S. domestic problems continues to interfere and endanger the multilateral mechanisms of the United Nations, the World Trade Organization, and NATO.

Applied to the political sphere as a whole, and promoted by the mass media and other public opinion leaders, "the majority shareholder syndrome" ends up looking like the only conceivable world view. The economic, financial and commercial data are the key criteria on which decisions are to be made in regard to international relations. They shape the strictly demarcated field of "market-based international policy," where the point of intersection between supply and demand dictates the great decisions.

Inherited from the Cold War, the U.S. policy of supporting Islamist movements — still in effect today — also impacts the "market-based international policy."

It is hard to interpret the various official entities' pronouncements on Islamism as a reflection of effective and operative political decisions. Important differences, if not contradictions, are expressed by the various think tanks charged with advising the policy-makers. The U.S. government's official doctrines are summarized rather well in Anthony Lake's (president of the National Security Council [NSC]), presentation to the Washington Institute on May 17, 1994. "Simply put, the U.S. policy on this matter is to seek to contain the States and the organizations that support religious or secular extremism. We are endeavoring to create a community of States in the Middle East, with all those who share our objectives of a market economy and broader democracy."[6]

In fact, the public debate on Islamism developed mostly after 1979-1980, in the aftermath of the Iranian revolution, and it was stepped up after the hostage incident at the U.S. embassy in Tehran.

Speaking at a conference organized by the Moshe Dayan Center for the Middle East at the University of Tel-Aviv in 1996, Robert Satloff, director of the Washington Institute, declared that the U.S. debate on Islam and its by-products, political Islam, Islamism and terrorism, comes down to only one question: "Why did we lose Iran?" This central question leads to a sad accounting. Terrorism then attacked U.S. interests directly: hostages were taken in Tehran (1980-81) and in Lebanon (1980); the GI's quarters in Beirut were bombed (1983); the World Trade Center in New York was hit (1993); the military training center in Riyadh was bombed (1995); the U.S. base in Dahran, Saudi Arabia was attacked (1996) and, more recently, the U.S. embassies in Nairobi and Dar es Salaam were bombed (August 1998). These events are interpreted through the lens of the Iranian threat, which continues to influence the United States' policy in the Gulf, in Egypt and in Gaza, in Algeria, and in Central Asia.

A Deputy Secretary of State, Edward P. Djerejian, entitled the speech he gave in June 1992 at Meridian House "The United States, Islam and the Middle East in a Changing World"; Robert Pelletreau, Deputy Secretary of State in 1994, spoke on the same subject under a different title: "Islam and the Policy of the United States"; another of Djerejian's speeches suggests, "The Policy of the United States vis-à-vis Islam, in a Crisis Zone." In 1995, he signed an article that opens on this warning note: "A coherent political approach vis-à-vis Islam is an essential need of our international policy in the crisis zone." Further, he raised the question, "What should be the United States' policy vis-à-vis Islam?"

Commenting on these examples, Robert Satloff wonders why the U.S. State Department should have one specific policy vis-à-vis Islam, when it does not have one vis-à-vis Judaism, Christianity and Buddhism. According to him, this formulation already betrays a form of "intellectual failure." "The United States must define its policy objectives vis-à-vis States, international organizations and universal principles like human rights," he adds, "but not vis-à-vis religions."

In an article in the *Middle East Quarterly* in summer 1995, Robert Pelletreau refined his approach. "We are confronted with Islamism in very different contexts. How does its impact influence the most important U.S. policy objectives, such as the peace process, the fight against anti-terrorism, the opening of markets, and respect for human rights? We should start by concentrating on our own interests and not on political Islam as such." This time, the director of the Washington Institute shares the Secretary of State's approach, adding that "the policy definition of a super power is worked out, initially, with its own interests as the starting point."[7]

Islamism, seen from Washington, also concentrates on extremism and its terrorist manifestations. Is there or is there not a continuum between radical Islamism and the Islamism described as "moderate"? The President of the National Security Council, Anthony Lake, gives an answer. "What distinguishes Islamist extremism from the other forms of extremism is not terrorism, but the nature of its goal, which is to take over the political power."

He added, in his final speech, that approaching Islamist extremism by its goal and not by its methods is the only adequate approach, "for it defines what is truly at stake with Islamism, whether radical or moderate, and that is the advent of an Islamic State. Insofar as both moderates and radicals share the same ultimate goal, the question of whether their relationships are continuous or discontinuous becomes purely academic."

In recent years, the State Department and its advisers have conducted their expert research in three areas: the relationship between economic underdevelopment and the assertion of Islamist ideology; the Islamist Internationale; and what kind of relations to establish with the Islamists — three perspectives all centered on defending "U.S. interests." Other experts at the Washington Institute and the Rand Corporation confirm this approach, figuring that "essentially, the actions of the United States government must correspond to principles of realpolitik; any other rhetoric is romantic."

In this respect, Satloff's final conclusion is extremely interesting. Not only does it summarize the dominant view at the State Department but, translated from the point of view of the intelligence and foreign operations services, it can be used as ideological cover for any kind of transgression — like Irangate — since the end justifies the means. "As a global superpower, the United States has the right, and often the responsibility, to be inconsistent in its approach to phenomena like Islamism," he explains, "because, in final analysis, the policy must be effective. Then, whether it can be regarded as intellectually coherent hardly matters."

In the context of these doctrines, while contradictions are legitimated in advance, it is on the other hand more difficult to justify incidents like Irangate or the World Trade Center. Thus, let us recall that the brains behind this clearly anti-U.S. attack, the Egyptian Sheik Omar Abdel Rahman, was allowed to settle in the United States thanks to a visa provided by the CIA, in return for services rendered during the Afghanistan war.

Satloff says the question must be viewed in its context. "It is very difficult to explain to the public — outside of the United States — that bureaucratic errors do not inevitably add up to a conspiracy. So, most Egyptians are thus persuaded that Omar Abdel Rahman was the guest of the United States before the attack at the World Trade Center. We know that he entered the United States with his papers in order. It is a fact that we admit, but that results from an error made by the administration in our embassy in Khartoum . . . . But one thing is sure. There is no conspiracy fomented by the United States that would secretly be helping the Islamist groups." The established facts, however, persist, and the federal administration cannot contradict the fact that the official at the Khartoum embassy who delivered the visa to Omar Abdel Rahman worked for the CIA.

Although it is not always expressed so clearly, the State Department experts, the National Security Council and the intelligence services are mainly informed by the think tanks and the research centers of the U.S. universities. With incentives from the federal government, study centers on the Middle East, especially those at Harvard, Texas, Georgetown, and the California (Los Angeles and Berkeley) Universities have developed programs specifically devoted to Islamism. New forums opened in the 1980's and many research institutes and foundations opened programs devoted to the political expressions of Islam. The US Institute for Peace, The Chicago Project on Fundamentalism, the US Information Agency, The Middle East Institute and many reviews regularly host workshops and conferences on "the challenges of political Islam, Islamism and terrorism."

Two schools of thought predominate. That represented by Daniel Pipes in particular (formerly a professor at the universities of Harvard and Pennsylvania and currently head of a private institute studying the Middle East) regards Islamism as a danger to the free world. This approach enjoyed its media apogee with Samuel Huntington's article, published by *Foreign Affairs* in 1993 and elaborated in his book *The Clash of Civilizations*. Its central thesis is that in our contemporary world, the greatest conflicts, the most important and most dangerous ones, will not take place between social classes, between the rich and the poor, groups defined according to economic criteria, but between people belonging to different cultural entities, in particular between the West and the Muslim countries influenced by the rise of Islamism. But for Huntington the West's major problem is not Islamism, but Islam. "Try to find a major conflict anywhere in the world that does not pit an Islamic society against a non-Islamic society," he asks. "The border of the Muslim world, from Morocco to Indonesia, is a continuous front line. Bosnian Muslims against orthodox Serbs and catholic Croats, Greece against Turkey, Armenians against the Azeris, the Russians against the Chechens and the Muslims of Central Asia and India against Pakistan. . . Not to mention the conflicts between Muslims and Catholics in the Philippines and Indonesia, between the Jews and the Arabs in the Middle East, and the bloody war between the Christians and Muslims of Sudan."[8] Revealing of the debate in America and the pendulum shifts that it manifests, this book succeeds Francis Fukuyama's, which brought an end to the great discussion on "the decline of America" by announcing *The End of History*, the triumph of capitalism and democracy. But terrorism and the Asian crisis having hit like a storm, Robert D. Kaplan also predicted the return of catastrophes in *The Coming Anarchy*, or how "scarcity, crime, over-population, tribalism and epidemics will soon destroy the social fabric of the entire planet." Ultimately, Huntington reactivates the idea of "each man for himself," founded on the old opposition between civilization and barbarity, a new trend that brings us back, once more, to the "higher interests of the United States," which are immediately translated in terms of domestic interests.

The second school of thought sees Islamism as a type of "liberation theology," waging a legitimate battle against autocratic and corrupt regimes. Previously at Holy Cross College and currently a professor at Georgetown University, John Esposito works on this basis from the point of view of a comparative study of religions. At Fordham University, John Entelis, whose research is focused on Algeria, takes the same approach and recommends establishing a political dialogue with the Islamists. A CIA analyst formerly at the Rand Corporation, Graham Fuller, author of the famous notes that led to Irangate, is part of this movement and finds it probable that the revolutionary uprisings in the Arab world will increase, if democratic openness does not give a significant role in political life to parties like the Algerian FIS. "Are these movements retrograde?" he asks. "Not necessarily, at least not in a political sense. While they are indeed socially conservative, they constitute the vehicle of the political aspirations of the middle class and the petty bourgeoisie, even if they also benefit from the support of the lower classes."[9] In this respect, Fuller sees Islamism as the expression of a social movement that is likely to bring in those who have been marginalized by modernization, and also those who seek a spiritual response to the loss of cultural identity. For him, the main question relates to how this social movement meshes with the economic, financial and commercial mechanisms of the market economy. If the Islamists gain control, insofar as they also represent the interests of the middle class, this evolution is perfectly likely to accord with America's economic priorities.

These two schools each have access to the executive and legislative powers, to the intelligence services and the lobbies. The diversity of expert opinion regarding international policy is disconcerting; it seems that everything and its opposite coexist at the same time. "It is difficult to make valid generalizations about the U.S. character and the nature of U.S. society that could shed any light, without ambiguity, on how Americans perceive Islamism," admits I. William Zartman, professor at Johns Hopkins University. "However, there is one characteristic that dominates the others in that it has such vast consequences: U.S. pluralism. In the United States, pluralism means recognizing the legitimacy of the differences existing within a great nation, given that, at the same time, these differences must be contained within the context of a certain cohabitation and of a certain degree of compromise . . . . That also means that the country is open to all beliefs and practices as long as they do not disturb the domestic tranquility of others . . . . But the way in which these beliefs are perceived only reinforces the general tendency toward openness and cohabitation, which underlies the attitudes towards Islam. University research about Islam and Islamism only reflect this same attitude."[10]

Does this blossoming of expert opinion (which we have to admire), does this research community apparently working in symbiosis with the political class, really make any difference to the course of events? Or does it, on the contrary, reinforce the unanimity of a political scene that appears smooth and consensual? Beyond their superficial differences, the "two schools" always end up converging on commonly acknowledged goals, in the name of the pragmatism and effectiveness of the policy-makers who look after U.S. interests. This is particularly the case in the Arab-Persian gulf, in Africa, in Central Asia and in the Middle East peace process. They prefer "low intensity conflicts" — the perfect theaters of operation for armed Islamists organizations.

Footnotes

1.  *L'Evènement du jeudi*, February 12-18, 1998.

2.  For example, on July 20, 1998, the House of Representatives adopted a resolution supporting Taiwan — that was necessary, according to the Republicans — to counterbalance the "counter-productive" statements of President Clinton during his last trip to China. This resolution, adopted by 390 votes to one, reiterates the U.S. support for the nationalist island, reaffirms the determination of the Congress to arm Taipei and reminds President Clinton of his commitment to require China to give up the threat using force to ensure that Taiwan is returned to China.

3.  It seemed clear that Irangate was above all the consequence of an Israeli manipulation, conceived and conducted by Shimon Peres and his team," writes Pierre Péan (*La Menace*, Fayard, 1987). "Israel's motives were clear: they were the same as the ones that pushed the Jewish State to deliver weapons to Iran from the very start of the conflict between Baghdad and Tehran, 'to stick' its Iraqi enemy in an extenuating war and to maintain divisions in the area."

4.  *Le Nouvel Observateur*, August 13-19, 1998.

5.  Jean-Paul Mayer gives a masterly study of this in *Rand, Brooking, Harvard et les autres — Les prophètes de la stratégie des Etats Unis*, Editions Addim, 1997.

6.  Islamic Activism and US Foreign Policy, United States Institute for Peace Press, 1997.

7.  The Islamism Debate, published by Martin Kramer, Tel-Aviv University, 1997.

8.  *Libération*, January 6, 1998.

9.  *Arabies*, No 136, April 1998.

10. *MARS*, Institut du monde Arab de Paris, No 5, Autumn-Winter 1995.

# Chapter IX
## Making Good Use of "Low-Intensity Conflicts"

> "One could do no better than to compare the United
> States' policy today, be it in Bosnia, Chechnya or
> Azerbaidjan, with what the United Provinces did in
> the 17th century with the Moors: they are using Islam
> for their own political purposes and if it helps them,
> they will support local *jihads*. That is how it was at
> that time and that is how it is today."
>
> Lucas Catherine

Never mind the official statements issued by the many U.S. foreign policy voices; the Pentagon's military experts have invariably followed the same course since the end of the Second World War by cultivating the best use of "low intensity conflicts." Islamism is one their favorite laboratories, in particular in Algeria, which is caught between high tensions, "low intensity" and major interests. On the privatized U.S. foreign policy market, human rights and religions are just so many alibis used in the pursuit of economic and financial interests alone. From this standpoint, the policy of sanctions is showing signs of fatigue, and the fight against terrorism is, too.

While theoretical expertise seldom goes beyond the borders of the microcosm of the policy-makers, military setbacks that cause the death of any "boys" inevitably lets loose a traumatic press campaign. In America more than in any other country, national cohesion is reaffirmed in these exceptional moments through the heavy media coverage of the drama. In addition to Vietnam, a partial list of these events is edifying: the failed attempt to free the hostages in Tehran, the bombing of the GIs' quarters in Beirut, the jets shot down over Lebanon, the notorious inadequacies of the invasion of Grenada, the air raid that missed in Tripoli, etc..

The vicious cycle stopped miraculously with the Afghanistan war, to which we must return if we are to try to reach any understanding of the U.S. approach to Islamism. After a whole series of attempts by the Pentagon and the Secret Service to manipulate Islamism, the Afghanistan war marked a departure from the past in three ways.

While the diplomatic position remained deliberately fluid, the war inaugurated a new U.S. military strategy founded on the return of the CIA to active operation, after it had been excluded from international operations following Vietnam and the Irangate scandal; finally, it provided a test laboratory for methods to be used later on, especially in Algeria and Central Asia.

Afghanistan was a perfect case study for low intensity conflicts. The Pentagon's score card is impressive, especially when it comes to personnel. First, this war, the first indirect conflict with the Red Army since Vietnam, could be carried out by proxy, using men from the Afghan underground who were themselves trained by the Pakistani army.

Second, this external engagement for the CIA, the biggest since Vietnam, didn't cost the U.S. taxpayer much. The amazing bill for the operations — $750 million from 1980 to 1986, and an equivalent sum every year until the in the early 1990's — was covered mostly by Saudi Arabia and other generous donors to the "holy war."

Some problems remain, however; they may be dormant today, but the Pentagon and all the federal agencies have not completely cleaned up past mistakes nor measured their full scope. As proof, one may consider the fatal bombings of the U.S. bases in Saudi Arabia (1995-96) and the embassies in Nairobi and Dar es Salaam (August 1998), the first steps of a new vicious circle. The fact is that the CIA has handed over the most sophisticated weapons to the most radical Islamists, including the famous "Stinger" missiles.[1]

In addition, the financial circuits that sprang up to accommodate the subcontracting arrangements of this war by proxy are taking on a life of their own, and will prove as long-lasting as they are unverifiable. Originally created to help fund the Afghan underground, the financial and distribution channels of the opium trade (primarily bound for Europe) will linger on to feed to coffers of the Taleban.

On top of the immediately beneficial effects of the "holy war" of Afghanistan, the second Gulf War in January 1991 put an end to a long series of military failures. "These conflicts were likely to accelerate instead of slowing down the transformation of the U.S. armed forces," according to Jean-Louis Dufour. "'Operation Desert Shield' rewarded everyone who had been struggling for ten years to give the Pentagon powerful and highly mobile means for intervening in external affairs. There is no doubt that the proponents of low intensity conflicts found the Middle Eastern events of the summer 1990 grounds for a considerable reduction of the traditional armed forces."[2] Though the European mind understood these two U.S. wars as the heralds of a "new military doctrine," "it was nothing more than the continuation of a defense and security policy initiated by John F. Kennedy, continued by Ronald Reagan, and amplified by President Bush," concludes Dufour. "The evolution that was taking place, with Iraqi impudence as a catalyst, was all headed in the direction of better adapting the U.S. forces to the thousand threats represented by low intensity conflicts."

Experts have defined "low intensity conflicts" in response to the traditional threats of nuclear war, direct confrontation with the USSR and conventional war between two States. They identify five types:[3]

1) insurrection or counter-insurrection; the two examples most often cited by U.S. military experts are the struggle between the Nicaraguan Contras and the Marxist regime of the Sandinistas and, obviously, the Afghan resistance against the Soviet army;

2) the fight against terrorism, including prevention as well as acts of reprisal such as those carried out by the U.S. Air Force in Lebanon (1983) and in Libya (1986);

3) the fight against drug trafficking, on home territory and abroad (the CIA's direct involvement with this objective is quite surrealist when one considers its notorious involvement in the Afghan and Colombian drug networks);

4) peace-time activities (also called "non-war operations") which cover hostage recovery operations, taking responsibility for civil populations displaced by a conflict, interventions following a natural disaster and air, naval or land-based displays of military force in order to impress the adversary;

5) finally, peace-keeping operations, whether conducted independently or under U.N. mandate. These operations imply interposing a force between two belligerents in order to make them respect a truce or a peace accord that has been negotiated beforehand.

Obviously, these various types of operations are not mutually exclusive.

The various situations of the Islamic countries and the Islamist movements correspond perfectly to the first two configurations of low intensity conflicts. As William B. Quandt (professor at the University of Virginia) explains, "None of these countries, none of these movements represents a threat to the United States comparable to that which the USSR was in the 1950's and 1960's. Most are economically weak and militarily under-equipped, and therefore are vulnerable to U.S. and Western forms of pressure."[4]

Requiring enormous intelligence gathering efforts beforehand, on-the-ground pursuit of low intensity conflicts entails a huge commitment of the information agencies, specifically directed to finding and interpreting "operative data," the essential fuel. "It is operative, because it can be used immediately and concretely," explains the criminologist Xavier Raufer. "Far too often in these realms, one receives information that is only the synthesis of remarks from 'fairly reliable sources,' personal assumptions and hypothetical constructs. Such poor data generally does not make it possible to defuse an attack that is being prepared nor to discover the real culprit behind an attack; and in the final analysis it does not give the 'active' elements the means of punishing this proven culprit. In short, it permits neither a definitive diagnosis nor an effective response."[5]

Consequently, and owing to the priority given to low intensity conflicts, the CIA emerged from the purgatory it was in following the Irangate incident, and it returned to the lead role in the foreign policy decision-making process. Thus, it is not a matter of chance that one finds CIA and other agency analysts at the heart of the international cases that are most important for the United States.

The Algerian conflict perfectly illustrates the rehabilitation of the U.S. agencies in the U.S. process of foreign policy decision-making. As in Afghanistan, the agencies recommend using the Islamist groups, or at least taking into account the areas where their claims converge with the projection of U.S. interests in North Africa, as in the Eastern Mediterranean and Central Asia.

At the end of 1995, a 120-page report, provocatively entitled *Will Algeria Be the Next Islamist State?*, was disseminated among the foreign relations ministries. The author answers clearly that Algeria will soon be controlled by the Islamic Salvation Front (FIS) and that "the question is not so much whether FIS will come to power, but how it will get there, to what extent it will control the power, and to what extent it will share it."

Published by the Rand Corporation (the semi-official CIA research center), the study was written by Graham E. Fuller, author of the briefing points that lay at the origin of the Irangate scandal. This support for the view that an Islamist regime was likely to arise in Algeria is not, in itself, a surprise.

The U.S. State Department is used to cooperating with this kind of regime in Saudi Arabia, and more broadly in the Arab-Persian peninsula, in Sudan during the Nimeiry dictatorship, Pakistan under President Zia, and recently with the Taleban of Afghanistan. That Fuller's report was an "event" is thus no accident and it deserves the greatest attention, insofar as his ideas directly dictated U.S. policy in the area until February 1996.

Seeking to persuade his backers that the U.S. government might find it very beneficial to collaborate with the Algerian Islamists, even to support their coming to power, Fuller concludes that such a possibility would not constitute a threat for "U.S. interests," but on the contrary, that it could in general "be a valuable example for the area. Indeed, how the FIS is treated would have a significant impact on how it would behave in a possible government role. It is not in the interest of the United States, nor in the interest of the area, that FIS be rigorously and illegally excluded from the electoral process or the government if it derives its power from the ballot boxes. An FIS that is perceived as having been excluded by definition as a political party (with the complicity of the West), simply because it is Islamist, would represent a dangerous force within the political body that would probably help to perpetuate the violence and extremism in Algerian politics."[6]

Using Algeria as an example, Fuller comes to a conclusion about "the nature" of Islamism, the quintessential "low intensity conflict," whose configuration corresponds to the Pentagon's priorities. "Islamism does not resemble Communism: it does not have a goal, or a central program. Islamist politics arise directly from the traditional local culture. The Islamist movements display a considerable diversity, and the undemocratic principle is not inherent for them. In addition, they evolve over time. . . . Finally, Islamist governments have every chance of proliferating in the Middle East in the years to come, taking many different forms. They will have to learn to live with the West, and the West will have to learn to live with them. This experiment with the Algerian FIS thus has a considerable scope."

Happy to see the Algerian Islamists preferring to learn English rather than French, Fuller talks mainly about the economic stakes, stating in particular that "The FIS would welcome any private U.S. investment in Algeria and would develop trade with the United States." Beyond the Islamists' "natural inclination" toward the market economy, Fuller is clearly impressed with the Algerian energy prospects, a billion dollar deal having been signed with the American company Arco. "It is extremely unlikely," he added, "that an FIS government would stop providing gas and oil to the West."

By the means of business, a priority for Islamist "Islamist power"— according to Fuller — the new Algeria would join the United States' Arab allies against Shiite Iran. "An FIS power would probably link up with the international network of Islamic banks based in Saudi Arabia and the Gulf. The Saudi bank Al-Baraka helped the Islamic National Front in Sudan for a long time and it is clear that it would do the same in Algeria, except if the latter adopted anti–Saudi policies, which is not very likely."

"The FIS maintained fairly good relations with Saudi Arabia, event though it lent its support to Saddam Hussein against Kuwait in the Gulf War. Saudi Arabia will seek to bring an Islamist Algeria back into the fold rather than allow it to drift toward Iran; financial ties are a key Saudi instrument in this respect."

A central element of Islamism as seen from Washington, Iran and all it represents lurks at the bottom of the Algerian question. "The realism of the Algerian Islamists could contrast enormously with the Iranian lack of realism. . . . Algeria would not act as a "revolutionary force" in the world as did Iran. . . . It might particularly seek to improve American-Iranian relations. But Algeria, if controlled by the FIS, might judiciously take on a kind of international leadership role for the Islamist movements, perhaps competing with Iran. The Algerian inclination to activism in foreign policy, particularly with regard to Third World issues, should not be neglected when one considers the future of the FIS."

Let us not forget that the Algerian authorities played a decisive role as intermediaries during the negotiations for the liberation of the U.S. hostages in Tehran in 1980-81.

Lastly, Fuller, who had already expounded upon "the moderating influence" that the FIS could have on the other Islamist movements of the Arab-Muslim world, ends with a strategic consideration that conforms to the Pentagon's doctrines on "low intensity conflicts," figuring that the FIS's stabilizing role could help the southern command of NATO, which was very much concerned by the crises in the Eastern Mediterranean. In this respect, it is not astonishing that Fuller produced an analysis of the Turkish Refah that was very similar to that conducted on the FIS.

Indeed, according to several briefing notes, the CIA considers that the FIS and the Turkish Refah would not be hostile to an increased NATO engagement in the Mediterranean. This bridgehead is considered vital for the projection of U.S. interests in Central Asia, and by extension over all the old Turkmen sphere of influence over the "silk route," encompassing the famous "Eurasia" so dear to Zbigniew Brzezinski, one of the principal proponents of the Pentagon's pro-Islamist orientation since the Afghanistan War.

Most of the views expressed in this report were the fruit of meetings and discussions that Fuller and other members of the CIA regularly conducted with Anwar Haddam, President of the parliamentary delegation of the FIS abroad, exiled in the United States since 1992. Several sizable contracts were signed between Algerian financiers and U.S. firms, in particular in the agro-alimentary sector, via this worthy representative of one of the great families of western Algeria.

And when *Middle East Quarterly* asked him whether he regularly meets members of the U.S. federal government, Anwar Haddam answered, "It is my job to meet this kind of person, especially members of Congress, but they are not in the habit of making the substance of the meetings public."[7]

During the same interview, the journalist asked him how it happens that no U.S. citizen has become a victim among the many foreigners assassinated in Algeria in the last few years. "Because in the particular situation that Algeria is experiencing, the Americans are perhaps more careful," Anwar Haddam answers; "you know, the Americans have better sources of information and thus know perfectly well who is manipulating these assassinations."

Seven thousand U.S. nationals, most of them employed by oil companies, live in Algeria, mostly along the periphery of the refineries and the terminals of the gas pipelines. Haddam has a perfect command of these data. He also knows the "internationalist" wing of the FIS which, with the help of Algerian veterans of the "holy war" of Afghanistan, would launch the first attacks claimed by the Armed Islamic Groups (GIA) in autumn 1994. According to several authoritative sources, Haddam oversees the connection between the FIS and the GIA, and he is the intermediary that would have given the GIA instructions to spare the energy infrastructure and U.S. workers operating in Algeria.

A competitor of Rabah Kébir, representative of the "Algerianist" faction and spokesman of the Executive Authority of FIS Abroad (IEFE) in exile in Bonn, Anwar Haddam, who would like to be the only international representative of the FIS, cultivates his relations with Graham Fuller. He "sold" him the idea of a meeting to bring together all the components of the Algerian opposition, to establish a common political platform.

The CIA "bought" it, especially since the plan received the approbation of Kashkett, a diplomat, head of the office of Algerian Affairs at the State Department and adviser to Robert Pelletreau, Under-Secretary of State for the Arab world. Organized by the CIA, with the assistance of the Catholic association Sant'Egidio (which has close ties to the Vatican), the meeting was held in Rome, November 21 and 22, 1994.

A second meeting was held in January 1995. The U.S. State Department asked its German homologue not to give an exit visa to the IEFE spokesman, in order to leave the field free for Anwar Haddam — who was traveling by U.S. Department of Justice jet.

Even though many of the historical leaders of the FIS disputed Haddam's right to represent them, he signed in the name of the Islamist party, jointly with the representatives of seven other political groups including the National Liberation Front (FLN), the Socialist Forces Front (FFS), and the Algerian League for Human Rights (LADDH), Rome's platform, calling for peace and a crisis resolution negotiated by the signatories and the Algerian leaders. The parties who did not agree to talk with the Islamists, the Gathering for Culture and Democracy (RCD) and the Communists under Ettahadi, were present but refused to sign the text. Knowledgeable observers of the Algerian scene did not miss the fact that most of the signatories were quite disconcerted to see

that Haddam's legitimacy was contested and that, under the circumstances, the meeting in Rome was likely to go nowhere.

The continuation of the story, which confirmed these premoni-
tions, makes Fuller's analysis seem all the more peculiar. "All of the important parties were represented, reflecting an exceptionally high proportion of the potential Algerian electorate; this confers a legitimacy on
this peace plan unequalled by almost any other political forum in Algeria for decades. By joining forces with other parties during the talks,
the FIS thus took a significant new step in the direction of
'normalization' into a traditional political group."

"This evolution was supported by the other parties, who saw it as
a legitimate if not essential element to any future dialogue with the
State," Fuller insists, adding: "In Algiers, the military junta denounced
the Sant'Egidio process as an attempt to usurp the government's
power. Actually, the challenge to the regime was powerful. The latter
prefers to deal separately with each party, to divide them by seeking to
cooperate with just a few of them. The unified front shown by the parties, having taken the liberty to hold their meeting abroad, was a challenge almost as great as a call for open and free elections.

"The parties also hoped that the international community could
support the Sant'Egidio process and force the regime to accept it. That
did not happen. Although foreign governments, including Washington,
made positive comments, calculating that Sant'Egidio indicated the
way to a peaceful solution, not a single European state took a step to
support the Sant'Egidio process in Algiers."

In Washington, this view of the matter prevailed until the autumn
of 1995, when it became obvious that the presidential election would
take place as envisaged in spite of the Sant'Egidio signatories' call for a
boycott. It became equally obvious that armed Islamism would not
win. Its transformation into blatant banditry succeeded in convincing
the State Department, in spite of the CIA's predictions, that Algeria
was definitely not Afghanistan.

In February 1996, Under-Secretary of State Robert Pelletreau, on
an official visit in Algiers, received some representatives of the main
opposition parties. The meeting took place at El-Biar on the heights of
Algiers, at the U.S. embassy. Pelletreau, who had been ambassador in
Bahrain, Tunisia and Egypt, is quite an expert on the Arab world. He
has a command of its language, history and customs; however, he found

it hard to hide his impatience. After twenty minutes, he made up his mind. None of his interlocutors, and consequently none of the current opposition factions, was likely to represent a credible alternative to the Algerian power. Long live Sant'Egidio! Recently discovered major oil reservoirs in the Algerian south may have had something to do with the State Department's change of position.

The U.S. benevolence toward the Algerian Islamists also waned when the Algerian leaders approached NATO. The Algerian military attaché in Brussels, General Saïd Bey, ex-commander of the principal military area (Algiers), headed up this policy. "NATO Approaches the Algerians," was the headline in the daily newspaper *El-Watan,* August 11, 1998. "Yesterday Lieutenant-General Mohamed Lamari, Chief of Staff of the Popular National Army (ANP), received Admiral Joseph Lopez, Commander-in-Chief of the U.S. naval forces in Europe and Commander-in-Chief of the southern command of NATO, at the Ministry for National Defense," reported the Algiers newspaper.

This about-face, a fresh opportunity for the Europeans to be amazed by the pragmatism of U.S. diplomacy, was principally inspired by the Americans' Africa policy. While remaining discreet on the categorical imperative of "U.S. interests," this policy strives to put an end to any situation that might be an obstacle to the opening of the raw materials market and the introduction of free-trade provisions.

Thus the State Department proceeded to liquidate Mobutu, who had been protected by Washington for years. Similarly, and again because of considerable oil stakes, U.S. diplomacy joined forces with the Marxist President of Angola, Dos Santos, against its old agent Jonas Savimbi, despite the fact that Savimbi had been its sub-contractor for operations in southern Africa throughout the Cold War.

Lastly, and for the same reasons, former Secretary of State James Baker invested heavily, through his private foundation in Houston, in seeking a solution to the last post-colonial conflict of the Western Sahara. Over Morocco's staunch opposition, Baker endeavored to have the United Nations endorse a solution supporting the recognition of an independent state for the Sahraouis of the Polisario Front. Protected by Algiers, the commander of the Polisario Front did not hide his surprise at this sudden and cordial solicitude, which went hand-in-hand with the new U.S. policy adopted with respect to Algeria since the discovery of new gas and oil reservoirs in the south of the country.

These last examples illustrate the CIA's and U.S. secret service' return to the forefront of the decision-making process in the field of foreign relations, in accordance with the primacy the Pentagon ascribes to low intensity conflicts. In addition, and to prevent any replay of the Irangate scandal, the secret services and other agencies now call on private companies, or large law firms, to take up operations that would have had to receive approval from Congress or the State Department.

The support that U.S. foreign policy grants to Islamist movements in several significant areas of the world remains hardly conceivable to the European mind, which vainly struggles to find the logic in it. This is a futile exercise, especially since the U.S. international choices now rely on a market for foreign policy, where the interaction of supply and demand determine the priorities, the views and the modes of action. One may reasonably consider that we are witnessing, since the end of the Cold War, a galloping privatization of the United States' foreign policy.

## Footnotes

1. See Chapter V, "The CIA's 'Afghans' and Their Networks."

2. Jean-Louis Dufour, *Les Vraies Guerres*, Editions La Manufacture, Lyon, 1990.

3. *Doctrine for joint operations in low intensity conflicts*, The Joint Chiefs of Staff, Washington, DC, September 12, 1988.

4. *Islamic Activism and US Foreign Policy*, *op. cit.*

5. *L'Express*, June 12-18, 1987.

6. Graham E. Fuller, *Algeria, the Next Fundamentalist State?*, Rand, Santa Monica, CA, United States, 1995.

7. *Middle East Quarterly*, September 1996.

# Chapter X
## THE PRIVATIZATION OF U. S. FOREIGN POLICY

> "A world in which the United States did not have primacy would see more violence and disorder, less democracy and economic growth. Maintaining the primacy of the United States is essential, not only for the standard of living and the security of the U.S., but also for the future of freedom, democracy, open economies and international order."
>
> Samuel P. Huntington

In order to make sure there can never be another Irangate, most of the foreign operations of the U.S. services and the Pentagon have been transferred to private companies whose activities are not subject to Congressional control. Most of them have extensive and diversified sources of financing, with a capitalization of several million dollars. Although their executives and employees are, generally, former employees of the CIA, retired officers from the "Special Forces" or former Pentagon workers, these companies are careful not to appear to be directly related to the CIA and the Pentagon.

The U.S. government, which encouraged the privatization of its agencies, finds this doubly advantageous. In the event of diplomatic interference, these "private" partners take the heat in place of the U.S. government; moreover, in a climate of budgetary constraints, this policy allows a substantial reduction in manpower without diminishing the Pentagon's capacity for influence and external projection. The Pentagon has a top secret ad hoc coordination group that supervises the these "private operations," the Special Operations Command (Socom), which also provides the interface with the "Special Forces" that can be committed in "mixed interventions" according to the context and the needs.

These "private" partners are supervised and coordinated by the

Defense Trade Control, a specialized organization in the State Department. Socom is a very opaque organization. Its chief, General Henry Shelton, defines Socom's objectives as follows.[1] "Whether by helping to evacuate U.S. embassy personnel from Liberia, Sudan or Congo-Brazzaville, or by broadcasting useful information over the airwaves of a hastily built radio station in Rwanda, the U.S. special military units baptized 'Socom' play a part in managing conflicts in Africa. The 47,000 soldiers of Socom are called 'diplomatic warriors'; they are responsible for peacekeeping missions and for safeguarding our economic interests throughout the world."

In 1996 alone, Socom was responsible for U.S. interventions in 140 countries. "In Africa," adds General Shelton, "it participated in humanitarian missions in Somalia, Sudan, Rwanda and the Democratic Republic of the Congo (formerly Zaire). Socom's involvement made it possible to establish mine-clearing operations after the end of several civil wars, in particular in Angola, Mozambique, Rwanda and Eritrea. Thus, in 14 African countries, local bomb disposal experts could be trained. . . "

Socom's involvement was critical during the crisis in the big lakes region, especially early in the rebels' offensive in eastern Zaire, which ended with the fall of Mobutu. It ensured vital logistical support for troops that were on the move: finding appropriate terrain for landing strips, securing watering holes and supply centers.

In Liberia, Socom provided security for the evacuation of 2,300 people fleeing civil war; in Rwanda, it handled communications for Paul Kagamé's troops, while he was training police officers for the new Congo of Laurent-Désiré Kabila.

Obviously, the "humanitarian" or mine clearance pretext for intervention is often used as cover for logistical or directly operational military missions. In 1995, several foreign ministries were advised that a U. S. mine clearing company, Ronco, was making regular deliveries of tanks and explosives to the Rwandan army, although the U.N. Security Council had just adopted a series of resolutions prohibiting any weapons delivery in the area.

Challenged, the Pentagon answered that it had indeed given its assent to Ronco which was conducting, of its own accord, deliveries to Paul Kagamé's armed forces. "The only difference between traditional mercenaries and these private companies," says Loren Thompson, a researcher at the Tocqueville Institute, "is that the latter have the government's approval and conduct their operations as one honors any private contract, with the imprimatur of the administration."

In addition to their engagement in Africa, these private companies altered the course of the wars in ex-Yugoslavia. Military Professional Resources Inc. (MPRI) created almost from whole cloth, and trained, the armies of both Croatia and Bosnia. Based in Alexandria, Virginia, MPRI was created by a retired U.S. army general, Vernon Lewis, in 1987.

Reading his advertising brochure, one learns that this company, consisting of some 2,000 former U.S. soldiers, defines itself as "the greatest private structure of military expertise in the world." Since April 1995, the decisive moment in the Gulf War, the MPRI has been providing its expertise to the Croatian army. John Dinger, a State Department spokesman, is obliged to acknowledge the company's involvement, which according to him was "responsible for helping the Croats to avoid excesses and the inevitable atrocities of civil wars." And he adds that this training would prove very useful the day that Croatia joins NATO. "Its army will then observe the same rules and methods as the other members of the club . . ."

This "assistance" had immediate effects. Just three months after the MPRI was hired, the Croatian army, very disorganized up to that point, conducted a series of victorious offensives. During the biggest one, "Lightning Storm" (conducted against the Krajina region), hundreds of Serb villages were plundered and burned, hundreds of civilians raped and killed and some 160,000 people dislocated.

The Bosnian government also called on the services of MPRI, starting in the beginning of 1996. And the training and preparation of its armed forces, estimated at $400 million, was mostly paid for by Saudi Arabia, Kuwait, Bruneï and Malaysia.

Ken Silverstein identifies two more companies that are particularly active in the arena of the most sensitive Pentagon and State Department dossiers: Betac and Vinnell. Created in 1980, following the failed attempt to free the U.S. hostages in Tehran, Betac supervised elite units specializing in clandestine operations, especially anti-terrorist activities, in training for local police forces, anti-drug operations and all other missions of safe-keeping and security. Vinnell oversees the management of the training of the Saudi National Guard.

The Pentagon pays very close attention to Saudi Arabia, whose "national army" depends today almost exclusively on private U.S. consultants. The Sang Company mainly looks after the security of the royal family, but also that of strategic sites such as the oil wells, the refinery installations and hydrocarbon forwarding depots. Since the Gulf War, Sang has doubled its manpower to reach 75,000 acknowledged workers today, all taking part in the daily work of Saudi institutions. Smaller but more specialized, Vinnell, which recruits primarily among former "Green Berets," veterans of the Vietnam War, trains soldiers for the National Guard, particularly in the use of new weapons and the tactical engagement of mechanized units.

The lessons of Irangate have been learned. The Pentagon is increasingly turning to these "private war companies" as an ideal cover for carrying out its most sensitive operations, independently of the heavy-handed Congressional oversight commissions and undesirable media coverage. Indeed, the Congress, which constitutionally retains control over external operations of the various Pentagon agencies, has no control over these private partners. The privatization of the Pentagon agencies is reinforced by a proliferation of security organizations and guard services employed by the large oil companies that, according to their own agendas, also conduct their own policies.

Without slipping into the fantasy of "plots," I might note that for the last ten years we have been witnessing the emergence of a clandestine U.S. international policy. Behind the State Department's press releases, international actions are undertaken that are unquestionably out of sync with the officially stated positions of the government of the world's premier power. "Clandestine U.S. international policy" or, rather, policies, for the various agencies and the interests of their private subcontractors do not always follow the same line.

A last significant sign that the United States' privatized foreign policy is gaining the upper hand may be detected in the general recourse to nongovernmental organizations, whose goals are not always consistent with humanitarian aid. In spring 1997, several U.S. embassies in Europe contacted the Education Ministries of their respective host countries to acquaint them with a vast program controlled by an NGO, "Civitas," which was intended to promote the topic of "democracy."

In 1995, the U.S. government organized an international meeting with the Federated Teachers of America (FTA), in order to create a worldwide network of pedagogues likely to be vectors of "democratic behaviors." Four hundred and fifty people, whose travel had been generously financed, in particular by George Soros and his foundation, took part in this forum. An Internet site accessible in several languages was created. Taking advantage of the same deep pockets, the organizers then brought together several hundred deputies from many countries in three other forums in Buenos Aires, Pretoria and Strasbourg, in order to organize regional groups.

In Washington, in April 1997, a synthesis meeting in the presence of the World Bank President and the general director of UNESCO, decided to transform the Civitas networks into an NGO headquartered in Strasbourg, near the Council of Europe. The elected president was none other than the head of the FTA. An official from the Hungarian Ministry of Education was named General Secretary.

Once this assembly was organized, the U.S. embassies in Europe got into action to promote the Civitas program. How does it get all this support? Where does it get its considerable funding? What are its activities and its objectives? Civitas has an impressive international breadth. It finances two newspapers in Togo. In Ethiopia, a network of lawyers and teachers is preparing a regional conference. To defuse inter-ethnic conflicts, it is workings with other NGO's and U.S. experts in South Africa. In Bosnia, Civitas heads up a training program for teachers with the assistance of the Council of Europe. It supports an association of teachers in Serbia and advises the local Ministry of Culture.

In the Czech Republic, Civitas is organizing exchanges between the teaching faculty of Prague and the Center for Civic Education in California. In collaboration with the Soros Foundation, it advises Hungarian universities. In Latvia, Civitas has a partnership with the Education Ministry and publishes civic instruction manuals. It finances school contests and media campaigns in Venezuela. Five British NGO's and universities are also paired with Civitas, while the Norwegian Ministry of Education and Ecclesiastical Affairs is working with Civitas on its reform of religious teaching, which needs to include new religions.

Other regional meetings were announced in Addis-Ababa, Maputo and Dakar in 1998-99. The Internet site, in its various linguistic versions, became a real forum of exchanges between teachers of the various continents. Without necessarily seeing this as a new CIA plot, one cannot not help but wonder about the nature of the messages disseminated by Civitas: the philosophical concept of democracy, citizenship and the State that it broadcasts internationally by every means possible. It is not clear that its concepts of secularity, of the role of the State and of religious communities absolutely match those of the European countries that were called upon by the U.S. authorities to take part in promoting the activities of Civitas.

Implanting Civitas in Strasbourg was the first step in a take-over attempt on the Council of Europe; it is now actively engaged in lobbying, in classic American style, with the new Eastern European countries as the intended audience. The methods used to promote Civitas resemble in every way those practiced by various U.S. NGO's within the Organization for Security and Cooperation in Europe (OSCE); the U.S. government's acknowledged objective being the rapid conversion of the new countries of Eastern Europe to the liberal political and economic designs that prevail in the United States.

Like other U.S. NGO's, Civitas's ultimate purpose clearly is the dissemination of liberal ideas (in their Anglo-Saxon version) to accompany the economic globalization that is underway.

The U.S. government chose to use an NGO, created in collaboration with the main U.S. teachers' trade union and the American-Hungarian Soros Foundation, all collaborating with a broad panoply of NGO's and public services in many countries, with the blessing of the World Bank. This technique exemplifies the new methods of influence, new transnational ideological apparatuses and the privatization of functions traditionally reserved as royal prerogatives.

"Intellectual influence has now replaced 'cannon diplomacy'," Robert Steele most aptly wrote. President of Open Source Solutions Inc., based in Oakton, Virginia, his not-for-profit group in the short run offers consulting services to government agencies and enterprises wishing to improve their information gathering systems. A former specialist in civil information for the Navy, and a former officer of the CIA, Steele adds: "A country that places its high-quality intellectual product at the disposal of a third country raises its international political status."[2]

In addition to the consensual set of themes of human rights, these new techniques of influence used by the U.S. government have actively persisted, in the last few years, in promoting the defense of religious minorities. Here one sees the connection with the State Department's official discourse on "moderate" Islamism, soluble in democracy and the market economy. Several think tanks, notably at Harvard University, have opened programs specifically devoted to "the geopolitics of religion." As with Civitas, they are already challenging the recognzied international organizations, such as the World Council of Churches (WCC).

"The religious field is now a priority of the U.S. government's private auxiliaries," explains a U.S. diplomat stationed in Paris, "because it offers doubly useful levers of influence. They are, on the one hand, powerful vectors for diffusing the principles of the market economy. Except for the old Catholic distrust of the accumulation of capital, most contemporary spiritual groups are objective allies of capitalism. In addition, the geopolitical translation of religious beliefs supports the atomization and the fragmentation of the arbitrary statist-nationalist configurations inherited from the old colonial empires."

In the long term it could be, concludes our interlocutor, that an intelligently managed defense — for example of the Bahaï community of Iran — would be more effective than economic sanctions against the whole country. In June 1998, the House of Representatives adopted by overwhelming majority, with the support of the democrats, a draft law on religious persecution, whose particularly broad scope will probably apply to Russia, China and several countries of the Arab-Muslim world. Strongly supported by the Christian Coalition lobby, this legislation is likely to succeed in the Senate as well.

In the context of this highly composite foreign policy, the proliferation of economic sanctions is the republican Congress's last weapon, and an increasingly disputed weapon that is beset by the contradictory protests of lobbies and other private interests. More than 75 countries, that is, two-thirds of the world population, are affected today by economic sanctions resulting from U.S. decisions. Used more than 100 times since 1945, 61 times since Bill Clinton arrived at the White House, they serve many purposes: to discourage nuclear proliferation, to dissuade terrorism, to stop the drug traffic, to prevent armed aggression, to replace governments, to fight against religious persecution, to protect the environment, to promote human rights and to conquer market share.

There are two laws decreeing sanctions on foreign countries: the

Helms-Burton Law, which targets companies that "traffic" with Cuba, and the D'Amato-Kennedy Law, targeting those investing in Iran or Libya.

Recent assessments of the various regimes of sanctions adopted by the United States cast doubt on their long-term effectiveness, and suggest that they fail in their objectives. They are expensive, and they produce very harmful secondary effects (especially against the civil populations, for example in Iraq), and they are based on a highly inequitable system of "two weights, two measures." Why is Iraq, which only partially applies the Resolutions of the U.N. Security Council, sanctioned, whereas Israel, which is quite as disrespectful of U.N. resolutions, is spared any reprisal?

Within the administration, the diplomatic repercussions of the Helms-Burton and D'Amato-Kennedy laws are becoming difficult to manage, since even the United States' the closest allies oppose them resolutely. In Congress, the deputies are torn between industrial interests (defended by the very powerful *USA Engage*, which represents 673 companies) and the ethnic lobbies that cover more or less every possible event in the world.

The Brookings Institution, one of the think tanks close to the Pentagon and the State Department, established a kind of guideline for the proper use of sanctions. The principal writer, Richard N. Hass, recommends avoiding unilateral action, since it allows the States that are under sanction to find alternatives. Cuba and Nigeria are eloquent examples. "We must avoid the phenomenon," explains Professor Hass, "of 'secondary sanctions' such as those imposed on Canada and the Europeans when they refuse to support Washington against Cuba, Iran or Libya.

"Sanctions must be applied in a targeted way; for example, in the event of nuclear proliferation, it is a question of striking the sensitive suppliers of products and the authors of illicit transfers of technology and not of suspending all diplomatic relations with the States concerned. We should always allow for clauses making exceptions on humanitarian grounds, as in the difficult cases of Cuba and of Iraq," Richard Hass adds. "In addition, and in collaboration with the Congress, we must also give better justification of the reasons for the sanctions, in accordance with the clauses of the Sanctions Reform Act, and include from the start an exit strategy guiding the end of the regime of sanctions, which should have been done for Pakistan and India after the measures taken following their respective nuclear tests. Lastly, the President should be able to suspend or stop a regime of sanctions if national security or the higher interest of the Union is concerned."

In conclusion, Hass calls for "a less reactive policy, making economic sanctions a serious foreign policy tool, one that can be used to avoid contradictions in the decision-making and the foreign policy options of the United States."

Always inclined to play the global cop, in multiplying the economic sanctions America ends up isolating itself, which of course goes against "the diplomacy of trade." Through this systematic reliance on sanctions, even the policy of fighting against terrorism is compromised by the constraints of business, by trade wars, and by the safeguarding of the sacrosanct "U.S. interests." This policy is a double-edged sword and even the Congress, constantly confronted by the powerful business lobbies, has admitted it. As a Chamber for drafting legislation that results from the juxtaposition of specific and often contradictory interests, Congress, too, is subject to the logic of privatization that underlies the entire foreign policy decision-making process.

This subservience is not accidental, and it corresponds to the traditional Baptist imperative that no one is free of sin. "But we believe in redemption and the need to move forward," President Clinton concluded, on a 60 Minutes (CBS News) program on adultery. Ultimately, Islamism as seen from Washington wavers between the cynical and devastating mix of business and politics, and the fascination that any sectarian reading of the world exerts in the heart of America.

For Jean Baudrillard, America is wed to the idea of religion, because it makes all the prospects for salvation concrete. "The explosive growth of individual sects should not delude us; the important fact is that all of America is concerned with the moral institution of religion, with its immediate requirement for beatification, its material well-being, its need for justification, and no doubt also by its folly and delusion."[3]

It is not only the manifold parallel foreign policies that make the United States an accessory to the rise of Islamism, but its short-term defense of its unilateral economic interests. This mercantile cynicism stripped of any guiding principle other than the economic inevitably produces contradictions and sometimes bloody snags. The extremists who take U.S. interests for targets today were trained by the CIA; the Iranians are also victims of the same Sunni activists; finally, while supporting Islamist activism, the United States remains Israel's best ally.

Footnotes

1. Ken Silverstein provided a very thorough study of these "companies" to *The Nation*, July 4 – August 28, 1997.

2. *Le Temps Stratégique*, Geneva, February 1995.

3. Jean Baudrillard, *Amérique*, Grasset, 1986.

Chapter XI

ISLAMISM AND ZIONISM: COMPLEMENTARY ENEMIES

> "We offered a little financial assistance to certain Is-
> lamic groups. We supported mosques and schools,
> with the intention of developing a reactionary force
> against the forces of the Left, which supported the
> PLO."
>
> General Segev, Military Governor of Gaza (1973)

How can the United States continue to sponsor the radical
Islamists that seek the destruction of Israel, when at the same time the
U.S. electorate considers the security of the Hebrew State to be a question of domestic policy? Are Islamism and Zionism complementary
enemies? In international public opinion, radical Islamism is identified
with Iran, an alibi of the United States ("the Great Satan"). Indeed,
since the ayatollahs came to power, all suspicion has fallen on Tehran
and the fundamentalist Shiites. However, the real threat comes from
somewhere else, in fact from the allies of the United States themselves.
Long before the bombing of the U.S. embassies of Nairobi and Dar es
Salaam, several Islamist attacks had targeted U.S. interests. The World
Trade Center in New York was bombed; two other attacks were made
on U.S. military installations in Saudi Arabia. Like so many overdue
bills from the Cold War, these lethal acts were all carried out by the
"Afghans" of Osama bin Laden, a former Saudi agent trained by the CIA.

The U.S. "sponsorship" of Islamism does not mean that we should
suspect the hand of Washington behind every Islamist organization,
association and group, behind every armed faction and terrorist clique,
behind every unexplained explosion. Admittedly, this is not a "U.S.
plot," not an Islamist *Internationale*, but a certain complicity that can be
explained by a "definite" convergence of economic and strategic inter-

ests. The tangle of economic circuits of the "globalization" that is underway is so convoluted that underwriters, executives, financiers, henchmen and "godfathers" end up merging in a kind of lawsuit that has no specific subject and where the theological-political motives often degenerate into a kind of transnational mafioso delinquency.

It is clear that United States remains implicated in the emergence, expansion and radicalization of Islamism, in spite of the end of the Cold War. The United States' responsibility for certain terrorist operations and other criminal activities is well established and proven. "You cannot catch the truth like a bird with glue," Hegel liked to tell his students. Defending the Jewish State remains a foreign policy priority for the U.S., so much so that most observers regard it more and more as a domestic issue, hovering over election times and continuously influencing the political and economic choices of the world's premier power. How, then, can the United States tolerate, or even encourage, an ideology where one of the categorical imperatives is the destruction of the State of Israel?

Zionism, a political and religious movement that was at the origin of the creation of the State of Israel in 1947, was recognized by the entire international community. This nationalism was primarily constituted on a religious basis, which makes Israel "a problematic theocracy," to quote the "new Israeli historians." Yeshayahu Leibowitz says, "The State of Israel is not a geographical or historical entity, it is a political entity. Its problem today is as follows: should it be the setting for the national independence of the Jewish people, on just one part of the territory of Israel; or indeed should it become, on 'all of the territory of Israel,' a binational state that, unlike Belgium, would rest on the violent domination of one people by another people?"[1] Above and beyond the Palestinian question, Israel — like Islamism, which also aims to become a theocratic state — faces the problems of power, sovereignty and territory. Perhaps it is for this reason that Zionism and Islamism share the same aversion for Arab nationalism and its secular bases.

Proud of the results produced by their financial and logistic support for the Muslim Brothers against Nasser, the U.S. agencies gave the method to their Israeli counterparts. From its new headquarters north of Tel-Aviv, in the greatest secrecy, Shin Beth (domestic security and counter-espionage) has been developing a plan since the early 1970's to support the emergence of Islamist organizations likely to compete with, if not to weaken and divide, the Palestine Liberation Organization (PLO). Shin Beth finances the Palestinian branch of the Muslim Brothers, to counter the development of Palestinian resistance inside Israel and the rise to power of Nayef Hawatmeh's Democratic Front for Palestinian Liberation (FDLP) and George Habache's organization, the Popular Front for the Liberation of Palestine — FPLP.

For the Islamists, the liberation of Palestine is not an end goal but a specific step along the course of a "regional holy" war including Egypt, of course, but also Jordan, Lebanon and Syria. Initially, the dangers of laicism must be resisted in all its incarnations, especially Palestinian. In addition to Israeli assistance, the Palestinian Muslim Brothers benefit greatly from Saudi generosity, which was inflated considerably by the abrupt increase in oil prices. Clandestine at first, the Israeli aid to the Islamists became public when the Hebrew state permitted them activities that it refuses to the PLO. "The Hebrew State in particular allowed the Gaza Brothers' main institution, the Islamic Center — Al-Mujam'a Al-islami — to function in the Gaza Strip since the early 1970's, and later accorded it official recognition." By thus opening clinics, sports clubs, nursery schools, hospitals, and schools with the approval of the Israeli authorities, the Islamists considerably tightened their hold on Palestinian civil society, and not only in Gaza but also in the northern part of the West Bank, as well as in Hebron.

The movement grew after the Islamic revolution in Iran in 1979, at the same time that the PLO was racking up defeats in Lebanon in the early 1980's. Still accompanied by Shin Beth, the actual political emergence of the Palestinian Islamists came two months before the "war of the stones," the *Intifadah*. Founded by a charismatic sheik with a handicap, Ahmed Yassin, the "Islamic Society" (1973) was changed in February 1988 into the Movement for Islamic Resistance (MRI), more commonly called "Hamas" ("enthusiasm"). In its charter, Hamas specifies that the nationalist goal is no longer incompatible with Islam and the practice of the true faith.

Tactically converted to the goals of nationalism, the Palestinian Islamists were now in direct competition with the PLO, in spite of the historical prestige of its chief Yasser Arafat. Hamas even took the initiative, condemning the PLO's acceptance of U.N. Resolution 242 and the coexistence of the two States. By also rejecting the Madrid and Oslo agreements, the Islamists sought to take over all that remained of the legitimacy of the Palestinian people's struggle. It is not absurd to consider that in so doing, they directly served the interests of the Israeli Right who also reject, even today, the peace accords, which they see as giving too much precedence to Yasser Arafat's PLO.

"Complementary enemies," Islamists and Zionists thus work toward the same ends. With Hamas "upping the ante," the Likud is all the freer to pursue its broad scale policy of establishing colonies using immigrants from the former Soviet Union, and completing the encirclement and Judeification of East Jerusalem — two means of pursuing the dream of "Greater Israel," which the "Oslo peace" was supposed to have definitively relegated to the quarrels of historians.

A new trick of logic, a combination of circumstances or an annoying coincidence? This ambiguous policy did not fall from the sky. On the contrary, it is implied in the downstream effects of Israeli strategy as it was already formalized by the Sharon and Eitan government, in the 1980's. Back in February 1982, a memo from Oded Yinon, a former official in the Israeli ministry of Foreign Affairs, details the geostrategic plan of this policy, in other words the fragmentation of the Middle Eastern ensemble into the smallest possible units, in other words the dismantling of the Arab States, Israel's neighbors.

As a preamble, Yinon wrote, "The Islamic Arab world is only a house of cards built by foreign powers — France and Great Britain in the 1920's — out of mistrust for the aspirations of the autochtones. The region was arbitrarily divided into 19 States, all compounded of different ethnic groups, of minorities, each one hostile to the others, so that every Islamic Arab State today is threatened from the inside by ethnic and social dissensions, and in some of them civil war is already at work."[3]

Relying mainly on a U.S. bibliography and on quotations from Israeli political leaders, the memo reviews these 19 Arab States by indexing the principal centrifugal factors that are supposed to herald disorder and possible disintegration. "Such is the sad *de facto* situation, the disturbed situation of the countries that surround Israel." Yinon's recommendation is perfectly clear. "It is a situation fraught with peril, with danger, but a wealth of possibilities, for the first time since 1967. The opportunities that were not seized then may turn out to be more accessible in the 1980's, under circumstances and on a scale that we cannot even imagine today."

The political analysis also deserves all our attention: "The policy of 'peace,' the restitution of territories under pressure from the United States, excludes this new opportunity which is offered to us. Since 1967, the successive governments of Israel have subordinated our national objectives to narrow political emergencies, with a sterile domestic policy that tied our hands domestically as well as abroad." After one final recommendation that invites Israel "to act directly or indirectly to re-take the Sinai as a strategic, economic and energy reserve," Yinon concludes: "Breaking up Lebanon into five provinces precedes the fate that awaits the entire Arab world, including Egypt, Syria, Iraq and all the Arab peninsula; in Lebanon, it is already an accomplished fact. The disintegration of Syria and Iraq into ethnically or religiously homogeneous provinces, like Lebanon, is Israel's top priority, in the long run, on its eastern front. In the short run, the objective is the military dissolution of these States. Syria will be divided into several States, according to the ethnic communities, so that the coast will become an Alaouite Shiite State; the Alep region, a Sunni State; Damas, another Sunni State hostile to its northern neighbor; the Druses will make up their own State, which will perhaps extend to our Golan, and in any case in Haourân and northern Jordan. This State will guarantee peace and security in the area, in the long run: that is an objective that is, now, within our reach."

According to this memo, "Israel's long term priority" is thus to encourage all the factors of disintegration in the Arab States, with dismantlement leading to the creation of "ethnically or religiously homogeneous provinces." Ten years before the Balkans went up in flames, ten years before the massacres, the mass graves and other "terrible processions" of Bosnia, this premonitory encouragement of "ethnic" and religious cleansing makes one's hair stand on end.

It also anticipates the benevolent assistance that U.S. and Israel would provide to the "Islamist brigades" engaged in ex-Yugoslavia, after having purposely scuttled the various peace plans successively suggested by the European Union and the U.N.. Using Islamist ideology as factor of disintegration of States was inherited directly from the British Empire's policy of "divide and rule."[4] Nevermind the historical ties, this recurrent theme explains, above all, the equation "Islamism + Zionism = Complementary Enemy."

A final element in this contradiction relates to Iran and the strange relations that Israel entertains with this "partner," considered by the Israeli Foreign Ministry (with cause) to be "a powerful divisive factor within the Arab-Muslim world." It was also in the 1970's that Israel, traditional an ally of the shah, aligned its relations with Iran on those of the Carter administration, which significantly encouraged the advent of the Islamic revolution.

During the first Gulf War, the Israelis delivered weapons bound for Tehran to the Ba'athist and secular Iraq of Saddam Hussein. This came to light in the public domain with the revelations of the Irangate scandal, that is, the illegal sales of weapons to Iran, jointly carried out by Tel-Aviv and Washington. Irangate was a major episode of the Cold War, a major incident in the East-West confrontation, like the installation of Soviet missiles in Cuba. This incident, which goes back to 1984, was not the only one of its kind. Several Israeli arms companies regularly sold military material to Iran during the 1990's.

More recently an Israeli businessman, Nahum Manbar, was tried in Tel-Aviv for "colluding with the enemy," for having sold Iran chemical weapons components. In July 1998, this trial became a new scandal for the Netanyahu government. Indeed, the financier, who always protested his innocence, established that he had conducted this trade with Iran "with the approval and support" of the Israeli secret service. Of course, these various examples should not be read as an assertion of a strategic alliance with Iran, but they are characteristic of Israel's ambivalent approach. Israel is continually warning the West of the dangers of Iran's program of weapons of mass destruction, while playing the Persians against the rest of the Arab world every time that it can.

Footnotes

1.  *Am, Eretz, Medina*, Shorashim & Keter Publishing House, Jerusalem, 1992.

2.  Wendy Kristiansen, "Les Contradictions de Hamas," *Confluences/ Méditerranée*, No 20, winter 1996-97.

3.  *Kivunium*, No 14, February 1982. Review published by the Department of Propaganda, World Zionist Organization, Jerusalem. This article was sent to the *Review of Palestinian Studies* by Israel Shahak and was published in No 5, autumn 1982.

4.  Alexandre Del Valle, *Islamisme et Etats-Unis — Une alliance contre l'Europe*, L'Age d'homme, 1997.

Chapter XII

IRAN, THE GREAT SATAN'S ALIBI

> "Exporting the Revolution was always a myth, be-
> cause revolutionary Iran never had much impact in
> the Sunni fundamentalist environment: the big or-
> ganizations like the Muslim Brothers always kept
> their distance from Tehran."
>
> Olivier Roy

Everybody looks at Iran when the subject of Islamism comes up.
Since 1979, its Islamic revolution has been the symbol of Muslim radicalism, and the arm wrestling with Washington lends credibility to the
false notion of the superpower's aversion to religious fanaticism. Indeed, how could the United States make a pact with Islamism, still embodied today by Iran, the absolute reference for many overly-hasty observers? How could the United States encourage — and on occasion
rely upon — an ideology whose sanctuary remains, in their eyes, the
top terrorist State in the world? The American list of States that actively support terrorism, unchanged since 1993, placed Iran at the top
of the charts in 1998. Denounced as the "State that most actively supports terrorism" by the last State Department annual report, Iran is still
public enemy number one. Then come Iraq, Libya, North Korea, Sudan,
Syria and Cuba. Appearing on this list precludes these countries being
given American aid.

It is true that by overthrowing the old Iranian monarchy, the Islamic Revolution of 1979 was a powerful catalyst for the expansion of
Islamist ideology, not only in the Arab-Muslim world, but also in many
Western countries. However, this dreaded revolutionary contagion did
not produce lasting effects among Sunni Islamists. A "revolution in just
one country," the Shiite revolution did not become the export product

to which its masterminds aspired. The bigger organizations like the Muslim Brothers always kept their distance and were wary of Iranian activism. The Sunni radical groups would take their inspiration from other sources, particularly in Afghanistan during the "holy war" against the Soviets.

The American demonization of Iran does not hold up very well under a careful examination and must be set in historical perspective. Didn't Washington have a hand in the beginning of the Islamic revolution in Iran? Indeed, it was the powerful Confederation of Iranian Students Abroad that organized the first serious disputes with the regime. Encouraged by President Jimmy Carter's declarations on the universality of human rights, and also by the financial largesse of generous American donors, the student organization waged several international protest campaigns. The shah experienced them personally during an official visit to the United States in November 1977. The extent of the demonstrations was such that the itinerary for the visit had to be modified *in extremis* on several occasions. Relations between the two governments deteriorated. The first dissensions on Iran's defense policy had appeared around 1960, under the Kennedy administration. By continuing to expand its military power and by proposing to the countries bordering the Indian Ocean a defense alliance independent from Soviet and American aid, the Shah caused growing mistrust on the part of the Pentagon strategists. Washington found it difficult to tolerate such a demonstration of independence, especially on the part of an ally that possessed the fifth largest army in the world. Given the degradation of the domestic situation, the danger of seeing the country falling into the hands of a coalition influenced by Moscow became an obsession with Jimmy Carter, who gave a green light to the "Islamic solution."

The "Shah cannot remain," Jimmy Carter predicted, trying to convince Messrs Schmidt, Callaghan and Giscard d'Estaing who were meeting on January 5, 1979 at the Guadeloupe conference. Even before the Shah was out, Washington started to negotiate with the representatives of Imam Khomeini, one of the central questions being the attitude of the army — since the quality of their equipment and training guaranteed the credibility of one of the linchpins in the American system of defense on the southern side of the Soviet Union. Deputy Commander-in-Chief of the NATO forces, the American General Huyser was dispatched on the spot, January 5, 1979, to negotiate the neutrality of the Iranian armed forces. The discussions, carried out directly with the revolutionary leaders, would also make it possible to accelerate the departure of the Shah and to guarantee that Ayatollah Khomeini came to power, without any intervention by the army.

"The Carter administration, in its idiotic desire to change Iran's political system, had put pressure on the Shah who, weakened, ordered his armed forces not to respond," explains the former chief of the French secret service Alexandre de Marenches. "Better yet, the unspeakable Carter dispatched General Huyser to Iran, who while making the rounds, told the Iranian armed forces, entirely outfitted with American matériel, that they would not see any more spare parts if they chose to response; thus, they put Khomeini in power and started the Shiite revolution."[1] The United States was among the first countries to recognize this regime that was independent of Moscow, led by students who obeyed an unknown patriarch, and who kept repeating that Islam had the answer to everything. Since his arrival in Tehran, the imam Khomeini had clearly stated that the purpose of the revolution was not the "overthrow of the imperial regime, but the introduction of a republic of divine inspiration."

Why did the idyll end so abruptly? In absolute violation of the most elementary international law, on November 4, 1979, shortly after the Shah arrived in the United States for hospital treatment, "students devoted to the imam" occupied the U.S. embassy. Taking the diplomats hostage, they basically declared war on the United States and the whole world, a kind of coup d'état that would shape the regime in the long term. The showdown lasted 444 days and Jimmy Carter lost a presidential election. The 52 hostages were released on January 20, 1981, a few hours after Ronald Reagan was inaugurated. The American humiliation was total. And it would last a long time.

Some of the "students" from the embassy favored a "social Islamism," sort of a Muslim third way, following the example of social Christianity and Christian democracy. Others were Marxists, heirs to the powerful Toudeh party. All, convinced Islamists and determined revolutionists, remembered the coup d'état fomented by the CIA in August 1953 against the government of Doctor Mossadegh (who had had the audacity to nationalize Iranian oil). They all harbored the memory of this original sin of imperialist America. But a strong national feeling also prevailed at the time of this hostage-taking, as the American embassy had become, during the months before the republic was pro-claimed, "a parallel government," a den of spies and specialists, consult-ants of every kind working to infiltrate the government, national com-panies, oil companies and other apparatuses of the Pahlavi reign.

The creation of the Pasdaran corps (revolutionary guards) corre-sponded to concerns on the part of an army that had been penetrated by American agents. And the "shredded files that were found in the embassy were patiently patched together by the students, who black-mailed those politicians who had entertained relations, inevitably guilty, with 'the Great Satan.' They published several dozen volumes of the American diplomatic documents, which contained in fact only rou-tine information. On Tâleqâni Avenue, in front of 'the nest of spies,' at the end of every afternoon popular demonstrations took place, like a permanent village fair, in which delegations from the provinces partici-pated, and companies and government officials came to shout both their hostility and their secret desire for America which they had taken hostage, frustrated at not being able to go there themselves."[2]

Mixed in with this confrontation with the world's leading power was a challenge to the Sunni majority in the Arab-Muslim world. Let us not forget that for many Sunni Muslims, the Shiites are seen as mar-ginal adherents of Islam, if not heretics. Consolidated in the 16th cen-tury by the Safavids, Shi'ism constitutes the real glue of contemporary Iran. Initially directed against the Abbassid, then the Ottoman, em-pires, this essential dimension of the Iranian national identity was reaf-firmed after the revolution and set itself up as a religious and political competitor to Saudi Arabia, the supposed guardian of Sunni orthodoxy. Thus one can understand the takeover of the great mosque of Mecca in November 1979, parallel to the American hostage episode. Besides its declared confrontation with the United States, the Islamic republic re-organized its strategy to focus on its competition with Saudi Arabia, ally of the "Great Satan" — a regional geopolitical competition, but above all a theological-political competition and an Islamist bidding war striving to embody the renascence of the "true faith."

This self-proclaimed political-religious legitimacy intending to supplant Saudi Arabia as the dominant pillar of the Arab-Muslim world was soon encouraged by two external events: the hardening of Israel's policy on the northern border of the country (leading to the in-vasion of southern Lebanon) and the first Gulf War. Giving the lie to

American prognostications that the regime would last only two years, paradoxically it is Iraq that probably saved the Islamic revolution of Iran. By invading the Iranian oil province of Khuzestan on September 22, 1980, Saddam Hussein reinvigorated Khomeini's entourage and brought new life to a revolution that was losing speed. Encouraged by the tacit support of the West after the American embassy incident, of the Soviets for the capture of the *mujaheddin* in Afghanistan and of the Arab countries that were worried by the risks of contagion of revolutionary Islamism, the Master of Baghdad went after Iran and confirmed its decision to wage a "war against all."

In Lebanon, where Tehran can use the Shiite party Hezbollah (controlled locally by Sheik Fahdlallah) and armed militia like the "Islamic Jihad," Iran started to apply this logic of all-out war. Shiite Islamism thus played a major part in the Lebanese civil war against Israel, against the Christian militia, and against Western interests — not only in Lebanon but also in Europe, and particularly against France (which was delivering weapons to Iraq). On November 13, 1983 in Beirut, a suicide truck bomb attack hit the camp at Drakkar and killed 58 French soldiers. Another suicide attack hit the American army quarters, killing 241.

Following the withdrawal of foreign troops from Lebanon in 1984, the Jihad and Hezbollah stepped up their terrorist activities, taking hostages, hijacking planes and planting bombs in Europe. Throughout this decade and until the death of the Imam Khomeini (on June 4, 1989), the Islamic Republic of Iran was the command center of international terrorism, inciting all the Muslims, both Shiites and Sunni, to fight the Western countries as "greater and lesser Satans." On every continent, and using the local Shiite communities as intermediaries, Iran supported and financed an impressive number of liberation movements and armed factions from Palestine to Northern Ireland, Sudan, the Ivory Coast and the suburbs of Europe's capital cities.

Reinforced by the death sentence for apostasy pronounced on the British writer Salman Rushdie, by a *fatwa* from Ayatollah Khomeini,[3] this overexploited media image of Iran as a great manipulator of world terrorism only added to the effects of a two-fold confusion. Even before the imam's death, the Iranian leaders quickly understood that this terrorist approach was a dead end, especially from an economic standpoint. But the image was convenient, and it was used for a long time to explain quickly and simplistically any terrorist tribulation that took place anywhere in the world. More serious, the Iranian bogeyman long obscured the endogenous origins of Islamism and its true funders and supporters, who were far more dangerous than an economically very much weakened Iran.

With the death of Ayatollah Khomeini, Tehran fell back into line. And, in spite of appearances, the mullahs' foreign policy was similar to that of the Shah, the latter being traditionally concerned with two principal objectives: maintaining national unity in spite of the multiethnic composition of the country; and safeguarding the regional balance, a necessary condition for the transport of oil in the Persian Gulf. With the passing years, Iran restored normal relationships with nearly every country in the world, even though the question of its being rehabilitated in the concert of nations was not entirely solved. Even Saudi Arabia ended up betting on Iranian moderation, and the decision to hold the Organization of the Islamic Conference (OCI)'s summit in Tehran, in December 1997, was a spectacular sign designating the end of Iranian isolation within the Arab-Muslim world. The effects caused by the demise of the "supreme guide" combined with those of the end of the war in Lebanon. As far as international terrorism, these two events together marked a break that inaugurated a new era. From now on different logic would be in place.

Indeed, the attack on New York's World Trade Center on February 26, 1993, the explosion that damaged the CIA's headquarters in Langley the same year, the assassinations of foreigners by the Algerian GIA and the killing of tourists in Egypt, the bombing of a military training center in Riyadh on November 13, 1995, and the blowing up of the base of Dahran in Saudi Arabia, June 26, 1996, all inevitably bring us back to the Sunni terrorist networks composed of former *mujaheddin* of Afghanistan, trained by the CIA for the most part, and mostly prepared and financed by the Saudi or Pakistani secret service, themselves trained by the United States!

As soon as one looks into the question of Afghanistan veterans, inevitably one comes across the Saudi Osama bin Laden, universally considered to be the "banker of the Jihad," patron of many Islamist associations and armed factions today that are engaged in Egypt, Algeria, Yemen, Somalia and Sudan in particular.[4] Currently, this benefactor of "new terrorism" is peacefully living in southern Afghanistan under the protection of his Taleban friends, in downtown Kandahar, where he has had a sumptuous palace built. And "Should I remind you that the U.S. State Department considered the capture of Kabul a 'positive step' in September 1996?" asks Olivier Roy.[5] "Here we have reached the height of nonsense: the Americans would support the Taleban, *inter alia*, because the latter strongly oppose the "Iranian terrorist State"; however, in fact, the Taleban give asylum to the most prominent terrorist of the day." This spectacular inversion to suit the circumstances is still not clearly seen by the general public.

The Iranian bogeyman, the best excuse available to the "Great Satan," is only a lure that noisily diverts attention from the true perpetrators, underwriters and backers of the "new Islamist terrorism" since the end of the war in Lebanon. They are the oil monarchies and Pakistan, combined with the "Great Satan" itself. The American government does not much appreciate being reminded that the cadres of the "new terrorisms" have, for the most part, been trained through his kind offices. The Iranian bogeyman is not only used to cover the CIA's latest intrigues, but it amplifies the apparent Iranian threat so that it can be used to justify military interventions similar to that deployed in Iraq, during the second Gulf War.

But Iran's prudent and reserved attitude during "Operation Desert Storm," the new relations engaged between Tehran and Moscow, and the "hole" that Iran has dug in the United States' patiently woven plan to secure control of the Gulf and Central Asian hydrocarbons, have led several leaders of the American government and the business world to doubt the State Department's policy. The strategy of "double containment" (consisting in isolating Iraq and Iran, without differentiation) is considered to be increasingly unsuited to the new economic-strategic reality of a region that is vital to American interests.

The State Department admits, moreover, that prolonged isolation of Iran can only constrain it to forge preferential relations with Moscow; an evolution that is potentially fraught with consequences in terms of regional stability and the risk of nuclear and ballistic proliferation. The tone is thus set for a change, certainly circumspect, but inevitable, of the policy the "Great Satan" must adopt with regard to the "public enemy Number One that most actively supports terrorism." Even if nothing currently makes it possible to affirm that there is a coherent and specific American policy with regard to Iran, business is picking up again at a brisk pace. Some 4,000 American businessmen or workers related to American firms — under various pretexts, using Canadian or multinational subsidiaries of the big industrial and financial groups as cover — have traveled to Tehran since March 1998.

"In Afghanistan, it is the 'Westerners' who support the most rigorous fundamentalists known to the contemporary Muslim world (the Taleban), while the Iranians, allied with the Russians and the Indians, lend a hand to the moderate and lay Islamists under General Doustom," adds Olivier Roy. "Iran is even a victim of Sunni extremist terrorists in Pakistan: in 1997, in Lahore alone, the Iranian cultural center was set on fire and the station chief and six Iranian subordinates were killed."

How could the United States seriously encourage an ideology whose terrorist operations were increasingly targeting American interests as well? A review of the facts is enlightening.

Friday February 26, 1993, in New York at 12:18pm: A violent explosion ripped through the walls and brought down the ceiling of the subway station under the basement parking lot of the World Trade Center. Since the Center was opened in 1973, a stone's throw from Wall Street, the 110 stories of the two highest towers in the "Big Apple" have become the hub of the business district. More than a thousand financial companies and institutions, including the Mercantile Exchange and the Commodities Exchange, are headquartered there. Some 55,000 employees work there more or less around the clock, and about 100,000 tourists head to the summit everyday to enjoy a stunning view of the Manhattan skyscrapers. The explosion set off a series of fires that, by chimney effect, went all the way to the 90th floor. A group of children from a vacation camp were trapped in an elevator for five hours. It took hours for the occupants of the top floors to evacuate the smoky offices; they had to walk down dozens of floors due to the lack of electricity. A major catastrophe was barely averted, and although the toll was too heavy by any reckoning (six dead, two missing, fifteen severely wounded and a thousand minor casualties), it was, fortunately, modest considering the nightmarish vision of a tower suddenly become infernal. In his short speech that was broadcast the following day, President Bill Clinton promised, "We will find the culprits, and we will find out why this happened. . . . Americans must know that we will do everything in our power to maintain the security of their streets, their offices and their houses."

In the hours that followed the attack, no less than twenty claims arrived at the various police offices. Why the United States? (And why not the United States?) asked the pundits, seized with a terrorist psychosis. You would have to go back to 1975 to find a trace of any previous terrorist attack (in that case, it was Puerto Rican separatists) in New York. And even though American interests were often the target of terrorist operations in Lebanon or elsewhere, the "forces of evil" never dared to act on U.S. territory, far from the complexities of the rest of the world.

The head of the investigation, the Deputy Director of Federal Security, James Fox, did not hide his embarrassment when he declared to the press that the research was likely "to go on for months at least." However, six days after the explosion, his colleagues made the first arrest, the result of a miracle as much as the admirable obstinacy of the FBI investigators. While clearing some 2,500 tons of rubble, they discovered a tiny piece of a license plate, from which they were able to reconstitute the number of the vehicle that was probably used to transport the explosive charge. It was a Ford van rented from a Ryder outlet in Jersey City, which was immediately subjected to close surveillance by FBI agents who were brought in to replace the usual employees.

A 26-year-old Palestinian holding a Jordanian passport, Mohamed Salameh, threw himself to the wolves when he lodged a claim that the vehicle had been stolen, and tried to recover his deposit of $400, on March 4, 1993. The same day, in Brooklyn, the FBI arrested another person, Ibrahim Elgabrowny, who was holding forged passports in the name of . . . Mohamed Salameh and al-Sayed Nosair (who had been implicated in the assassination of the far right rabbi Meir Kahane, in November 1990 in New York).

Some time later, American justice issued a warrant for the arrest of a new suspect, Mahmoud Abu Halima, who, in another "miracle," had just been arrested in the suburbs of Alexandria by the Egyptian police force, then expatriated to the United States on March 24, under circumstances that are not clear. Meanwhile, the FBI identified a chemist, Nidal Ayad, who could have prepared the charge and the fuse.

Dubbed "Islamist militants" by the federal security agency, these four suspects regularly attended the al-Salam mosque of Jersey City, where the Egyptian Sheik Omar Abdel Rahman officiated. Rahman, an eminent Islamist preacher, served as spiritual guide for many armed organizations who were in open conflict with several Arab governments. An international warrant for arrest was served for a fifth man who was in hiding — Ramzi Ahmed Youssef, an Iraqi native about whom little was known (other than that he had shared a room with Mohamed Salameh several months before the World Trade Center bombing, and that he might be the commandos' chief).

On August 25, 1993, Sheik Omar Abdel Rahman was indicted by the American courts. He was accused of being the "brain" behind Islamist terrorism in the United States and of having "directed" the terrorist organization that was responsible for the explosion at the World Trade Center. In addition, he was supposed to have supervised the preparation of a series of bombings, against the U.N., the FBI headquarters, the George Washington Bridge and the Lincoln and Holland Tunnels. He was also accused of having prepared an attempted murder against Egyptian President Hosni Mubarak during a visit to the United States in March 1993. The same criminal charges were pronounced against eleven other people.

At the end of a farcical manhunt across several continents, the fifth man, Ramzi Ahmed Youssef, supposedly the commando chief and bomb expert, was captured on February 7, 1995 in Islamabad. President Clinton greeted his arrest as the "greatest success recently recorded in the fight against terrorism." Wearing the complete regalia of the successful businessman, a dark subtle plaid suit, white shirt, silk tie and French eau de cologne, this 28-year-old (originally from Pakistani Baluchistan) presented himself two days later before a New York court as the principal defendant in the attack on the World Trade Center. At his side appeared the blind Sheik and the eleven other fellow defendants. When the judge who asked him what he intended to plead, he answered "Not guilty," in an extremely calm voice.

Ramzi Ahmed Youssef does not come across as a lost soul or a fanatic ready to make the supreme sacrifice; he is characterized rather as "a top terrorism professional," according to the FBI's notes. Youssef had a collection of forged passports and borrowed names (Mahmoud Abdelkarim, Ali Khan, Naggi Haddad, Abdelbassat Mahmoud). A former *mujaheddin* of the Afghanistan "holy war," he apparently learned the arts of bomb-making, urban guerrilla warfare, disguise and forged identity papers in Peshawar, Pakistan. A classified FBI file indicates that he was recruited by the local branch of the CIA. A great traveler, he became "a lecturer" very much in demand at various Islamic arts centers, in Karachi, Islamabad, Khartoum and Mayotte. He also visited Bangkok and the Philippines, where he tried to mount an attack against the Pope.

"In the Philippines, Ramzi Youssef and his team, made up of 'Afghans' from various countries such as Kuwait, Morocco and Pakistan, relied on another group (known as Abou Sayyaf) that was established in the Muslim islands toward the south of the archipelago (the cadres of this group and even its 'emir,' Abou Bakr Djandjalani, are 'Afghans,' familiar with the camps around Peshawar), and seem to have had contacts with the Moro guerrillas."[6] He also made several clandestine visits to Egypt. His itinerary was quite emblematic: in September 1992 in New York, holding Iraqi papers. At that time he told the immigration department at John F. Kennedy Airport that he was Kuwaiti by nationality and that he was actually engaged in the resistance to Saddam Hussein during the Gulf War.

Identity checks were carried out, but the American government granted him political asylum at once. Welcomed like the prodigal son by Sheik Abdel Rahman, he moved into the community of the al-Salam mosque in Jersey City, where he answered to the name of "Rashid the Iraqi." This was the time during which he was sharing a room with Mohamed Salameh. Lastly, a new disconcerting fact came to light: it was with a Pakistani passport, delivered in record time by the consulate, that he fled New York on February 27, 1993, just before the attack. "Now, that is a lucky boy," the judge blurted out; he, too, could not contain his astonishment.

The route of the blind sheik Omar Abdel Rahman is even more diverting. Born in 1939 in a village along the Nile delta, he lost the use of his eyes when he was only ten months old. He suffers from diabetes, but is nonetheless a great fan of Swiss chocolate. He knows the entire Koran by heart, and has since he was eleven years old. After theological studies at the very prestigious al-Azhar University, he joined the Muslim Brothers in the 1960's. At that time, he assumed the ministry of a small mosque in the province of Fayoum, in Upper Egypt. He became acquainted with the Cairo jail system during Nasser's great repression against the Islamists in 1954. Upon the death of the Raïs in 1970, he was a beneficiary of the policy of Islamization that Nasser's successor

Anwar al-Sadat inaugurated in order to get rid of the Nasserians and the Egyptian left.

Taking part in the emergence of the "Gama'a islamiya," the Islamic associations that were flourishing on university campuses, Omar Abdel Rahman was named professor at the University of Assiout, a big city in the south. In 1977, he visited Saudi Arabia several times, where he became friendly with the financier Osama bin Laden, and other countries of the Middle East where he met with several Islamist leaders including the Sudanese Hassan el-Tourabi, chief of the Islamic National Front (FNI). Playing up his aura as a visionary, and using his physical handicap "willed by God" to increase his authority, he encouraged and radicalized the Islamic associations that were initially only university organizations.

In October 1981, shortly after the assassination of President Sadat, he turned up in the dock with the protagonists of the attack Abboud Zommor and Mohamed Chawki al-Islambouli. He was accused of having pronounced a "*fatwa*" (an Islamic directive), a kind of legal opinion governing the creation of the "Jihad," which financed and carried out the assassination. But he was released for lack of evidence. Two other trials would more or less confirm his central role as "murchid al-ruhi," spiritual guide of "Gama'a islamiya," a new armed faction, born from a scission of the Jihad. There again, the evidence was inadequate for a conviction, and he continued to emit *fatwas* from abroad that specified the priority targets of the "holy war," such as the assassination of the secular writer Farag Foda, June 8, 1992, as well as attacks against the Copts or the tourist sites. Produced from his American exile, his sermons and directives are videotaped and are shown in most of the mosques in Egypt.

"How (and why) did you settle in the United States?" asked the judge. That was a critical question that underlay the entire inquiry conducted in the context of the World Trade Center bombing. The defendant answered with the enlightened statement of some select *suras*, while his lawyer tried to explain that he had received death threats from the Egyptian intelligence services and that escape to the New World was the only way out. The reality is more complex. Indeed, shortly after the Soviet intervention in Afghanistan, Sheik Omar Abdel Rahman asserted himself as one of the principal recruiting agents of the "holy war." Using his considerable political-religious authority, he organized the collection of funds for the Brothers' anti-Communist crusade in several countries, especially in the American Muslim communities. To stay beyond the reach of Egyptian justice, the sheik settled down close to Sudan. From Khartoum, he also pursued (by videotape) his holy war against the "impious regime" of Cairo. But the friendship of the Sudanese Islamists was not flawless and his entourage, fearing a crackdown by the Egyptian secret service, urged him to leave this too risky place of exile.

For several years, he had been "tracked" by the American intelligence agents who were responsible for supporting the Afghan *mujaheddin's* war effort. In 1986 and 1987, he was already going to the United States to participate in Islamic conferences. Every time, he spent a few days in Saudi Arabia. Now taking refuge in Khartoum, he was interviewed by the CIA station chief in early March 1990 in a villa near the airport. A few days after this secret meeting, the sheik got his visa for the United States, to which he repaired after a quick tour of the *mujaheddin* camps in Peshawar during summer, 1990 (where he was received by Gulbuddin Hekmatyar, one of the most radical Afghan Islamist chiefs).

*Newsweek* confirmed this version of the story, revealing that the American consular agent in Khartoum who provided the visa was in fact a CIA employee stationed in Sudan. In Washington, this news caused a commotion. The CIA and the State Department were constrained to admit that the official who had delivered the visa was, indeed, employed by the CIA. But, continues the official press release, his assignment to the consular service responsible for visas was sheer coincidence. . . As for the formalities leading to long term residence on U.S. territory, including obtaining the legendary green card, these were carried out as a result of "a tragic series of administrative errors, computer glitches and spelling errors," but not from any intervention by the CIA. Welcomed by the Muslim community in Brooklyn, he moved into the training offices of the Alkifah Refugee Center, directed by an Egyptian emigrant who was also leader of a recruitment center for Afghanistan. Offering *mujaheddin* candidates training in weapons and explosives handling, the center had a training camp nearby in the state of Connecticut. Although the Afghanistan "holy war" was over, the center nevertheless continued its military activities!

The Alkifah Refugee Center had huge expenses, estimated at several million dollars, which were covered by various benefactors including an old friend of the sheik, Osama bin Laden. Several former officers from the active service of the CIA were employed at the training camp as "expert consultants." The names of Elgabrowny and Abou Halima also come up — the same people we find in the defendant's box after the World Trade Center bombing. Several former Afghan *mujaheddin* who were graduates of the same "school" took part in the fatal attacks against American targets in Riyadh and Dahran.

November 13, 1995: a bomb explodes at the Saudi National Guard headquarters (where the emir Abdallah Bin Abdelaziz, designated heir to King Fahd of Arabia, was director). Seven people are killed by the blast, including five American military instructors. Riyadh immediately points a finger at Iran. Tehran is supposed to have chosen this means of expressing its dissatisfaction with the increasing U.S. presence in the Gulf — 35,000 American soldiers in Saudi Arabia. Four months later, the culprits are arrested: Khaled Ibrahim Saïd (29 years old), Abdelaziz al-Mouathem, Moslih al-Chamrahni and Riyadh al-Hadjiri (all three 24 years old); they give televised confessions, broadcast by the national channel. Television viewers are stunned to discover that they are not Iranian, Yemeni or Iraqi fanatics, but four sons of honorable, well-connected commercial families in Riyadh and Jeddah. They admit the facts. Claiming that they were "working on their own," they say they bought the explosives in Yemen and were linked with Egyptian Islamists. The four were riflemen against the Russians in Afghanistan and are said to be close to the principal opponent to the monarchy, Mohamed al-Masaari, chief of the Committee for the Defense of Legitimate Rights (CDDL), in London, and to bin Laden.

The Khobar airfield, close to Dahran, east coast of Saudi Arabia, June 25, 1996: A key strategic station during the second Gulf War, Khobar is also the center of the kingdom's oil industry. 9:15pm: an oil tanker stops in the parking lot of the building that serves as the living quarters for the approximately 3,000 American soldiers who oversee the air embargo against Iraq. Two individuals quickly get out of the cab of the truck and dash into a white Mazda parked nearby. The guard instantly sounds an alarm and the evacuation starts immediately. But, exactly four minutes later, the truck explodes with an outrageous violence that tears off the building's façade. The following day, at the site of the attack, Secretary of State Warren Christopher said that it was "a miracle that the losses were not greater." By evening, there were 19 dead — all American — and 386 wounded Americans, Saudis and Bangladeshis. The drama sadly echoed the April 1983 bombing in Beirut that devastated the headquarters of the American contingent of the multinational force and killed 241 GI's, marking the end of the foreign intervention in Lebanon.

A few hours later, the Israeli the Prime Minister Benjamin Netanyahu declared that "Iran encourages this type of actions." At his side, the President of the State of Israel, Ezer Weizman, said he was "ready to bet that Iran is behind this business." Washington abstained from making any comment on the Israeli statements, whereas Tehran officially denied "any responsibility in this act," suggesting that it had to do with an "internal Saudi matter." The Iranian Minister for Foreign Affairs Ali Akbar Velayati deplored the attack during a press conference, affirming, moreover, that the "leaders of U.S. diplomacy immediately accused Iran. . . . We are astonished to see the foreign policy leaders of this great country making baseless statements against other countries."

One year later, while the FBI was complaining about the lack of cooperation from the local authorities, the investigation was still lost in a sandstorm when the American justice system ended up hauling in a Saudi, Hani Abdel Rahim al-Sayegh, suspected of having participated at the sites and of having given the signal to start the attack. Extradited on June 17, 1997 to the United States by Canada, where he had been arrested in March after seeking political asylum, this 28-year-old claimed to be member of the Saudi Hezbollah. The brains behind the mission was another member of Hezbollah, Ahmed Ibrahim Mughassil, who had taken refuge in Syria, then in Iran. This trail cast suspicions directly on the repressed Shiite minority of the Dahran region, which then replaced Tehran as the chief suspect. But the rest of the investigation hit a dead end and in Riyadh, several foreign offices hypothesized (with considerable confidence) that the attack originated among the Saudi Islamists, inside the country itself.

However, an Islamic revolution did not appear very likely, given the Saud family's proven ability to control internal crises and the American strategic interest in the area. The situation was not comparable to that which had existed in Iran before the revolution. "The bombing does not necessarily, and only, mean a rejection of the American presence, but rather that the Americans are being used in the power struggle between the Crown Princes, thus confirming the bitter struggle that is heating up for the final succession to the throne," reckoned a European diplomat. The strength of the American presence, its cost, and even its disputed effectiveness was turning into a series of domestic questions on which the Princes and the tribes were strongly divided. How could they maintain the security alliance with Washington while safeguarding the economic and political sovereignty of the kingdom; in short, how could they bring up to date the "Quincy Pact," the act that founded the monarchy? That was the heart of the question for Prince Abdallah Bin Abdelaziz, designated heir since the abdication of King Fahd.

In this incomplete succession, the veterans from Afghanistan played a preeminent role. Indeed, those who had come back were not just sitting on their hands. Some were placed at the disposal of the officers of the National Guard. Controlled by the Crown Prince called Abdallah — half-brother to King Fahd — the Guard embodies the legitimacy of the regime and ensures its stability. Its cadres almost all belong to the Dawiche, Qahtan or Oteiba tribes, which constituted the bulk of the "Ikhwan" battalions, the personal guard of the Saud family, during the conquest of Arabia (1905-1928) and the introduction of the monarchy at the end of the 1920's. Constrained by their tribal allegiances, other "Afghans" preferred to join forces with the powerful Sudairi clan and to side with Prince Sultan Bin Abdelaziz, Minister for Defense and Aviation since 1962. This latter also enjoyed the preference of Washington and of bin Laden (on whom the course of the Sudairi clan's business was heavily dependent).

Beyond the contentious Saudi succession, another contradiction originated in Afghanistan, through the showdown between the Saudi Islamists on one side and the monarchy and the United States on the other. One cannot repeat often enough that the Saudis — approximately 5,000 of them — were the most numerous of the "Arab internationalists" to join the Afghan underground. They joined the boldest special units, including the famous "Ansars," of whom bin Laden was one of the combat chiefs. But these "international Arab brigades" never formed a homogeneous unit, neither on the religious nor on the political plane. And although some of these units choose to wage "holy war" today on American or Saudi soil, they do so according to their view of the Jihad and their respective economic interests.

One cannot manipulate the mechanisms of the Jihad with impunity. Therefore the attack on the World Trade Center, like those of Riyadh and Dahran, must be racked up to the account of unpaid arrears from the "holy war" of Afghanistan, an unfinished war. The United States, just like other Arab and Western countries, is the target of "new terrorisms" today whose activists were motivated, armed and financed by the American intelligence agencies during the war with Afghanistan. The attacks made by Egyptian Gama'a, the slaughters perpetrated by the Armed Islamic Groups (GIA) in Algeria and their bombings in France (July-September 1995), as well as several more recent terrorist acts in Somalia, Ethiopia, Pakistan and the Philippines are, in most cases, carried out, financed and supported by former "Afghans." To this syndrome of the sorcerer's apprentice we must add the overwhelming American responsibility for obstructing, if not killing, the Middle East peace process and especially for creating the apartheid situation that is being consolidated today within Israel proper, between the Jewish and Arab populations, as well as between Israel and the occupied or autonomous Palestinian territories.

These old debts from the Cold War, these "dysfunctions" or snags that are so unacceptable in a democracy, don't seem like a high price to pay for the big American oil companies that have engaged former "Afghans" in their service. Started under Carter, the support for the Nicaraguan Contras expanded under Reagan, as did the assistance to the most Islamist of the *mujaheddin* of Afghanistan. The same policy is being pursued in Central Asia today, and all along this "new silk road," where these "rehabilitated" Afghans play watchdog for globalization.

The U.S. is concentrating these days on Eurasia. It covers three key areas: Ukraine, with its 52 million inhabitants and a strong sense of sovereignty vis-à-vis Russia; Azerbaïdjan, the promised land of petroleum, the linchpin between the Black Sea and Central Asia and between the Caucasus and Turkey, with an opening on the Caspian Sea; and finally, the former Soviet republics of Central Asia, guardians of the southward and westward flow of hydrocarbons from Kazakhstan and Turkmenistan (the key country of the area being Uzbekistan). While the Afghanistan war contributed to the break-up of the Soviet Union, one of the American priorities remains to seek the long term weakening of Russia, on a regional level, by creating a Tashkent-Baku-Tbilisi-Kiev axis: pursuit of Cold War by other means.

And "it was inevitable that the political elites as well as the populations of these countries should loudly declare their national identity and their adherence to Islam," adds Brzezinski, who clearly delineated the geopolitical axis that should be consolidated by relying on his old Islamist friends. "It is hard to imagine that the states of Central Asia, which entertains the best relations with Turkey, Iran, Pakistan and Saudi Arabia, would exchange their very new political sovereignty for the benefit that the possible integration into a great economic whole under Russian aegis could confer upon them."[7]

More imperialistic than ever, the U.S. wants to garner the dividends from the end of the Cold War, which it interprets as solely America's victory. Thus, it claims to be fulfilling an imaginary new world order that conforms only to America's own interests. To make this happen, the United States is turning back to the pioneering spirit and religious faith of the first American colonists. In accordance with this mindset, the "Afghans" who helped them to overcome the Soviets can still render many services. And however regrettable they may be, they are not "dysfunctions" that might obstruct the path of this God-given destiny. Neither will they stand in the way of the oil prospects for the next millennium. For this reason, the kingdom of Saudi Arabia remains the requisite partner of the United States.

Footnotes

1. Alexandre de Marenches, *Dans le secret des princes*, Stock, 1986.

2. Jean-Pierre Digeard, Bernard Hourcade and Yann Richard, *Iran au 20me siecle*, Fayard, 1996.

3. Ten years after the religious decree launched by Ayatollah Khomeini (February 1989) condemning the author of *The Satanic Verses* to death for blasphemy, Iranian president Mohammad Khatami stated on September 22, 1998 that the "fatwa is completely finished." In this way, Tehran was trying to bring the Rushdie matter to closure. "The Iranian government dissociates itself from all the premiums that were offered and does not support them," added the Iranian Foreign Minister Kamal Kharazi, after two days of sideline negotiations with Great Britain during the U.N. General Assembly in New York. The writer, who still remains at the mercy of a fanatic, was delighted by the Iranian position and observed, "I wish that from now on my name would appear on the literary page of the newspapers, rather than under the international news heading."

4. See Chapter VI: "Osama bin Laden, Our Man in Kandahar."

5. "Faut-il diaboliser l'Iran?", *Politique Internationale*, No 78, winter 1997-98.

6. Abderrahim Lamchichi, "Islamisme et violence politique," *Confluences/ Méditerranée*, No 20, 1996.

7. *Le Grand Echiquier — L'Amerique et le reste du monde*, Bayard Editions, 1997.

Chapter XIII

Why Saudi Arabia Finances Islamism

> "Not much remains today of this dream, just the
> memory of what could have been, if luxury had not
> slackened the bonds of the former discipline and had
> not swept away the ideals of the great puritan belief
> that had made virtue a necessity and had proclaimed
> its faith in the moral and spiritual values, in the face
> of a world that was increasingly dominated by mate-
> rialism and the hideous development of its mechani-
> cal inventions. It should be recognized, in all hon-
> esty, that these grapes were too green. For religious
> fanaticism had no sooner reached the height of its
> development, it had no sooner celebrated its material
> triumph, than the infidels offered advantages and
> benefits that at once started to sap the convictions of
> the winners."
>
> H. St John B Philby

Saudi Arabia plays the lead role in financing contemporary
Islamist movements, within the Arab-Muslim world but also in Africa,
Asia and Europe. In August 1996, an "influence" meeting was held in
Madrid during which Riyadh endeavored to get a grip on the "Islamic
centers" that were the beneficiaries of its largesse. Saudi Arabia finances this "checkbook diplomacy" to buy legitimacy and peace while
exerting its hegemony over Sunni Islam; only Shiite Iran seeks to dispute its control. Obsessed with this goal, upon which the survival of
their dynasty depends, the Sauds have created a whole battery of powerful financial tools. Dar al-Mal al-Islami (DMI), the "Islamic financial
house," is a kind of model. Other banks, innumerable foundations and
"humanitarian organizations" ensure continuity between the checkbook and policy decisions, the most visible of which is Riyadh's unfailing support for the totalitarian regime of the Taleban. The Sauds' "Arab
diplomacy" focuses on three areas: the Arabian Peninsula; the Middle
East; and the Western world. The "American insurance policy" guarantees this diplomacy in exchange for direct access to the greatest oil reserves in the world. The security of the kingdom of Saud is thus part of

the "vital interests" of the United States.

The cradle of Arab identity and of Islam, Saudi Arabia asserts these two claims with pride. It seeks to foster a double network of influence and solidarity — one that considers the Muslim world as a whole, and the other targeting the Arab world, starting with the Peninsula and, to an degree that declines over the distance, extending to the gates of the Near East. Consequently, the House of Saud invests a great deal of money in "Muslim" and "Arabic" diplomacy, two different concepts, the stakes and the developments of which do not, in the long term, coincide. Islamism and its factions are influenced by both these spheres of influence, which are themselves dependent on the special relationship entertained with the United States since the kingdom was founded.

Islam and "Arabity" are not one and the same thing. Even if most Arabs are of Muslim faith (Arabic being the sacred language of the youngest monotheist religion), most Muslims are not Arab. Indonesia, with its 220 million inhabitants, is the most populous Muslim country, ahead of even the Muslim communities of India and Pakistan. Thus the Muslim world is far greater than the Arab world, in terms of both quantitative and qualitative stakes. Its demographic weight and its geopolitical importance open opportunities upon which the Saud dynasty, obsessed with security and survival, wants to be able to rely if necessary. Indeed, the fact that Saudi Arabia is one of the richest countries of the world makes it extremely fragile and vulnerable.

Occupying most of the Arabian Peninsula and covering some 1.4 million square miles, its population hardly exceeds 12 million, including 4 million immigrants. By way of comparison, its turbulent neighbor Yemeni claims 15 million inhabitants on a territory smaller than France (330,000 square miles). This disproportion is even more salient when measuring wealth. In Saudi Arabia, the GNP per capita is thirty times superior to that of Yemen, ten times greater than that of Egypt and five times greater than what Syria claims. In such a context, one can easily understand that the House of Saud, managing the country like its own property, seeks to contain its neighbors' envy and prefers influence over confrontation.

Looking for "diplomatic" ways to secure a position of central influence within the Muslim world as well as in the Arab world is one of the country's major concerns. This partially explains the constant aid that Saudi Arabia has rendered to Islamist movements since the foundation of the kingdom. "The Saud family," wrote Alain Chouet, "pays particular attention to all those in the Sunni world and in Arabia proper who, like the Muslim Brothers, could elevate the debate over who holds the reins of power to the plane of religion; for that reason, Riyadh strives to fill the role of religious leadership to the greatest possible extent."[1] To fill the religious space completely, to preserve the peace and maintain its monopoly over the political arena, those are the main objectives of the Saudi Club.

"Don't start your examination of Saudi reality with the everlasting account of decapitations by the saber of justice on the Bazaar plaza," an Egyptian diplomat advises me. "You will never do it better than Benoist-Méchin, and you will only get caught up in describing the superficial oddities of this country, of which there is a plethora .... You can do better than that, in particular by taking a close look at the administrative apparatuses of the House of Saud. By familiarizing oneself with how they function, one reaches a certain depth of the system, one of the most opaque political systems today. Lastly, to understand why and how Saudi Arabia helps, supports, finances and protects so many Islamist movements throughout the whole world, it is necessary to also look into its parallel diplomatic efforts directed toward the Arab-Muslim world. There too, discretion and opacity are rigorous, because its attitude is contradictory to the preferential relationship that the kingdom, since its creation, has maintained with the United States."

These words came back to mind while I was going down Gran Via to meet a Saudi friend who had come to Madrid to take part in a conference that he was particularly keen to discuss with me.

Indeed, in Madrid in August 1996, an interesting meeting was held that went completely unnoticed by the public. A conference of "the directors of the Islamic Centers of Europe" took place in a large hotel at Puerta del Sol. The vague denomination "Islamic Center" actually covered schools, institutes, foundations and Islamic arts centers of Saudi financing or allegiance. The presence in the Spanish capital, at that very moment, of Prince Turki (chief of the Saudi intelligence services and contact officer of the famous "Afghans") would appear to be more than coincidental and gave this scientific "congress" a very specific connotation that was quite intriguing to the agents of the DGS (Servicio de información de la dirección de seguridad).

This meeting, presided over by Dr. Abdullah Bin Saleh al-Obaïd, General Secretary of the World Islamic League, brought together leaders from nine countries of Europe (Spain, Italy, Great Britain, Germany, France, the Netherlands, Belgium, Switzerland and Sweden). This gathering was the second of its kind, the first having been held in France, in May 1993, at Château-Chinon. Placed under the auspices of the Islamic Organization for Education, Science and Culture [Isesco] (a special agency within the Organization of the Islamic Conference [OCI] which is headquartered in Rabat), the conference's official topic was, "To support dialogue, mutual understanding and cooperation between cultures and religions."

The four principal workshops offered were devoted to "the role of cultural centers and schools in spreading Islamic culture, the education of imams and their awareness of the needs and the problems of Muslims in Europe;" "the role of Islamic centers and schools in Europe in the training, teaching and education of youth, in accordance with the obligations of the Muslim culture;" "the role of the European Islamic arts centers in fostering dialogue and understanding between different religions and cultures;" finally, "the problems experienced day-to-day by the Muslim communities of Europe and how to respond to them."

According to the Saudi press and in particular *al-Alam al-Islami*, the weekly gazette of the World Islamic League, several speakers cited various vexatious and discriminatory measures practiced by the governments of their respective host countries. Others fervently criticized the various attempts to integrate young Muslim immigrants, comparing them to campaigns of cultural negation, if not to more or less disguised forms of evangelization.

Without officially calling for the formation of closed communities, the conference proposed a certain number of techniques aiming at promoting the "acceptance of the Islamic veil in the public school," the opening of Koranic schools, and the creation of cemeteries specifically reserved for Muslims. These various "legitimate claims," the conference recommended, must always be expressed in "suitable forms" starting with "the right to be different" and the themes of "openness and dialogue."

These expressions, so dear to the Muslim Brothers, require explanation, as the vague semantic territory that they cover historically has set the scene for not a few misunderstandings, and not only in the context of inter-religious dialogue. "Indeed, how shall we interpret these calls for mutual understanding when they come from the political-religious leaders of such a religiously intolerant State as Saudi Arabia?" asked a diplomat who had spent his entire career in the Gulf countries. "Never forget that the debate over ideas has less to do with exchange and a search for common ground than with the possibility of making someone accept the viewpoints that one considers to be the only truths, and the practices conforming with Islam whose juridically dictated totality can neither be modified nor negotiated."

By the end of the conference, the President, Doctor Abdullah Bin Saleh al-Obaïd, was in addition elected Chairman of the Board of the Islamic Religious Organization of Geneva, the oldest Saudi institution in Europe. This center, whose goal is "to maintain the Islamic religious feelings by ensuring the teaching of the Koran and the dissemination of the Muslim culture," was founded by King Fayçal and was inaugurated by King Khaled, June 1, 1978. Its various activities are financed by a "waqf," a pious foundation — mainly intended to manage revenues — especially created by King Fahd.

The conference closed with the announcement that it would be held again regularly (without further detail). Scrupulously observed by most of the European foreign offices concerned, the event illustrated Saudi Arabia's efforts since the second Gulf War to take control of the Muslim communities of Europe. Scalded by the pro-Iraqi choice of many Islamic centers that had fallen under the influence of political-religious factions from the Maghreb or from Palestine, Riyadh intended to affirm (or reaffirm) in this manner a hegemonic authority derived from its interpretation and its practice of Islam, as well as from financial maneuvers that would be controlled better than in the past.

Riyadh pursues neither a restoration of a "caliphate" (like the Ottoman Empire) nor a hegemonic intention to control the whole Arab-Muslim world; it strives to produce the influence necessary and sufficient to give legitimacy to the House of Saud, guardian of the holy places of Islam. This is a fragile and disputed legitimacy that rests neither on a historical commitment to the Arab cause, such as Nasser, for example, could claim, nor on any form of election.

Islam remains the essential source of internal and external legitimacy of the Sauds since the kingdom was founded in 1932. Religion is used as the main basis for their Arabic and Muslim policies (which do not necessarily overlap). Thus, most of Saudi Arabia's activities related to the outside world are tied to "Muslim diplomacy." It is all the more dependent on managing the oil supply and its relations, as privileged as they are ambiguous, with the United States.

Even before it radiates outside the country, "Muslim diplomacy" expresses the very essence of life within the country. Every traveler who goes to Jeddah or Riyadh is immediately struck by the verticality of the constructions; these are cities with no apparent memory, where smoked glass, the most sophisticated concrete and metals combine in a multitude of airy constructions furrowed by the continuous flow of al-most silent traffic. Along the streets, fast-food outlets and other "delicatessens" follow one after another, as is so characteristic of American metropolises. But once the call to prayer is launched, all movement is suspended. And "you can hear the monotonous chant of the muezzins going up, on the terraces of the mosques, inviting all be-lievers to pay homage to the Creator and to thank Allah for the new day."[2] This public spirituality that so impressed Jacques Benoist-Méchin infiltrates every aspect of life, like the ever-present desert. The innumerable agents of this transcendence that pervades everything in the country are recruited, managed and paid by the dynasty, which as-sumes the burden of all the costs of worship and all the investments necessary to the correct operation of religious practice. In 1993, a few dozen muezzin wrote an open letter to the King, asking for greater autonomy for the religious sphere. It was a strange paradox to see these Muslim "clerics" thus requesting, although not in so many words, a certain separation of the Church and the State. Dismissed from their jobs, they were immediately thrown into jail.

Beyond this intangible geometry, Saudi Arabia has woven a net-work of international, governmental and nongovernmental forces, secu-lar, religious, economic, humanitarian and political organizations, to relay its influence throughout the Arab-Muslim world. Superimposed on this cartography of interlocking apparatuses, the private initiatives of the House of Saud and the Princes form only the most visible layer of the complex construction of the kingdom's "Muslim diplomacy," a dis-creet diplomacy that advances under cloak and mask. It is imperative that we examine this cartography if we wish to comprehend the "masked strategy," which is the main beneficiary of contemporary

Islamist movements.

Within this nebula, the Organization of the Islamic Conference (OCI) plays a central role, since it represents a kind of U.N. of the Muslim world. Created after the Islamic Summit of Rabat (1969) to divide and the unmanageable and "too socialist" Arab League, the OCI is the kingdom's latest tool for imposing its diplomatic priorities. Thus, from the very start of the Soviet intervention in Afghanistan, the OCI launched a call to "holy war" against the infidel invader. Some time later, it condemned "Khomeinism and Shiite activism," before passing along the kingdom's views favoring the Muslims of Bosnia, Chechnya and more recently Kosovo. With some fifty member countries, its permanent secretariat is in Jeddah.

Equipped with considerable financial clout, the Conference controls several "technical agencies;" the main one is the Islamic Development Bank, created in 1973 to finance infrastructure and development plans in Islamic countries. It is a semi-secular, semi-religious institution. 25% of the bank's capital is held by the State, and its financial strategy is aligned with the kingdom's political-religious decisions. Lately, the BID raised the ceiling on its loans to Pakistan from $150 to $400 million to help it handle the sanctions imposed following its nuclear tests.

There are other instruments in this Islamic financial toolbox. "Development funds from OPEC for international businesses, with 30% Saudi capital; the Arab Bank for Economic Development in Africa (24.4% Saudi capital); "Arab Funds for Economic and Social Development;" and, with a capital of $21 million, the "Saudi Development Fund," which is fully funded by the kingdom. Until now, the principal recipients have been Pakistan, Tunisia, Algeria, Syria and Lebanon.

Let us add the specific or regular granting of direct budgetary aid that is a means of influence on recipients like Egypt, Syria (especially after the Israeli-Arabic war of 1973) and Yemen. Obviously, the amount of these donations is a "state secret." Generally, Saudi Arabia uses its own financial instruments and its investments in international organizations to encourage "brother countries" and its own objectives.

Copied on the system of the United Nations, the other major "agencies" of the OCI are the Academy of Muslim Law and Isesco, the Islamic Organization for Education, Science and Culture, created in Islamabad in 1981 as a kind of Islamic UNESCO. Its sponsorship of the

Madrid conference is perfectly in line with its areas of concern, which relate to the protection of Muslims living in non-Muslim countries. In opposition to UNESCO, it formulates its interventions in terms of clashes and confrontations; in spite of its calls for a "dialogue of cultures and civilizations," its creators have very well grasped the geopolitical impact of cultural activity.

In order to create a shadow of the U.N.'s system of international organizations with Islamic equivalents, Saudi Arabia sponsored the drafting of "an Islamic Declaration of Human Rights," opposing the "Universal Declaration of Human Rights" of 1948. Although it was a founding member of the U.N. in 1945, Saudi Arabia did not ratify this declaration and has no intention of recognizing it. Examining the kingdom's tools of "Muslim diplomacy" in this way illustrates one of the major principles of the House of Saud. "The dynasty and the great families," explains a European military attaché, "share the conviction that the universality of Western culture is factitious and that to escape its influence it is necessary to promote a Muslim counter-culture that will redeem all of humanity."

The World Islamic League[3] is one of the principal tools by which they exploit Islam at the international level. Created in December 1962, as an outgrowth of the "Islamic summit" convened that year in Mecca by King Fayçal Bin Abdelaziz, its statutes provide that its General Secretary must be of Saudi nationality and have a diplomatic passport. In 1995, King Fahd himself nominated Abdullah Bin Saleh al-Obaïd. One of his predecessors became the vice-president of the Majlis al-Choura (the Consultative Assembly); the grand mufti of the kingdom, Abdulaziz Bin Baz, is president of its legal committee. Represented in 120 countries, it remains an essential foreign policy tool of the Saudis.

"The League, or the organizations that depend on it, has to its credit several spectacular constructions in Europe: the Islamic Center of Brussels and the mosques of Madrid, Rome, Kensington and Copenhagen," writes the journalist Antoine Sfeir, editor of *Books of the East*. "In France, the League does not directly intervene in financial arrangements. It is used as an intermediary for advising and directing possible investors. It thus lent a hand to the National Federation of Muslims of France (FNMF) when it needed it. It helps projects that are on the verge of bankruptcy: the mosque of Mantes-la-Jolie, launched with the joint generosity of Morocco and Libya, was finished thanks to that of the Saudis. Similarly, the mosque in Evry proved to be a financial black hole and cost the League nearly $5 million."[4]

A small part of the oil revenue is thus devoted to the construction of mosques and Islamic centers everywhere in the world: Ottawa, Quebec, Toronto, Brasilia, Lisbon, Gibraltar and Zanzibar. . . the mosque of the Islamic Center of Rome caused a great fuss because the plan for its minaret was higher than the dome of Saint-Peter (as well as the giant mosque of Bethlehem). Indonesia, Japan, South Korea, New Zealand, the Fiji Islands, Argentina, Mauritania and Djibouti have also benefited from Saudi generosity. Today, the kingdom finances 875 Islamic societies and centers in the world.

The Sauds' "Muslim diplomacy" is also expressed through the financing of charitable societies and other charitable institutions whose activities always fall somewhere between the religious, the political and the humanitarian. It would be tiresome as well as useless to enumerate an exhaustive list. Let us cite only the World Association of Muslim Youth, and the Organization of the International Islamic Relief Organization — IIRO, whose publications are particularly aggressive with respect to other religions, especially Christianity.

This last organization, which funds many "missionaries" abroad, uses them as the intermediary in maintaining relationships with most, if not all, of the known Islamist groups. A subsidiary organization of the World Islamic League, the IIRO was deeply involved in Bosnia, and President Izetbegovic regularly traveled to Riyadh to request financial aid from his co-religionists. The material and financial support available to these "missionaries" makes one wonder whether one of their roles, and perhaps their primary objective, is to acquire the favor or the neutrality of the impoverished countries toward which they are directed, toward the Iranian intrigues and competition from Shiite expansionism.

"In the same way, Saudi 'charity' with regard to 'minority or oppressed Muslim populations' in Palestine, Afghanistan, Somalia, in Bosnia at one time, in Chechnya and Kosovo today, is hard to see as being disinterested," explains an expert in Islamic finances. He adds: "Nevermind what all the official statements claim, it is not Islam but money that is at the heart of the Saudi system." In addition to the State apparatuses and the official foundations, these "diplomatic funds" require such fluidity and such silence in the face of any probing that it became necessary to create banking fronts as discreet as they are effective.

In 1981, in the backrooms during the Islamic summit in Taëf, Mohammed Bin Fayçal al-Saud, brother of Prince Turki's brother, brought together major investors from Saudi Arabia and the United Arab Emirates to create a private Islamic bank, Dar al-Mal al-Islami. DMI, the "Islamic financial house," shares a headquarters in the Bahamas with the bank of the Muslim Brothers. The Sudanese Islamist leader Hassan el-Tourabi took part in setting it up. One year later, King Fahd charged his brother-in-law, Sheik Saleh Kamel, with launching another private Islamic bank, Dallah al-Baraka ("the blessing").

Thus opened a new axis of Saudi financing for Islamism. Via these two banks the innumerable Islamic nongovernmental organizations, the Saudi agencies of influence for "Muslim diplomacy" would be funded.

Mouaouia Mokhtari, public relations director for DMI, suddenly gets very nervous when one broaches the question of the financing of Islamist movements. Algerian by origin, he hastens to point out that "DMI and its group arrived on the market well before the fundamentalist wave and they proclaim a moderate version of Islamic. Besides, the staff is hired without regard to religious belief," he concludes, while announcing that my visit with the general manager Ali Omar Abdi, a Somali and a great specialist in Islamic finance, has just been cancelled.

Dar al-Mal al-Islami (DMI) is an investment consortium made up of various economic and financial institutions like Faysal Finance, the Islamic Investment Company of the Gulf, etc. Based in Geneva, DMI has subsidiaries in ten countries (Bahrain, Pakistan, Turkey, Denmark, Guinea, Senegal, Niger and Luxembourg). The King Faysal Foundation of Riyadh figures among the principal shareholders. Created by the heirs to the late King of Arabia, this foundation is known for its many activities of religious proselytism, especially the financing of Koranic schools, Islamic arts centers and mosques. DMI is also one of the principal shareholders of Bank A.T. Limited, the Muslim Brothers of Egypt's bank,[5] which also plays a central place in financing many Islamist organizations.

The financial concept of DMI, in conformity with Islamic precepts, does not release profits on interest-bearing loans. The holding company chooses to invest in activities that produce profits by adding value. The investors who entrust their resources to DMI subscribe to shares (of an average par value of $100,000 dollars for the first, $20,000 for subsequent ones). Today, DMI manages $3.5 billion dollars, as opposed to $852 million when it began in 1982. The profits are distributed 80% to the shareholders and 20% to DMI, which in addition charges an overhead of 1/1000$^{th}$ of the sums entrusted to it.

Lastly, the subscribers commit, when they purchase their shares, to turn over the annual "zakat" — the religious tax — on their funds, according to the legal regulations of Islamic law. It is mainly this last provision that enables DMI to play a significant role in financing many Islamic activities in Europe and elsewhere. Its last activity report shows more than $2 million in "zakat." The same report gives no indication whatsoever of how this sum was used, nor could anyone at the bank tell us anything about it. According to experts, this religious tax is precisely what feeds the financing of Islamist groups, under cover of religious and humanitarian activities.

During the 1990's, DMI experienced major financial reverses due especially to ill-considered speculation in gold and currency trading; to the rising interest rates that ate up the profit margins on which it was founded; to the repatriation of liquidities by many Saudi subscribers after the Gulf War; and to the collapse of oil revenues. These difficulties led DMI to conduct a deep reorganization at the beginning of 1994 and to let go several dozen executives and employees. In addition, the bank undertook to diversify its recruitment of subscribers and decided, during its last general meeting, to recruit in the Maghreb (Morocco and Tunisia), in the Levant (Syria and Lebanon), and in non-Arab Muslim countries: Pakistan, Indonesia and Malaysia.

Officially concentrating on extending credit without charging interest, these Islamic banks started to get involved in securities trading in early 1997. Thus, Dallah al-Baraka launched al-Safwa International Equity Fund, an investment fund equipped with $2 billion. Anxious to display a partnership that would be recognized on this market, the Saudi bank appealed to Rolls & Ross Asset Management, an American investment firm specialized in the valuation of companies, for guidance. Dictated by the globalization of the financial circuits, as well as by the desire to "melt" into the traditional financial scene, this evolution came along some twenty years after the appearance of the first so-called Islamic banks.

On the strength of these various financial relationships, the Sauds' "Muslim diplomacy" now began to strike out into ventures that were not directly related to the kingdom. In July 1998, the Saudi Council for the Interpretation of Islamic Law formally and publicly condemned the possibility of the civil wedding, a plan that was at the time under discussion in Lebanon. This initiative was all the more surprising given that the question of the civil wedding absolutely does not come up in Saudi Arabia. Until this time, only institutions that were universally recognized in the Sunni world such as the al-Azhar University allowed themselves to make this kind of statement. Obviously, this step illustrates the increasingly clear desire of the Saudi authorities to affirm their influence in the Arab-Muslim world.

In this way the Sauds were pursuing a two-pronged objective, to promote both Muslim proselytism and the monarchy's propaganda. "They want to prove that the immense wealth of the country — a blessing from Allah which the royal family uses largely for its personal comfort — is also used for the glory of Islam," adds the diplomat who had warned to us against making blind clichés about Saudi society.

The Sauds' "Muslim diplomacy" cannot be reduced to their financial relationships; it ties in with political choices, which may be limited but are publicly acknowledged. In the aftermath of the first war of Afghanistan against the Soviets, this more traditional practice of international relations was illustrated significantly through Saudi Arabia's unconditional support for the Taleban, a regime that it was the only one to recognize (except for Pakistan and the United Arab Emirates).

This political positioning is explained as much by the sympathy the Saudis feel for these theology students, anticommunists promoting an "Islamically pure" plan, as by an alignment with the Pakistani attitude. Islamabad is the guarantor of a decisive religious and political alliance against Shiite Iran. Iran is the Sauds' biggest problem, and it affects the central core of their "Arab diplomacy": the great desire for hegemonic control of the Gulf. Enemy brothers (brothers as Muslims, enemies as Shiites, i.e. heretics), the Iranians remain the Sauds' most serious threat. And the royal house never forgets it: the Saudi Shiite minority experiences discrimination in this regard on a daily basis. This will no doubt continue to be the case as long as Tehran claims to play the role of a regional power in the Gulf.

The question is, admittedly, symbolic, but how well the climate of

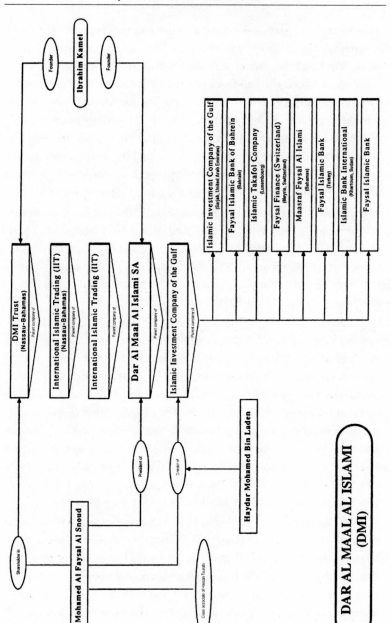

distrust that continues to reign between the two countries is revealed by the question of whether the Gulf should be described as "Persian" or "Arabian." Every time this question re-surfaces, it is treated as a major issue by the two parties. It embodies a distrust that is embedded in the geography, the history, the culture and, worse, the religion of both sides. The Saudis always qualify the Iranians as heretics, and the latter never speak about the Saudis but of the Wahhabis, a way of reducing these arrogant Princes to their minority religious practice. By comparison, the opposition to Iraq is more clear. Tied primarily to the personality of Saddam Hussein and to the economic situation produced by the Gulf War, the dispute is not irremediable and must be managed carefully so as to avoid breaking Iraq into two or three pieces, which would destroy it as the essential "buffer" with the Iranian enemy brother.

Except for its "Iranian obsession," Saudi diplomacy supports every Muslim cause on principle, as was the case in Bosnia, and then in Kosovo and Albania. President Sali Berisha established diplomatic relations with the kingdom in 1992, although there is practically no trade between the two countries. Like its Bosnian homologue, he undoubtedly hopes to benefit from Saudi subsidies.

For the moment, it does not seem that Saudi Arabia is officially very active in the new Muslim States that resulted from the collapse of the Soviet Union. Its charitable and humanitarian representatives are engaged there. And in counterpart, Uzbekistan, Kazakhstan and Azerbaïdjan have opened representations in Riyadh. An exchange of goodwill that nothing justifies objectively, if not Islam. There is an office for Asia and an office for Africa at the Saudi Ministry for Foreign Relations, but their activities are confidential, except for the countries with a strong Muslim minority like Senegal or the Philippines. Indeed, since they are not actually Islamic, these countries are regarded as "Islamizables," i.e. worthy of medium- and long-term interest.

While "Islamic matters" may be the foremost political office in the ministry's organizational chart, the Saud do not claim to impose their Wahhabi orthodoxy on all the Muslim world. They know very well that Wahhabism will remain a minority current of Sunnism on the dogmatic level and a marginal school of Hanbalism in the terms of the legal interpretation of the dogma. King Fahd, who no longer calls himself the "guardian of the holy places of Islam," prefers to make the more modest claim of being the "servant of the two holy mosques." The regime finances, as we have seen, an impressive number of Muslim institutions that are far from adopting Wahhabi rites.

"In fact, it is more a question of the Sauds justifying the exploitation of their immense wealth by financing the '*da'wa*', the 'propagation of Islam,'" explains another diplomat familiar with the palace, "and thus of making the enormous wealth of one Muslim country a little less scandalous (compared to the others that are stagnating in underdevelopment). The exact amount of the development aid financed by the kingdom is unknown. But it is certainly far lower than the believers would have the right to hope for, given a strict interpretation of the responsibility of mutual aid between good Muslims."

So the Sauds' "Muslim diplomacy" is not intended to bring about a fantastical unification of the Muslim world; rather, it has to do with establishing their legitimacy, which can rest neither on a democratic basis nor on an incarnation of Arab nationalism (which the dynasty deplores). Purely defensive, this policy aims at countering any possible meddling in terms of modernization, openness and respect for international law, particularly in the field of human rights.

"Three basic principles apparently guide their policy," continues our diplomat. "First, and above all, to keep a low profile. Second, that everything can be bought, for a price. And finally: Butt out." The Saud hold rigorously to their Wahhabi practice, which is the guarantor of dynastic continuity and of control of oil revenues and their investments throughout the world. "The opiate of the people," decried by Karl Marx, religion here functions more as a type of intercontinental bank secrecy preserving the privileges of a dynasty that is worried about tomorrow.

This Saudi attitude which, ultimately, amounts to buying good behavior and peace, has often led (and still leads them) to finance Islamist groups over which they do not exert any particular control, in the hope that these groups will not call into question the power of their dynasty. More traditional, their "Arab diplomacy" corresponds to the same imperative.

In terms of traditional foreign policy, Saudi Arabia's ambitions are shaped according to the impact they can have on the Peninsula and the Gulf region. They thus delimit a strictly finite arena centered on the geographical cradle of the dynasty. This area opens three angles whose amplitude increases as one moves away from the center from gravity.

*The first angle* is formed by the Peninsula, baptized the island of the Arabs, "Jazirat al-Arab." For most Saudis this constitutes the true center of the world, because it is the home of the Arab people chosen by God to disseminate the revelation of his benificence. "This 'insular' conscience should not be underestimated," explains a European diplomat stationed in Riyadh. "It adds to the meaningfulness of the vision according to which the Arabs (in particular) and the Muslims (in general) are surrounded by a hostile world against which they must defend themselves." The political, economic and cultural independence of the Arabic peninsula, backdrop of Islam's two holy places, is clearly the primary objective of the Saudis' "Arab diplomacy". And to demonstrate that he is still on his own territory, the King does not delegate to his powers to the Crown Prince when he visits a country on the Peninsula, whereas he usually does so whenever he travels abroad.

This "sovereignty by proximity" rests on making the small Emirates into satellites and dividing or isolating Yemen, which is too large and too populous to be neutralized in the same way. The "satellization" of the smallest neighbors, in particular Bahrain, Qatar and Kuwait, has not encountered any major difficulty up until now; but the same cannot be said for the United Arab Emirates (UAE) and Oman, which have the means to assert an economic and political autonomy. Since the discovery of the first oil reserves, the Saudis have sought to create more than a simple union of oil-producing nations, a sort of oil patriotism. "The expression 'Arab oil' has quite a precise meaning, both political and economic. It is the sense of jointly sharing a resource, and a wealth that gives the Arabs strength vis-à-vis the Western powers that dictated their law to them for centuries."[6]

This "oil patriotism" benefited from the Iran-Iraq war (1981) by being formalized, through the creation of the "Council of Cooperation of the Arab States of the Gulf" (CCG), from which Yemen is naturally excluded. Financed mainly by Saudi Arabia, the CCG (whose headquarters is in Riyadh), actually functions like a sound booth to record and broadcast the decisions of the House of Saud, which is thus ensured of maintaining its undivided supremacy over its "private preserve," whose only unknown factor resides at Sanaâ. "The good fortune of Arabia depends on the misfortune of Yemen, as light is dependent on the sun," the Princes heard this historical pronouncement from King Abdulaziz on his deathbed. It is true that since this last word, Riyadh has not spared any effort in seeking to divide Yemen into two mutually hostile States. Therefore the reunification of July 1994 is seen in Riyadh as a policy failure.

The Saud continue, in any case, to talk tough in Sanaâ, on the frontier dispute that opposes the two countries as well as on the million Yemeni immigrant workers expelled from Saudi Arabia during the Gulf War. Having taken sides with Saddam Hussein, Sanaâ lost a major source of foreign currency. Hostile on principle to international arbitration, Saudi Arabia wants to treat these questions as a "package," and in a strictly bilateral way. Thus it is ensured of being able to take advantage of the Yemenis' unfavorable financial situation while "buying," here again, security, allegiance and peace from neighbors who are proud, savage, and unpredictable, and who regularly hold — horror of horrors — legislative elections.

*The second angle* delineates the "Near Middle East." Here too, "Arab diplomacy" can be summarized as "buying and dividing, to rule." Pan-Arabism was never very much favored in Riyadh, which remains indifferent if not frankly hostile to the Arab League which it suspects of latent laicism. The Nasser version of Arab nationalism is seen as the devil incarnate by the kingdom, which was always hostile to the United Arab Republic (Egypt-Syria), playing a subtle balancing game between the two ba'as-ist enemy brothers, Iraq and Syria.

Today, the Sauds entertain good relations with Syria, which preserves a traditional reverse alliance against Israel, and against Iraq since 1990. If necessary, this could prove useful against the Hashemites of Jordan, historical enemies whom the Sauds dispossessed of Hedjaz and the holy places at the beginning of the century. Everything augurs well for future relations with Damascus, since one of the designated Crown Prince's wives — Hassa al-Chaalane — is Syrian and, what is more, sister of the wife of Rifaat el-Assad, the brother of the Syrian president, who is thus the brother-in-law of the next King of Arabia. These family and tribal relations can only consolidate a Riyadh-Damascus axis.

Relations with Egypt are currently characterized by non-aggression and by economic cooperation; more than a million Egyptian nationals work in the kingdom. Over time, this work could be threatened with "Saudization" in order to give jobs to the kingdom's youth: more than half the population of Saudi nationality, today, is under the age of 30. The kingdom would compensate for this loss by increasing its direct subsidies of the Egyptian budget. Indeed, several foreign ministries acknowledge that Cairo is already given substantial Saudi aid, although no numbers are given.

"In fact," a former French ambassador to Riyadh summarizes, "Saudi Arabia forms (with Egypt and Syria) a self-sufficient 'decision-making triangle' for everything that generally relates to shaping the Arab attitude with respect to the Palestinian question. It is an undeniable success of the Sauds' 'Arab diplomacy'." Indeed, it is traditionally admitted that no war against Israel is possible without Egypt, and no peace without Syria. In spite of its significant funding capacities, Saudi Arabia — a giant banker, but a dwarf soldier — is in no position to be a major actor in the Israeli-Palestinian process. But, in this "decision-making triangle" with Egypt and Syria, it is placed on an equal footing with two Arab partners that are strategically much greater than itself.

Lebanon is emblematic of the immense Saudi capacities of financing, and is a tactically key for Saudi sponsorship of Islamist movements. Having little strategic importance — even though it is on the front line vis-à-vis Israel — Lebanon indeed arouses Riyadh's interest completely out of proportion to its weight on the regional scene. All the great Saudi families are economically omnipresent in Beirut, and Riyadh regularly supports the exchange rate of the Lebanese currency. The principal pan-Arab newspapers, initially Lebanese, are controlled today by Saudi finance; the Lebanese former Prime Minister Rafic Hariri himself owes a good share of his personal fortune to the royal family, which conceded to him a quasi-monopoly over the construction and maintenance of innumerable Princely palaces, as well as major public works projects. Furthermore, he holds a Saudi passport, thus making an exception to the rule that formally precludes dual citizenship with Saudi Arabia.

Having become one of the principal financial outposts of the kingdom, Lebanon is located at the crossroads of the Sauds' Arab and Muslim diplomacies. In Lebanon, a Saudi "financial protectorate", all the underwriters and the beneficiaries of Saudi "generosity" meet. To counter the pro-Iranian Hezbollah engaged against Israel in southern Lebanon, but now represented in the Lebanese parliament, the Saudis employ the same "recipe" they apply everywhere: they use money. This is a perilous approach, because the benefit is not always proportional to the cost. Thus it sometimes happens that Islamist factions financed by the Saudis turn against their benefactors.

Here we are touching on a major difference between the Iranian school and the "Saudi" approach. Until the end of the war in Lebanon, Iran's approach guaranteed it complete control of the distribution channels, from the origin of the funds to the execution of the operations, even the material organization of influence and its political dividends. The Sauds too often consider, even today, that giving money is enough to control the whole process. In short, "checkbook diplomacy" à la Saud does not provide for after-sales service.

The last angle embraces the Western world. Most of the countries comprising this area remain little known, or unknown, to most Saudis (including members of the royal family) except as seen through the American prism. Saudi diplomacy does not follow any particular principle vis-à-vis the West; rather it displays a thorough sense of pragmatism in defending its interests, particularly through very large investments. Indeed, money from the State and from Saudi private individuals is heavily invested in various sectors of the developed economies.

It is not the least paradox that Wahhabi money thus participates in the prosperity of a Western world that is not only laic but is regarded as diabolical; the royal family and the Princes encourage the development of this "antimonde" that is decadent, even dangerous for the future of the Arab world and the religion of the prophet. "Islam does not have an evangelical contempt of wealth," write Simonne, Jean Lacouture and Gabriel Dardaud. "The prophet was an active and prosperous merchant. The Koran, which does not include any 'sermon on the mount" and which takes care not to praise the state of poverty, does not place any man above the honest tradesman."[7]

According to several financial experts, the amount of money the Sauds have  invested in the West is incomparably greater than the amount devoted to the propagation of Islam. More awkward for the Saudi dynasty, the monarchy's detractors use this "blasphemous" imbalance as a basis for their argument.

In fact, it is precisely to seek to exonerate themselves of this charge that Saudi Arabia continues to finance the most radical Islamist movements. The monarchy hopes thus to bring into better balance its commercial activities and its religious investments. The "profane part" of a system based on money, made up of unverifiable gifts and return gifts, the financing of Islamism ends up melding into a swirl of interconnected financial and commercial activities.

This system that the Saudis ended up generating was built for more than fifty years under the eaves of American protection. The United States has pursued this policy since it first began to exploit the Saudi oil concessions. Unconditional protectors of the House of Saud, they take care of any internal and external problems. While seeing the kingdom's stability as part of its "vital interests," the United States endeavors not to interfere in the monarchy's Arabic policy. The CIA is, however, omnipresent inside the kingdom, and in the external operations of the Saudi secret service.

In spring 1998, according to various reliable sources, the palace gave a $25 million check to Sheik Yassin, the chief of the Palestinian Hamas. Although they were perfectly well aware of what was happening, the U.S. agencies strangely did not do anything to prevent this payment being made, even though anything that strengthens the hand of Hamas weakens the Palestinian authority of Yasser Arafat. In spite of the U.S. State Department's appeals and efforts to reinforce the economic aid to the Palestinian Authority, the CIA continues to preserve, if not to promote, the interests of Hamas. In this sense, the U.S. agency plays the same role as its Israeli homologue, going along with an approach that was largely favored by Netanyahu's entourage which, in the long term, was counting on an intra-Palestinian war.

In this respect, the Israeli secret services also remained passive in the face of major weapons deliveries to the armed branch of Hamas during 1998. A military attaché stationed in Tel-Aviv explains that "Shin Beth (Israeli internal security and counter-espionage) is persuaded that the death of Arafat will inevitably start a Palestinian civil war that will blow the Palestinian Liberation Organization apart, as well as the political and military leadership of the Islamists."

You would scarcely be able to detect this convergence of views with the United States and Israel if you looked only at the official positions taken by the monarchy. And yet, pragmatism and respect for power, which are the two invariables of Saudi diplomacy, always lead the palace to tacitly maintain its alliance with Washington as the intangible guarantor of the kingdom's independence. "The only ambition of the Sauds is to remain master at home. To do that, no matter what happens, they need the United States," adds our military attaché, "while internal stability is, for the moment, maintained through a flawless ballet between the religious and police authorities." The alliance with the United States is as much in place now as it ever has been. Year by year, the alliance is renewed, with Washington guaranteeing Riyadh absolute immunity to any external threat, while Riyadh guarantees Washington a sure and tightly controlled source of energy for the Western world.

While nothing currently states that the alliance sealed on board the *Quincy* in 1945[8] soon may be called under question, its "sacred" status could suffer from the succession to throne, an as yet indeterminate process that conditions the future of the country and all of the Arabian peninsula. The designated crown Prince, more inclined toward pan-Arabism than King Fahd, is convinced that in the long run this alliance requires some modification as it is not in the kingdom's interest to prolong an exclusive tête-à-tête with the United States. However, this inclination toward emancipation is opposed on two counts. King Fahd, who has not gotten over his great fright during the Gulf War, remains infinitely grateful to the Americans for having taken care of him; he stayed in hiding throughout the entire conflict. Sultan, the second-in-line crown Prince, remains the United States' best ally within the royal family. His personal fortune has been accumulating for more than thirty years, starting from the commissions made on the innumerable deals signed with Washington, which has made him a particularly ardent defender of American interests in the area.

After the cerebral accident that befell King Fahd in 1994, Prince Abdallah took on a more active role in the administration of the kingdom. The approach remains pro-American overall, but since 1996 several spectacular shifts have been noted. While he nourishes a personal Bedouin resentment against Saddam Hussein, Prince Abdallah seeks to attenuate the harshness of the economic sanctions that affect primarily the Iraqi people, to whom he feels close. And every time a new crisis sets Baghdad against the United Nations, every time the United States tries to resort to force again (as it did at the end of 1997, and in February and November 1998), the Saudis show a weakness that reflects on all the Gulf States, including Kuwait.

The various American advances toward improving relations between the countries of the area with Israel have encountered a stone wall in Saudi Arabia. Like most Arab States, the kingdom spurned the economic conference of Doha (November 1997), but it was quick to attend the summit of the Islamic Conference of Tehran (December 9-12,

1997) where its absence would have surprised no one. Since the election of the new president, Mohammad Khatami, this renewing of relations with Iran — politically very incorrect, in Washington's eyes — is also put to the personal credit of the crown prince.

The Saudi authorities' refusal to cooperate seriously with the FBI in the context of the investigations concerning the anti-American attacks of Riyadh and Khobar (November 1995 and June 1996)[9] adds to the frustration of the Americans. The United States also wished to see the Sauds increase their support of the Hashemite kingdom of Jordan, which they see as being too dependent on Iraqi oil (which continues to supply Amman in spite of the embargo). There again, the Saudis claimed to be short of cash as a pretext for putting off the American request.

Lastly, Riyadh's purchase of a Chinese missile in order to circumvent the American refusal to sell it mid-range weapons — a threat to Israel —irritated Washington, which is regularly attacked by the Saudi press in any case. Indeed, not a day of summer 1998 went by without the Saudi gazettes taking a shot at the leniency Washington showed to Netanyahu, in particular vis-à-vis the withdrawal of colonists from the Jewish settlements, and making clearly anti-Semitic attacks against Mrs. Albright and Messrs. Cohen, Ross, Indyk and others, "the ten Jews who carry out American policy in the Middle East," as the headlines read in one Saudi daily.

If these various demonstrations of emancipation cannot all be directly ascribed to Prince Abdallah, they could not have been expressed without having received his blessing beforehand. Admittedly, the designated Crown Prince is not about to jeopardize the "Quincy pact," but he has clearly decided to interpret it with a little more distance. "Since American policy outside from the Arabian peninsula does not feel constrained by its engagements towards the kingdom," says the military attaché, "why should the kingdom feel obliged to adhere to this policy outside the aforementioned peninsula?" But, let us repeat, this change of tone (which recalls King Fayçal) does not prevent the Crown Prince from essentially reaffirming the pact sealed in 1945 with the United States, by which the U.S. remains the gendarme of the Gulf: absolute protection against any external threat, in exchange for oil at a moderate price.

For its part, the United States seems to have gotten used to the idea that one day Prince Abdallah may rule, even if it has not lost hope of shifting the balance of power within the kingdom in favor of "their man," Prince Sultan, by fostering the kingdom's internal oppositions and by betting on the Saudi Islamists (whose leader Osama bin Laden was an agent of the CIA). Another major American asset: the royal family is becoming more and more involved in speculation and deal-making, and continues to invest in American Treasury bills. In recent years, the murky way the great Saudi families combine business and politics has directly fed the progress of the Islamist movements. This has been a determining factor in the current mutation of several of these movements, as the Saudi ambiguity has allowed for many "Afghans" to be rehabilitated. The latter have by no means laid down their weapons and they pursue the "holy war" today by means of criminal businesses. They are found in the traditional sectors of economic crime — money-laundering for drug- and arms-dealers — as well as in new branches of organized crime, through the Islamist maffias and the ethnic-religious mercenary bands.

This recent evolution has not been achieved only through under-hand maneuvers, but has been given semi-official and benevolent support from the Saudi and American secret services, that are always inclined to make use of the Islamists and their never-ending wars — wars against international Communism, then today the new commercial wars in Latin America, Africa and Asia (particularly Central Asia, where the Taleban is a major player in the "new great game" in progress).

## Footnotes

1. "L'Islam confisqué: stratégies dynamiques pour un ordre statique," in *Moyen Orient: migrations, démocratisation, médiations*, Presses universitaires de France, 1994.

2. Jacques Benoist-Méchin, *Un printemps arabe*, Albin Michel, 1959.

3. See Chapter V: "The CIA's 'Afghans' and Their Networks."

4. Antoine Sfeir, *Les Réseaux d'Allah — Les Filières islamistes en France et en Europe*, Plon, 1997.

5. See Chapter VII: "The Muslim Brothers' Holy (and Financial) War."

6. Gabriel Dardaud, Simonne and Jean Lacouture, *Les Emirats mirages*, Le Seuil, 1975.

7. *Les Emirats mirages, op. cit.*

8. See Chapter II: "An American Friend at the Palace of Nations."

9. See Chapter X: "The Privatization of U.S. Foreign Policy."

## Chapter XIV
## The Taleban, Mercenaries of the American Oil Companies

> "By her very nature, woman is a weak being and vulnerable to temptation. If she is allowed to go out on her own, without the supervision of her father, her brother, her husband or her uncle, she will soon permit herself to be led into the ways of sin. . . . A woman who leaves her home to go to work inevitably comes into contact with men who are foreign to her. As the experience of the Western countries shows, this is the first step toward prostitution."
>
> Mullah Mohammad Omar.

"It is not we who created the Taleban," exclaims Mr. Riedel, special adviser to the U.S. president, in the aftermath of the anti-American attacks in Nairobi and Dar es Salaam (August 7, 1998). "And just because Pakistan supports them does not mean that we do," he added. In singular contrast to Washington's unyielding position on Iraq, the State Department's remarks are suffused with concern for not alienating the new Masters of Afghanistan, and they do nothing to contradict the action of the CIA and the big American oil companies. After having financed, armed and trained the anti-Soviet factions of Afghan resistance, the CIA pursued the same policy with the Taleban. In the name of Allah, these "religious students" set up a regime of terror. The grotesque regulations weigh particularly against women. This totalitarian regime that is conducting a second war in Afghanistan is also responsible for forming the "Pakistan-Taleban terrorist sanctuary," which destabilizes the entire area and attacks the Shiite minorities. Surrounded, Iran threatens to take military action, especially to help the Shiites of central Afghanistan. This area shelters vestiges of ancient Buddhist cultures that have been classified as part of the "patrimony of humanity" by UNESCO. The Taleban has sworn to destroy them: the mad king does not like Buddha. In fact, control of Aghanistan is the key to the roads that give access to the exceptional wealth of Central Asia. Across the Atlantic, this "new great game" is described as "America's principal interest." From the Mediterranean to the Far East, this strategic axis of the next millennium inspires great covetousness. Perhaps the "new silk road" will open the doors of China.

Islamabad, July 23, 1998. The Chargé d'Affaires for Southern Asia at the U.S. State Department, Mr. Inderfurth has no choice but to meet the local press following the conclusion of his two-hour interview with the General Secretary of the Pakistani Ministry for Foreign Affairs, on the situation in Afghanistan. "Is this really essential?" he asks the embassy advisor who accompanied him. It would be difficult to avoid — the correspondents from the international news agencies had been standing around for over an hour. They were waiting for a comment on the expulsion of nongovernmental organizations from Kabul issued two days earlier by the Taleban.

Very awkwardly, Mr. Inderfurth began his press conference with a long-winded speech on the American disposition to encourage the resumption of dialogue between the Afghan factions, and Washington's support for the Pakistani Prime Minister's initiatives to put an end to the conflict. The exercise had its limits. A stream of questions was hurled at him, regarding the humanitarian future of the Afghan capital, the fate of women and the series of prohibitions emitted by the religious leaders in Kabul. *"No comment!* I can only reiterate the hope on the part of the Americans and the Pakistanis that the recent decision of the Taleban concerning the NGO's will find a resolution soon," Mr. Inderfurth answered, before diving into his air-conditioned limousine to return to the embassy. These statements do not even register disapproval for the attitude of the Kabul government. The Pakistanis themselves were not even invited to use their influence to try to bring the Taleban around to an attitude more in conformity with the standards of international human rights and the basic principles of the United Nations charter.

The American government was, however, quite well-aware of the real nature of the regime founded by the Taleban in Afghanistan. Secure in his seasoned age of 32 years, his religious certainty and his recent military successes, their supreme chief, Mullah Mohammad Omar, serenely spouts his strange truths. In an interview published by the review *International Political*, he justified the shocking fate reserved for Afghan women, particularly the obligatory wearing of the "burqaa" (or chador), that super-veil that covers the entire body except for a mesh-covered opening at eye-level. "The *burqaa* keeps men from knowing how a woman looks, and even her age, for any woman with whom they do not have family ties," he explains; "Thus temptation disappears purely and simply. As for the women, they don't have to be concerned any more with their external appearance... since nobody will see them, so they can develop their spiritual resources, instead of enduring the sad fate of Western women who have been transformed into painted mannequins and sex objects." In addition, Mullah Omar's so-puritanical movement had no intention of giving up the considerable revenues that it derives from controlling the poppy cultivation intended for the foreign drug trade. "If non-Muslims want to buy drugs and poison themselves," he remarked, "it is not up to us to protect them." Was he so unconcerned with the fate of the world outside? Certainly not, but the opening of the Taleban's conscience to the world must proceed in an orderly and gradual manner. "We must purify our Muslim societies before we worry about the rest of the world, divert it from the path of Satan and make it look squarely at the truth," he concluded. "The most outstanding event of the current era is not the invention of the computer or other equally absurd machines, but the revival of Islam and its mission: to save the world from *Jahiliyah* (ignorance) and to civilize humanity that has returned to the savage state."[1]

Two weeks before Mr. Inderfurth's sparkling presentation, and in contrast to the previous years, the Afghan representative of the Taleban stationed in the Pakistani capital appeared among the American ambassador's guests of honor during a reception given on the occasion of the anniversary of the independence of the United States. This official reception, with a very restricted guest list (some two hundred people — very few of them Pakistani) added to the discomfort felt by several European diplomats and representatives of U.N. agencies. Indeed, during the evening, the American ambassador publicly thanked the Taleban representative for "his presence and the cooperation established between Kabul and Washington during the recent visit of a State Department delegation in April 1998."

This American diplomatic signal is quite intriguing, given that at that very moment the Taleban was reinforcing its prohibitions on women in their daily life and was stepping up the number of incidents to encourage the international organizations to leave Afghanistan. It was primarily with regard to women that relations between the "students" and the humanitarians ran aground. Many of the Taleban are orphans. Indeed, many of them were abandoned at the doors of the mosques by parents in distress. Raised and educated in the shadows of the ulemas in a closed universe, many of them reached adulthood without ever coming across a woman. This fact, on top of a highly sexist theological training, would explain the fear inspired in these virgin students by the simple sight of a woman and the delirious measures that they take to deal with their overwhelming emotion. In response to the positions taken by certain NGO's that denounced the prohibition on women regarding work, study, and even access to medical care, about thirty organizations that were active in Kabul received an order on June 29, 1998 to relocate to the ruins of the old polytechnic school, which had neither water nor electricity. On July 14, this order was transformed into an ultimatum and a threat, which obliged the humanitarians to leave. "We could not accept the retaliatory measure of parking us in a ghetto, an uninhabited neighborhood far away from the zones where the populations live with whom we work daily. This symbiosis of life with the people whom we help is one of the founding principles of our work," summarized a local leader of Doctors of the World (MDM). At its clinic, MDM collected upsetting testimonies that may lie at the origin of the confrontation.

S., 35 years old:

"Before, women had to obey the rules imposed by the family; now they have to obey the laws imposed by the government, too. Already, the earlier governments had wanted to impose Islamic rules, but since the arrival of the Taleban, it is worse! The *chador* is like a bag, you are almost blind in it. In the beginning, they said that with the *chador* we could go out in the street. We accepted. But now, we do not even have the right to go out unless we are accompanied by a family member. The only family I have is my husband. If he is not there, I cannot go to buy food for my children. My husband cannot always go with me. We accepted the *chador* for our children: 'OK, we'll wear the *chador*, but you open schools for our children." They closed the schools for girls. . . .

"In the villages, the women live like animals. They have no rights, they cannot take care of themselves. They do not have clothing, food, or medicine. They are forbidden to go out in order to take care of themselves. If they are sick and their husband is away, they stay in the house until they die. It is forbidden to go to see the doctor alone. And sometimes, even, the husband refuses to take his wife to the doctor. It is not worthwhile to look after her: if she survives, so much the better, if she dies, so what. Like animals.

"Of course, before the Taleban, it was already like that for some women. But there was the hope of changing things through education. Now, that is no longer possible. As women, we are losing ground. . . . I have a graduate degree. But now, my children are illiterate."


M., a doctor (a man), 40 years old:

"I think it was last Friday, I was on duty, and this woman arrived who had been turned away by the other hospitals. I did not have the right to admit her, because it is a political decision and because there are no more beds for women in this hospital. I said out loud, in general: "Here is a woman who is wounded, and I do not have the right to hospitalize her." I nevertheless made her some bandages and I advised the parents not to take her to another place, because I know that, over there, they would not find a female surgeon to look after the wounded woman, either. I recommended they transfer her to Peshawar. . . .

"I was waiting in front of the office for Professor X to arrive, when a Taleban accompanied by two men-at-arms made me follow him. . . . I tried to run away but the Taleban caught up with me, beat me and brought me to their barracks . . . . One tied my feet and a Taleban said to me: "Now I will show you what is men's rights and women's rights." First I was beaten with a Kalashnikov, then with an electric cord. There were ten or fifteen of them. Some beat me, others insulted me."[2]

The interdiction on treating women dates back to March 6, 1997, when the Afghan Health Minister, Mullah Abbas, signed a decree forbidding all the public hospitals in the capital to accept women except for emergencies judged as such by a religious authority. The female personnel who remained in the capital's hospitals found themselves constrained to follow an absolute prohibition on providing care. From that time on, the only place that was likely to accommodate women was the Central Polyclinic, a decayed, un-modernized hospital with a

45-bed capacity. That's on the small side for the entire female population of a city with more than a million inhabitants.

The European Union (EU), which devoted $200 million to Afghanistan in 1996 and 1997, responded at once by blocking its payments to Kabul, while maintaining the assistance intended for the other areas of the country. In reprisal, the Taleban immediately closed the EU representation despite its diplomatic status. This strong-arm approach came shortly after an agreement was reached between the Kabul regime and the U.N. agencies that implicitly ratified the sexually discriminatory measures imposed by the Taleban. UNICEF, the World Health Organization (WHO) and the World Food Program (WFP) continued to work in Kabul, and the Taleban would say, after the NGO's departed: "God and the United Nations will fill the vacuum."

"Divide and rule: the Taleban know the formula well. They are not such illiterates, unaware of international laws, as we are sometimes given to believe," comments Emma Bonino, European Commissioner for humanitarian action. "But it is true that there can be two possible attitudes to this sort of situation. One can accept the conditions of dictators who are uninterested in human rights and one can be an accessory, or even the tool of the powers that be. . . . Or one can refuse any complicity in the name of universal humanitarian principles, and walk away. But the population suffers then, and that too is intolerable."

"I will always remember these Afghan women," concludes Bonino. "Some of them came to see me in a hiding-place in Kabul to tell me: 'We know that you are doing everything possible within your principles, but do not leave. You are our only witnesses and our only hope.' They lifted their veils. They were very heavily made up. In response to my astonishment, they explained: 'It is our only way of expressing that we are people, not objects.' It was upsetting. And instructive. Humanitarian action must display its values today, but must also recognize its limits."[3]

From Somalia, Rwanda and former Yugoslavia, we know it only too well: humanitarian action does not replace the political and diplomatic intervention of States, the central and recurring question of all the intra-national, civil, ethnic and religious wars that have flourished since the end of the Cold War. By pushing this question even further on the scale of totalitarianism, the lunacy of the Taleban has come up with something new. How did this happen?

The term "Taleban" or *Talebs* literally means "student of religion." They come from the "medressehs," the Islamic schools of Hanafite interpretation,[4] which appeared in 1867 in Deoband, the seat of a famous faculty of Muslim theology, located near Delhi, India. In the 19th century, this movement extended to Baluchistan and the province of the North-West — two Pakistani areas bordering on Afghanistan. Like the populations of this region, the Taleban belong exclusively to the Pashtun ethnic group from which the cadres of the army and the Pakistani government also come.

Their appearance on the political-military scene as an armed movement did not happen overnight; it results from the sudden reversals at the end of the first Afghanistan war, in February 1989, with the evacuation of the Red Army. Although one would have expected a rapid victory by the resistance, instead we witnessed its collapse, which degenerated into a new civil war.

Once united against the Soviet enemy, the various Afghan factions — in which the Taleban took part separately — now burst apart in a power struggle. And so the "second Afghanistan war" started, with the usual amount of violence and plundering. Weakened by more than twenty years of combat, the civil population itself appealed to the students who had just returned to their studies and prayers. Many were the inhabitants of the southern valleys — pashtun as well — who thought that only the pious students could bring the chiefs of the factions back to reason. Legend has it that one of Taleban professors, Mullah Mohammad Omar, received a call from God, enjoining him to put an end to the fratricidal combat that was devastating Afghanistan.

Lastly, the Gulf War completed the consolidation of their position as arbitrators, since the principal factions of the former Afghan resistance chose to support Saddam Hussein against Saudi Arabia and Pakistan. Consequently, the special services of the Pakistani army (ISI) withdrew all their help to the old factions of Afghan resistance and gave it to the students, who were trained in armed militia. By mid-October 1994, they took over the town of Kandahar, which controls the south of the country, without any difficulty. The civil population welcomed them enthusiastically as liberators. The Pakistani support for the "theology students" mainly comes from the Interior Minister Nasrullah Babar, himself a Pashtun, and is implemented on the ground by the ISI. The Pakistani services did not have any trouble selling the idea to their Saudi backers and their American homologues at the CIA.

Indeed, the Taleban option seemed to have three things in its favor. In the immediate future, it ensured the Pakistanis the continuity of strategic depth vis-à-vis India. In addition, this Sunni movement guaranteed the Saudis an obstruction of any pro-Iranian Shiite projection. The theological-political proximity of the Taleban to Saudi Wahhabism is obvious, and the "schools" were in any event mainly financed through private Saudi channels. Lastly, it guaranteed the CIA and the armed militia of the big American oil companies direct access to the new States of Central Asia, rich in hydrocarbons and promising sizable markets for infrastructure projects and equipment sales.

In October 1994, the American Ambassador to Pakistan, John C. Monjo, made a tour of southern Afghanistan with the Pakistani Minister for the Interior, in the hands of the Taleban, and the U.S. State Department published a press release calling the victory of the "students" a "positive element likely to bring stability back to the area." As Olivier Roy (director of research at the CNRS and a specialist in Afghanistan and Central Asia) emphasizes, "In Afghanistan, the United States used the Aramco formula again from Saudi Arabia in the 1930's: Islamic fundamentalism + tribes + oil."[5]

Feeling strong, with its new godfathers and a fistful of financial and military options, the movement grew from 2,000 men (in autumn 1994) to nearly 25,000, at the beginning of 1995; it was equipped with heavy weapons, armored tanks and ten combat planes. The Taleban were thus ready to carry out, with drums beating, the second war of Afghanistan against the coalition of the old resistance factions, baptized by foreign offices "the Coalition of the North," in reference to the Tajik stronghold of the famous commander Masoud. In less than two months, the Taleban seized a dozen provinces, that is to say one third of the country. On February 14, 1995, they arrived at the gates of Kabul, after a lightning-fast advance. According to the files at one European intelligence agency, these military successes can be explained mainly by "strong military training, not only by the Pakistani services, but also by American military advisers working under humanitarian cover."

According to the Turkish weekly magazine *Aydinlik*, the CIA's involvement was confirmed by a confidential report given in July 1995 to the staff of Ankara by one of its military attachés in Kabul. The document analyzed the Taleban's military organization and specified in particular that "their principal base is in Quetta, the main city of the Baluchistan province of Pakistan. From there, they cover all of Afghanistan under the cover of humanitarian action. They have vehicles equipped with computers and special antennas enabling them to maintain permanent contact with their base by satellite connection."

"Their officers, well trained in the techniques of war," continues this report, "were recruited among former officers of the Afghan army (for wages of $1,000 per month) by the Quetta and Peshawar (Pakistan) offices of the Organization for Disarmament and Peace, an NGO that placed classified advertisements. Coordination was managed by the former president of the Pakistani Popular Democratic Party, who also worked for the U.N.." As for the Pakistani secret service, in close connection with the CIA, "they collaborate closely with the Taleban and organize their contacts with other countries, above all the United States and Saudi Arabia. What ties the latter two to the Afghan business is their desire to contain the Iranian presence in the area."[6]

September 5, 1995: The Taleban seize the town of Herat, which controls the north-west of Afghanistan. On June 11, 1996, for the first time, the movement sends a delegation abroad — to Germany and the United States — in order to explain its political-religious views. Lastly, on September 26, the Taleban captures Kabul and hangs the former communist president Najibullah and his brother, who had taken refuge in the United Nations offices. European military observers gave a report on the presence, within the ranks of the Taleban in Kabul, of "paramilitary groups, originally made up to feed the resistance to Kashmir (the Harakat ul-Ansar movement)." Lastly, in May 1997, a top-secret meeting took place in Riyadh between the Taleban military command and its Pakistani advisers, the Saudi intelligence services and a delegation of American top military advisers, according to an Arab diplomatic source. On this occasion, the Taleban is thought to have sworn it would conquer the entire territory before the end of the year.

All this helps one understand the difficulties faced by the United Nations, charged by the Security Council with engaging in talks between the Taleban and the Coalition of the North for a cease-fire. For several months, the U.N. emissary shuttled between Kabul and Mazar-i-Sharif, the Coalition of the North's fortified camp. The notion, put forth by Paris and Bonn, of a peace conference to be organized in Germany by the United Nations with the support of the two capitals "was diplomatically undermined by Pakistan and scorned by the United States," comments a European diplomat who is a specialist in this matter. The relations between the U.N. negotiators and the Pakistani representatives were execrable, and the Islamabad press regularly accused the U.N. of being "anti-Islamic."

It was not until the United States became directly involved that the diplomatic situation could be resolved. At the end of an eight-hour trip through Afghanistan, the American ambassador to the U.N., Bill Richardson, President Clinton's special advisor for coordination with the United Nations, extracted from the Taleban the principles that would be the basis of a truce and was able to set up a meeting with the Coalition of North, on April 27, 1998, in Islamabad. This was the first time that the Taleban and their opponents agreed to meet under U.N. auspices. This visit, the first by an American of ministerial rank since 1974, unquestionably marked the increasing control of Kabul by the United States, and made obvious their renewed interest in the area.

The American envoy extracted other concessions from the Taleban, who made a commitment to relax certain restrictions on women. "According to Mr. Richardson, the Taleban promised 'to tighten the screws' on Saudi billionaire Osama bin Laden and to prevent him from using Afghanistan as a base for terrorist activities," noted Françoise Chipaux in *Le Monde*, April 19-20, 1998. "This question gives the United States more and more concern, as it fears the consequences of Islamist activism on the stability of Pakistan, and this also explains the renewed American interest in Afghanistan."

These repeated warnings to the Taleban concerning the use of their territory by terrorist Islamist groups were transmitted on several occasions by the U.N. special representative, Algerian diplomat Lakhdar Brahimi. A confidential memo addressed to the Secretary General of the United Nations in April 1998 stated that the "reactivation of the centers of terrorism in Afghanistan, on the Pakistan border, is alarming. An increasing influx of people from the Maghreb and Egypt can be observed; they often carry Belgian passports, since the Pakistani have told the relevant countries they would no longer give visas to their nationals."

A few days before this memo was sent, the Uzbek Minister for

Foreign Affairs directly accused the Islamist organizations based in Pakistan of several murders of police officers made in his country in December 1997. According to him, more than 400 Uzbek, Kirghiz and Tajik men were trained in camps (either in Pakistan or in Afghanistan, in the areas controlled by the Taleban), before being infiltrated into Uzbekistan, via Tajikistan and the Kyrgyzstan. They were ideologically educated beforehand in Islamabad, in the medressehs governed by the Taleban. Every year, added the Uzbek leaders, an assembly of Islamist extremists is held in Peshawar; young people from many countries of the Arab-Muslim world receive weapons, clothing and money. This subversion apparently started in 1991, following a three months visit to the Pakistani capital by several Wahhabi theoreticians, including Amjed Ali, who was well-known in Saudi Arabia.

In Afghanistan, the terrorist training camps are under the supervision of the radical Islamist parties, under the international organization of the Muslim Brothers in connection with bin Laden. These camps offer training in bomb-making, car-bomb attacks, and other techniques of urban warfare; they operate with the approval of the Taleban leadership. In the area of Peshawar, the camp of Pabi (with approximately 200,000 people) is the command center in the organization of the secondary camps of Warsak, Saada and Miram Shah. There are two other important camps in Quetta, in the tribal border area near Afghanistan. This nebula is supported and financed by various pro-Saudi Wahhabi factions, various radical Sunni groups and the Taleban Supreme Council, which considers it a good breeding ground to stock its war against the opponents from the North.

Many other camps line the road connecting Kandahar to Khost, where one of the headquarters of Saudi Osama bin Laden is located; "Afghans" are quartered there, and Pakistanis, but also Kashmiris trained directly by the ISI (the intelligence services of the Pakistani army). "Markaz al-Daawa Wa al-Irshad," the official Islamist combat movement in Kashmir, whose armed branch is affiliated with the Pakistani Sunni sect "al-i-Hadith," has its headquarters just 20 miles north of Lahore. Similarly, the Harakat ul-Ansar movement, a radical Sunni organization made up mainly of Kashmiri and Pakistani mercenaries, veterans of the "holy war" of Afghanistan, has a network of both training camps and religious schools which are affiliated with Kashmir, Pakistan and Afghanistan. Egyptian and Algerian nationals also pass through these institutions.

Generally speaking, many Maghrebians, Egyptians and natives of the Republics of Central Asia take theological-political courses completely openly, either at the international Islamic university of Islamabad, or in the thousands of Koran schools run by the Pakistani and Taleban Islamist religious parties. The most famous is that of Jamiat-Ulema-Islami de Sami-ul-Haq with Akkora Khattaq, a Déobandie Hanafite revolutionary Islamist school from which most of the Taleban dignitaries graduated.

"The U.S. agencies are perfectly aware of this explosive situation," according to a military attaché European stationed in Islamabad. "If the Taleban reject all these international warnings," he continued, "we will have to wait and see whether the Pakistani government, after supporting the birth and the development of the Taleban for far too long, can still control everything that is taking place on its own territory. Certain Pakistani leaders go as far as to affirm that the Saudi monarchy is using Pakistan and Afghanistan in an actual war against Iran, using Pakistani and Afghan intermediaries." It is true that in spring 1998 there were frequent clashes between Sunnis and Shiites, causing several dozen deaths.

Time is on the Taleban's side and their expansion has shuffled the cards for everyone in the region. By autumn 1998, the Tehran press was expressing great concern over the threat represented by the recent Taleban military victories around the strategic city of Mazar-i-Sharif. This city represents an essential, vital point of support for Iran's logistic assistance to the factions that it supports within the Coalition of North. According to a military observer in the area, there is at least one military air link per week between the airport of Mashad, in northeastern Iran, and Mazar-i-Sharif. "If the Taleban take over this key city of northern Afghanistan it would be a serious reversal for Iran," say several Arab ambassadors stationed in Tehran. To summarize the situation they say, "Wahhabism would be virtually at their gates."

. The daily newspaper *Djomhuri Eslami* ran a headline, "Our National Security is in Danger." Breaking with the usual practices of the Iranian press, which generally have emphasized only the victories of the Coalition of North, the lead article stressed the importance of the advance of the Taleban militia and denounced Pakistan for its role. Certain officials of the Iranian Defense Ministry went as far as to assert that, the Taleban not having the logistic capacities to assemble such offensives, in fact it was beyond doubt that Pakistani troops were involved in the battles and in this way were securing control of entire zones of Afghan territory.

"The town of Mazar-i-Sharif, the last stronghold of the opposition in Afghanistan, has fallen to the Taleban," the Iranian press agency Irna announced on Saturday, August 8. "Large explosions were heard in Mazar-i-Sharif and the opposition leaders have fled the city," Irna wrote. "The population is fleeing the center; several districts are in flames," added the agency, giving an account of "limited resistance," in certain streets of the metropolis. The same day, a dispatch from the Agence France-Presse began: "Quoting a spokesman from the fundamentalist militia, the Afghan agency AIP (whose headquarters is in Pakistan) announced Saturday morning that the Taleban had penetrated Mazar-i-Sharif. 'At the present, there is major resistance in several districts,' the Taleban spokesman declared."

Finally, the Iranian radio and several newspapers reported that skirmishes had taken place at the border between Afghanistan and Iran, in the area of Herat. Taleban combatants were said to have fired on Iranian border guards who fired back. In Tehran, emotions were running high, dominated by concern over the fate of eleven Iranian diplomats who had been in town and by the bitter report of the failure the Tehran's policy.

The Foreign Ministry spokesman deplored the "massacre of innocent people," and the president of the Parliament called the Taleban attack on the Iranian consulate and the arrest of diplomats "regrettable;" he said that he considered it "a hostile act towards the Islamic Republic of Iran." The acceleration of the historical process sometimes produces an odd resonance; therefore it may be pertinent to mention also the comment made by Iran's ambassador to Uzbekistan, Mr. Mohsen Pakaeen, who deplored this "sign of aggression," specifying that "taking diplomats hostage goes against international laws and the diplomatic code of conduct." Everyone remembers, indeed, that one of the founding acts of the Islamic revolution of Iran in 1979 was the 400-day sequestration of 52 American diplomats.

Pakistan's ambassador in Tehran was, for his part, called to the Iranian Ministry of Foreign Affairs by Iran's Special Representative for

Afghan Affairs, Mr. Alaeddin Burudjerdi. Burudjerdi blamed the Pakistani government for the fate of the Iranian diplomats and also stated that "Iran has established contact with the Taleban directly and via the intermediary of Pakistan, in order to achieve the liberation of the diplomats." According to various foreign ministries, the Iranian Minister for Foreign Affairs, Kamal Kharrazi, asked in a letter addressed to the Secretary General of the United Nations "for an urgent intervention by the U.N." to liberate the diplomats, adding that he "regards Pakistan as responsible for the life of the members of the Iranian mission and the security of the diplomatic buildings in Mazar-i-Sharif."

Lastly, according to the Iranian press, "In response to recent events along the Iran-Afghanistan border, General Rahim Safavi, commander of the Pasdarans, set out on August 9 to inspect the defense situation in the frontier area." It affirmed that "Iran would never tolerate instability and insecurity along its borders and would resist any aggression." In mid-August, the main diplomatic representations of the region sent the same message to their respective capitals: 'We are on the brink of an Iranian intervention, which is likely to start a third war of Afghanistan.'

Obviously, this Iranian foreign policy setback had consequences on the internal confrontation between the "moderates," who support the new president Mohamed Khatami, and the conservatives, opposed to any accommodation with the Shiite regime. *Tehran Times,* for example, called for "more realistic and more aggressive policies" than the previous ones that had been revealed as leading to "a complete fiasco." Under the heading, "Passive Diplomacy," *Djomhouri Eslami,* hostile to the Khatami government, took on the Minister for Foreign Affairs in virulent terms, saying that he "could not find anything better to do than to leave the Pakistanis responsible for the safety of the diplomats and any Iranian nationals still in Mazar-i-Sharif." The newspaper also noted that Iranian diplomacy had allowed itself to be abused by Pakistan since the fall of Kabul; and concluded by calling "for a radical revision of the support we have hitherto granted to Pakistan, on the regional scale in the Kashmir incident, as well as the international scale," referring to the nuclear tests Islamabad had conducted in response to those of India in July 1998.

A setback for Iran, the fall of Mazar-i-Sharif also threatened what remained of Russian influence in this zone. Independently of its eco-

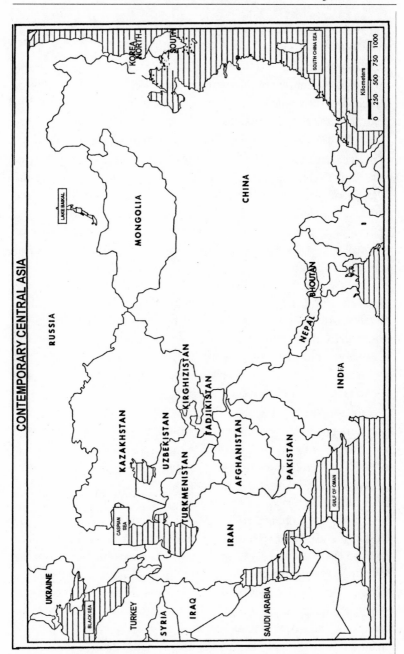

CONTEMPORARY CENTRAL ASIA

nomic interests in the area, and scalded by the war in Chechnya, Moscow indeed is very worried about the risk of Islamist contagion in the new States of Central Asia. In a status report to his ministry, the Russian ambassador to Pakistan reckoned that the Taleban would continue the war for two or three years and would strive to get rid of the Pakistanis by sparking a "holy war" in their own country. Become increasingly intransigent due to their military successes, and ideologically entrenched in their religious restrictions, they will end up with military control over nearly all the Afghan territory.

"The Taleban continue to enjoy a powerful and effective network of external assistance," declared the Russian ambassador; "The flow of men, arms, vehicles, petroleum and various equipment crossing the Pakistan-Afghan border, especially at Chaman (between Quetta and Kandahar), is continuous and completely free. Pakistani aid, be it governmental or private, remains substantial, even if it cannot quite be equated with a regular army supply process." The Russians also had very alarming information on the foreign assistance to the Taleban, in particular on the Islamist networks that are financed (if not under government control) by the Saudis, the United Arab Emirates, Kuwait and Qatar. Lastly, the memo states, the Taleban have considerable financial means derived from the drug traffic, which enables them to buy the necessary individual cooperation, in particular that of Osama bin Laden's "Afghans" who had previously been engaged as mercenaries in the wars in Yemen and Somalia.[7]

In the heart of the country, in the Hindu Kush mountains, the Taleban's bombs fell on Bamiyan, the capital of Hazaras. But this Shiite minority put up a savage resistance to the "students" who swore to extinguish the heretic redoubt. However, few invaders have dared to venture into these inhospitable mountains. Only Gengis Khan and his Mongolian riders succeeded in invading Hazarajat, in the 12th century. The current inhabitants are descended from these warriors and the Turkmen and Tajik tribes that still preserve their autonomy from the pashtun leaders of Kabul. Bamiyan was once an important stop on the Silk Road connecting the Roman Empire to Central Asia, India and China. Major pilgrimages of the faithful from all these remote regions would converge on the capital of Hazaras to adore two enormous seated Buddhas. Approximately 400 meters apart, they rise at the bend in a narrow gorge, in an abrupt sandstone wall. Carved from the very ribs of the mountain, under the vault of two immense artificial caves, one is 160 feet high, the other 100. Pocked with holes and bearing the patina of the centuries, their gaze was erased for a long time. The only ones of their kind, they were probably created between the First and the Third century after Jesus Christ. "After the Fifth century, the caves were enlarged and included a sanctuary, meeting halls, and one or more cells and rooms which opened out above the cliff. Some were given ceilings of false beams, cut in the rock and laid out in corbelling, a fashion that is also found in the basin of Tarim at Kazil, and at Kan-sou in T'ouen-houang. Other caves, larger yet, are painted with effigies of the Buddha and his assistants; blue is the dominant color. Long ribbons, very Sassanid in style, are enough in themselves to justify the use of the sometimes disputed term of Irano-Buddhic art."[8] Contrary to the traditional style common to all the Buddhas of the subcontinent, they are draped in ancient tunics, wedding the techniques of Greece and traditional India. Brought in the carriages of Alexander the Great's armies, who invaded Asia and Afghanistan from 334 to 327 BC, this "Gandhara" style flourished in the northwest of what is now Pakistan.

Several times, the Taleban tried to bombard them. By reproducing the human body and the face, these Buddhas diverge from the "students'" interpretation of the Shari'a; they strictly prohibit this kind of representation. But the sandstone statues especially remind them of the pre-Islamic past of Afghanistan, a past that they would like to wipe away entirely. UNESCO, which classified the site as part of humanity's cultural heritage, recently sent a delegation of experts to study what measures should be taken to protect the statues from missiles. The Hazaras who, at the moment, are storing weapons in the bottom of the Buddhas' niches, are persuaded that no possible negotiation will prevent their destruction if the Taleban manage to take military control of the site. Allah entrusted these Buddhas to them. They will defend them until the end, they say.

Challenged on the fate of these statues, the United States embassy in Islamabad was far more reassuring. "As always, and even on the most absurd questions, even the most humiliating for a global spirit, the United States semi-openly advises the international community to establish a dialogue with the Taleban," comments a European diplomat posted in the Pakistani capital. "The Americans maintain an ongoing dialogue with them, in any case, right in their headquarters in Kandahar, and give the impression that they really believe that some compromise, some improvement can result from this in the course of time."

Having been first in line to defend the NGO's engaged in Kabul, the European commissioner for humanitarian action Emma Bonino considered, just prior to the fall of Mazar-i-Sharif, that Afghanistan was not "prey to an internal war, but to a regional war for strategic position with respect to the energy resources of Central Asia." The United States obviously counts on the Taleban to give them the keys of this gem-studded cave of Ali Baba. Since the first war of Afghanistan, the CIA has maintained and preserved its contacts with the "Afghans" that it itself trained.

As so often happens, the CIA and the big oil companies banded together again and then presented the State Department with a *fait accompli*. Indeed, since the Taleban captured Kabul these companies, and particularly Unocal, have been directly implicated in buying off the local warlords. Since the end of the First World War, the oil companies have exerted a decisive influence on U.S. foreign policy (when they do not, in fact, make their own foreign policy).

"Few American industries sing the praises of free enterprise more than the oil industry. However, there are few that count as much on special privileges granted by the government. These privileges are defended in the name of national security," explains the journalist James Hepburn, recalling that since 1920 Standard Oil of New Jersey — symbol of the incipient American oil empire — had its own secret service "six times greater than that of General Electric. It had about thirty special agents, former CIA or FBI." These old ties between the American "agencies" and the oil companies were de-nationalized, and are beyond any political control from Congress.[10]

The CIA and Unocal's security forces have provided military weapons and instructors to several Taleban militia that are fighting, in fact, for Allah as much as for the Dollar god. This direct military involvement has been confirmed by several foreign ministries, by various intelligence agencies and oil industry experts; it is a partial explanation for America's diplomatic leniency with regard to the "students."

Having seriously underestimated the capacity of the Pakistan-Taleban terrorist sanctuary to do harm, as well as that of its principal underwriter, Saudi Osama bin Laden, and his Egyptian, Yemeni, Somali and Sudanese networks, the CIA got the United States ensnared in an Afghan trap; the August 7, 1998 bombings only marked the beginning. Since Irangate, the American agencies had revised their working meth-

272

ods by privatizing their "operational services," so as not to be trapped anymore by Congressional committees. Nevertheless, in Afghanistan under the Taleban, in full complicity with Pakistan and Saudi Arabia, the CIA objectively created the conditions for a "Bin-Ladengate" to come.

The two wars that have successively torn up Afghanistan remind us that it is a buffer state that, at the end of the last century, crystallized the confrontation between two empires at the height of their power: that of the tsars of all the Russias and that of Queen Victoria, who kept a jealous watch (from London) over her monopoly of the road to the Indies. At that time, the fate of the world was so much tied to Afghanistan that Arthur Conolly, an intelligence agent for Her British Majesty and an army captain in the Indies, said that the area had become the theater of the "great game," an expression made famous by Rudyard Kipling. The collapse of the Soviet Union left a vacuum in this fabulously area of fabulous wealth. Besides Russia, Turkey, Iran and the new regional republics, the United States, India and China now compete to impose their influence on this Central Asia, the field of maneuvers for the "new great game."

Implying a merciless fight for political influence, the primary goal of the "new great game" is to grab the local riches. "Central Asia has considerable resources, especially in the earth: oil, iron ore, zinc, copper, coal in Kazakhstan; gold, mercury, uranium, coal in Kyrgyzstan; natural gas, oil again, copper, gold, silver, zinc, coal in Uzbekistan; natural gas and oil in Tajikistan. Its oil reserves are thought to be equal to those of Arabia. Its agricultural output is significant but is overspecialized in cotton (Uzbekistan is the third-largest producer in the world). Industry has been developed, with metallurgical plants, heavy machines and machine tools, chemistry, agro-alimentary, and textile factories). It has sufficiently skilled labor and well-trained business managers."[11]

Most of the proven petroleum reserves are in deposits that border the Caspian Sea. Derricks already lined its shores in Baku at the time of the October Revolution, but the Bolsheviks preferred to exploit Siberia first, and to keep the Caspian deposits as a kind of reserve for the future. Although many sites have not yet been assayed, most experts agree that the reserves are considerable, even if "publishing such figures is always an extremely political act," as one expert emphasizes. According to proven estimates, the largest deposits — especially in Kazakhstan and Azerbaïdjan — vary between 6 and 10 billion tons; optimists even advance the figure of 25 billion tons. That represents approximately 18% of the world's reserves, evaluated at some 136 billion tons. By way of comparison, the Arab-Persian Gulf holds some 85 billion tons and the North Sea, 3 billion tons.

In addition to a battle of often whimsical statistics and estimates, the international status of the Caspian Sea remains a highly controversial question that has divided experts for seven years. Indeed, the distribution of resources depends on how this is interpreted. Two views are in conflict. If the Caspian is, indeed, a "sea" then its floor belongs to every resident, who can exploit it within the boundaries established by the international law of the sea. This option is preferred by Azerbaïdjan, Kazakhstan, and more recently Turkmenistan (which changes its view on a regular basis). On the other hand, to the west and the south, Moscow and Tehran want to see it defined as a "lake," which would mean shared exploitation, in the form of a condominium guaranteeing them a right of veto. Moscow's position is, however, weakened by the participation of Russian companies in the oil consortia of Azerbaïdjan and Kazakhstan. The United States supports the "sea" partisans, since the D'Amato-Kennedy law prohibits its tankers from collaborating with the Iranians.

The proven reserves of the Turkmenistan gas deposits vary between 12 and 21 billion cubic meters, representing approximately 10% of world reserves. Other important deposits are located in Uzbekistan, Azerbaïdjan and Kazakhstan. As far as mineral resources go, Kazakhstan is the premier world chromium producer. It holds ninth place for silver and tenth for lead. Uzbekistan is the eighth world producer of gold and Tajikistan has strategic raw materials such as tungsten.

For oil and gas, the crucial problem is not the delimitation and the exploitation of the deposits, but the choice of delivery routes toward the global markets. Preliminary solutions have been agreed, as for example the "contract of the century" relating to the "Early Oil" of Azerbaïdjan, which parallels the Russian (Baku-Novorossiisk) route with a route through the southern Caucasus, then the Turkish (Baku-Ceyhan) route. The number of alternatives keeps increasing and changing according to the perceived seismic dangers and the risks of Chechen and Kurdish flare-ups. The American companies have less and less faith in this approach, the final plan for which is constantly being delayed. This option will become irrelevant anyway, if the perennial sanctions are ever lifted from Iraq and Iran.

On the other hand, a serious plan for east-bound transport of the Caspian resources is confirmed. The American company Unocal's plan, via Afghanistan toward Pakistan, is more than a simple idea. In addition to the financial and military support that Unocal continuously provided to the Taleban militia, the company has already invested considerably in feasibility studies and in stock purchases of the Russian company Gazprom. A major question remains as to Pakistan's capacity to serve as a real terminus for this pipeline. Lastly, the political-military situation remains, particularly the evolution of the Pakistan-Taleban terrorist sanctuary, which can compromise Unocal's plans at any time.

On July 27, 1997, *The Washington Post* announced that the United States would not be opposed to the construction of a trans-Iranian gas pipeline that would transport natural gas from Turkmenistan to Turkey and Europe. According to U.S. government leaders, the plan does not technically violate their economic sanctions on Iran and Libya. This 2,000-mile gas pipeline, which will cost $1.6 billion, is the first major infrastructure plan since the fall of the Shah in 1979. The American leaders, still according to *The Post*, explained Washington's position by "the will to contribute to the emergence of capitalist economies in the former Soviet Republics of Central Asia."

A few months later, the Deputy Under-Secretary of State for Economic Affairs for energy, raw materials and sanctions, Mr. Ramsay, called on the ambassador from the Netherlands in Washington to have him dissuade Shell Company from getting too involved in this plan. Recalling that Shell's assets in the United States are among the largest in the group, Mr. Ramsay made his interlocutor understand clearly that the Netherlanders would have every interest "to play a special role in supporting American policy."

Officially, this policy is still organized around the need for surrounding and isolating Iran. Nevertheless, the latest shifts in American-Iranian relations might not be unrelated to the slow progress of the Turkish (Baku-Ceyhan) route. Several experts pointed out the central importance of Iran in any plan for the development of Central Asia resources. Burned by the American pressure in February 1998, Shell's staff does not hide its fear of paying the price for a sudden American political reversal with respect to Iran, in which case it would see its American competitors making a return in force to that country. Lastly, several experts feel that the only way to interpret the repeated deferral of the Turkish plan is by a planned termination of the American policy of economic sanctions and a renewal of American interests in Iran.

But the stakes are larger still on the strategic level. The United States considers that a rival to their unilateral global hegemony might emerge: in the long run, a Russian revival is always possible, and China is starting to wake up. "The principal interest of America is thus to make sure that no single power takes control of this geopolitical space and that the global community can enjoy unlimited economic and financial access," says the former security adviser to President Carter, Zbigniew Brzezinski (who is also a consultant for American oil companies). These last are now fundamental actors on the new strategic scene. In Central Asia, where the Cold War is not completely finished, the shifting relations in the area between the Caucasus and the Hindu Kush will have repercussions on the economic and political future of Russia and Turkey, on the regional and international position of Iran and, obviously, on the future of energy supplies for the West.

While the United States may have stepped up its use of the most radical local Islamist factions to push its pawns, the general framework is neither a confrontation of civilizations à la Huntington, nor a new Cold War in which the new republics would return to the Russian bosom. The model of relations that is developing tends rather to resemble the traditional diagram of the balance of power between the various States involved. All in all, this configuration outlines two axes of contradictory interests and movement: west-east, from Turkey toward Central Asia, passing through the southern Caucasus, and north-south, between Russia and Iran.

"Central Asia is the Balkans, with oil," explains a European diplomat who is a specialist in the region; "the question is whether the 'great game' will, as in the last century, lead to a draw, which is always liable to degenerate into a huge battlefield in the future, or whether it can be used to create a stabilizing balance of interests for the entire region. The fact that several players have already made very substantial investments lends hope to the second idea, which would encourage integration and economic cooperation."

Several factors stand in favor of stabilization. The most significant concerns the political evolution of the new States. The majority of them established their sovereignty more quickly than expected. Even if it was established at the expense of certain "universal values" of democracy, the establishment of authoritative presidencies for all these regimes has prevented, for the moment, their ethnic-religious fragmentation. While their GDP has fallen by approximately 50% since 1990, the forecasts for 1997 indicated economic growth ranging between 2 and 8% (except for Uzbekistan), and an average rate of inflation of 25% (except for Turkmenistan). In spite of these vicissitudes, added to those of President Yeltsin and the ruble's woes, the Russian government and economic decision-makers continue to conduct a pragmatic foreign policy, attentive to the economic evolutions, in particular with regard to the Caspian zone. With the exception of Tajikistan, the new States of Central Asia share a feeling of common ethnic identity going back to the old Turkmen era. "Our Turkestan home," the political leaders like to say.

Lastly, whereas the Commonwealth of Independent States (CIS) ruled by Moscow failed to unify these countries who were anxious to affirm their new national/State existence through emancipation from the old Russian overlordship, new approaches to regional cooperation seem to be emerging. Only partially, admittedly, but nevertheless with unquestionable pragmatism, these States have begun to cooperate together. Perhaps this is the context in which we should consider the happy news item echoed in *The Wall Street Journal* of July 20, 1998. "On Sunday, Aidar Akaïev, 23 years old, eldest son of the president of Kyrgyzstan, took as his wife Alïa Nazarbaïev, 18 years old, the younger daughter of the President of Kazakhstan." Officially, it is a love match. But in the backrooms, the families are pleased with this alliance which cannot but reinforce the two countries vis-à-vis Moscow. The reception was supposed to remain simple; but among the two hundred guests, it was noted that the presidents of two other States of Central Asia (Uzbekistan and Tajikistan) were in attendance.

This petit-four politicking however appears quite ridiculous compared to the existing and brooding conflicts. Contrary to that of Chechnya, which sometimes appears to have been stabilized, the conflicts in Abkhazia and Tajikistan still have not been resolved, in spite of several international mediations. "For too long, Russia kept these little regional wars down, so as to preserve its power of influence in the area," explains a diplomat stationed in Baku. The Nagorno-Karabakh war, which takes the Azerbaïdjani oil deposits hostage, can always degenerate and draw in the players ever more deeply.

The "second war of Afghanistan" and the Pakistan-Taleban terrorist sanctuary have not yet fully lived up to their potential. This is significant for it relates precisely to the strategic poker-game that is being played for control over the raw materials of the Caspian region. Will the support of Saudi Arabia, the United States, and Pakistan for the Taleban hold steady in the face of American feminist lobbies and, especially, the terrorist "blow-back" effects that started to show up after the Gulf War? In addition to plans made by the CIA, Unocal and Saudi political-religious organizations to construct a pipeline going from Turkmenistan to the Indian Ocean, by-passing the Taleban kingdom, this touches on the "principal interest of America," according to Brzezinski, who always regarded an alliance with Sunni Islamism as the most powerful lever for political influence in this region.

On the verge of open conflict, the Caspian remains very vulnerable to crises, especially given the lack of any political culture for the peaceful settlement of conflicts. The nations still in formation and the search for national identity going on in the post-Communist States still conceal many uncertainties. Parallel to this "fabrication" of new nations, to quote Olivier Roy, the entropic tendencies characteristic of ethnic-religious minorities are far from being suppressed. The ethnic antagonism that affects the whole area, setting the Turkish populations in conflict with the "Aryan" communities (Iranian, Armenian and Tajik) is superimposed on all the arms and drug trade, as well as on considerable migration of populations. A million people, for example, fled Azerbaïdjan, and Iran is now home to 2.5 million refugees driven out by the "second Afghanistan war." A water shortage has struck several republics that are frequently in conflict over upstream diversions and appropriations that remove water from the great rivers, Syr-Darya and Amu-Darya.

Lastly, Muslim extremism is one of the principal factors of destabilization, even if Islamist radicalization, harboring a plan to conquer the State (as in Tajikistan) gives way to cultural conservatism that tends rather to seek to reform the society. In the long run, the growth of Muslim extremism depends primarily on economic and social devel-

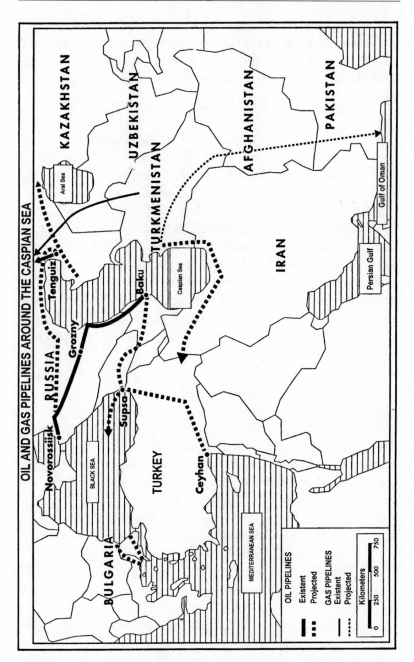

opment. "This evolution is reinforced by the part played by Saudi financing and the educational institutes or associations of preachers that come from abroad. . . . What is at stake is not only political, but cultural: attacks against weddings where drinking and music are allowed, the promotion of a strict practice of the Islamic rites without reference to national culture, criticism of Sufism and traditional religious practices. Wahhabism is substituted for Hanafite Sunnism, in the sectors of society that are suffering an identity crisis."[12]

What are the principal players up to? Russia continues to view the Caspian as its vital sphere of influence and wants to preserve a hegemonic position in the area. In the process of disintegration, the CIS is being replaced by a network of bilateral relationships, through which Moscow pursues its policy, "divide and conquer." Russia absolutely makes a point of preserving its position as principal country of transit for the wealth of Central Asia. The former Soviet empire still has considerable levers for accomplishing this end. Direct economic aid is putting certain republics increasingly into debt; they are dependent on Russian transit routes for oil and gas; and Russian troops are stationed in the southern States of the CIS. Thus Moscow has retained its determining role, but is losing ground as the United States consolidates its involvement.

Indeed, the United States has stepped up its presence, especially via the oil companies. Chevron invested $20 billion in Kazakhstan and controls 38% of the Azerbaidjan oil consortia. To reinforce this policy Washington has three principal goals: it gives unconditional support for the sovereignty of the post-Communist States; it pursues its own economic interests; and it seeks to diversify its energy sources. Washington is counting on Turkey, on the temporary isolation of Iran, and on the rise of radical Islamism. "Thus it is the Americans who have made inroads in Central Asia," concludes Olivier Roy, "primarily because of the oil and gas interests. Chevron and Unocal are political actors who talk as equals with the States (that is, with the presidents). The oil companies have come to play a greater and greater role in the area. When the Taleban took power in Afghanistan (1996), it was largely orchestrated by the Pakistani secret service and the oil company Unocal, with its Saudi ally Delta. And the Saudi dynasty-Aramco duo, from the 1930's, has not changed much, especially in Turkmenistan."

Like the United States, Turkey is betting on the assertion of independent States, converted to the market economy, emancipated from their Russian overlords and beyond the influence of Iran. Turkey's economic interests are also concentrated on the energy reserves and plan for a pipeline connecting Baku to the Turkish port of Ceyhan. It sees the emergence of the new States as an opportunity to forge major commercial and financial partnerships. Ankara has been systematically involving itself in Azerbaïdjan and turkophone Central Asia, at the risk of causing anti-hegemonic reactions in Uzbekistan and elsewhere. Relations with the republics of the southern Caucasus, including with Armenia, are more profitable and more subtle. Ankara is placing less emphasis on pan-Turkism and counting more on cultural and educational cooperation, in particular by giving scholarships.

Iran is Russia's most important ally in the "new great game." The two countries, who share the "lake" view in the battle over the legal status of the Caspian, regard each other as essential counterweights to the growing American presence in the region. Of course, Washington officially continues its policy of quarantine for Tehran, although lately Brzezinski and his petro friends have been recommending a thaw in relations (American pragmatism dictates that they should soon be restored). Indeed, America's policy of isolating Iran is less and less understandable to the republics that have concluded agreements on the construction of the gas pipeline between Turkey and Turkmenistan. Tehran has signed gas contracts with Turkmenistan and Kazakhstan, and is part of the Azerbaidjan oil consortia.

Iran, which is seeking by this means to strengthen its economic ties with the republics, finds it very beneficial to work toward stability in the region. That is what it is doing, with some success, by mediating in the Tajikistan civil war. While still committed to the propagation of Islam, Iran is not so much exporting its revolution as seeking to dam up Sunni radicalism. In the final analysis, geography always ends up being right; therefore Iran remains an important and central actor the region and it has to become regain its full share in the near future. Tehran's declared objectives include not only the exploitation and transport of Caspian energy reserves, but also the re-establishment of the old shopping streets of the great silk route that extends all the way to China.

If the silk route to Sin-Kiang manages to survive the wear of time, if the restoration of this ancestral axis of communication becomes a reality, China could indeed be holding the best cards in the "new great game." It would be in a good position to steal the pieces needed to meet its increasing energy needs as an emerging country. After decades of stagnation, under Deng Xiaoping in the 1980's China launched an ambitious program of economic reforms. This beginning of openness and economic success soon recorded record-breaking results, with a growth rate of 9 to 10% over ten years.

Following on the heels of 1988, a new boom drove the Chinese economy up by 13% in 1993 and investments, especially foreign, took off. Foreign investment reached an aggregate total of $44 billion. Thus, more than 60 million Chinese would have an annual income right now of $1,000 dollars, and the population, mostly urban, is tripling at the end of 2000. Obviously, fuel consumption constitutes the engine of this "great leap forward." Therefore, the problem of energy supply is a question of survival. According to *The China Business Review* of September-October 1996, China has increased its energy consumption by 5% every year since 1980. While its present needs are already more than 10% of the global energy demand, they could reach 20% by 2010.

Will the 21$^{st}$ century be the Chinese century? While it waits to find out, Beijing is working to develop various strategies founded mainly on diversifying its energy sources, increasing its imports and increasing exploration of its potential reserves. "In this sense, the Chinese strategy of establishing interests abroad, particularly in Central Asia, in order to guarantee a stable source of energy in the long run, could enter into competition with the energy interests of other powers, first and foremost the United States," underlines Valerie Niquet, Director of Research at IRIS.[13] This new inclination for buying interests abroad is manifest in Central Asia, especially in Kazakhstan where the Chinese company National Petroleum has invested more than $4 billion, thus gaining control of 60% of the capital of the country's second-largest oil company.

China shares 1000 miles of borders with the republics of Central Asia. And the bridgehead of the openness that is starting to take place there and in Iran is based on the oil reserves of the province of Sin-Kiang. According to the regional planning policy that currently prevails for all of China, the central government wants to spur local development in this area (which remains one of poorest in the country).

But this openness and the local development that it encourages should not, according to Beijing, be carried out in such a way as to hurt "productive China," that is, the great industrial basins in the east of the country. "There is a plan to construct a pipeline between Sin-Kiang and the great centers of the oil industry in the northeast, where 90% of the country's refining capacity and petrochemical industries are concentrated," adds Valerie Niquet. "However, the cost is estimated at more than $9 billion and it is far from being a sure thing. Today, oil is still transported from Sin-Kiang by tanker truck, then by one-way rail (not electrified) toward Lanzhou, then eastward." This route follows that of the caravans described in detail by Marco Polo, connecting remote China, Central Asia, the Middle East and the gates of Europe since the dawn of history.

The extreme west of China is one of the pivots of this eternal road. Its name, Sin-Kiang, means "new border," a reminder that the province has really been under the influence of Beijing only since 1950, after the brief rule of an ephemeral Turkic republic under Soviet protection. Mainly populated by Sunni Muslim Uighurs, Sin-Kiang's military apparatus has been reinforced considerably because Beijing fears that, with the independence of the republics of the former USSR, this turkophone population will be infected with a breakaway tendency. The Tajik conflict awoke a sense of Islamism and separatism among the Uighurs, who hate the Chinese. Two clandestine organizations (seven, according to other sources) are leading a fight for independence that has intensified since 1995. This activity is currently centered on the destruction of the infrastructure; it is a major headache for Beijing, which keeps a close eye on the activities and the relationships of Uighurs abroad.

"The 'Uighur diaspora' covers Kazakhstan (200,000), Kyrgyzstan (5,000), Uzbekistan, Turkmenistan, Turkey and finally Saudi Arabia," says Patrick Karam. "Three big Uighur organizations have their main office in Kazakhstan, with branches in Kyrgyzstan and Uzbekistan. . . . In December 1992, the Uighurs of Saudi Arabia financed the organization of a World Uighur Congress in Istanbul, and created the National Council of the Uighur People."[14]

The Taleban, oil and silk: this unique triumvirate comes together in Afghanistan, epicenter of the "new great game." Led by Pakistan, Saudi Arabia and the CIA, the Afghan shock wave is propagated all along the old, the new, and the future silk routes. Indeed, one can hardly doubt the rebirth of this great axis of communication connecting the Far East to the Far West. But one must take into account the persistence of Sunni Islamism, with its fundamentalist and terrorist factions. Its fragmentary effects, based on identity and territory, have not yet exhibited all their contradictions.

The inhabitants of Upper Egypt know something about that. On November 17, 1997, an Islamist commando massacred 58 tourists, three police officers and a guide in a temple at Luxor. This attack, conducted by students who came from that area, was financed by the "Afghans" of the Pakistan-Taleban sanctuary.

Footnotes

1.   *Politique Internationale*, No 74, winter 1996-97.

2.   These testimonies were captions on photographs in an exhibition entitled "Lifting the veil on Afghan women," by Médecins du Monde, on March 8, 1998, International Women's Day, during a campaign launched by the European Union.

3.   *Le Nouvel observateur*, July 5-30 August 1998.

4.   The Hanafite school is one of the four law schools of Sunni Islam. Founded in the 8th century in Iraq, it is a leader in Afghanistan and southern Asia, as well as among the Sunnis of Pakistan, of India and China.

5.   "With the Taleban, *Sharia* plus the gas pipeline," *Le Monde diplomatique*, November 1996.

6.   Cited by *Courier International*, No 311, October 23, 1996.

7.   See Chapter V: "The CIA's 'Afghans' and Their Networks."

8.   Jean-Paul Roux, *L'Asie Centrale — Histoire et Civilisations*, Fayard, 1997.

9.   James Hepburn, *Farewell America*, Frontiers Publishing Company, 1968.

10.  See Chapter VIII: "Is There a Pilot Onboard the American Aircraft?"

11.  Jean-Paul Roux, *L'Asie Centrale — Histoire et Civilisations, op. cit.*

12.  Olivier Roy, *La Nouvelle Asie centrale, ou la fabrication des nations*, Le Seuil, 1997.

13.  "La Question énergétique en Chine," *La Révue Internationale et stratégique*, No 29, spring 1998.

14.  Patrick Karam, *La Retour de l'Islam dans l'ex-empire Russe — Allah après Lénine*, Harmattan, 1996.

Chapter XV

BEHIND THE LUXOR MASSACRE, BIN LADEN'S "AFGHANS"

"In Egypt, political Islam was born at the end of
1920's, but it only recently began to draw inspiration
from a similar ideology born in the Indian sub-
continent. In this region so beset with contradictions, following a complex series of historical circumstances, an Islamist movement has appeared that
combines the inferiority and persecution complexes
characteristic of minorities, hatred of colonialism,
and a poor comprehension of Islam."

Muhammad Saïd Al-Ashmawy.

November 17, 1997: 62 people are massacred by an Islamist commando in a temple at Luxor, in Upper Egypt. The killers disguised
themselves as police officers in order to get to the site. The slaughter,
which went on for over an hour, revealed serious lacunae in the Egyptian security apparatus. "The Luxor incident" had begun . . . The investigation was going nowhere and the authorities were hiding key elements in the case. The organization that took credit for the attack was
close to the fraternity of the Muslim Brothers and the university-based
Islamic associations that Sadat had used to "break" the Egyptian Left.
Indeed, it was Anwar Al-Sadat, backed by the Americans, who opened
the Pandora's box of Egyptian Islamism. . . To avoid acknowledging its
own responsibilities in a war against the religious fanatics that had
been going on since the beginning of the 1990's, the ruling power re-
verted to the old theme of a "foreign plot" and accused London of having become the world capital of Islamist activism. Although its intention was only to divert attention from its own inadequacies, Cairo's
point was, however, well-made. Bin Laden's "Afghans" were behind the
Luxor slaughter. They planned the operation from London, under the
nose and in the face of the British secret service. A turning point in the
military strategy of the armed Islamist groups, the Luxor massacre set
off a chain of other mutations within the movement.

The sun has been flooding the Valley of the Queens for more than two hours. An almost cool air rises up from the Nile, and the morning light neatly carves the watershed, revealing the famous terraces of Deir el-Bahari where the temple of Hatshepsut is enshrined.

Hatshepsut, the only Pharaoh-Queen of the 18$^{th}$ dynasty. Dressed as a man and wearing a false beard, she took the throne from her own nephew Thutmose III, whom she had married. She had this monumental temple built to glorify her own power. Every year, some two million tourists pass through this holy of holies among the sites of Egyptian history; they come to admire the bas-reliefs that relate the story of her reign.

Six strange men, who are apparently neither casual strollers nor employees of the site, get out of a tourist agency bus. Dressed in worn black trench coats with zippers, they divide into two groups. The first four move toward the main access ramp to the temple. The other two remain stationed close to the retaining wall; they open their coats and pull out collapsible Kalashnikovs, and open fire on a police officer, then on a guard who collapses in turn . . .

The echo of the gunshots that rip through the valley reaches the first terrace, where a group of tourists is visiting the side chapel. After a few seconds of surprise and indecision, four people jump over a low wall to take cover, while the detonations come closer.

Under their trench coats, the attackers are all wearing the black uniform of the Egyptian police, with the front crossed by a white band marked in red letters: "Section of Death and Destruction." Having reached the foot of the ramp leading to the second terrace, the attackers train their machine-guns on the temple columns, behind which several tourists are cowering. Another group is overtaken as they try to run away. "They forced us down on our knees, then started to fire again," says a stupefied Rosemarie Dousse, who miraculously survived the massacre. She was interviewed by a press agency, and her testimony was read around the world. "A very large man fell on top of me and the lady behind me also covered me. I had nothing showing anymore but an arm and a leg that were sticking out. They shot me in the arm and the leg. Then, they started again. Anyone who was still alive, they gave a death-blow in the head . . . And they took away the very young girls who were lying among the dead, before disappearing. I do not know where they went afterwards, but we heard them crying. . . cries of pain. They were hurting them . . . Then I heard the lady behind me say, 'Don't move, they're coming back.' Then I hid under the big man; I soaked the scarf that I had on my head in blood and I wiped it all over me. I kept my head hidden, and I didn't move any more. But it was a long time before help came. Between an hour and an hour and a half. The terrorists kept coming back. . . Finally, somebody pulled me by the legs. I thought that it was the terrorists again, but it was the people who had come to help us. They took me away in an ambulance." On her hospital bed, this 66-year-old Swiss woman spoke mechanically, almost clinically, as if this story had just happened to someone else.

The massacre went on for nearly an hour. Passing by again and again in the rooms and on the terrace, the gunmen completed their work by knife. The sun had almost reached its zenith when one of the temple souvenir-shop owners dared to venture onto the esplanade. Discovering the extent of the carnage, he did not believe his eyes: 58 dismembered bodies, torn apart by bullets and the knife blows, or both . . . Contrary to several of the news reports, none the torture victims had had his throat cut, nor been mutilated, but the murderers obviously vented themselves on their poor hides. "They were very very young," adds Rosemarie Dousse, "they danced, raising their arms to the sky, and sang: Allah, Allah, Allah."

Obviously, the commandos did not prepare their retreat very carefully, for after having held up two taxis, they commandeered a tour bus that was circulating in the vacuum. The kidnappers ordered the driver to take them to the Valley of the Kings, about three miles from there, where hundreds of other tourists should be walking, but the driver drove around for more than half an hour, hoping to come across a police patrol. In vain . . .

Increasingly nervous, the killers finally understood that he was going in circles, and began to hit the driver. Believing his final hour had come, the unhappy man finally turned in the direction required. But, in the valley, news of the massacre had spread. The inhabitants had spontaneously armed themselves with sticks, stones and tools, and went on a hunt. They all more or less made their living off tourism, these guides, these shop-keepers, these craftsmen and taxi drivers; and they not only wished to defend their "livelihood" but to wash away the insult made to their legendary tradition of hospitality. They raised several barricades of rubble on the access roads to the temples, especially the exit from the village of Gurna that controls the crossroads of the Valley of the Kings.

A hail of stones met the bus when it approached this junction, obliging the vehicle to turn back in the direction of the Valley of the Queens: a dead end. The heroic driver knew it well and drove his bus right into the next barricade, before losing consciousness.

There followed an intense fusillade and a chase through the mountains, with several police officers guided by inhabitants of Gurna pursuing the hard-pressed commando. Reinforcements arrived and the pursuit became more systematic. Following the instructions of the villagers, who know every nook of the valley, the security forces flushed out the terrorists and drove them to seek refuge in a narrow cave. Several gunshots resounded inside the rock, and the Egyptian police rained fire through the entrance. After a lull of several minutes, during which a heavy silence descended upon the valley once again, the chief of the detachment (at the villagers' insistence) led his men through the cleft in the rock.

It was over! The six members of the commando were lying on the ground. Each one had a bullet in his head. The investigation would conclude that they took their own lives before the prosecutors could do it for them. The police officers had to prevent the villagers from dismembering and burning their bodies. It was approximately 1:00pm, on Monday November 17, 1997. The nightmare was over, but the affair of the "Luxor massacre" was just beginning. The Egyptian authorities have never published an official assessment of the Luxor slaughter. According to several European embassies, 10 Egyptians and 58 tourists were killed: 35 Swiss, 11 Japanese, 4 Germans, 6 British, and 2 Colombians.

The following day, Egypt's premier television news program played down the event during its main evening broadcast, devoting only a few minutes to it. Filtering the domestic news as usual, the station did not even mention the number of victims. No image was shown of the scene of the slaughter, only the visit by three ministers who went to the military hospital where the survivors were being treated. Then the program passed on to an interminable report on the travels of Beatrice, Queen of the Netherlands, who was visiting the new control tower of Cairo's airport with the Burkinabe president Blaise Compaoré, guided by their host, the head of the Egyptian State Hosni Mubarak.

The newspaper industry was more vindicatory, especially the newspaper of the liberal opposition *Al-Wafd*, whose lead article suggested that this was "the most serious terrorist attack ever made in Egypt." "Terrorism has entered a new stage. It is now obvious to the public that security at the most famous tourist sites in the world is seriously flawed."

Close to those in power but still wishing to express criticism, *Al-Gumhuriya* condemned "the massacre of the innocent." "All Egyptians are responsible," declared the editor Mahfouz Al-Ansari. "It is our society which has sheltered these criminals. We are collectively their guardians since they live, hide and kill, before returning to live in our midst." He took issue directly with the leading institution of Egyptian society, Al-Azhar, the prestigious and untouchable university and its various religious faculties, which he labeled "so many terrorist factories who stuff people's heads with Islamist teachings, a virtual brainwashing." Mahfouz Al-Ansari concluded by comparing his country's situation with the scene in Algeria, where the scholars of Al-Azhar have never clearly condemned the terrible massacres.

As for the economic daily *Al-Alam al-Yom*, it blamed the big American protector. "The assassins were used by the most hegemonic of the foreign powers: the one that wants to damage our economy in order to punish Egypt for its attitude towards the peace process, for the Doha Summit, and for its refusal to take part in a new operation against Iraq." Lastly, the very official *Al-Ahram* ran the headline: "Catastrophe on Western Bank of the Nile." This institution of Egyptian journalism demanded that an example be set by "sanctions against the enemies of Allah and all of humanity."

Shortly after the massacre, President Mubarak personally made headlines in the national press by going to the foot of the temple of Hatshepsut. His sunglasses could not hide the strain he was feeling. The soldiers and security officers around him were uncomfortable. Surrounded by several of his ministers, the president set foot on the access ramp to the first terrace, the very spot where the main scene of the drama had unfolded. "This tragedy could have happened anywhere," he declared, a little self-consciously, to the television cameras. "No country in the world can absolutely guarantee 100% security." Carefully avoiding the qualifiers "terrorist" and "Islamist," Mubarak solemnly condemned this act by "criminals who have nothing to do with real religion," while promising to take exceptional measures in order to reinforce the protection of the archeological sites.

Behind these conventional remarks, the presidential entourage was aware that was having trouble concealing one of his legendary rages. A career officer — a former air force intelligence chief — he immediately took the real measure of the disaster. Clearly, the local police force was behind it all. The Interior Minister, Hassan Al-Alfi, hopelessly struggled to come up with explanations. When the President ordered him to organize a meeting with the villagers who had assisted in neutralizing the commando, he already knew that his career would not survive their testimonies. The Interior Minister spluttered that at this hour the shops were closed and the guides were gone, but the President coldly reiterated his request and specified that he wanted to see them "immediately."

The shopkeepers and the temple guards told the President everything: the laxity of a security force headquartered miles away from the site; the lackadaisical attitude of the police; the way the terrorists had kept coming and going during a massacre that had gone on for over an hour. They poured out their rage, spilling out what had lain in their hearts for too long, and acknowledged to him that the police officers spent more time in racketeering than in doing their jobs. The officer in him rebelled. "This security plan was conceived and managed by irresponsible parties," he concluded. Within a few days, nearly every executive in the Interior Ministry (a score of senior officers) as well as the Hatshepsut security chief found themselves re-assigned to positions managing the challenges of traffic flow.

The Interior Minister himself was constrained to resign at once and was replaced by General Habib al-Adli, vice-minister of the Interior and chief of the State Security Services — the very one who, alerted by his colleagues as well as by some of his European counterparts for several weeks, had vainly tried to warn the presidency of the risks of new terrorist operations against tourist sites.

The Egyptian police knew that something more was involved, but the chief did not want to risk catching the presidential entourage off guard — they were so convinced that they had definitively eradicated "criminal violence." The Egyptian leadership, indeed, had just opposed a truce that, for the first time, had been proposed by five imprisoned leaders of the country's principal armed Islamists organizations. "We do not negotiate with terrorists," Minister Hassan Al-Alfi had essentially answered.

Was it to celebrate this "final victory" over terrorism that, October 12, 1997, the entire Egyptian government and a passel of foreign guests, businessmen, actresses in evening gowns and tuxedo'd diplomats had attended an exceptional evening of opera? That event, held on the same terrace of the temple of Hatshepsut, featured a performance of Verdi's *Aïda*, with police security that was also exceptional. For the comfort of the guests, tents and tarpaulins had been requisitioned and confiscated from their initial recipients, the villagers, who had received them from humanitarian organizations following a series of floods. "The local population was overcome with frustration and resentment against this scandalously sumptuous party that had been organized, partly, on its back," explained a British diplomat posted in Cairo. By killing on the same spot where this official ceremony had taken place just one month earlier, was the commando trying to prove how ridiculous was this showy demonstration of a hypothetical return to civil peace?

In five and a half years, these acts of violence killed 1,334 people, including 100 Westerners. Criminal violence, terrorist violence, Islamist violence? How can we characterize this war between the Egyptian government and religious activists that has persisted since the assassination of President Anwar Al-Sadat, October 6, 1981? In a flyer left on the steps of the temple of Hatshepsut, the killers claimed the attack in the name of "Gama'a islamiya," the Islamic associations that started to appear in Upper Egypt in the early 1970's. At that time, the term "Gama'a islamiya" indicated the Islamic associations that were proliferating in the Egyptian universities, with the blessing of President Sadat himself. Indeed, it is Anwar Al-Sadat, the key man of the Camp David accords, "the hero of the West," to whom we owe this irruption of religion into the political sphere. After rejecting the heritage of Nasser, Sadat was looking for new allies to dismantle "the Egyptian Left." Thus he called upon the Muslim Brothers and their networks that had been banned by Nasser. The bonds between Sadat and the Muslim brotherhood go way back. Before overthrowing King Farouk in 1952, the "free Officers" tried to ally themselves with the Brotherhood. They appointed Anwar Al-Sadat to approach the guide Hassan Al-Banna. The two men met regularly until 1942, without leading to any agreement. But Sadat never broke the contact completely.

By registering Islam in the 1971 Constitution as the State religion, Sadat thought he was pulling the rug out from under the Islamists. He broke with a certain consistent policy that had begun well before Nasser, when the monarchy, imbued with the heritage of the Enlightenment, had worked to dissociate religion and the State and to build a modern Egypt. One touches here on the very essence of Egyptian identity, and the nature of the Egyptian State, epicenter of the Arab world. Sadat thus opened the Pandora's box that would end up destroying him. In so doing, he also contributed to the destabilization of more or less every regime in the Middle East.

Encouraged by his new American and Saudi friends, Sadat simultaneously supported a profound Islamization of the society, in particular the education and health sectors, and the emergence of an Islamic economic sector with its own banks and investment firms. Following the same policy, President Hosni Mubarak goes even further, giving over whole facets of society to the Islamists, while nourishing the illusion that he can thus maintain undivided control of the apparatuses of State.

Visitors who have been going to Egypt over the last ten years have noted the rise of a patriotic-Islamic tone used by a population that is more and more pious, and that is confronted with the brutal effects of economic liberalization. Today, 13.7 million Egyptians live below the poverty line. The annual per capita income is still only $1,100, and 23% of the population lives on less than $240 per annum. Lastly, the unemployment rate exceeds 20%. The public education and health systems function very poorly. This context has largely contributed to the radicalization of President Sadat's "objective allies": the Gama'a islamiya, which are still expanding on the social plane, monopolized until now by the Muslim Brothers.

Since its founding in 1928 by a teacher from Upper Egypt, the Brotherhood has been the dominant political pillar of Islamism not only in Egypt, but in most of the Muslim countries where it has local branches.[1] Without being direct offshoots of the Muslim Brothers, Gama'a islamiya and other armed groups like "Jihad" (the holy war) — which specializes in anti-Copt attacks in the southern part of the country — use the same watchwords as the Brotherhood. Many chiefs, leaders of the military and religious training of these groups, were educated by the Brothers and still maintain direct ties with them.

The Jihad and Gama'a were divided over how to behave toward the American ally after the Soviet withdrawal from Afghanistan, and especially after the war of the Gulf. Gama'a stayed in touch with their case officers at the CIA, while the Jihad recommends the "holy war" against the Americans, too.

Taking advantage of the dismantling of the Jihad in the early 1990's, Gama'a temporarily became the main armed organization in the country by federating the combatants lost by other groups that were in the process of dissolution (Soldiers of God, Al-Takfir Wa'l Hijra and Shabab Muhammad). The Gama'a are mainly based in Upper Egypt, with bastions in Assiout, Miniah, Sohag and Qehna. They are organized in some twenty groups of five to six cells, strictly compartmentalized, of ten or twenty of people each, under the command of "an emir," a religious and military commander.

"The Gama'a's armed activity has grown since 1991 and today it is the major challenge facing the Egyptian government," notes Olivier Roy. "Contrary to the Islamist movements of the 1970's and 1980's, the Gama'a seem very decentralized, lacking any uncontested chief, and they recruit in a much more popular and less intellectual milieu than the other Islamist movements. The movement also has a powerful base in the city of Cairo because of rural exodus."[2]

Since 1992, the Gama'a had been stepping up their attacks against Copts and police officers, then they began to favor touristic targets, symbols of the Western way of life: hotels, cruise ships and travel agencies. The organization is theoretically directed from the United States by the former spiritual leader of the Jihad, Sheik Omar Abdel Rahman. Jailed for having been part of the assassination plot against Sadat, the Sheik had been pardoned by President Mubarak. Celebrated in Islamist milieux throughout the world, this blind preacher was sentenced to prison during the trial of the perpetrators of the World Trade Center bombing that killed six and wounded a thousand more on February 26, 1993.

Orphaned by their sheik spiritual guides, the Gama'a have also been abandoned by most of their regional military commanders, decimated after the violent crackdown that followed the waves of attacks in 1992 and 1993. Crippled, the young activists of Gama'a nevertheless continue their fatal activities through other organizations, such as the Young People of Paradise (Chabab Al-Janna), which appeared early in 1994.

The macabre team at work in Luxor could have come from one of these new cliques. Written by hand, the text claiming credit for Hatshepsut linked the operation to the start of a trial, the same day, in Cairo, where the Islamist leader Moustafa Hamza was the principal defendant in the attempted murder of President Mubarak on June 26, 1995 in Addis-Ababa.

Moustapha Hamza, one of the principal figures of the Gama'a ismaliya military organization, is a kind of living legend. . . the requisite hero-model of all young militants for the Islamist cause in Egypt. Better than a legend, Hamza is the prototype of the religious activist. An academic, a graduate in management and commercial studies, he served seven years in detention after the assassination of Sadat. When he got out of prison in 1988, he had only one dream: to get the assassins of "Pharao" in action again and cut down "the new impious one" who was governing Egypt. Twice, he has been condemned to death *in absentia* — for taking part in the attempted murder of the Minister for Information Safwat Al-Cherif in 1993, then for the attempt on President Mubarak in 1995.

A member of the Muslim Brothers, his father brought him up in accordance with the watchwords of the cult, looking forward to the time when an Islamic State would prevail in Egypt and in all the countries where the Brothers were established. But the Brotherhood's teaching and its long-term strategy no longer met the immediate need for action. Thus, young Hamza has engaged in armed combat since the age of sixteen. Upon the disappearance of the founder of the military wing of Gama'a — Talaat Yassin Haman — and that of his official spokesman, Talaat Fouad Qassem (who disappeared in Croatia in 1995[3]), he became the key man of the organization. In 1989, he left Egypt and moved to Peshawar, like many Islamists, and then to Afghanistan. It is there that the movement's "military planning group" was established.

The Egyptian president asked for a new report, complete and detailed, on this group during the first 48 hours of the new Minister for the Interior. Having done the intramural homework, it was now time to deal with the affair at the international level. Indeed, in the foreign press emotions were very heated, and comparisons with Algeria were rife — very bad for foreign investment, and of course for tourism, the chief export activity.

The President's right-hand man, Dr. Ossama Al-Baz, from the Camp David agreements, the most respected political adviser, suggested that an occasion should be found that would allow for "a presidential statement laying the responsibility for the massacre on the foreign countries that accept, finance and ultimately support terrorists." Several advisers of the president's public relations team worked night and day to come up with a plan to save what was to have been one of the best tourist seasons ever.

The President's cabinet chose the inauguration of the Nubian Museum in Aswan for the occasion, on Sunday, November 23. It would be the President's second public appearance, one week after the drama of Luxor; it was a symbolic inauguration to launch the opening of the economically vital tourist season. It came as no surprise that the presidential speech returned to the theme of a "foreign plot" to explain the drama. His criticisms targeted the neighboring Sudanese and their Islamic regime, as well as Iran under the mullahs (the usual whipping boy since the Islamic revolution of 1979). But this time, the president hit Great Britain the hardest, officially accusing it of "protecting" terrorists, financing them, and establishing connections with Afghanistan, Pakistan and Sudan. "Sudan is not as great a threat as in the past, for the criminals who give the orders and the money today are in Europe," Mubarak lashed out, adding, "On many occasions, we have challenged John Major and his administration. They always find excuses for preventing the extradition of these people who have committed crimes, in particular against the former Prime Minister Atef Sedqi. We have gotten nowhere. Thus, we solemnly ask once again that Tony Blair and his government hand these people over to us." The Head of the Egyptian State also addressed himself privately to the French Minister for Foreign Affairs Hubert Védrine, while he was passing through Cairo, November 26, and repeated these remarks to the editors of all the major Egyptian newspapers that accompanied him during his hurried visit to Saudi Arabia, December 3, 1997.

At the strong urging of the General Information Directorate (DRG), which is a direct subordinate of the President's chief of staff, the Egyptian press seized on the topic and created a stream of articles and special broadcasts talking about the financial circuits and linkages tying together "the criminals who want to weaken Egypt and the whole Arab world." The press campaign lasted several weeks. According to the magazine *Al-Mussawar*, "500 terrorist leaders live abroad." Mostly based in London, they are devoted primarily to propaganda and collection of funds, under cover of humanitarian activities, well-disguised by an Egyptian community of 50,000 in the British capital and its suburbs. The journal blamed six leaders, including Yasser Tawfiq Ali al-Sirri, who had lived in London since 1994 (after staying in Yemen from 1988 to 1993, and then in Sudan). This member of the Egyptian Islamic Jihad was in charge of the military wing of the organization Tala' i Al-Fatah ("guardians of the conquest"), associated since 1995 with a new movement dubbed the Organization of the Jihad. In London, he runs *The Islamic Observatory*, which officially condemned the Luxor attack while mentioning that it is "the logical result of the failure of Egyptian security policies and the product of the equation violence + counterviolence." *The Islamic Observatory* has ties with sister organizations in Saudi Arabia and in the United Arab Emirates. Along with Al-Sirri, the magazine named Ahmed Hussein Ajiza (his lieutenant within the military wing of the Jihad) and Adel Abdel Magid Abd al-Bari (who runs the "International Office for the Defense of the Egyptian People" and manages considerable funds raised by the businesses of Saudi billionaire Osama bin Laden. Within this maze, one stumbles across the trail of Hani Siba'i, spokesman of the Organization of the Jihad; of Mohammad Mokhtar Mustapha Goum'a, head of the "Islamic League of the Workers of the Book and Sunna"; and of Moustapha Kamil, who serves as liaison with the Algerian Islamists who have taken refuge in London and a writer for the periodical *Al-Ansar*, a quasi-official organ of the Algerian Islamic Groups (GIA).

According to the newspaper, the London sanctuary was in cahoots with Afghanistan and Pakistan, where ten military leaders are circulating, including the top emir of Gama'a islamiya, Rifai Ahmed Taha, as well as Mohamed Chawki Al-Islambouli, another known leader of Gama'a. According to the Egyptian intelligence service, the Afghan-Pakistani sanctuary also shelters Tharwat Salah Chata, 37 years old, the member of the Jihad who looks after relations with the "brain" of the organization: Ayman al-Zawahiri, the only true chief of the Jihad.

At the age of 47, al-Zawahiri deserves our very close attention for he embodies "the Afghan" *par excellence*. Respected for his intelligence and his skills at dissimulation, he holds Egyptian, French, Dutch and Swiss passports; for a long time he pretended to have taken refuge in Switzerland. Admittedly, he has reliable places to go on the territory of the Swiss Confederation, and he frequently passes through, but his last traces were seen in Bulgaria. A grandson of Mohammad Ibrahim Al-Zawahiri, he studied medicine in Cairo. Currently, Ayman al-Zawahiri is the personal doctor, the intimate friend and the right arm of Osama bin Laden. An Islamist activist since 1970, he was implicated in the assassination of Sadat, arrested and sentenced to three years of prison on October 25, 1981. Released in 1984, he traveled to Saudi Arabia, then to Pakistan and Afghanistan, where he took up with other Egyptians in the Arab volunteer units. It is there that he became acquainted with bin Laden, who has kept him at his side ever since. Following a falling out with the Sheik Omar Abdel Rahman, the Gama'a islamiya's guide, he reorganized the Jihad, which was being directed by Abou Zomor from his prison cell in Egypt. Ayman al-Zawahiri wrote several books including *Bitter Harvest*, where he denounces the economic strategy of the Muslim Brothers and preaches armed struggle. In the early 1990's, after the Gulf War, he developed the military wing of the Jihad, "guardians of the conquest."

Lieutenant to Zawahiri, who fled Egypt in 1991, Ahmed Ibrahim En Naggar is another top-ranking "Afghan." He was condemned to death *in absentia* in Cairo, in connection with the case known as "Khan Khalili." Also sentenced to death during what is known as the trial of "the veterans of Afghanistan" in 1992, Othman Khaled Es Saman is member of Gama'a, like Ahmed Moustapha Nawa and Othman Ali Ayoub, who were convicted in the same trial.

A collaborator and friend of the famous Moustapha Hamza, who was also in Afghanistan, Islam Al-Ghoumri stayed in Sudan and conducted many expeditions and "training courses" between Yemen and Somalia. Lastly, Hussein Chimit, an engineer by education, the Gama'a explosives expert, was also implicated in the murder attempt on President Mubarak in Addis-Ababa. After having vainly requested asylum in Austria, Adel Said Abdel Qoddous, another member of the military wing of the Jihad, returned to London six months before the Luxor attack. This character is a major part of the apparatus of the Egyptian

Islamists, for he maintains ties with the leaders of the groups in Upper Egypt and the chiefs abroad.

This list, which reprises that of the Osama bin Laden's chief collaborators, should include Ossama Rushdi Ali Khalifa: one of the best-known leaders of Gama'a, director of communications logistics. After staying in London, he settled in the Netherlands where he married the daughter of Abassi Madani, the historical chief of the Algerian Islamic Salvation Front (FIS). The Dutch authorities have refused him political asylum, a decision that he has appealed.

Well-known to the police, due to their stays in Egyptian jails, most of these activists had been released or pardoned at the beginning of Hosni Mubarak's presidency. Today, the Egyptian authorities have difficulty to explain why so many Islamists that belonged to criminal organizations could thus have been let go and, especially, why they were not at least put under police surveillance. Cairo turns on the foreign capitals and claims to have submitted requests for extradition against most of them. A spokesman for the British government answers that no request in due form ever arrived in London, and reckons that the Egyptian charges are more a matter of "media/diplomatic gesticulation intended to divert attention from the true causes of Islamist terrorism."

However, warnings from Egypt keep multiplying. Visiting Paris for the 50th anniversary ceremonies for UNESCO, on November 16, 1995, Hosni Mubarak gave a premonitory warning, declaring: "I do not understand the countries, like Great Britain, Germany and others, that grant political asylum to these criminals. One day, they will pay very dearly." Mubarak developed the same argument during the anti-terrorist summit at Sharm el-Sheik, in March 1996., and during the G7 meetings in Lyon, the same year, and then in Denver in 1997. The Egyptian warnings would be greeted with polite approval by the apparently unanimous international community.

On an official visit to Paris on May 18-20, 1998, Mubarak declared in *Paris-Match*: "You should be aware that, under the current conditions for international terrorism, the attack that took place at Luxor could happen anywhere in the world. And we already know who fomented it: the residues of the war between the Afghans and the USSR, the alleged *mujaheddin* that are financed by the CIA and the inexhaustible source of drug money." It is the first time that the leader so specifically pointed a finger at the American "big brother," who gives more than $2 billion in direct assistance to Egypt every year.

In spite of the repeated intimations of international complicity with the Egyptian Islamists, the responsibility for "the Luxor incident" has still not been clarified. Some observers think it was a completely impromptu operation and maybe the swan song of the armed Islamists: as if there is nothing but competition between the various chiefs in exile, who have no real power over day-to-day operations that are now abandoned to uncontrolled cliques. "The attack at Luxor was the spontaneous initiative of young activists from Upper Egypt, backed into a corner and driven by a desire for revenge after the recent death sentences," underlines an American diplomat in Cairo. "The extent of the slaughter does not prove anything," says Olivier Roy. "There is an enormous gap between the scope of the damage and the simplicity of logistical means. It is easy to find a group of tourists in a bus, then to massacre them." Clearly, the escape plan was not thought through and the execution of the Hatshepsut tourists did not require a particularly thorough military training. . . A significant observation, indicating that men who used to be trained at length in Sudan and Afghanistan are now being trained on the job, and are increasingly young. Outside commanders, then, would only have taken advantage of the political aspects of the operation, thus gaining the opportunity to return to the forefront of the domestic scene, in order to negotiate their return to Egypt or the liberation of their incarcerated comrades.

However, according to several European foreign ministries, the Luxor attack lends credibility to the idea that there is a terrorist mini-*Internationale*, where the assignments are distributed between the leaders in exile and the soldiers on the ground, with "cells" from Upper Egypt directing the practical aspects of organizing the operations. "The date of the attack appears to have been too carefully selected to be simply the work of actors with no real experience," explains a European military attaché posted in Cairo. But the most rational explanation is that an order came from abroad, namely, to strike a tourist target in a spectacular way. This last analysis comes from the American intelligence agencies. It was not until the two attacks against the U.S. embassies of Nairobi and Dar es Salaam that the CIA decided to communicate certain elements that are essential to the comprehension of the massacre. On August 24, 1998, the U.S. chargé d'affaires at the United Nations, Peter Burleigh, affirmed that Osama bin Laden's network is linked to a series of eighteen attacks, including the Luxor massacre. Without giving more details, he revealed this capital information at an *in camera* meeting of the Security Council, and emphasized bin Laden's Egyptian connections and the military instructions that his "Afghans" have been following since autumn 1997: to return a blow for a blow, every time Muslims are threatened . . . everywhere in the world.

Furthermore, several weeks before the Luxor massacre, the Gama'a had issued warnings following a series of death sentences that were pronounced on several of their militants. The attack would thus appear to be consistent with the tactics of a vendetta, favored by the Egyptian Islamists.

By lending credibility to the version of "lost soldiers from a residual terrorism," the Egyptian investigators themselves did not help further anyone's comprehension of the event. Indeed, the identity of five of the six perpetrators shows that armed Islamism is still very attractive to Egyptian youth. Four of them were, indeed, very young students, and rather bright: two in agronomy at the university of Assiout; one in medicine; the fourth was training as an engineer. All came from families that, locally, are not in the lowest stratum. And, according to sources close to the investigation, Gama'a islamiya had recruited them long ago; the Gama'a organizations are a long way from fading out, even if their forces are divided between four principal "branches":

1) The historical leaders (for the most part imprisoned in Egypt, except for the Sheik Omar Abdel Rahman, the spiritual guide of Gama'a, who is jailed in the United States); they have decided on an unconditional halt to violence after Luxor.

2) The leaders of the expatriate refugees in Europe (primarily in Great Britain, but also the Netherlands, Austria and Germany), who oscillate between suspension and resumption of the armed struggle.

3) The leaders of the refugees in Osama bin Laden's camps in Afghanistan (in particular the one who is known as the emir Mohamed Rifai Taha, as well as the military planner, Moustapha Hamza); they clearly choose to pursue "the Jihad" on Egyptian territory, and everyplace where brothers are in difficulty.

4) Finally, the home-grown militants, weakened considerably by the security operations that were launched after Luxor; they remain

unpredictable. According to the Egyptian intelligence services, there are not more than twenty leaders and a hundred combatants.

However, according to several knowledgeable sources, these figures do not correspond to reality. One European intelligence service estimates the number of the Egyptian activists at more than 1,000, and believes that their Sudanese weapons supply channels are functioning perfectly.

This state of affairs is interesting in more ways than one; does it herald the resumption of armed Islamism in Egypt? Will it serve as an example for militant groups in other locations? Clearly, one year after the slaughter of Luxor, Egyptian armed Islamism has preserved a very real and unpredictable capacity to cause harm. Under surveillance and even driven into retreat, the militants on the ground have little more than their weapons to prove that they still exist, whatever progress and successes of repression. "This will probably not manage to achieve a total eradication of armed violence," says Dia Rashwan, an expert from the Center of Strategic Studies of the newspaper *Al-Ahram*. The same research center confirms that the thousand combatants of Gama'a islamiya had merged with the military wing of the Egyptian Jihad a few months before the slaughter at Luxor. And the Egyptian authorities are not mistaken in blaming British laxity in regard to the Islamist networks, for the logistics of the slaughter had indeed been planned from London . . .

A big, clandestine meeting was held on October 10, 1997 at 94, Dewsbury Road in Wembley (London NW, 10) — in the house of Khaled Al-Fawwaz, spokesman of the ARC (Advice and Reformation Committee), the London antenna of Osama bin Laden. This is when Luxor was selected as a target. The Saudi billionaire had been working for months to reconcile the Egyptian enemy brothers who had been torn apart over internal questions of power and strategic choices since the end of the war of Afghanistan.

Principal backer of the two armed Islamist branches, Osama bin Laden was leveraging his financial assistance to encourage a military recasting of Gama'a islamiya and of the Jihad, under the sole control of the Jihad, whose more centralized military command answered directly to his right-hand man: Ayman al-Zawahiri.

Three sources confirm that this meeting was held: several members of the Saudi opposition in London, the Egyptian secret service and, last but not least, Scotland Yard (which received instructions of strict confidentiality on this case that was so likely to involve catastrophic political consequences for the United Kingdom). David Veness, head of the "Special Branch," the anti-terrorist section of the British police, could not believe his eyes when he read the report on this major reorganization of the Egyptian armed Islamist groups.

This information radically contradicted the official discourse in London on Islamist terrorism in recent years. Regularly accused of being the world capital of Muslim extremism, London very officially takes umbrage every time such a charge is levied, since it goes against the freedom of expression of the kingdom, and especially since it discredits the legendary infallibility of Scotland Yard.

In fact, the negligence of Her Majesty's secret service is stupefying. Everything took place just a stone's throw from the City. The Saudi billionaire's private jet was allowed to land without hindrance at Heathrow. He was welcomed there by Yasser Tawfiq Al-Sirri, one of the chiefs of the military wing of the Jihad and a direct collaborator of Ayman al-Zawahiri, residing in London. At the ARC, they met a third man, Adel Saïd Abdel Qoddous, who oversees communications with the advisory council (Choura) of the external Jihad. They had not met since April, but it was clear what had to be done. The members of Choura were in prison, the Gama'a islamiya groups were scattered and left to their own devices. It was imperative to gather the forces and to strike a great blow to cement a new alliance, to defy the Egyptian authorities and to support the second front of "the global holy war," in support of the Afghanistan brothers.

It is thus decided to place all the Gama'a and the Jihad combat units together under the sole command of the military wing of the Jihad — the Tala'i al-Fatah, "the guardians of the conquest." Communications and coordination would be handled via the satellite system of the Osama bin Laden networks. On October 13, 1997, three days after the London meeting, the new unified command did not rule out a large-scale operation to show "Pharaoh" that the "holy war" was still going on.

This communication was transmitted between Cairo and London and was intercepted by the British intelligence services. When we asked for confirmation, David Veness's assistant precipitately left her office and called us back from a telephone booth. Apparently thrown into a panic that such information could have filtered out, and without confirming anything officially, Miss Floira Maninring admitted never-theless that "the news of a communication giving notice of the prepara-tion of a spectacular action did lead to a telegram being immediately transmitted to the highest British authorities."

The speech given by the U.S. chargé d'affaires on August 24 to the U.N. Security Council was based on this telegram. And it was further confirmed by the American services: the weapons used by the Luxor commando came from Sudan and were conveyed to Upper Egypt by channels working directly for bin Laden's companies, based in the sub-urbs of Khartoum. With the slaughter of Luxor, we enter a new era for armed Islamism, better organized at the international level, and mainly financed by Saudi funds (which do not come from the fortune of Osama bin Laden alone).

In Egypt, superimposed on the strong "Saïd" (Upper Egypt) tradi-tion of family vendettas, the major causes of Islamist violence are in no way declining. Moreover, the emphasis on suppression through secu-rity measures brings entails a political crackdown. One of the first vic-tims is the press, which had guaranteed heretofore one of the last free-doms of the civil society. One thus seems to be moving toward a petri-fied society, increasingly dominated by a puritan viewpoint built on two axes — the fight against corruption and an increasing Islamization of the public space, with a form of Islamism that is buttressed by a se-ries of "Islamically correct" pillars.

This trend certainly does not encourage the disappearance of po-litical Islamism, but opens a new period characterized by changing methods, networks and financial channels. This shift already seems to have been integrated into the Egyptian authorities' current discourse. Indeed, according to several foreign ministries, Egyptian media cover-age of the British responsibilities goes well beyond resentment towards the old colonial power. Supporting the notion of a "foreign plot," so dear to President Mubarak, it suggests the complicity of other Euro-pean countries, and thus more global interference, and hints at a certain configuration of the "Western camp" in its Atlantic version. The slug-gishness, not to say the death, of the Middle East "peace process" is cer-tainly not unrelated to this evolution, in spite of the recent agreement at the Wye Plantation. Feeling that they are the main victim in a mar-ket of dupes, the Egyptian Raïs, who had bet heavily on the dividends expected from the "peace of the brave," is now trying to preserve a certain popularity by taking a pro-Palestinian standpoint vis-à-vis the State of Israel (which is used as scapegoat for the growing frustrations of the majority of the population). But for two years, the Oslo agreements have been in tatters and the amplified effect of their failure on Arab public opinion is opening the door wider and wider for Islamism.

After the 50th anniversary of the creation of the State of Israel, only an equitable re-equilibration of the Near Eastern crisis would be likely to hold back the populist expansion of the Islamist groups. To be credible and effective, such a re-equilibration must be directed surely and concretely toward the creation of a Palestinian State. Edward W. Saïd ([a Palestinian] professor of Comparative Literature at Columbia University) is right to say, "The only peace worthy of the name is an exchange of territories based on parity between the two parties. There can be no peace without a sincere effort from Israel and its powerful guardians to take a step in the direction of the people which they have injured, a step which must be accomplished in a spirit of humility and reconciliation, and not with fine words and inhuman behavior. . . . One cannot expect people who have neither a home, nor rights, nor hope, to behave like well-bred diplomats. . . . What we need now — and the United States can certainly do this — is to go back to the fundamental principle that there can be peace only if land is given back and if the goal is independence and a home for two peoples in Palestine."[4]

Beyond repairing a historical injustice, this change would not only stabilize the region, but it would deprive Islamist ideology of its central figure: that of a monolithic West, the unconditional ally of radical Zionism, synonymous with the negation of the rights of the Palestinians to self-rule.

A direct inheritance from the end of the East-West confrontation and an ascending phenomenon, Islamism today has a significant impact on the future of several Arab-Muslim countries that will soon be confronted with (or are now confronting) questionable successions (Saudi Arabia, Syria, Jordan, Algeria, Morocco, Libya, Afghanistan, Sudan). Beyond these "national" situations, Islamism is one of the major social and political components of one of the key strategic areas of the next millennium: Central Asia.

Lastly, by profoundly shifting the new political context in several emergent countries of Southeast Asia, Islamism is turning out to be one of the principal actors in the new "great game" that has been engaged in this area of the world since the end of the cold war.

From this point of view, Islamism is less likely to produce a "clash of civilizations," as the American political scientist Samuel Huntington predicts, than to consolidate the mafia channels of organized crime and the far-reaching networks of the businesses built under globalized capitalism.

Footnotes

1. See Chapter VII: "The Muslim Brothers' Holy (and Financial) War."
2. Olivier Roy, *Généalogie de l'Islamisme*, Hachette, 1995.
3. See Chapter V: "The CIA's 'Afghans' and Their Networks."
4. *Le Monde*, September 5, 1997.

## Chapter XVI
### ISLAMIST DEAL-MAKING AND ORGANIZED CRIME

> "Islam is in a sense, overall, a synthesis of the religious and military forms, but the military king could leave the religious forms intact, alongside his position. Islam subordinates them to the military, it has reduced the sacrifices, limiting religion to morals, alms, and the observation of the prayers."
>
> Georges Bataille

The Afghans were "invented" by the American intelligence services. Their successors enjoy more or less the same protection. By redeploying their international sanctuaries, the "new Afghans" are drawing up a new crime map. They now influence the political future of several countries in Southeast Asia, including Indonesia and Malaysia where Islam is very much on the ascendant. The "new Afghans" have a military and financial base in the southern Philippines. In the heart of the Indian Ocean, Madagascar has become a hub for their drug traffic. In the cauldron of southern Africa, the "new Afghans" played an active part in the gang wars and in the groups in Niger that feed the racketeering of the Algerian Armed Islamic Groups (GIA). Far from being confined to the Arab-Muslim world, these networks are also established in the "Islamic-Latino-American Triangle." Add to this non-exhaustive cartography the tax havens and the offshore business zones. The "Swiss friend" and other money-launderers play a crucial role. The entire lot of today's Islamist movement often goes through the three stages of the same evolution: armed groups transform themselves into mafioso networks, seeking to rehabilitate themselves, sooner or later, in the world of big business. The "holy war" can definitely be absorbed into global capitalism.

Here, at the start of the millennium, the specter of Islamism is still haunting the United States. The terrorist attacks that hit the United States since the beginning of the 1990's originated at the very heart of the economic, political and military logic promoted by the Americans. A certain continuity exists, from the first attacks that struck the American soldiers in Somalia, to the explosions of the Nairobi and Dar es Salaam embassies, plus the World Trade Center and the military bases in Saudi Arabia.

The Pentagon strategists never changed their approach since the end of the Second World War. By "inventing" the Afghans, the CIA was only responding to an emergency situation governed by the great confrontation with the USSR; but it opened the way to international chaos. As Alain Joxe emphasized, after the Gulf War, "While controlling the disorder has been essential in the long run for the alliance of America and the Old World, the disorder in the Mediterranean and throughout the Islamic world does not represent a failure of current American policy but precisely the required effect. The disorder, indeed, creates a self-managed line of fire between the North and the South, which can quite handily replace the iron curtain and allow the survival of NATO as an alliance of the North."[1]

This new international disorder started, in part, in Afghanistan. The post-Cold War world is rooted there and derives its principal characteristics from there. In the 1980's, in collusion with Saudi Arabia, the United States endeavored to turn Sunni Islamism against the USSR and Iran. It not only invented the "Afghans," but also systematically encouraged all the Islamist movements against the statist-national regimes of the Arab-Muslim world.

These organizations encourage an intransigent trend toward re-Islamization which is certainly anti-Shiite, but also anti-Western in the broad sense. "We are not dealing here with the tail of a movement whose days are over, but with a new dynamics: a Sunni communitarianism anxious to cleanse the *Oumma* of heretics and to establish a clear break with 'the Christians,'" explains Olivier Roy.[2] "The Islamist movements (and often the religious environments) have been 'Wahhabized' and for the worst. There is an insistence on the strict observance of Islamic precepts and on puritanism (the veil), attacks against the Sufi brotherhoods and everything that smacks of a Muslim or national culture. Neo-fundamentalism is combined with Islamist activism (which is very 'anti-imperialist' and recruits in the modern milieux) and Wahhabi scripturalism, to become the basis of a new 'war of cultures.'"

This evolution does not inevitably mean there will be more new Islamic States but it encourages the propagation of Islamist ideology, which becomes an inescapable component of the governments of Arab countries, and also of several countries in Central Asia and the Far East. By making social and humanitarian claims, the Islamist organizations put more pressure on the political powers and call for the gradual application of Islamic law. Even though the Islamic State is not always proclaimed as such, the Islamist social movement founds its existence on asserting a bond dogmatically established between religion and State affairs.

Even when it fails to infiltrate the political power by electoral or military means, as the Taleban try to do, Islamism generates confrontations that are likely to lead to an "Islamization" of the most restrictive social and economic processes (dressing, eating, sex, the legal system, banking).

This strategy — baptized "Islamization from below" by Gilles Kepel — explains the perceptible social shifts in Jordan and Egypt in particular, in the last ten years, and the evolution of Algerian society since the interruption of the December 1991 legislative elections. Salient features are the maintenance of a family code that discriminates against women and the law on Arabization. While there may not be "Islamism in power," this amounts to an "Islamism of the power" that strongly affects current political developments, especially in those States where the succession is in doubt. This includes more than thirteen countries in the Middle East. From Morocco to Syria, with Saudi Arabia, Jordan and Turkey, the Islamist trend is seeking to influence the procedures of succession and the political, economic and social shifts likely to accompany them.

The middle class on the whole supports this rise of the "Islamism of power." Without being directly involved in any decision-making, they try nevertheless to be associated with the process in every way possible, thus obeying a dominant practice of Sunni Islam. (It recommends staying close to the prince in order to inspire his choices and to correct his errors.)

There is no break between the armed struggles to put "Islamism in power" and the social expansion of the "Islamism of power." As

Georges Bataille says, "The holy war is always at the borders of Islam." "No real peace is possible between the Muslims and the infidels," adds Bataille. "That is a purely theoretical notion that cannot stand up to the facts, and a legal expedient, the *hila*, had to be concocted in order to avoid it while conforming to it. The doctrines allowed the Muslim princes to conclude truces with the infidels for up to ten years, in the event of insurmountable weakness of the Muslim State and in the latter's interest. They are free to break the truces as they like, as long as they make reparations for violating their oaths. How can we not see in these precepts a means of extension — of indefinite growth — that is perfect in its principle, its effects, and the duration of its effects?"[3] The analyses of the author of *La Part maudite* remain particularly apt, in that they show how Islamist ideology manages to generate economic strategies in support of its theological-political goals.

In the Hindu Kush, the CIA's "Afghans" make war. The Afghan shock wave awakens the dormant conflicts in Chechnya, in the Caucasus and in Central Asia. Having become a giant thanks to drug money, Afghanistan under the Taleban nurtures an Islamist coalition that has waged an armed war against the old Communist power of Tajikistan since May 1992. As one lever in the Islamist dispute, the Tajik minorities of Uzbekistan fuel the rebellion in the Ferghana valley. Encouraged by Pakistani and Saudi missionaries, several Islamist brotherhoods pursue goals similar to those of the Muslim Brothers: developing clandestine religious and economic groups organized in mafia-like networks. The Uzbek leaders continually struggle to contain this growth by prohibiting foreign preachers and by trying to control the Pakistani-Saudi financial flows. The same financial backers now support the Uighurs of Sin-Kiang, who are sawing down telephone poles and blowing up railroad lines. . .

In accordance with the rules of guerrilla warfare, the new 'Afghans' have adopted tactics that change according to the characteristics of the natural and human environments. At the fringes of open military conflicts, further toward the extreme East, they influence the political evolutions that are underway. Sometimes, these new 'Afghans' take control of the social and protest movements. In Indonesia, the largest Muslim country (by population — 88% of the 220 million inhabitants are Muslim), the Islamization of power is in full swing, and the old political castes have to take that into account. In Malaysia, this power passes through an extended financial network that relays Saudi financial clout to southern Asia, while in the Philippines, a sanctuary of bin Laden's "Afghans," Wahhabism represents an Islamism of countervailing power that seems more closely related to the traditional forms of guerrilla warfare.

**Indonesia.** Although the collective expression of the Muslims of Indonesia is less radical, it leads just as often, and on a regular basis, to outbursts of extreme violence. Owing to old social grudges, the Islamism of power shows up especially in the form of an ethnic confrontation with the Chinese.

All the area of Banyuwangi — the east most point of the island of Java — was so devastated it seemed a typhoon must have just passed through. At the beginning of 1998, and for several weeks, popular riots tore apart the Chinese stores. From small shops to major supermarkets, no sales outlet run by Chinese tradesmen was spared. On the façades of the few strangely untouched buildings, protective inscriptions were scrawled in white paint: *"Keluarga Muslim"* and *"Toko Muslim"* ("Muslim family" and "Muslim house"). The others were systematically ransacked because they belonged to the *"Cokim,"* a pejorative name for the Chinese.

This popular emotion was sparked by the budgetary adjustments demanded by the World Bank and the IMF. Since August 14, 1997, Indonesia was forced to allow its currency to fluctuate, following the example of other Southeast Asian countries that had been struck by a serious financial and monetary crisis. By autumn, it felt the effects of the "Asian crisis" even more, and became subject to an IMF restructuring plan to the tune of $40 billion. Brutally applied by President Suharto and without any collateral measures of social protection, this resulted in the fall of the rupee, which immediately caused a substantial rise in the prices of gas and rice. The country had not seen such troubles since the riots of 1965 when Sukarno was thrown out. But rather than directly attacking those in power or the rich Muslim owners of the fisheries and the canning factories, the inhabitants of the most impoverished districts attacked the Chinese tradesmen, the traditional scapegoats of Indonesian society.

Although it had been expressed through this openly racial impulse, it was not long before the political and social rancor was expressed directly against President Suharto and his family, who had kept the country on a short leash since the Communist pseudo-coup of 1965. Facing an aging military *nomenklatura*, the students were protesting, strikes were held in the industrial centers and revolts in the country-side began to be commonplace in the early 1990's. Besides being involved in an ongoing repression against the national liberation guerrillas of Timor and Irian Jaya, "The Indonesian army has come forward a half-dozen times since the autumn 1995 in Java, Sumatra and Sulawesi, killing several demonstrators."[4] As it did during the riots in Banyuwangi, the Islamic component invariably re-appears during these events without, however, leading to the formation of permanent armed groups.

If, today, the armed struggle is not underway, the Indonesian Islamist movement has nonetheless resorted to violence several times since the end of the Second World War. "In 1947, Hizb-Allah took the name of Dar ul-Islam — the House of Islam — and its militia that of Tentara Islam Indonesia (Islamic Army of Indonesia). This army of former resistance fighters waged a ferocious campaign against the nationalists and the former pro-Japanese collaborationists, in the north of Sumatra, in the southern part of Kalimantan, and Sulawesi, holding to its sanctuary in the west of Java (proclaimed Nagar Islam Indonesia, the Islamic State of Indonesia), until the beginning of the 1960's."[5] At the end of the 1970's, the Indonesian army arrested approximately a thousand people throughout the archipelago; they were suspected of being part of, or of helping, several Islamist armed organizations.

In October 1984 and July 1985, a wave of Islamist terrorism targeted the banks and shopping centers of the Chinese districts of Jakarta, as well as Christian churches and Buddhist monasteries in Java. "The most virulent springboard of the Islamic rebellion Indonesian is Aceh, Sumatra — and the capital, Aceh Bandar. A bastion of the faith at the westernmost tip of Sumatra, it was Islamized in the 13th century and is known throughout the archipelago as the Gate to Mecca, because of the religious enthusiasm that reigns within a population of some four million inhabitants. In 1982, Aceh Sumatra was the only area in Indonesia where an Islamic party obtained a majority."[6] Sporadically, a clandestine Islamic Jihad makes its appearance in Jakarta via the publication of press statements calling for a "holy war" and via threatening letters sent to various Western embassies.

In spite of these marginal manifestations, Indonesian Islamism was deeply marked by the Near Eastern influence in the 1980's, and especially since the early 1990's. At that time, Indonesia became the target of assiduous efforts of Saudi Arabia's "Muslim diplomacy." The monarchy and the great families extended many public and private gifts to the "largest Muslim country in the world," considered to be a priority because it was too lax according to the police of Wahhabi orthodoxy. The construction of mosques and Koran schools increased. Girls began to wear the veil more often, and the middle class, especially the bureaucrats, displayed an ostentatious puritanism. A previously unknown segregation between men and women became the rule at public events and on university campuses. The 1980's confirmed an increasing Islamization of education and legal practices.

The re-Islamization of political life was consolidated in 1990 with the creation of the Indonesian Association of Muslim Intellectuals (ICMI), whose recognition by Suharto contradicted the laic tradition of the Indonesian State. "An improbable mixture of moderate Islamism and radical Islamism, the ICMI is divided into two wings, but anti-Western and anti-Christian Islamist discourse has acquired a new legitimacy. A re-interpretation of Indonesian history has become common practice," says Andrée Feillard. "Furthermore, the broad themes of world Islamism have made their appearance among the intelligentsia: the conviction that there is a Western plot against Islam, the repression of Muslims in Europe and particularly in France (for the veil), the great cruelty of "the Christians" throughout history (Bosnia being only the latest proof, Nazism the perfect proof), the "well-deserved" deaths of the Frenchmen in Algeria (for the French support of the regime), etc.. It is hardly possible for the secular national press (judged to be "too Christian") to run any rebuttal to such comments without immediately being subjected to trial by the mob."

A series of anti-Suharto demonstrations erupted in May 1998, accompanied by the traditional plundering that comes with price hikes. From May 12th to 15th, fifteen people died in the violence in Jakarta. After some friendly pressure from the U.S. Secretary of State Madeleine Albright (inviting the patriarch "to make a historical gesture as a statesman"), Mohamed Suharto announced his resignation on May 21, live on television, and turned over his powers to the vice-president, Bacharuddin Yusuf Habibie. Spear-carrier for the protest movement and defeater of Suharto, the student movement was also strongly Islam-ized. The leader of the students, Amien Rais, is a professor at Trisakti University. At the age of 44, he gained their support by being one of the rare Indonesian personalities to publicly declare himself against President Suharto's re-election for a seventh five-year term, in March 1998. A political science graduate of the University of Chicago, Rais usually speaks English. He is head of the second largest Islamist organization in the country, Muhammadiyah, which claims to have 28 million members. Founded in 1912 and conceived on the model of the Muslim Brothers, this Sunni association pursues a social and religious goal. Members are encouraged to conduct their studies at the best Western universities, especially in America, "in order to become part of the world elite," explains one of its leaders. Managing his public image like an American, Rais spends his time visiting the various islands of the archipelago (13,000 of them), inaugurating Koran schools, Islamic hospitals and mosques. He begins all his talks with "Allah akbar" — Allah is great — and punctuates his speech with prayers that he invites the audience to repeat: "May Allah forgive us and save us from darkness and evil." His populist argumentation goes over all the better with the disinherited since he sprinkles it with racist remarks against Chinese tradesmen, the Christian and Buddhist minorities, and the Jews.

Abdurachman Wahid is the leader of the other Islamist association, Nahdlatul Ulama (rebirth of the ulemas), which boasts 30 million more moderate and primarily rural members. He regards Amien Rais as "dangerously mad, and his only ambition is to attain the presidency of Indonesia by whatever means necessary." In the course of the conversation, this wise old man points out one of the directing principles of his association: "to avoid mixing religion and politics. . . A dangerous confusion that can bring nothing good. It is reasonable that the government should govern and the religious leaders should deal with religion, without combining the two. Islam should not intervene in everything." He concludes by warning against the political use that Amien Rais has made of the Islamic religion.

By the way, Rais has just formed a new political party, the Party of the National Mandate, and everywhere in the archipelago groups are emerging that bear the colors of Islam. The new Habibie government is affected by this movement too, and has clearly engaged in an effort to synthesize the military basis of the old power, the Indonesian Association of Muslim Intellectuals (ICMI) and other vectors of this "Islamism of power" that is flowing through the society. This movement cuts across the whole political class, which aspires more and more to an "Islamization" from the top, to an "Islamic power," following the example of its Malayan neighbor.

**Malaysia.** In Malaysia, the Moslem religion serves as the State religion, and through its assistance to the educational and economic sectors the government openly discriminates against the other communities, especially the Chinese. Islamism is particularly radical in Malaysia since it is confronted with a population that is 50% non-Muslim.

The Islamism in power in Malaysia[8] has an especially strong effect on all the Muslim communities in the region because the country is enjoying exceptional economic success. Malaysia has recorded the highest growth rate in the world since 1990, and has often been cited by the IMF and the World Bank as the example for developing countries to follow. Giddy with these results that have made his country the most envied "little Asian dragon," Prime Minister Mahathir Mohamad let loose an attack on the Western countries during the traditional speech of Member States before the General Assembly of the U.N. in September 1995. Accusing the Security Council of not intervening in Bosnia because the victims are Muslim, the Malaysian Prime Minister castigated the U.N., saying its "image is in tatters and the moral authority has evaporated."

"Despite the first hopes for a world order that would be just, at the end of the Cold War, we note that the U.N. is still dancing to the gratifying music of the great powers, and completely ignoring the great principles and objectives proclaimed at its creation. We must conclude that the U.N. is still guided by the narrow national interests of the few," he declared, and then stunned the assembled delegates by launching into a long diatribe against the sexual freedom in the West that was sapping religious values. "Sexual freedom makes the concept of fidelity meaningless, and it renders marriage anachronistic," concluded Mahathir Mohamad. This radical criticism of the West brought him inexhaustible electoral goodwill, and helped to bring him closer to the new strongman of Indonesia, Bacharuddin Yusuf Habibie, who was also known to give way to religious fervor. Over time, the two Malaysian and Indonesian presidents would seek to formulate a Malayan-Muslim bloc that would be both anti-Western and anti-Chinese.

The Malaysian Prime Minister, known for using extreme language, achieved new heights during the monetary crisis. He ascribed the 35% devaluation of the ringgit (the national currency) to a "Jewish plot." Speaking before a crowd of partisans, in the vicinity of Trengganu, on the eastern coast of the peninsula where the local political leaders were agitating for a strict application of the Shari'a, Mahathir Mohamad declared: "We are Muslim and the Jews don't like to see the Muslims making progress... the Jews stole everything from the Palestinians but, since they cannot do the same thing in Malaysia, they are trying to depreciate the ringgit."[9] The idea of a Jewish-Western plot, so favored by the Malaysian Islamists, was also pleasing to the Saudi financiers who were omnipresent in the Prime Minister's entourage.

Indeed, the majority of the big Saudi banks had invested heavily in Malaysia. The real estate boom of the 1990's was also fruitful ground for the application of Koran financial principles. After having experienced some political and doctrinal reverses in several countries of the Middle East, Egypt in particular, the main tools of Islamic finance found Malaysia to be an extremely favorable outlet. Furthermore, the most prominent experts of Islamic financial law are based in Kuala Lumpur, which now set the tempo for new Islamically correct products and techniques. In a parallel development, secondary products to this financial sector blessed by the Mahathir government were flourishing, specifically educational, religious and charitable associations.

The "zakat" (the religious tax) was invested in a multitude of Islamist foundations and associations, reproducing the organizational nebula of "Saudi diplomacy" in Southeast Asia.[10] As well, many Near Eastern armed groups, and "Afghan" and "new Afghan" networks, organizations linked to the Muslim Brothers of Egypt and the European Islamist institutions, derived a considerable part of their incomes from the Malaysian eldorado. The Malaysian and Indonesian sultanates trained and financed the Muslim guerrillas of the southern Philippines.[11]

**The Philippines.** Following a violent suppression of a mutiny by a (mostly Muslim) army corps, the indignant population first began to call for the creation of an independent State encompassing the islands of Sulu, Palawan and part of Mindanao. In 1969, young academics from the MNLO founded the MNLF, the Moro National Liberation Front, which entered into conflict with President Marcos's tight control over law and order. The confrontations sharpened and spread throughout

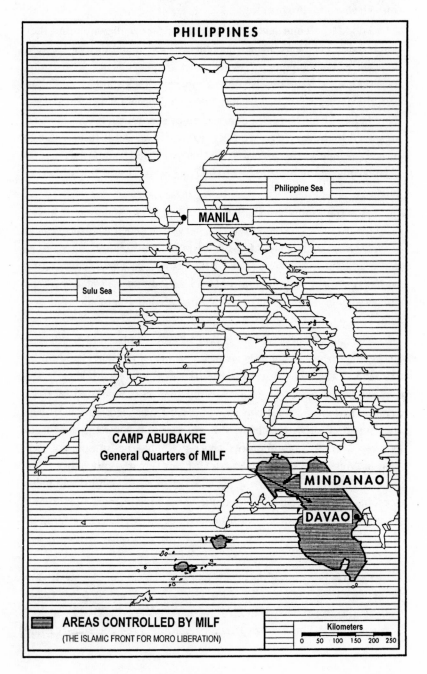

PHILIPPINES

Philippine Sea

● MANILA

Sulu Sea

CAMP ABUBAKRE
General Quarters of MILF

MINDANAO

DAVAO ●

AREAS CONTROLLED BY MILF
(THE ISLAMIC FRONT FOR MORO LIBERATION)

Kilometers
0   50   100   150   200   250

the region in 1974-75. Colonel Kadhafi, the principal backer of the MNLF, together with the Manila authorities, organized the signing of a cease-fire agreement that recognized the administrative autonomy of thirteen southern provinces.

The MNLF considered the agreement to be ambiguous, and they boycotted it. The agreement was quickly broken and hostilities went on until the beginning of the 1980's, when the movement fell apart due to scissions and a progressive abandonment by Libya and Malaysia. In 1978 the MILF (the Moro Islamic Liberation Front) was formed. Far more radical than the MNLF, influenced by the Iranian revolution, and organized by leaders who were located in Cairo, the MILF resolutely turned the fight in the direction of a "holy war" and sought the creation of an Islamic State. It claimed 120,000 partisans, of which 10,000 were active.

"A certain number of officers were trained in Malaysia, Pakistan or Afghanistan. Its headquarters, the heavily defended Abubakre camp, are located at Mindanao, at the borders of the provinces of Maguin-danao and Lanao del Nor. The MILF has no major problems getting weapons. Apparently it even obtained anti-aircraft missiles (perhaps Stingers, from Afghanistan). It also has a good communication system."[12]

The fall of Marcos and the eclipse of Libya, replaced by Saudi Arabia, opened new possibilities for negotiations. Talks were held under the aegis of the Organization of the Islamic Conference (OCI). In the context of the policy of national reconciliation inaugurated by Cory Aquino, in January 1987, the Jeddah accord was signed between the Filipino government and the MNLF, granting autonomy to the Muslim provinces. A referendum ratified this autonomy: the Autonomous Region of Muslim Mindanao, the ARMM, was created officially in November 1990; but the guerrilla attacks began again. Shortly after his accession to power, the Filipino President Fidel Ramos re-started a peace process with the military command of the MNLF. Sponsored by the OCI and Indonesia, a new agreement was signed in November 1993 in Jakarta.

Other series of negotiations took place, also in Jakarta, starting in September 1994. These talks led to the signing of a new peace treaty between President Ramos and Nur Misuari, chief of the MNLF, on September 2, 1996. But an increasing atomization of the guerrillas, certain

of whose components specialized in drug traffic, gun deals and kidnapping for ransom, quickly cast doubt on how representative the MNLF
might be. In addition, the Moro Islamic Liberation Front (MILF) did
not recognize this peace, since it was not a participant. In June 1997,
the MILF rebels captured 43 employees of the Philippine National Oil
Company, who had been drilling in the zone of Cotabato, on the island
of Mindanao. The army launched a great offensive throughout the region on June 16. A spokesman for the Muslim separatist movement
then announced that the MILF peace talks that had been planned for
the end of June in Cotabato were postponed indefinitely,

A situation of generalized civil war again set ablaze the Muslim
provinces of the southern Philippines, especially since a third radical
Islamist component had emerged. This one preached an eternal "holy
war" until the advent of an authentically Islamic State. "The Abu Sayyaf group developed on the island of Basilan. . . . Its extreme standpoint
and the violence of its methods quickly made up for its lack of repre-
sentativeness. The chief of the group, Abubakar Abdurazak Janjalani,
defied the MNLF leadership and set out to recruit all the disappointed
Muslims."[13] In 1995, this group massacred the hundred inhabitants of
the Christian village of Ipil, on the island of Mindanao. The Abu Sayyaf
group ("the sword-bearer") had approximately a thousand combatants
including "Afghans" trained in the Taleban camps in Pakistan, Yemen,
Somalia and Sudan.

During the trial of the World Trade Center bombers (1993), the
explosives expert of the team — Ramzi Ahmed Youssef — admitted
having planned the operation together with "Afghans" at one of the
Abu Sayyaf group's bases. According to various police sources, the
same organization was also behind the attack against a Philippine Airlines Boeing 747, flying the Manila-Tokyo route, in December 1994.
The toll: one dead and 20 wounded, mainly Japanese. It apparently
also prepared an attack against the Pope, in Manila, during the pontifi-
cal visit in January 1995. According to the Thai intelligence services,
the Abu Sayyaf group is financed by Osama bin Laden, through his
brother-in-law Mohamed Jamel Khalif, regional manager of a Saudi
NGO. The Philippine *Daily Inquirer* of August 23, 1998 adds that "in recent years Bin Laden was a frequent visitor to the Philippines, in particular in the area of Mindanao."

However, the Saudi does not show up on the Philippine authorities' black list. Established at the request of Interpol, this list counts 519 terrorists and international criminals from 19 countries. The Philippine president's chief of staff even recalls that in the Philippines "Osama bin Laden is known for his philanthropic activities in several Muslim organizations that are active in the south, where they support the poor Muslim population."

According to same sources, bin Laden's brother-in-law is said to bring financial help to the Gama'a islamiya (who claimed to have been behind the Luxor massacre). His collaboration with Osama bin Laden also means that he must have worked with the Palestinian and Jordanian Muslim Brothers. Lastly, bin Laden's import-export companies in Sudan were one of the principal business outlets of the two partners.

These connections often parallel those of the drug trade. In the Philippines, experts estimate the annual production of marijuana at $1.5 billion a year, going up by approximately 10% yearly. For that alone, the narcotics traffic would be more than $10 billion, that is, half of the Phillipine State budget. Admittedly, the Islamists do not control all of these flows, but the Abu Sayyaf group plays a big part. Its mercenaries look after the protection of transport and the shipping of cargoes via jungle airports in the islands of Basilan, Sulu and Jolo. By the same air channels, and also by sea, weapons are delivered for the group's combat units. This supply chain is managed by Pakistani intermediaries who are trained directly in the Afghan camps around Peshawar.

For a few years now, the religious dimension of the fight carried out by the Abu Sayyaf group has been subsumed in activities that are closer to organized crime than to revolutionary Islamism. Raised in the context of a "holy war," the "new Afghans" often end up as mercenaries of the traditional circuits of organized crime. And conversely, some find the religious alibi a good means of "whitewashing" their primary activities that relate purely and simply to organized crime. Terrorism can lead to anything, as long as you can get out. . . These narco-Islamist currents emerge in the Indian Ocean, "the new heart of the world" that opens the routes to Europe, from the southernmost ports of Sind and Baluchistan, from southern Africa and Latin America.

**Madagascar.** Traditionally watching over the oil and trade routes that use the channel of Mozambique and the east coast of Madagascar, the great island is regarded today as "the sick man" of the Indian Ocean.

The traditional tension between the Merinas, who are anglophile and Protestant, and the "Coastals," francophile Catholics, is exacerbated by new ethnic-religious conflicts that erupt on a regular basis with the Muslim communities from Comoro that have cropped up in the north and the west of the island. In this area in 1995 a local branch of Hezbollah appeared, which also found some supporters among the Indian Shiite communities that control the retail trade of the principal cities.

"The arrest in Madagascar, in January, of seven members of the local *khoja* community (Muslims Shiites) and their accomplices implicated in kidnappings for ransom may have brought to light the visible tip of an international network of criminals."[14] The money made by the group is said to have been invested in drug and weapons smuggling, then "laundered" on the black market for currency exchange, before being transferred to bank accounts in La Réunion. "Family ties within the *khoja* community were used to relay these transactions," adds *La Lettre de l'océan Indien*.

According to experts, these denominational ties have contributed significantly to the emergence of an international "criminal elite" that is deeply involved in the narcotics trade, and is clearly in a phase of "pre-cartellization" that recalls Colombia of the 1970's or Mexico of the 1980's. "These former small-caliber delinquents now lead a life of luxury, with a fleet of fancy cars, building establishments that facilitate money-laundering (hotel-restaurants) and making spectacular gestures of charity to propitiate the disinherited areas where they prevail," says a confidential report from a narcotics research center. "These traffickers move about, followed by a troop of bodyguards who are both young and obvious, and have a strong power of corruption over rural populations with scant resources."

According to the relevant Malagasy agencies, the internationalization of this "criminal elite" can especially be ascribed to the Filipino narco-Islamists of the Abu Sayyaf group, as well as to their Pakistani intermediaries who, with the assistance of Osama bin Laden's oceanic shipping companies, oversee the convoys of opium leaving the Taleban redoubt. Thus, according to the experts, the Filipinos and Afghan narcotics routes follow three principal axes: one toward Turkey, gate to the European market; the second aiming for the Horn of Africa, starting from Somalia; finally, towards Sudan, bound for sub-Saharan Africa and southern Africa. Madagascar plays a crucial role as hub for all three routes, and is especially effective since the island has its own channels by which it can distribute local production (which is in full expansion).

Heavily concentrated in the north of the country, the production of cannabis reached 150 tons in 1996. But the area of Analabé and the peninsula of Ampasinda, where the plant is heavily cultivated, are mountainous, and cannabis seedlings are often camouflaged in fields of corn and manioc. The local harvest is thus seriously underestimated. Other plantations probably exist in the cliff zones and are wedged into the "Triangle of the North," where the plantings and the harvest, worked by hand, are extremely hard to find. In 1996, the Malagasy *gendarmerie* eradicated 100 acres of cannabis — a negligible proportion of the area actually cultivated — and destroyed 86 tons of product. Opium culture has also taken root in the north of the island, on slopes up to 2600 feet high, in the area of Ambodilaitra, Ampisara and Ampolovantsambo.

Here is an illustration of the internationalization and the sophistication of the drug trade networks operating from the western basin of the Indian Ocean, and particularly from Madagascar. According to a September 1997 Interpol report on "The Summary of Heroin Seizures in the World, 1996-1997," the Mauritius police dismantled one of these networks and arrested seven people: five Mauritians, one Tanzanian, and a Kenyan. The chief of the gang is a Tanzanian who operates out of Sofia (Bulgaria). The "way stations" used in the traffic of heroin produced in the Afghan "Golden Crescent" are Mauritius, Nairobi, Istanbul, Munich and London . . . the Malagasy police force recently established that the traffickers maintain close contact with the crews of trading vessels and large yachts registered in the Comoros, South Africa (Durban), in Zanzibar and the Philippines.

As if the two centers were communicating vessels, the impetus of the Malagasy hub comes primarily from the production of heroin in the Afghan "Golden Crescent." Since the Taleban have controlled the country, production has almost doubled, reaching an estimated turnover of more than $5 billion per annum. According to a report dated April 1997, written by Dr. Mahbul ul-Haq, former Minister of Finances of Pakistan, approximately 5% of the Pakistani adult population uses narcotics regularly, accounting for 50 tons of opium, that is to say 4 to 4.5 tons of pure heroin per year. These figures contradict the assertions of Mullah Omar, chief of the Taleban, who justifies the Afghan production on the grounds that it is sent exclusively to destinations with non-Muslim populations. As for exports, the same report indicates that consumption of heroin exported via the ports of Sind and Baluchistan is going up equally quickly in other adjacent countries such as India and the Maldives. And, in addition, the eastern coast of Africa is also affected, through the distribution channels of the Indo-Pakistani diasporas.

Before being redistributed at the Malagasy hub, another share of the heroin traffic transits the international airport of Karachi, where *passeurs* — "mules" — generally African, are arrested every day. They carry the heroin from Afghanistan via the Horn of Africa and Madagascar to Europe and North America, in quantities of one to three kilos. Most of these "carriers," previously natives of western Africa, i.e., Nigeria, Benin or Sierra Leone, now mainly come from Tanzania, Kenya or Zambia, and the airports of eastern Africa are seeing a steady increase in heroin traffic: at the Jomo Kenyatta and Nairobi airports in Kenya, Kampala and Entebbe in Uganda, and Zanzibar in Tanzania. The same applies to sea-borne traffic, the ports generally concerned being Mombasa in Kenya and those of the east coast of Madagascar.

From Karachi, the principal Pakistani port, amphetamines are also being distributed, to Asia, Africa and the rim of the Indian Ocean. In Mozambique, in 1995, the first clandestine laboratory of metaqualone discovered on the African continent — Mandrax — was dismantled. Since then, other organizations have been liquidated in South Africa, Kenya, Mozambique, Swaziland and Zambia.

**South Africa.** The transnational, even transcontinental, nature of this traffic makes up the largest share of the most tightly-knit organizations (in terms of logistics and ideological purpose). Organized crime is never so effective as when it develops its networks in the name of a cause to defend, or better yet some imaginary notion that is in tune with the local populations. In this regard, political-religious ideologies constitute the best cover and the best guarantee of effectiveness and adherence to specified procedures, according to experts who have been following the emergence and the assertion of the "narco-Islamist" phenomenon for four or five years. As in Afghanistan, which remains the test laboratory and the driving force behind the growth of Sunni Islamism, we are witnessing in Southeast Asia, in the Indian Ocean and in southern Africa, a proliferation of Islamist networks where the race for dollars is gradually taking over the "holy war," (which is also transnational, de-territorialized and, on the whole, increasingly indeterminate).

For the "new Afghans," the culture of the dollar is replacing that of the "holy war" to a greater and greater extent and organized crime is supplanting the Islamism of power. Osama bin Laden's networks are examples of the redeployment and "privatization" of Sunni Islamist activism, whose specific circuits end up melding into those of organized crime. This evolution is particularly detectable in South Africa, where narco-Islamism and organized crime have given rise to the formation of a Shiite counter-banditry that claims to fill in for the deficiencies of the State. The Sunni narco-Islamism that merges with organized crime is now met in South Africa by a denominational reaction, based on Shiites communities, that organizes gatherings of citizens against gangsterism and drugs.

Pagad ("People Against Gangsterism and Drugs") first appeared in January 1996. One of its founders, Achmat Cassiem, had already created the fundamentalist group "Qibla," strongly influenced by the Iranian revolution, in 1979. Although it cannot be reduced to these terms alone, the South African criminal situation nevertheless reflects the resurgence of a Sunni-Shiite confrontation.

The Republic of South Africa is "one of the most violent places on the planet. The murder rate is six times that of the United States, five times that of Russia. The rate of unemployment is close to 33% and much higher among young people. For every police officer hired by the State, there are ten armed watchmen hired through private security companies. That's an important base for the intercontinental drug trade." This picture, drawn by Robert Kaplan,[15] is not contradicted by Sydney Mufamadi, the South African Security Minister, who describes his country as being prey to "a criminal epidemic," with some "192 organized gangs," while several foreign ministries count some 500 armed gangs.

Jean-François Bayard also describes "a striking increase in criminality, the growth of connections with various foreign Mafias, the privatization of violence. . . . South Africa has become the target of the big international crime syndicates, especially those based in Nigeria, but also further afield, in Russia and China. It has become a major importer and re-exporter of cocaine and heroin, as well as a gravitational center for money laundering . . . It is, in fact, the African capital of organized crime, with a turnover estimated at $9 billion per annum."[16]  The South African gangs began their history in the 1930's as security companies ensuring the safety of goods and people.  Concentrated at that time in the 6th district of the Western Cape province, they multiplied and diversified their activities, and now are active in drug trafficking, smuggling and extortion.

In the 1970's, the apartheid policy caused population shifts toward the "Cape."  This evolution reinforced the growth and the diversification of the gang activities on new territories.  For years, the South African police ignored the gangs because their various activities did not directly affect the white population.  The State agencies even made use of these organizations.  This situation persisted until in the 1980's, a period when a fatal war between rival organizations revealed their existence to the public.  Created in the early 1990's, anti-gang units have really been operational only since 1996, a record year during which the authorities listed some 500 groups and identified more than 1,500 criminals.  Most of them, now, are established in the areas of Port Elizabeth (Eastern Cape province); Cape Town (Western Cape province); Johannesburg and Pretoria (Gauteng province).

Suspected of international activities and institutional links with organized crime, in particular the Nigerian, Colombian and Chinese networks, sixteen of these organizations were targeted by intense investigations since 1998.  For the area of the Cape alone, one hundred gangs were identified, involving (to varying degrees) some 100,000 people — according to South African police estimates.  Set up along the tribal model, these gangs take names that are picturesque and revealing: "Bornfree Kids," the "Cape Town Scorpions," "Casbas," "Backstreet Kids," "Genuine TV Kids," the "Pipe Killers," "Sexy Boys," or "Turtles." In the area of Port Elizabeth, the principal organizations are "The Untouchables," "Bon's Gang," "The Invisibles" or "Vatos Locas." Five criminal organizations share the area of Pretoria: "The Mafia," "Dixie Boys," "Super Boys," "Fila Boys" and "Bad Boys."

Given this "cartellization" of crime and a too timid reaction by the powers that be, the Shiite Muslim communities have created militias in self-defense. Calling for "an Islamism of power" and evolving into an anti-organized-crime criminal organization, they now openly call for the Islamization of society as the only viable response to violence. This movement immediately won broad support from the South African Muslim communities, whose out-of-work youth constituted one of the principal targets of the gangs. On the strength of this support, which ensured it a broad social and logistical base, Pagad launched out in spectacular armed operations against the dealers and their gangs, in the name of the "holy war." A climax was reached on August 4, 1996, with the public execution of Rashad Staggie, the chief of the gang of "Hard Livings."

Gaining in notoriety since the end of 1997, this holy war against the gangs gradually turned into a "holy war" plain and simple. Forsaking its actions against organized crime, Pagad now directs its attacks against the South African apparatuses of State. In the context of a pro-Islamist fight centered on the claim of sovereignty of the "communitarian" type, Pagad's actions clearly aim to introduce a specific administration for all the populations and the districts with a Muslim majority. Giving up its initial objectives of self-defense, Pagad is now used as the armed branch for movements that are more overtly political such as, for example, MAGO ("Muslims Against Global Oppression") which demonstrated recently against President Clinton's visit to South Africa. CAG ("Concern Action Group") also calls for Islamization as an answer to crime, unemployment and poverty, while the "National Muslim Youth Forum" (NMYF) officially admits training its members in self-defense and in handling firearms.

The South African police force ascribes to these movements the August 25, 1998 bombing of Planet Hollywood, an American restaurant on the waterfront, in the port of the Cape. It was a beautiful evening and the dining room was packed, when a violent explosion tore through the building. The blast killed one woman and wounded 27 customers. A few minutes later, an anonymous representative of MAGO took credit for the attack. "The holy war is declared," he specified, adding that this explosion was just a warning of others that would respond to the American bombing of Sudan and Afghanistan on August 20. Those raids, on the orders of the White House, were made in response to the August 7, 1998 attacks against the American embassies in Nairobi and Dar es Salaam.

The police force apprehended one member of Pagad and two women, while they were on the point of boarding a flight bound for

Cairo. Pagad denied any involvement in the Planet Hollywood attack and mobilized several hundred sympathizers to demonstrate at the Cape, in front of the residence of the Minister of Justice, to protest the "illegal" detention their co-religionists and to serve a warning to the authorities. "If blood flows from the veins of our brothers, because of punishment inflicted illegally and un-constitutionally by malevolent members of the police force, then the police will have to face the rage of the community."

Under these conditions, the religious authorities of the "Muslim Judicial Council" quickly disassociated themselves from Pagad and condemned its "Jihad" actions as inappropriate to the situation of the Muslims of South Africa. Nevertheless, Pagad continued its armed activities and sought to recruit more broadly (until this point it had addressed primarily the Shiites) by negotiating agreements with the "narco-Islamists." Indeed, police investigations show that while the gangs — now represented by big law firms — were seeking to extend their territories, Pagad was trying to join forces with the Sunni traffickers who were established in South Africa.

On both sides, this search for alliances called for new strategies in the field of narcotics. Schematically, the gangs divided up the sales markets and the channels of export for Mandrax (metaqualone), crack, ice (methamphetamine hydrochlorate) and cocaine; meanwhile, Pagad attempted to enter into the service of the heroin godfathers (including certain collaborators of Osama bin Laden) by playing on the idea of denominational solidarity. From their Sudanese stronghold, the heroin chiefs are heavily involved (according to several police sources) in the Nigeria and Niger distribution chains, essential components of the African segments of organized crime.

**Nigeria.** The new Afghans use the distribution chains in Niger to supply the GIA. Like the Algerians, they currently prefer to develop their own business circuits over the pursuit of "holy war" for its own sake.

Like the South African Pagad, the "Vigilance Committees of Tassara" (VCT) of western Niger are armed groups constituted on the basis of an "Islamism of power," and are metamorphosing into mafioso structures. These militia were formed on the initiative of the central power in 1992, in the hope that they could supplement the Niger army that was engaged against the Tuareg rebellion. But, very soon, these well-armed and well-trained units were converted into gangs that specialized in various illicit trafficking, especially drugs, weapons, cigarettes and stolen cars.

Islam in Niger, however, had had a long tradition of moderation and tolerance. Nothing predisposed this country a priori to becoming a sanctuary for radical Islamist networks. Established long ago, the traditional brotherhoods of Quadirriya and Tijaniya never really got involved in the political field and, up until the end of the 1980's, there was only one official Muslim association, the Islamic Association of Niger, which was used as quasi-institutional intermediary between the government and the Muslim communities. Today, no fewer than fourteen Islamic associations have offices in Niamey.

Using the customary tactics of the Muslim Brothers, these semi-official organizations take advantage of the grave economic and social situation that the country is going through, and of the ruling power's inability to fully discharge its responsibilities — in particular in the medical and social fields — to gain influence among the most disadvantaged populations. Moreover, thanks to their financial clout (which cannot be accounted for, locally), these associations have now managed to forge high-level alliances within the apparatuses of State.

The Association for the Appeal for Islamic Unity and Solidarity (Anausi), created in July 1992, is at the forefront of the Islamic landscape in Niger, together with Anasi (The Association for Islamic Appeal and Solidarity) as well as the "Nasratou Din" and "Jamiyat Nassirat Din," women's associations that were founded in March 1997. These new arrivals are definitely less moderate than the Islamic Association of Niger, and according to several African intelligence agencies they are riddled with partisans of theocracy and armed struggle. Thus, Anasi is considered to be close to the Algerian Islamic Salvation Front (FIS) and the women's associations controlled by the "izalists," a Nigerian sect with Wahhabi leanings. In July 1991, they were authorized to preach on the territory of Niger, but due to their radicalism and their attitude towards the authorities this was retracted in 1994. They are still very influential in the southern part of the country, in particular around Maradi.

All these organizations exert their influence through sermons in the mosques, but even more so through a very tight network of Koran schools. The Niger national education system provides education for only 35% of the boys and 20% of the girls. Nongovernmental organizations with a social vocation enable them to reach the most desperate. Many activities are sponsored by four large foreign organizations: the World Islamic League, the World Association for the Call to Islam, the Agency of the Muslims of Africa, and the International Islamic Benevolent Foundation. These organizations, traditional tools of Saudi Arabia's "Muslim diplomacy," are funded publicly and privately, directly from the Gulf.

In addition, the local police have established that certain Niger preachers who are renowned for their extremist and antigovernment propaganda were trained in Sudan or in one of the three theological training centers that Khartoum financed in the north of Nigeria, in Zaria, Gari Tudu and Angouan Malam. These centers have the peculiar characteristic of offering both religious education (led by Sudanese masters) and training in the handling of explosives, taught by military operatives from the Algerian GIA. Indeed, for several years, the Algerian activists have had an important base in the area of Azawak, in the west of Niger. The GIA made an alliance with the Arab militia of the VGC (Vigilance Committees of Tassara) on the basis of their common interest in various kinds of dealing and clandestine sales.

Heavily armed, highly mobile and beyond the control of Niger's soldiers and police officers, these militia allow the GIA commandos to transport the necessary weapons, communications equipment, food and drugs to the Algerian Islamists. According to several military sources, the weapons and radio equipment supply the Nigerian rings and made possible several attacks on the Libyan army's depots. Moreover, the Algerian extremists apparently have no difficulty in obtaining false birth certificates in Niger, which enables them to get real passports and identity cards. Several times, the Algerian authorities have alerted the authorities of Niamey so that they could break up these channels. The Niger police force then conducted some symbolic operations, without much tangible result.

Arrested in Niamey for weapons smuggling in spring 1998, a well-known chief of the Algerian GIA, Larcen Bega, was released at once when one of the principal financial backers of the Arab militia, Sidi Mohamed, intervened. Tourad Sidi Mohamed is closely related to the current Niger Minister of Agriculture, Idi Omar Ango, who is also a past

Interior Minister. It was in a villa belonging to the financier that Lar-cen Bega stayed when he was living in the capital of Niger. Sidi Mo-hamed is not only one of the backers of the Arab militias and of the GIA, he has business connections with the presidency of his country and with the Agency of the Muslims of Africa, and with the Saudi fi-nanciers via the World Islamic League.

For their part, the Arab militias of Niger are interested in the vari-ous traffics managed by the Algerian GIA, for two reasons. They take their percentage on the transit of goods heading for Algeria, and the benefit from the GIA's investments in many import-export companies recently created in Algeria. "In Niger as in Algeria," explains a Euro-pean diplomat stationed in Niamey, "to establish their influence and to weave their networks the radical Islamists exploit the thirst for money at least as much as the ideological thirst. In any case, the results they obtain are obviously very quick." This "thirst for money" has shaped and controlled the tactical evolution of the Algerian Armed Islamic Groups (GIA) for several years.

Indeed, the marriage of the economies of the GIA underground to the financial activities of their chiefs, the "emirs," is one of the main en-gines driving the pursuit of violence in Algeria. Meticulously analyzed by Luis Martinez, the most disadvantaged layers of society consider the figure of the "emir," the chief of an armed group, to be the symbol of perfect social success combining both the control of violence and the accumulation of wealth. "In fact, the 'emirs' of the armed bands are more interested in changing the social relations (in the territories that they control) to their own benefit, than in carrying out the final battle against the regime and replacing it by an Islamic State."[17] In that, their war tactics differ from those of the traditional liberation movements that aim at political change on the national level.

Targeting the national companies and service organizations sym-bolizing the central State, the GIA accelerate the privatization of the economy and consolidate the emergence of the "emirs" as new socio-economic actors. Those who do not succeed in "managing" their terri-tory, either because they exhaust the resources, or because of military setbacks, are often rehabilitated into all kinds of dealing. A GIA sanctu-ary in western Niger forwards weapons as well as heroin (which will be shipped to Europe via Italy, France and Spain). Other flows of narcotics heading for the same destinations transit the Moroccan border. Once they are in Europe, these goods are exchanged for stolen cars, sent to Algeria by networks with accomplices among the customs and military officials.

Several times, these car-thief rings protected by the Algerian government have been used by the GIA to introduce weapons into Algeria. During the autumn of 1996, a ring dealing in Skorpio machine pistols between Slovenia, Switzerland and Italy was broken up. "Imported Fiat Pandas were blocked in the ports until a new order came from the Office of Counter-Espionage. Precise information indicated the existence of a network actively dealing in weapons and well-organized in Switzerland and Italy. The dealers sending guns to the Islamist underground took advantage of the mass of vehicles to ship their goods clandestinely. . . . But in spite of the firmness of the blockade order from the highest authorities, certain Fiat Pandas succeeded in leaving the ports, Algiers in particular. Well-organized and obviously benefiting from complicities among the customs officers, the traffickers changed the license plates of the vehicles and drove away."[18]

These rings provide the "emirs" and their soldiers with opportunities to revive a flagging "holy war" by recycling it in the market economy. Since the end of 1994, this evolution has led to a spectacular growth in the number of Algerian import-export companies. They are not required to justify their sources of funding and can represent foreign firms in all legality. "Thus, by grafting themselves onto the trading industry, the Islamist armed groups have freed themselves from the local economic contingencies," concludes Luis Martinez. "As part of the commercial flows between Algeria and its foreign partners, they can shelter their organization from financial woes. The policy of trade liberalization encourages the intermediaries of this policy in Algeria, as well as the Islamist groups that are fighting the regime. All things considered, Algeria's entrance into the globalization of exchanges fuels all parties of the civil war. In 1994, the establishment of a market economy, with all its economic reforms, helped consolidate the armed Islamist groups. It encourages a "pillaging economy" for "the good of the Mafias" — the "emirs," military leaders and other notables exploit the transition toward a market economy to further their interests."

The evolution of the Algerian civil war is emblematic in more ways than one. Its many stages recall the mutations of Osama bin

Laden's networks; the transformation of the Algerian "emirs" corresponds perfectly to the economic functions to which the "new Afghans" aspire. From this perspective, the armed struggle now defines its objectives in terms of quickly accumulating capital and other resources. There again, the objectives of the "holy war" yield to the imperatives of the predatory systems and rentier mechanisms of a transnational mafioso economy. And now, we must consider one final example of this Islamic-mafioso development. Far from defining the limits of the sanctuaries of the "new Afghans," the "Islamic-Latin-American triangle" shows the extent to which they intend to enjoy the fruits of a globalization that goes far beyond the limits of the Arab-Muslim world.

**Latin America.** Once an obligatory way-station for war criminals and other fleeing Nazis, the region known as "the three borders" (Brazil, Argentina, Paraguay) is considered by anti-terrorist experts to be a new base of radical Islamism. Often, intelligence agencies have traced the leaders of Hezbollah, Hamas and the international organization of the Muslim Brothers to this area. Forming a triangle between the towns of Puerto Iguazu (Argentina); Foz do Iguaçu (Brazil) and Ciudad del Este (Paraguay), the area holds a population of more than 400,000, a quarter of them foreigners, with strong Near Eastern communities, especially Lebanese.

At the center, the site of the marvelous waterfalls of Iguaçu hosts more than 40,000 visitors a year, which makes the identification and the monitoring of people particularly difficult. In addition the topography, crisscrossed by innumerable rivers and streams, makes it impossible to get an overall view. This tormented physical and human geography encourages all sorts of traffic. Ciudad del Este has thus become the Latin-American capital for counterfeiting and for the smuggling of weapons and explosives. Weapons come from the United States via Paraguay, and are mainly destined for the markets of Rio de Janeiro and São Paulo; they follow the route to Foz do Iguaçu and cross the border of Paraguay at Mato Grosso do Sul. Small landing strips in the region are also used for delivering cargoes, and drugs.

A non-producing country, Brazil is today the main regional transit center for the cocaine trade from Colombia and Bolivia, heading for the United States and Europe, via Cape Verde, the Ivory Coast and South Africa. Experts estimate that 80% of Colombian cocaine passes through the Islamic-Latin-American triangle. The Latin-American, Chinese and Near Eastern mafias have made their headquarters there. The mosque of Foz do Iguaçu, which also has a Koran school, regularly receives visits by religious dignitaries and Saudi businessmen, although the communities are mainly Shiite. In 1997, the Lebanese former prime minister Rafic Hariri was the honorary guest of the Arab community of Ciudad del Este. Accompanied by a delegation by Gulf financiers, he was mainly interested in Near Eastern investments in the region. At the time, the police services identified a close collaborator of Osama bin Laden in his retinue.

Certainly, the Lebanese former prime minister is not considered to be a dangerous terrorist himself, but his many business engagements often lead him to mingle with intermediaries who are directly involved in Islamist mafia operations that generate international terrorism. The "Lebanese cauldron" alone deserves a close investigation into the gray areas of finance where private banking, international businessmen and major offshore criminals meet. Whether in Latin America or in Beirut, these business milieux reveal the osmosis that is going on between the criminal hierarchies and the legal structures of economic and financial activity worldwide. It is symptomatic that when one finds the heads of various criminal groups, one reaches the limit of the criminal activity at the same time.

The influence of the Mafias is never so great and so dangerous as when they leverage their criminal activities to ply all the levers that legal society offers in order to subvert that legality itself. Money laundering is not only a monetary activity aiming to legalize dirty money by injecting it into licit economic sectors; it is also exerted on organizations and elite groups that also wish to be made respectable. "One point is essential: organized crime is not only a problem of criminality anymore. It is a too broad a topic, these days, to be entrusted solely to the criminologists. The economy of crime was based in the legal economy. If you make a clean distinction between organized crime and the sphere of finance, you are condemned to not understand either one. Certainly, it is more comfortable to regard the Mafias and the criminal organizations as malevolent foreign powers. Reality is less appealing and more complex: criminality has become an essential gear in the engine of contemporary societies."[19]

While it is based in the structures of organized crime, whose con-

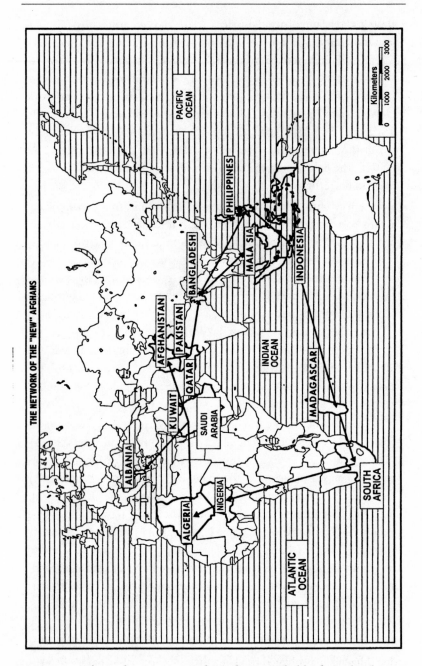

THE NETWORK OF THE "NEW" AFGHANS

sortia are themselves increasingly indistinguishable from legal economic and financial activities, the networks of contemporary Islamist
terrorism pass through the offshore banks of the tax havens. To the

partial cartography of the sanctuaries of the "new Afghans," we must add these financial harbors that have developed on the periphery of the industrialized countries. Half of these territories may be under British sovereignty, but Switzerland too plays a central role in capital flight and money laundering.

**The Swiss Confederation.** After London, Switzerland is the biggest outlet for the Gulf's petrodollars and offers the best private fund management services in the world. It is generally estimated that of the $500 billion that have left the Gulf to seek shelter in tax havens, more than half is in Swiss banks — which hold 40% of the $12,000 billion world market of private fortunes under management.

When tracing the various financial connections of Osama bin Laden, the Muslim Brothers and the Saudis' "Muslim diplomacy," one invariably finds oneself back at the door of the "Swiss friend." The big Italian and Russian mafias, too, for the most part, have founded corporations in Switzerland. On March 28, 1998, during an event at the federal Polytechnic School of Zurich, Mrs. Carla del Ponte, the Attorney General of the Confederation, admitted that money-laundering cases went up by 200% in Switzerland between 1996 and 1997. "We are all the more sensitized to the various questions touching on laundering dirty or criminal money since the financial flows that pass through our premises are constantly increasing," she said.

Indeed, enjoying rock solid monetary and political stability, as well as a long tradition of rigorous and discreet banking know-how, the Swiss Confederation remains one of the most attractive money markets in the world, even if bank secrecy is more absolute these days in Liechtenstein, Austria and Luxembourg. Since July 1, 1991, the Swiss banks can no longer accept dummy names for the famous numbered accounts. In contrast to an ordinary account, a numbered account offers all the guarantees of bank secrecy since fund transfers are never ascribed to the customer, but to a simple number. Up until now, people holding dubious funds have systematically hidden behind the anonymity of these accounts, behind their lawyers, their notaries, their fiduciary agencies and other fund managers. Since 1992, a convention on due diligence has obliged the banks to verify their customers' identity, including those who prefer numbered accounts.

In theory, the Swiss banks are now required to make sure that the identity of the person truly corresponds to the person who is really the bearer of the account. However, the concept of "ultimate beneficiary" of an account does not exist in Swiss law, and thus the banks must be satisfied with the information the customer provides. This obviously does not prevent the use of imaginary names and other ruses, which are frequently used by the mafias and terrorist organizations. "Swiss bank secrecy is not absolute at all," underlines Jean-Claude Buffle, a member of the Geopolitical Observatory of Drugs. "From time immemorial, the curtain could be lifted on a judge's order, to facilitate criminal investigations, for example, to seize the accounts of a drug trafficker or a gangster. In 1967, Switzerland became part of the European Convention of legal mutual assistance on criminal matters. Under the terms of that agreement, a Swiss magistrate can eliminate bank secrecy to help a penal investigation opened by foreign magistrates."[20]

But, he adds immediately, "A Swiss judge can issue a compulsory measure such as lifting bank secrecy only in the pursuit of an infringement that is recognized by Swiss law as a criminal matter." The Swiss penal code has considered money-laundering an offence since August 1, 1990. Adopted in 1994, another law encourages the banks to take control — via the Federal Commission of Banks (CFB) and the Federal Police Office (OFP) — when they come across funds of doubtful origins. Lastly, a law passed on April 1, 1998 extends the field of application of the preceding texts to the para-banking sector; now, all financial intermediaries, business lawyers, estate managers and fiduciary companies are (in theory) constrained to denounce any suspect operations.

When a legal authority that is internationally recognized issues a letter of request, Swiss justice can freeze the banking assets. This is what happened to certain accounts belonging to outcast dictators such as Duvalier, Marcos, Noriega, Ceausescu and Stroessner. In certain cases, such as the former president of Mali, Moussa Traoré, some of the funds were even reassigned to the new Mali leaders. This happy outcome remains the exception, however, because of the sluggishness of the procedures which leaves the suspect all the leisure he needs to transfer his money elsewhere. And in spite of the evolution of the legislation, the para-banking sector, where financial intermediaries continue to play an important part, is still a wide-open gateway for bringing illicit money into the Swiss money market.

For example, in June 1997, two fiduciary companies were officially added to the Trade Register of the canton of Geneva, although the declared owners of these companies were suspected by the federal police force (Bern) to be the leaders of a dormant network of the GIA that operated out of Switzerland. The names of the same people (who had every legal right to found these two fiduciary companies) also shows up in the briefing book on the gun- and car-theft-ring that was broken up during the autumn of 1996! The many dysfunctions governing relations between the federal authority and the cantonal administrations add every shade of gray to the shady side of the Swiss banking structure, which is fully exploited not only by the launderers but also by the business networks behind international terrorism.

Many times, we asked the Attorney General of the Swiss Confederation to account for these "shady areas" and how they are used by the business networks that finance Islamist terrorism. Invariably, the answer led to an admission of great impotence. "If you do not have concrete elements, if there is no duly formulated request, we can't do anything," admits Carla del Ponte. She does not hide that she is more concerned with fighting against the Russian and Italian Mafias. This hierarchy of priorities in the fight against organized crime is eminently political, and the scant eagerness expressed by Switzerland with regard to international cooperation against terrorism is not unrelated to the weight that Saudi finance carries in the Swiss banking environment.

While precise calculations are limited by the "secrecy defense," the most serious experts estimate the volume of Saudi capital injected into the Swiss banking structure at between $150 and $200 billion. From Osama bin Laden's networks to the racketeering channels of the Muslim Brothers, to the various networks of the Near Eastern mafias, most of the investigations completed or in progress reveal that Gulf capital, usually Saudi, is involved to varying degrees. These enormous funds are characterized by their fluidity; therefore competition is sharp with London and Luxembourg to "fix" them for a term. "So, it is important not to upset such large accounts with legal annoyances that might encourage them to place their investments under more clement skies," admits a big Swiss banker, under cover of the strictest anonymity.

The affair of the "Nazi gold," and the fact that Swiss banks have recently been obliged to return funds to several Jewish associations, have encouraged Gulf financiers to prefer the Swiss money market, according to several financial experts who confirm that Saudi capital plays a central role in Swiss banking circles. The publication of a confidential report from the Foreign Office on September 10, 1996, relating to the deposits of Nazi gold in Switzerland (estimated at the end of the war to be between $200 and $500 million), set off the powder keg and launched the affair known as the "Jewish funds." Switzerland took on the commitment to restore several billion dollars to the World Jewish Congress. "In return, this event has caused a sympathetic reaction among certain Arab financial milieux, especially Saudi, for the Swiss money market," the banker adds. "But independently of this incident, Saudi funds are regarded as vital for the future of Swiss finance."

Admittedly, the Swiss money market does not have a monopoly on money-laundering, but its Arab tropism has placed it at the center of the mechanism for creating offshore companies for the Islamist business networks. "In any case, most of the money-laundering fronts are set up with the assistance of professionals, either financial or legal, who take care of the administrative requirements (the legal formation of the company, opening the bank accounts, etc.)," explains Marie-Christine Dupuis. "Most of them are import-export companies; commercial firms are established in several countries simultaneously, which makes it possible to open banking and investment accounts in their names and to transfer funds back and forth on an apparently legitimate basis."[21] Thus, between 1989 and 1997, some $800 billion dollars seems to have disappeared from the planet's accounts. According to the International Monetary Fund, the worldwide addition of dirty money in 1997 was over $500 billion, that is to say approximately 3% of the gross world product.

With their logic of economic deregulation, the United States has given a big boost to the establishment of these "offshore" commercial zones, beyond the control of central banks and national legislations. Consequently, it is no surprise that the majority of these zones cropped up within the old British Empire. "The creation of offshore companies," adds Marie-Christine Dupuis, "is precisely the specialty of the British Virgin Islands which, since the formation of the first IBC (International Business Company) in 1984, have called themselves one of the leaders of this market. Approximately 145,000 IBC are registered in the Virgin Islands." The Anglo-Normans islands, the Cayman Islands, the Bahamas and other tropical paradises of the old sterling zone and the dollar zone have also become centers of the offshore economy.

This offshore economy, which siphons off huge amounts of money, is on the way to becoming integrated into the legal economy. One understands better the embarrassed remarks of the Attorney General of the Swiss Confederation when he was asked about Islamist deals. One understands better why no government attacks these parallel mechanisms head-on, and why it has become increasingly difficult to fight the financing of terrorist networks. It's a terrible state of affairs: "From the most impoverished to the most powerful, including the middle class whose professional activities provide the logistics and the infrastructure of the banks and financial services, everyone, to some degree, whether he knows it or not, is put to the service of the criminal economy." Islamism and its various forms of organization take full advantage of this process of economic deregulation and globalization.

We should consider once again the difference between Islam and Islamism. While there is no inherent doctrinal antagonism between Islam and the general mechanisms of the accumulation of capital, Maxime Rodinson did not discover between them the causal relationship that Max Weber suggests between Protestantism and capitalism. "For example, the precepts of Islam did not create the propensity for commercial activity that one observes in many Muslim societies," he concludes. "The leaders of the Muslim expansion were, even before their conversion, the tradesmen. They conquered societies where trade was highly developed before the conquest. The precepts of Islam did not seriously block the capitalist orientation of the last century and nothing in them is really opposed to a socialist orientation."[23]

Rodinson was analyzing Islam. Islamist ideology produces very different conse-quences. The morals and the order of things that Islamist ideology postulates are more in sync with liberal ideology. They are easy to reconcile with the economic models that derive from it (the same ones that the United States is trying to impose on the rest of the planet).

Islamism and deal-making always fit together well. The economic schemes of the Muslim Brothers are a strange echo of Guizot's exhortation, "Get rich." The great Saudi families were able to invest their petrodollars in the growth industries of the developed economies, including in their tax havens, while financing Wahhabi proselytism on a planetary scale. In the paradise of the international and privatized "holy war," "everything can be bought; everything is for sale," rejoices the Saudi billionaire Osama bin Laden. He invented a form of terrorism listed on the Stock exchange... Educated at the American intelligence school, his primary identity is that of a businessman and the "holy war" is his business.

In the majority of the current conflicts where Islam plays a part, the Algerian paradigm of Islamism-speculation, elucidated by Luis Martinez, is spreading. The entire contemporary Islamist movement is going through the stages of the same evolution, more or less: that of armed groups transforming themselves into mafioso networks, which seek to rehabilitate themselves, sooner or later, into the respectable world of business.

In Egypt, Algeria, Saudi Arabia, Pakistan and elsewhere, it is significant that Islamist ideology first appeared in the engineering schools, in scientific faculties, among computer specialists and medical interns; i.e. in the most modern sectors and those that are most open to the external world. Among Islamist propagandists, e-mail has replaced *noms de guerre*, satellite phones have replaced secret letter-drops; and sermons and military ambushes are immortalized on videotape, while a proliferation of Internet sites drives an electronic "holy war" in real time and promotes the advent of the virtual Islamic State.

These various exhortations to a total political-religious assertion are not calling for the preservation or the restoration of a tradition that was damaged by historical progress. On the contrary, they are founded in that very evolution, they adapt to its rhythms and they take advantage of the most avant-garde mechanisms. Heirs to the Enlightenment, to Alain and Auguste Comte, we have erred in viewing the idea of progress as ascending in a straight line. By locking reality into all kinds of sub-Hegelian equations such as, "modernity is rational, rationality is modern," our comprehension of History has ignored the inevitable ruses by which every advance is accompanied by a resurgence of retrograde details, where every modernization brings back archaisms that one believed had been forgotten, where every step of progress is matched by a subjective step backward that marks the assertion of an inassimilable self-awareness.

Indeed, it is self-awareness that lies at the heart of the matter, that is, control of one's own intimacy in a world that has been expanded to its ultimate limits. Georges Bataille, an acute visionary, had a presentiment of it when the Marshall plan was being launched. "First of all, the paradox is carried to the extreme, owing to the fact that the envisaged policy, based on "the dominant international economy," has as its goal only an increase in the global quality of life. That is disappointing and depressing. But it is the starting point and the basis, not the completion of self-awareness."[24] Establishing the market economy and its financial activities throughout the world deprives us, indeed, of the great legends, their epic accounts and ultimately of any form of imagination.

Rather than the advent of the mystical 21st century heralded by Malraux, this tension between the famous universal (which, for the moment, and for want of anything better, we may call "globalization") and the specific, in all its states, brings us back to the inherent evidence of the movement. This call to order of reality summons up its contradiction, and we are once again engulfed in history, whose radiant demise had been promised to us.

Far from attenuating the forms of archaism, the evolution of history — let us say the modernization of the economic, social and cultural structures — of our societies exalts conflicts of differentiation, space-time particularisms and all kinds of makeshift forms of more or less shared self-awareness. While this trend is relentlessly at work all across the planet, the economy as understood through its neoliberal mechanisms requires the accompaniment of spiritual values expressed as so many phenomena of compensation in a world governed by the cold law of merchandise. These centrifugal expressions do not hamper the centripetal trend of the economic logic about which we speak. Rather, they reinforce its daily and inescapable progress.

The implosion of the States and the territorial fragmentations that result from the political-religious claims, fanaticism, intolerance and xenophobias that they generate do not in any way restrict the economic globalization. On the contrary, these ideological manifestations encourage the international deployment of the laws of the market and justify the worldwide integration of the economy. Like a principle of thermodynamics, exponential economic integration corresponds, almost organically, to an equal and opposite political disintegration. Islamist ideology does not postulate, as its hasty and easily manipulated observers claim, a kind of liberation theology, progressive and liberating, but a static theological-political order founded on a neocommunitarism with totalitarian tendencies.

Far from raising obstacles to the new configurations of global capitalism, Islamist ideology is becoming part of its new superstructures. It provides them not only with fantasies of substitution, but more important, with military-racketeering networks that merge very easily into the filaments of the networks of organized crime, the supreme stage of capitalism. In a fantastic twist in meaning, religious fanaticism no longer merely ensures the salvation of the ignorant, denounced by Spinoza, and religion is no longer just the opium of the people . . . Through Islamism and the other political-religious ideologies, the spiritual revival acts as a tranquillizer for the misfits, who are the losers in the game of globalization.

To quote Georges Bataille again, "Going from the perspective of a finite economy to the economy as a whole is really a Copernican shift: it overturns thought — and morals. From the outset, if some of the resources, whose worth can be estimated approximately, are dedicated to a loss-maker, or an activity with no possible profit, to unproductive use, then it is necessary, it is even inescapable to give up goods without anything in return." One can, indeed, consider corruption, the disappearance of a billion dollars from international account books, the mafioso and terrorist crimes, as so many necessary evils, consubstantial to the imposition of a total hegemonic economic model. This working hypothesis actually opens up some real possibilities.

"Now," Bataille concludes, "nevermind pure and simple waste, like the construction of the Pyramids, the possibility of pursuing growth itself would have to be a gift: developing industry throughout the whole world would require the Americans to grasp the fact that an economy like theirs would have to have an operating margin that does not produce a profit. Managing an immense industrial network is not like changing a tire. . . . It expresses a cosmic flow of energy and is dependent upon it, a flow that cannot be limited, and the laws of which cannot be ignored without consequences. Woe to anyone who persistently tries to control the flow, which is something greater than he is, with the limited mindset of the mechanic who changes a tire."

In responding to Islamism with missiles, the United States is not only working on the wrong tire, it is reinforcing that against which it claims to be fighting. By bombing bin Laden's bases, the United States sought above all to shoot down the specter of duplicity that has haunted its foreign policy since the end of the Second World War.

344

However, the U.S. knows that you cannot trap the truth in glue like a bird; it knows better than anyone else that you don't respond to terrorism with bombs.

## Footnotes

1. Alain Joxe, *L'Amérique mercenaire*, Stock, 1992.
2. Conference at the Institut des hautes etudes internationales (HEI), Geneva, October 13, 1998.
3. Georges Bataille, *La Part maudite*, Editions de Minuit, 1967.
4. Jean-Marc Balencie and Arnaud de La Grange, *Mondes rebelles — Acteurs, conflits et violences politiques*, Editions Michalon, 1996.
5. *Atlas mondial de l'islam activiste*, under the direction of Xavier Raufer and Philippe Rondot, La Table ronde, 1991.
6. *Ibid.*
7. Andrée Feillard, "L'Islam comme nouvel enjeu dans la politique indonésinne," *Hérodote*, No 88, 1st quarter 1998.
8. The Islamization of the Malaysian peninsula began in the 14th century with the establishment of the sultanate of Malacca. Today, "In Malaysia one finds the most militant form of Islam in the Malayan world: fasting for Ramadan, justice inspired by the Shari'a, wearing the *hijab*. A Muslim resurgence that goes back to the 1970's and affects peasants as well as the students of major universities, especially that of Kuala Lumpur" (*Atlas Mondial de l'Islam activiste*). In 1951, the Malaysian Islamic Party (PAS) was created, whose youth organization was active in Islamist propagandizing that culminated in the 1980's. These excesses have been co-opted by increasingly Islamized apparatuses of State, and the federal legislative elections of 1990 provided a comfortable majority to outgoing Prime Minister, Mahathir Mohamad, who saw himself as the incarnation of "Islamism in power" in Malaysia. Even today, PAS maintains relationships to sister parties in Indonesia and activists movements in the Philippines.
9. *Le Monde*, October 12-13, 1997.
10. See Chapter XIII: "Why Saudi Arabia Finances Islamism."
11.. Blocked by the Spanish colonization of the 16th century, Islam's expansion in Southeast Asia stopped at the eastern border comprised of the islands of Mindanao, Basilan, Sulu and Tawi-Tawi. Representing 40% of the territory, these islands are home to approximately 5 million Muslims, that is to say 8% of the Philippine population (which is predominantly Catholic). Initially, in the 1970's, the Muslim rebellion had more to do with the desire for regional autonomy vis-à-vis the colonization by Catholics from the north than with any claim to establish an Islamic State. Thus the MNLO was created, in 1966 — the Moro National Liberation Organization (the name given to the Muslims by the Spanish colonists).
12. Jean-Marc Balencie and Arnaud de La Grange, *Mondes rebelles, op. cit.*

13. *Ibid.*

14. *La Lettre de l'Océan Indien,* April 18, 1998.

15. "Was Democracy Just A Moment?", *The Atlantic Monthly,* December 1997.

16. Jean-François Bayard, Stephen Ellis and Béatrice Hibou, *La Criminalisation de l'Etat en Afique,* Editions Complexes, 1997.

17. Conversation with Luiz Martinez, author of the *La Guerre civile en Algérie,* Editions Karthala, 1998.

18. *Algérie Confidentiel,* No 79, 1996.

19. *L'Atlas mondial de l'argent sale,* by Jean de Mailard, Renaud Van Ruymbeke, Antonio Gialanella, Benoit Dejemeppe, Bernard Bertossa, Stock, 1998.

20. Jean-Claude Buffle, "Double jeu— Les Etats-Unis, la France and et les banques suisses," *Revue des relations internationals et stratégiques ,* winter 1995.

21. Marie-Christine Dupuis, *Finance criminelle, comment le crime organisé blanchit l'argent sale,* Presses universitaires de France, 1998.

22. *L'Atlas mondial de l'argent sale, op. cit.*

23. Maxime Rodinson, *Islam et capitalisme,* Le Seuil, 1966.

24. Georges Bataille, *La Part maudite, op. cit.*

# Chapter XVII

## Afghanistan and Sudan are the Wrong Targets

> "Washington prefers the spectacular military maneuver, but combating terrorism is a long-term process, inevitably secret, difficult and dangerous, and to be effective it requires close international cooperation."
>
> Jean-Louis Dufour

The United States did not wait long to respond to the August 7, 1998 attacks against the American embassies in Nairobi and Dar es Salaam. On August 20, cruise missiles hit several military camps in Afghanistan and an industrial plant in Sudan. During a short televised speech, President Clinton gave the official reasons for the action. An urgent investigation apparently had established Osama bin Laden's direct responsibility. During the attack, American interceptors violated Pakistani airspace. Classified "top secret," the actual results of the bombing were disappointing. Not only was the anti-terrorist objective not achieved, but the Sudanese target, a pharmaceutical factory, causes a word-wide furor. Was it, or was it not, part of bin Laden's military apparatus? The answer to this question and the explanation for the attacks in Nairobi and Dar es Salaam are related to the Sudanese political imbroglio. The religious guide of the Islamist regime of Khartoum, Hassan el-Tourabi, who had been seeking a rapprochement with the United States, was attracting lightning bolts from the regime's hawks. It was to thwart his initiatives that they, with the assistance of bin Laden, had financed and organized the two attacks of August 7. FBI investigations revealed several connections between the CIA and the Saudi billionaire's networks. "Bin-Ladengate" was underway. Causing a wave of protest in the Arab world, the American response only confirmed Islamism in its distrust towards the West. This military re-

sponse was unsuited to today's terrorism. The current priority for international cooperation in anti-terrorism is clear: to counter the financing of terrorism by punishing those who finance it.

Washington, August 20, 1998, 1:30PM. It is time to launch the
operation "Infinite Reach." It is 10:00PM in Afghanistan and 7:00PM in
Sudan. Fifty-five Tomahawk cruise missiles, launched from four light
cruisers and a U.S. Navy submarine crossing the Sea of Oman, rained
down on Afghan camps near the Pakistani border, less than 100 miles
south of Kabul. Twenty more, fired from two vessels that were crossing the Red Sea, targeted (at a distance of nearly 2500 miles) a factory
in the outskirts of Khartoum.

A spokesman for the U.S. navy stated that the objective was the
Al-Shifa industrial pharmaceutical center; it was suspected by the
American intelligence services of being used to manufacture chemical
weapons. This story was confirmed by various centers of the Sudanese
opposition in Cairo. "Indeed, this factory specializes in manufacturing
chemical weapons with the assistance of foreign experts, mostly Iraqi."

In Afghanistan, the targets hit were part of a complex close to
Khost, composed of the Aswa Kali Al-Batr base camp, a logistics base
and four training camps used not only by Osama bin Laden's "Afghans"
but also by Gama'a islamiya and the Egyptian Islamic Jihad, according
to Pentagon sources. "These bases are used as refuges for the terrorists,
they house the financial infrastructure of various organizations and are
used to give fighters the technical and tactical training for international
terrorism," said General Hugh Shelton (head of the Joint Chiefs of Staff
of the U.S. army). According to the CIA, the Afghan complex housed
approximately 600 people.

From his vacation spot on Martha's Vineyard, President Clinton
announced in a statement broadcast by the major television networks
that the United States Air Force had bombed "terrorist sites in Afghanistan and Sudan," in retribution for the events in Nairobi and Dar
es Salaam.

"I ordered these strikes for four reasons," said the U.S. president.
"First of all, because we have convincing evidence that these groups
played a key role in the attacks against our embassies in Kenya and
Tanzania; secondly, because these groups have already conducted terrorist attacks against Americans in the past; thirdly, we have information that they were planning new attacks against our citizens and those

350

of other countries, whose victims we so tragically acknowledge in Africa; fourthly, because they were seeking to get chemical weapons and other dangerous weapons. The terrorists should have no doubt that, given their threats, America will protect its citizens and will remain at the head of the global fight for peace, freedom and security."

The president's third reason was the determining factor, according to several diplomatic sources. A CIA memo suggested that an Islamist group was preparing a new attack against the United States embassy in Tirana, where the U.S. secret service took part in the arrest and extradition of several Egyptian Islamists. The memo explains that the Islamists, together with members of Gama'a islamiya and of the Egyptian Jihad, established in Bosnia, also work in Albania under the cover of several Islamic nongovernmental organizations, in particular "Mercy International," an organization of the Muslim Brothers that is headquartered in the United States and has an office in Zurich, Switzerland.

On August 18, the United States ambassador to Tirana and the head of the Albanian government had an hour and a half long private conversation about the Muslim extremists' local sanctuaries. The following day, the U.S. State Department announced that it was reducing the personnel at the embassy to the bare minimum and recommended that Americans in Albania "should consider their personal safety and leave Albania, if they can."

The same measurements were taken, following specific threats in Islamabad and Sanaâ arising out of an overall situation of insecurity, in Uzbekistan and Azerbaïdjan because of more traditional conflicts endangering the embassy's security personnel, and in Asmara and Kinshasa. The State Department added that "these embassies will be reopened on an individual basis, as the situation evolves and as security improves."

A few days later, the State Department's "antiterrorism coordinator," Chris Ross, transmitted to his NATO colleagues the first conclusions of the investigation that was opened after the Nairobi and Dar es Salaam attacks.

Ross confirmed that the United States, without eliminating any possibilities, was particularly interested in Osama bin Laden's networks. A suspect had been arrested, the very same day of the attacks in Karachi, while he was trying to get to Afghanistan with a forged Yemeni passport. According to the Pakistani police, he had already admitted participating in the team that had prepared the Nairobi attack. A Jordanian of Palestinian origin, 34 years old, Mohammad Saddiq Howaida (also known as Odeh), was sent to Kenya at once where he was questioned by FBI investigators.

Very quickly, the man named bin Laden as his boss. Presented by the press Kenyan as the principal organizer of the attack, on August 4 Odeh went to Hill Top Lodge, a seedy hotel in Nairobi where he met with three accomplices who had arrived the day before. Hill Top, a rundown little establishment located in the poor district of River Road, belongs to a Yemeni who settled in Kenya about thirty years ago. The commandos occupied rooms 102 and 107, and it is there that they are supposed to have started building the bomb with 800 kilos of TNT. During two searches conducted by the Kenyan police force and fifteen FBI inspectors on August 18 and 22, the rooms were dusted with carbon powder to look for fingerprints.

On August 7, the day of the attack, the Islamists are supposed to have completed the preparation of the explosive device in a van; then they drove across the city to the embassy. Odeh, who had a Kenyan passport, had lived as fish merchant for several years in Mombasa, on the Indian Ocean, before marrying a young Kenyan from Malindi in 1994. Odeh admitted to being part of a team of seven men, including Egyptians and Lebanese. Three of them died in the explosion.

Arrested two days after the attack by the Kenyan police, Khaled Salim, of Yemeni origin, admitted having launched a grenade at the security agents at the American embassy, before fleeing at the moment of the explosion. A third man, Abdallah Nacha, a Lebanese national, was also questioned by the FBI in Nairobi. According to the *Daily Nation*, the three men were seen filming the American embassy four days before the explosion. On August 26, the Attorney General of Kenya announced that Odeh and Khaled Salim had been extradited to the United States while, on the spot, the FBI investigators were keeping very quiet about their investigations.

Several police raids were carried out in Nairobi, at the site of a nongovernmental organization that assisted Somalian refugees. Two Saudis were arrested. The manager of the hotel Heron Court, a 5-star establishment, was suspected of having rendered logistical assistance to the commando. This individual, of German extraction, left Kenya

the day before the attack. He was being sought by Interpol. Other suspects were arrested in the Muslim district of Pangani and the coastal
cities of Mombasa and Malindi.

On the ground, several foreign ministries reported that in November 1997, the Kenyan police had arrested and expelled ten members of
the Saudi foundation Al-Haramain. Described in the bulletin of the
Saudi embassy in Nairobi as being financed by the kingdom's philan-
thropists, this foundation is very active in Kenya and in Somalia, where
it has created many Koran schools, orphanages, hospitals and mosques.

Lastly, in spring 1997, the Kenyan police also dismantled several
Islamic NGO's in Mombasa and in the Sudan border area, including an
office of "Mercy International." We have noted that this when this
"humanitarian organization" opens new branches, it generally coincides
with the presence of dens of "Afghans," as in Albania and Bosnia. According to investigations by a European intelligence service, this organization centralized the money collected in Muslim communities in
the United States and several European countries, including Switzerland and Italy.

These funds are intended for the financing of Osama bin Laden's
networks. The American services have known of the existence of these
networks, and have observed their evolution, for several years. This
knowledge, if not this complicity, explains why bin Laden's trail was so
quickly picked up by the American investigators.

The phenomenon of public enemy number one is reassuring for
the public. Like the legendary Carlos and Abou Nidal, it has, however, a
blinding effect so that in the end everything is blamed on one culprit
while valid questions are not raised that might have made it possible to
track down real operatives. Once there is an ideal culprit, he is pun-
ished in the name of self-defense.

Resorting to force, inflicting on the culprit the same treatment
that he has given his victims, has three aims: to establish reciprocity, in
conformity with the idea of retaliation that governs international relations; and to protect the dogma of the infallibility of the State. Lastly,
while operating in the name of "peace, freedom and security," the terms
used by Clinton, to improve universal public morale through these reassuring actions.

The mechanism functioned perfectly for the Afghan targets, the
terrorist camps protected by the Taleban. Even if such bombings are

contestable from the perspective of international law, they can be politically justified by self-defense, recognized by the Charter of the
United Nations (article 51). Favorable opinion polls, public support
from both the democrats and the republicans: a wave of approbation
washed over the White House.

The Republican president of the House of Representatives, Newt
Gingrich (a good barometer of American opinion), applauded the reprisals and said that "the raids were the best thing to do." "They were carried out at the right moment," he declared on CNN TV, adding, "I
strongly support these operations, for we have an obligation to strike
terrorists everywhere they are."

The very conservative president of the Senate Foreign Affairs
Committee, (the republican) Jesse Helms, also emphasized in a press
announcement that there "should not be any refuge for the terrorists
who assassinate innocent U.S. citizens. . . . I hope that the bombings
were successful and I am extremely proud of the courage of the U.S.
armed forces that did their duty." Lastly, senator Arlen Specter (R,
Pennsylvania) indicated during a press conference that he "supports
every strong response against terrorism," but that now he was waiting
to hear the administration's arguments for making the raids; "for we
need irrefutable evidence before undertaking such action," he concluded.

A consequence of the bin Laden effect, there was almost complete
unanimity in the United States in favor of the bombardments against
the Afghan camps, even if some things are not clear in how the U.S. response was deployed. Many questions remain as to the exact conditions in which the bombing was carried out, and particularly about the
part (real or imaginary) played by the Pakistani government in the
preparation and execution of the response.

Tomahawks, the cruise missiles with a range of 1000 miles, are
guided by a GPS system (a satellite-based homing system); they do not
require guidance or support from combat planes to reach their targets.
They fly at low altitudes (from 10 to 100 meters) and are not easily detectable by even the strongest radar systems. However, many eyewit-
nesses contradict the Pentagon's official story. In an article from Pakistan's The News, a journalist known for his relationships with the secret
service reported that nearly all the wounded people stated to the local
Pakistani authorities that the bombings were closely followed by over-

flights by combat planes. The same newspaper quotes another eyewitness, in its August 23, 1998 edition, who confirms that there were air raids simultaneous with the missile attack.

After issuing several contradictory public statements, the Pakistani government instructed its permanent representative at the U.N. to lodge a complaint with the Security Council for violations of Pakistani airspace made during the U.S. bombings of the Afghan camps. In addition, the government admitted to having found a Tomahawk missile in Shatingar, Baluchistan, some seven miles from a population center. According to information in the possession of the Pakistani government, the missiles were launched by U.S. naval units 120 nautical miles off the Pakistani coast, and were accompanied by sixteen fighter jets. One of them was damaged in Pakistani territory, 160 miles from the coast.

Following the lead of the religious parties, the Islamabad press speculated over the Pakistani government's possible involvement in the operation. Several military experts stationed in the area confirmed that sixteen American jets had flown over Pakistan. "The U.S. attack could not have been a surprise to the Pakistani government," one of them stated, under cover of anonymity. "These air strikes were preceded by two telephone discussions between Prime Minister Nawaz Sharif and President Clinton between August 7 and 14. The U.S. Secretary of State Madeleine Albright called the Prime Minister right before the attack." In parallel, in the United States, a series of meetings took place between the chief minister of the Punjab, Shahbaz Sharif (brother of the Pakistani Prime Minister) and Pentagon officials.

Lastly, the Pakistani press confirmed the presence in Pakistan of the U.S. General Joseph Ralston (a senior officer in the U.S. Air Force) a few days before the attack. His role, apparently, was to make sure that when the Pakistani army learned about the operation it would not mistake if for an Indian attack. On August 23, Qazi Hussain Ahmad, chief of the religious party "Jamiat-i-islami," publicly accused the government of not having heeded the Pakistani Navy's warnings about the presence of several combat units of the U.S. Navy near their territorial waters.

Given the tense political atmosphere, punctuated by popular demonstrations supporting Osama bin Laden, it is probable that Islamabad's decision to accuse the U.N. of violating Pakistani airspace was made under pressure from the religious parties. In any case it demonstrates the Pakistani desire to exonerate itself from any direct implication in the U.S. retaliation, whereas others, Arab diplomats, speculated as to whether the United States was not also attempting to strike the Pakistani nuclear test site. Much was uncertain, and there were additional questions concerning the number, the identity and the nature of the victims of the raids in Afghanistan.

According to The News (Pakistani) of August 22, the American raid on the area of Khost killed sixteen people including five Pakistanis. The same day, The Nation reported 26 Afghans dead and six Pakistanis. The latter, all natives of the Punjab region, were supposedly militants of the religious party "Harakat ul-Ansar." The intelligence agencies of the Pakistani army added that bin Laden had escaped the bombardment himself, after having hastily cancelled a dinner that he was planning to host in his camp in Khost.

According to other sources close to the Pakistani government, Prime Minister Nawaz Sharif declared a state of maximum alert to the security forces after receiving a report that, of the three camps struck by the American missiles, two were actually run by Pakistani monks and that several dozen armed Islamists, also Pakistani, had been killed.

A second report from the intelligence services of the Pakistani army supplemented that information a little later, informing the Prime Minister that the authorities of the frontier town of Miranshah had found several dozen severely wounded people and the bodies of at least eleven Pakistanis. According to the same source, the U.S. missiles actually hit three military camps in the area of Khost. In addition to bin Laden's "Afghan" training center, that of "Harakat ul-Ansar," a few miles away, was especially targeted for having trained hundreds of Islamist activists who fought in Bosnia, in Kashmir and alongside the Muslim rebels in the Philippines. The chief of the camp, a Pakistani identified as Saïf Akhter ul-Islam, was also killed. The U.S. Deputy Secretary of State Thomas Pickering confirmed that this "terrorist base" was indeed a priority target.

Directed by another Pakistani, Mufti Bashir, the camp of "Jamiat ul-Mujahidin" (the third target concerned) trained combatants for Kashmir. Forty Kashmiri soldiers were killed.

According to The Nation, which quoted an Arab diplomat stationed in Islamabad, the Pakistani army closed all "rest camps" in the tribal zones bordering on Afghanistan, where the Islamists were accustomed to spending some time before and after their training in Osama bin Laden's centers. Lastly, the Pakistani government apparently decided to prohibit passage to volunteers looking for military training in the other networks controlled by the Saudi billionaire.

The aftermath of the American bombings confirmed the Pakistani secret service's complicity in the organization of Osama bin Laden's networks, and also revealed the extent of the support, spontaneous or organized, that the Taleban enjoys in many circles within Pakistani society.

While this information did not directly affect American public opinion (unanimous in thinking the bombing had been appropriate), the details relating to Sudan continue to raise many questions. The puzzle over the Al-Shifa industrial pharmaceutical center goes well beyond the question of whether or not the factory manufactured chemical weapons. The choice of the target and the political message to which it corresponds must be examined attentively, because they lift the veil on the true investigation that is only now getting underway. In the long run, it could generate a resounding "Bin-Ladengate." This potential scandal is lurking in the old and deeply ramified connections between the CIA and Osama bin Laden. It is based in the brouhaha caused by the very choice of the Sudanese target.

U.S. authorities justified the destruction of the pharmaceutical plant by affirming that it manufactured components that went into the manufacture of chemical weapons. They also accused the factory of collaborating with the Iraqi military-industrial complex and of serving the interests of Osama bin Laden. Lies! responded the Sudanese authorities; and to prove their good faith, they declared they were ready to welcome a board of inquiry on the spot.

"We are not opposed to the arrival of a U.S. delegation that could be directed by somebody as respected as former president Jimmy Carter or a member of the Congress. On the ground, this delegation would have all the necessary room for maneuver in order to investigate the true activities of the Al-Shifa factory," stated Moustafa Osman Ismaïl (the chief of Sudanese diplomacy) on CNN, shortly after the bombing.

On August 22 in Amman, three engineers introduced as Ahmed

Salem (responsible for the design of the factory since 1993), Eid Abou Dalbouh (a pharmacist), and Mohammad Abdul Wahed (design leader for the drug manufacturing equipment ), held a press conference. Ahmed Salem stressed that "there is no possibility that this factory could produce chemical weapons, for it was designed exclusively for pharmaceutical and veterinary products." According to Abou Dalbouh, employed in the factory until November 1997, the production of toxic gases would have required industrial ducts and separate buildings, which is not the case at the Al-Shifa factory. An engineer still employed there, Ali Jaber, stated that no modification had taken place at the factory in recent months, that would have permitted a reorientation of its production.

According to Jordanian engineers, the factory, at a cost of $32 million, was financed by a Sudanese businessman, Bashir Hassan, who then sold it because of financial difficulties. "The factory was designed in Jordan and Jordanian experts supervised the entire building site, because of the industrial relationships established between the Jordanian pharmaceutical company and businessman exporting to Sudan," they said, adding that "Osama bin Laden was never seen on the site of the factory, during the four years that construction was going on." And finally, the three engineers affirmed that an expert from the World Health Organization (WHO) had visited the site in December 1997.

The German weekly magazine *Der Spiegel* brought in a new angle by printing a diplomatic telegram in which Werner Daum, the German ambassador, confirms the Sudanese story, to wit: the Al-Shifa factory never manufactured chemical weapons. The truth is apparently halfway between the U.S. and the Sudanese positions.

Indeed, an expert from the French Defense Ministry brought some clarity to the debate by concluding that the factory could have produced chemical ingredients which, individually, remain inert, but which, joined together, might go into the design of "a weapon of mass destruction."

These ingredients are organophosphores. "Ethyl (disipropylamino) ethylmethylphosphonite, which along with other components like dimethyl polysulphide, can go into the composition of the toxic agent VX. VX, in very small amounts, causes a lethal cutaneous reaction," explains Jacques Isnard. "This class of poisons — in a liquid state, close to that of oil — appeared in the 1950's."[1]

358

The Pentagon experts added, for their part, that they had "soil samples" collected on the site several months before the raid that proved that the Al-Shifa factory manufactured components of chemical weapons. On August 25, the U.S. Deputy Secretary of State Thomas Pickering explained that Sudan was collaborating with the Iraqi program to produce the nerve gas VX.

The last element to add to this dossier comes from Khartoum, where the lawyer Ghazi Suleiman, a renowned and flamboyant figure of the opposition, caused a sensation by giving the press an unexpected view. As a board member of the company operating the Al-Shifa factory, he claimed to know personally all the shareholders and he assured them that the billionaire Osama bin Laden did not own a single share.

Without being quite as categorical as this representative of the Sudanese Bar, directly associated with the management of the factory, other opposition leaders also contributed to the beginnings of an explanation, which was confirmed by several chancelleries. Thus, the former governor of the Bank of Sudan, Farouk el-Magboul, proposed that Washington was less concerned with the specific choice of the Sudanese target than with delivering a strong political-military signal to the entire Sudanese political class.

Indeed, besides Osama bin Laden, some of the reasons for the American response are related to the Sudanese imbroglio. Its various actors and the stakes are the true key to the anti-American attacks of Nairobi and Dar es Salaam.

The U.S. intelligence agencies know exactly where bin Laden's Sudanese companies are installed. They know perfectly well the agricultural farms that the Saudi has developed near the airport, and the military training camps that he finances in the suburbs of Khartoum. In Sudan, Osama bin Laden still has thousands of miles of poppy fields in the Damazin area, as well as a dam and an electrical power plant not far from the Eritrea border, in the southeast of the country, that supplies the Sudanese capital. Thus, there were plenty of targets.

Why, under these conditions, was an operation like the one carried out in Afghanistan not carried out against these targets that are directly tied to the terrorist complexes in question?

"The scandal caused by the bombing of the Al-Shifa factory is not a diplomatic game," says the former governor of the Bank of Sudan. "You should find out who bought the factory, for he is a central character in the political conflict that is dividing the central power." A Saudi of Sudanese origin, the new owner of the Al-Shifa pharmaceutical complex is the businessman Salah el Din Ahmed Idriss, right-hand man to an important Saudi financier; he saved him $600 million during the Islamic Bank scandal (BCCI). Close to the Saudi monarchy, Idriss is related to bin Laden through one of his wives.

On the Sudanese political scene, the current owner of Al-Shifa is a known member of the opposition to the Islamist regime of Khartoum. Although he maintains good relations with President Omar Hassan el Bechir, he has a regular column in *El Khartoum*, a Sudanese opposition newspaper that is printed in Cairo. Sudan is complicated . . . this businessman passes for an ally of the hawks in the regime, opposed to Hassan el-Tourabi, the religious guide and the real strong man of the country. The leader of these "extremists," the former number two of the Sudanese Islamic National Front, Ghazzi Salah Ed-Din Atabani, is part of bin Laden's team.

Salah Ed-Din began his career in the 1980's within the Islamic League under Colonel Kadhafi, a unit made up of Arab anti-imperialist "internationalists" that never saw action outside of the Libyan borders. After this military training, Salah Ed-Din participated in the "holy war" of Afghanistan in one of the Arab volunteer units trained by bin Laden. Having become a friend of the billionaire, he represented his interests Sudan after the withdrawal of the Soviet army. Leader of the Party of the People, the extreme wing of the Islamic National Front, for several years he was in charge of the Sudanese special services. For this reason, he has many ties in Uganda, Eritrea and in Ethiopia where he coordinated the attempted murder of Egyptian President Hosni Mubarak in Addis Ababa, in June 1995.

Shortly after this botched attempt, the Ethiopian police got busy and broke up several armed factions that had been working for Khartoum. Salah Ed-Din then had to reorganize the international antennas of the Sudanese services. He chose Tanzania, in particular Zanzibar, where several Islamist groups made their facilities available to him, as well as the near part of Kenya, and particularly the coastal area of Mombasa and Malindi, easy to access because of tourist transit. These same networks were useful, after the first Afghanistan war, facilities for the mercenaries and Osama bin Laden's trading companies. This Salah Ed-Din conglomeration was actually used as the logistical base for the

August 7, 1998 attacks against the American embassies.

Nairobi and Dar es Salaam are more or less comparable in terms of urban organization, the distribution of neighborhoods and the type of social relations that govern them. While it would be hazardous to try to reduce these capitals to villages and to claim that everyone knows everyone there, it is nevertheless difficult to imagine that anyone staying in these cities could organize any clandestine operation or transaction whatsoever, without having diversified and longstanding local relationships. Owing to the civil wars of Ethiopia and Somalia, Salah Ed-Din's agents worked with several Islamic NGO's, financed by Saudi Arabia, and they ended up completely controlling them.

Consequently, and for several years, the Sudanese services have had a foot in both capitals. Thus, it was relatively easy for them to materially organize the anti-American attacks, which one must regard as heavy military operations, requiring well-developed and tightly organized logistics. And that takes care of supplies.

Supplies: a capital question when it comes to fighting terrorism! Indeed, if the type of the explosive is the first question considered by the investigators, the next one has to do with the inventory of the local actors, factions, groups and movements that could carry out such attacks, which — we repeat — are analogous to actual military operations.

While the material elements form the basis of any investigation of a terrorist operation, still we must reconstruct the political motives and the calendar according to which they were performed. In fact, this relates to the inter-clan power struggle in Khartoum and the Sudanese civil war, in which the government army has been fighting the animist rebellion of the southern provinces since 1983.

Since the beginning of this conflict, the Sudanese National Islamic Front (the NIF) associated with the Muslim Brothers in Egypt, has opposed any negotiated solution that would honor the south's call for returning Sudan to secularity, or any possible secession of the southern provinces, rich in oil. This defense of Sudanese unity, guaranteed by the supremacy of the Muslims in the north, constitutes the historical base of the power of the Sudanese Islamists.

On the very eve of the negotiations scheduled to begin on July 4, 1989 with the rebellion in the south, the army, infiltrated by the NIF and the Brothers, fomented its coup d'état. "A group of 300 soldiers led by the General Omar Bechir, supported by the directorate of the NIF and the director of Faysal Islamic Bank (Mohammad Youssef Mohammad), took over in Khartoum," writes Alain Chouet. "The new regime, immediately recognized by Saudi Arabia, claimed to be virtuous. Under the cover of a supposed fight against corruption, and pursuant to the stipulations of the International Monetary Fund, it proceeded to fire some 10,000 civil servants and 9,000 soldiers. In fact, these State employees were not on the Brothers' side and were therefore discreetly replaced by NIF clients; this disastrously reduced the professionalism of the government but gave Tourabi the means of taking over the entire apparatus of State."[2]

To start a transition toward a civil regime, Tourabi fostered the creation of institutions like the Transitional National Assembly, a self-proclaimed Parliament created in February 1992. At the same time, the NIF activists and those close to Tourabi moved into the administrative offices and the business organizations, and set about arranging matters so that the entire country would be run in the interests of the Muslim Brothers. At the time, all sensitive issues began to come under review by Ghazzi Salah Ed-Din, considered to be a mentor of General Bechir. With the support of his friend Ali Osman Mohamed Taha, number two at the NIF (and serving as Prime Minister), he represented Tourabi in the pursuit of the Islamization of the society and in taking over all the Sudanese economic and financial circuits.

"And we can add to this racketeering-based economy," Alain Chouet continues, "a de-professionalization of the government administration and several large companies, which were brutally purged to the make room for the privileged few, relations and clients of the NIF, along with their families. Lastly, the Sudanese diplomatic network was urgently mobilized to ensure the success on foreign markets of the spoils effected by the Brothers which constituted, in selected money markets, a "war chest" that enabled them to deal with any eventuality. Certain close collaborators of Hassan el-Tourabi were thus entrusted, for various periods of time, with the function of ambassador in capitals renowned for their commercial and banking facilities." This management style established by the Brothers in Sudan very quickly exposed its political limitations. The foreign-exchange reserves evaporated, exports broke down and external debt went up alarmingly.

With the Sudanese Islamic State on the verge of bankruptcy,

Tourabi seized the occasion of new peace talks with the south to begin negotiating with the American armed services to oversee the containment of the rebellion. In response to the regime's political opening, the American emissary guaranteed Tourabi that his personal financial network would survive. In spring 1998, a series of secret talks was held in an attempt to draw a definitive map of the provinces of the south, and to establish the methods for creating a separation between the religious and the State sector and for the introduction of the pluralism.

Carried out by Tourabi's trusty comrades, this negotiation, if it succeeded, would have meant the end of the NIF's business networks and would have been the political death of General Bechir and his friends, including the indispensable Salah Ed-Din. Anxious to defend their system of emoluments, the NIF "hawks" then entered into resistance against Hassan el-Tourabi. During the last congress of the NIF, in November 1997, Salah Ed-Din, still General Secretary of the party, was relieved of all significant political responsibility at the instigation of Tourabi. The ideologist of the regime looked to be a turncoat, and the Sudanese armed services lost their patience and began to prepare their revenge.

For the people who were favored by the system, it was time to try anything they could to strengthen their hand, even if it required the most unsavory actions. . . Thus, by financing the attacks against the American embassies of Nairobi and Dar es Salaam, the NIF "hawks," who opposed any negotiation with the southern rebels, were certain to compromise the talks and to isolate Tourabi.

Even in the wake of the bombing of the Al-Shifa pharmaceutical factory, Hassan el-Tourabi thought that relations between Washington and Khartoum, so often strained over the past ten years, could only improve. "I am convinced that we have hit bottom and that we can only go up from here. That is what I think, and I don't see that as wishful thinking; and I am persuaded that that it will not take long," he declared in an interview with the Associated Press Agency. The same day, Washington proposed to Khartoum "a program of cooperation on security matters" and the return of the Sudanese ambassador to the American capital. The furor caused by the bombardment of the Al-Shifa factory came to an abrupt halt.

"Concerned not to hurt Tourabi politically, the Pentagon experts had to choose a marginal but nevertheless significant target. It had to send a sufficiently clear signal to the "NIF hawks," explains a European military attaché stationed in Khartoum. "Thus, by bombing Al-Shifa, the Americans said very distinctly: we do not want to destroy the economic base that is vital to the country, but only the interests of those who are obstructing the peace process with the rebellion in the south. We know who the "hawks" are, who are opposing this process. We also know perfectly well where their economic interests lie."

Admittedly, the principal silent partner of the Nairobi and Dar es Salaam attacks, the Sudanese Salah Ed-Din, is Osama bin Laden's man, and indeed the Saudi billionaire financed these operations; but one cannot seriously, now, suggest that he was "the brain" behind the attacks.

Questioned on Khartoum's support of the billionaire, Tourabi affirmed that he is not a terrorist and that he left Sudan of his own free will in 1996, after five years of presence in the country without incident. At the time, Khartoum had just handed over to France the terrorist Carlos. Judging that his Sudanese refuge was no longer very secure, bin Laden had then returned to Afghanistan; this transfer which was carried out, according to several qualified sources, under the protection of the Saudi services, with a green light from the CIA.

In Nairobi, the FBI was mainly working to sort out the tangled web of ties between the Sudanese secret service, the Osama bin Laden organization and the Islamic NGO's. Going from one surprise to another, the investigators ended up focusing on two American connections. The first relates to the organization Mercy International Relief Agency, whose direct involvement in the financing of the "Afghan" networks we have mentioned on several occasions.[3] Active in Bosnia, Chechnya and Albania, this subsidiary of the Muslim Brothers was able to establish its headquarters in the United States, in the State of Michigan, with the assistance of . . . the CIA. The Agency provided significant logistical and financial support to this "humanitarian" organization, enabling it to act clandestinely in the various Balkan conflicts as well as within the Muslim communities of several Russian republics.

On the basis of the FBI's conclusion, the Kenyan government announced the dissolution of Mercy International and five other Islamic NGO's that had probably also enjoyed Saudi and CIA support. The second organization in question is the Al-Haramain Foundation, whose nine members had been expelled from Kenya in November 1997. The

International Organization of Islamic Salvation, Help Africa People, the Saudi foundation Ibrahim Bin Abdul Aziz Al-Ibrahim and the local outpost of the World Islamic League were also shut down. The Kenyan authorities explained their decision by stressing that "these organizations are involved in activities that are unrelated to their stated purpose and contrary to the interests and the security of the Kenyan State."

At the end of a private interview with the ambassador of Great Britain, President Moi expressed his "deep concern with regard to the rise of fundamentalism," stressing that the Kenyan authorities "had assessed the dangers of a certain type of Muslim proselytism, with significant financial backing, in particular within a pluri-religious society that is very vulnerable to corruption." The Supreme Council of the Muslims of Kenya (Supkem), traditionally moderate, immediately denounced the persecution of Islam by the public powers and called for demonstrations and public prayer meetings all over the country to force the government to reconsider these prohibitions.

The second American connection is more serious, for it directly touches the family relations of Osama bin Laden. One of his six wives is Philippine. Since 1991, bin Laden's brother-in-law Mohamed Jamel Khalif had overseen the management of the International Islamic Relief Organization (IIRO), a nongovernmental organization that acts as cover for the financing of the Muslim Philippine guerrillas on the island of Mindanao, particularly the terrorist group Abu Sayyaf. Confronted with armed violence on the part of the Islamists in the south of the archipelago, Manila expedited an expulsion order against the brother-in-law in 1994. He had to leave the country and he managed to enter the United States with a visa that was delivered with help from the CIA. This affair, reminiscent of the visa that was obtained under similar conditions by the Egyptian sheik Omar Abdel Rahman (implicated in the World Trade Center attack), had already caused a crisis between the FBI and the CIA. The CIA had not been able to justify its willingness to support a Filipino suspected of financing terrorist organizations.

On August 30, 1998, the *Counter-Terrorism and Security International Journal* organized a round table bringing together several antiterrorist experts, including the former federal prosecutor Anders McCarty, Patrick Eddington, private consultant and CIA agent for nine years, and Eduard Balato, president of "International Association of Counter-Terrorism and Professional Security." The discussion makes it clear that the FBI and the CIA had engaged in "a war between the police forces," since the Gulf War, with the FBI reproaching the information agency for its "too great leniency with regard to its 'Islamist partners.'" To keep the situation from degenerating, the CIA requested that bin Laden's brother-in-law leave the United States in December 1994. One month later, he boarded a flight bound for Jordan, before reaching Yemen. During the same round table, it was learned that Omar Bakri Muhammad, a personal friend of Osama bin Laden and chief of the Al-Muhajiroun party, residing in London, was in possession of several specimens of the famous Stinger missiles provided to the Afghan resistance by the CIA. Today, everyone is passing the buck as far as who is responsible for these various scandals.

"Bin-Ladengate" had already begun. . . while the American response kicked up an international wave of protest. By setting up Osama bin Laden as public enemy number one, the United States the best thing for the terrorists: it crowned the Islamists' biggest "hero" as the greatest adversary of the world's leading power.

On August 21, 1998, throughout the day that followed the American bombings of Afghanistan and Sudan, Arab capitals were passing messages to the Egyptian presidency to ask for its reaction and "to set" their position based on that of Cairo. President Mubarak's official declaration was, in addition, communicated to all the Arab capitals.

Egypt renewed its traditional call for an international summit, under the auspices of the U.N., to examine the ways to fight terrorism, and, consequently, it invited the Security Council to adopt "resolutions in conformity with the charter of the United Nations in order to counter terrorist violence." Torn between the difficulty of accounting for its indistinct support for the American response and the impossibility of condemning it explicitly, the Egyptian government chose the middle way, to no one's surprise, calling once again for an international conference.

During the meeting of the Council of Permanent Representatives of the Arab League (held on August 24), the Egyptian delegate joined the consensus on the text pointedly condemning the bombings, and stressing that the behavior of the United States "can only encourage violence and counter-violence."

The state-run press was unanimous in emphasizing Egypt's condemnation of terrorism, but several articles also underscored the idea that "collective action in the fight against this plague is preferable to unilateral action, which is liable to have only specific and limited effects." The evening edition of *Al-Ahram* described the American response as "barbarian and stupid," while emphasizing that the Sudanese and Afghan regimes had a share in the blame for this incident. In addition, most of the editorialists echoed the Arab man on the street, who was convinced that an equitable solution of the Palestinian question, and especially of Jerusalem, would be the only event likely to defuse one of the principal causes of Islamist terrorism.

"We are against aggression aimed at civilians, as in the case of Sudan and of Afghanistan," Mohammed Sayyed Tantaoui (the sheik of Al-Azhar) declared to the press. He is the supreme authority of Sunni Islam. In addition, the Muslim Brothers condemned the American attacks in a press statement, declaring that they were a "diversion from the scandals confronting the president of the United States," referring to the President's sordid affair with a White House intern, Monica Lewinsky. And the Brotherhood invited "the Arab and Muslim Heads of State to close ranks in confronting American aggression."

As one might expect, the Saudi authorities remained particularly discreet, restricting their comments to a condemnation of terrorism "from wherever it might come," while the press was much more critical; it presented the bombings as a diversion to the Lewinsky affair and an initiative contrary to international law. The lead articles were unambiguous: "The Wrong Approach" in *Arab News*, "Irresponsible American Actions" in the *Saudi Gazette*, "Terrorism Against Terrorism" in *Al-Hayat*, "Washington and Its Motives" in *Al-Madina*, and "Terrorism Confronted with Vague Positions" in *Al-Charq al-Awsat*.

The press of the United Arab Emirates (UAE) also criticized the attacks, which had "poor objectives," and awaited explanations of the links between the selected targets and the real authors of the attacks. Syria, too, denounced the "ineffective air strikes," observing that they would elicit "acts of revenge." The official Sana, quoting the remarks of a "reliable source," said that "such actions undermine the International Conventions as well as the U.N. charter, and do not make much difference in controlling the difficult problem of terrorism."

In Djakarta, the new Indonesian president Yusuf Habibie deplored the raids, and several hundred people representing various Islamist organizations demonstrated in front of the United States embassy.

Lastly, the Algerian government deplored that innocent civilians were victims of the American air strike. "Any retaliation must fit in the context of international legality," said an official statement from the Foreign Affairs office, stressing that the United States had acted "unilaterally." Algiers also called for "the early conclusion, under the auspices of the United Nations, of a General International Convention on the Fight Against Terrorism." Such a tool would constitute "the appropriate context for community action by the States to oppose the authors of terrorist acts and those who back them."

Most of the Algerian political organizations stressed the negative impact that the American response would inevitably have on relations between the Arab countries and the West. And, a spin-off of the former Islamic Salvation Front (FIS), the Front of Socialist Forces (FFS) thought that the bombings would lead to "a hardening of public opinion in the Arab and Muslim countries, with unfortunate consequences for the reinforcement of radical Islamism to the detriment of peaceful and democratic forces."

Beyond these unanimous political reactions, and on a purely technical level, there is indeed room to doubt that the military response is the best approach to a transnational phenomenon that requires a long-term fight, that requires secrecy, with the presence of agents on the ground, and that must be articulated and coordinated at the international level.

The United States prefers information based on its technological superiority in satellite surveillance and phone-tapping over operational information and the leg work represented by information from human sources. The CIA and the other American intelligence agencies are reluctant to work in collaboration with their "allies," although the operational and legal tools exist. Indeed, while there may be no "global doctrine," since no definition either of terrorism or of a terrorist act has been adopted at the international level, the tendency is to define terrorism by its effects.

From this point of view, general agreement has allowed regional conventions to be adopted. They are adapted to specifically established threats, and they rest on three key elements: the nature of the act itself, which may be "characteristic" of terrorism; its gravity; and the intended goal.

The international standard for the fight against terrorism is basically composed of fifteen International Conventions. There are four regional texts, and eleven that have been adopted within the United Nations. Four of them relate to acts of terrorism targeting airplanes and airports; two, ships and ports; one, acts committed against certain people; one, the taking of hostages; three, the use of certain products or devices with terrorist intent.

A twelfth convention, concerning acts of nuclear terrorism, is currently being studied by the sixth commission of the General Assembly of the U.N.. A "global convention" against terrorism soon may be proposed by India, Turkey, Egypt or Algeria.

International law now recognizes the need to "depoliticize" the most serious terrorist attacks, without prejudice to "the right of the people to self-determination" which must, in addition, be assured. That means that the "political motive" cannot be used any more to refuse requests for legal cooperation and extradition. The principle of "judge or extradite" means that there can be no more "certain shelter" for the perpetrators of attacks.

Lastly, it is universally accepted to facilitate legal cooperation, and in particular legal mutual aid. To speed up investigations, and to facilitate the execution of requests for extradition are among the objectives of these conventions.

At the 1978 summit in Bonn, the G8 started to take an interest in the question of terrorism; it created a task force and assigned them to look into airplane hijackings. Terrorism as a whole has only been tackled since the Tokyo summit in 1986.

The acceleration of the G8's work resulted in the development of the "25 recommendations for fighting terrorism," presented at the summit in Halifax in 1995, under the Canadian presidency, and then under the French presidency in 1996. The recommendations were adopted at the time of the ministerial conference in Paris, July 30, 1996. They are centered around six priorities:

— improving cooperation and antiterrorist capabilities;

— dissuasion, pursuit and sanctions against terrorists;

— re-considering asylum, border control and travel documents;

— broadening the scope of treaties and other international agreements;

— improving information exchange;

— examining the financing of terrorism.

The G8 "terrorism group's" work has shown real progress right now, in particular in the field information exchange. In addition, steps have been taken in more than a hundred countries to invite the governments to ratify the eleven International Conventions on countering terrorism.

Under the last British presidency in 1998, the experts concentrated on four subjects: preventing hostage-taking, controlling the export of weapons and explosives, reinforcing air security, and blocking the financing of terrorism. It is precisely in this last field that international legislation is most cruelly lacking.

The Nairobi and Dar es Salaam attacks could not have been committed without a large organization and complex logistics, which consequently required financing. The evolution of the Islamist networks, through their transnational racketeering circuits and their offshore companies, also constitutes — in addition to the existing legal apparatus — a specific tool for the fight.

Since the wave of Islamist attacks that occurred in France during the summer and the autumn of 1995, the French Foreign Ministry started working on a specific International Convention against the financing of terrorism. Announced by the French President on August 26, 1998, then by the Minister for the Foreign Affairs before of the U.N. General Assembly, this instrument would envisage several concrete mechanisms of legal cooperation to counter the financing of terrorism.

For example, an inquest could not be blocked on the grounds of bank secrecy or to protect the anonymity of numbered accounts. Heavy financial penalties might also be provided, such as the seizure or the freezing of the assets of any organization or individual suspected of taking part in terrorist activities.

Countering the financing of terrorism, whether the money comes from "legal" activities — commercial, industrial and charitable — or "illegal" — racketeering, drug traffic, procuring, slavery and theft — is a top priority for the intelligence services that are engaged in the day-to-day fight against terrorism. Indeed, the international terrorist organizations' power, range and, indeed, their capacity to cause harm depend largely on their financial means.

"To deprive them of these resources, or at the very least to make those clearly illicit, would confirm that the States engaged in combating terrorism intend to fight it in all its forms," explains one of the authorities who helped to author the convention. "Moreover, this measure would make it easier to get the 'clients' and could possibly dissuade certain States from subsidizing terrorism."

We have seen the extent to which Osama bin Laden's financial companies and business contacts have contributed to the invention of transnational terrorism, privatized and dissimulated behind the stated objectives of innumerable offshore companies and organizations. In concrete terms, a convention such as the one described above (which applies particularly to cases like the Nairobi and Dar es Salaam attacks) could, for the first time, allow these offshore centers to be treated as elements in the financial apparatus that supports transnational terrorism.

The definition of the "material elements" in the crime should include all the means of financing, "illegal" as well as "legal," private, public or semi-public, associative financings. On the other hand, this would apply only to the financing of the most serious actions, those that endanger the life of others. The "moral" element of those responsible — intent — should also appear in the text. Since intent is what makes the funding part of a terrorist action, this would make it possible to exclude those people who made donations in good faith. Lastly, the competence of the States should also be taken into account, through the various questions of the territory where terrorist activity takes place, such as the nationality of the perpetrators and the victims.

The acts to be subject to this convention could include financing and the search for financing, but also the holding, the transfer and the use of funds with terrorist intent. The people who would be liable to these provisions would include not only the authors and the perpetrators, but also the accomplices, the clients, and even any person who knowingly and voluntarily took part in any of the stages of the financing.

"Such a public action could be modeled on the one covering terrorist attacks involving explosives: 'Judge or extradite,'" adds our authority. "The regime of sanctions should be particularly dissuasive and should include provisions for the seizure of the goods and the assets, the banning of associations, and, for the duration of the investigation, the freezing of assets. Moreover, above a certain sum, the responsible financial institutions could be sanctioned for dereliction of their duty of diligence."

Until now, the American response to terrorism has take three principal approaches: the publication of a list of "rogue states;" the adoption of economic sanctions against these States and others; and "cannonball diplomacy," such as was applied on August 20, 1998 against Afghanistan and Sudan.

These measures are anachronistic today, for they rest on the outdated concept of "State terrorism," whereas the current terrorist organizations are transnational networks. And furthermore, they lead to outcomes that are very different from curtailing terrorism. Washington's partners have long understood that this obsolete approach ahs more to do with economics than with politics.

Indeed, hiding behind the alibi of the fight against terrorism, behind the convenient scapegoat of the State as hooligan, we find the intransigent and sacrosanct doctrines of "defending American interests"; a new commercial and financial war; and an ongoing battle to conquer new markets.

An "International Convention on Combating the Financing of Terrorism" would represent an entirely different approach, one that would be far more effective against terrorism that is run by networks; it would give precedence to judicial cooperation in two principal senses. The first must formalize a prohibition on the anonymity of bank accounts when there is a legal request for the names of the people or organizations involved in the financial transactions. The second must hold the financial institutions responsible for their obligation to make a "declaration of suspicion," above a certain amount.

Following the attacks in Nairobi, Dar es Salaam and Omagh (in Ulster), the British and Irish Parliaments took up a new legislative arsenal against terrorism. The adopted measures will simplify the trying of people suspected of belonging to a terrorist organization, allow the courts to draw conclusions from a suspect's refusal to answer questions from the police concerning his terrorist membership, extend police custody, authorize the confiscation of goods from people found guilty of belonging to terrorist groups and enhance witness protection. It is a step in the right direction.

Advised by the investigators of the FBI, of which the investigations in Nairobi and Dar es Salaam are just a start, the Secretary of

American State Madeleine Albright herself admitted the pressing need for reinforcing the international cooperation as regards the fight against terrorism, and particularly for improving the tools to combat its financing. Beyond the adoption of a new International Convention, as relevant as it may be, it will be up to the signatory States to apply it effectively and to see to it that the financiers of death are combated, not protected.

Parallel to this ongoing construction, we should offer political answers to the Islamist ideology, and in particular we must not compromise on the principle of the separation of the religious and the political. It is in danger of being compromised, but we must insist that this principle is not negotiable.

Footnotes

1.  *Le Monde*, August 27, 1998.

2.  Alain Chouet, "L'Islam confisqué: stratégies dynamiques pour un ordre statique," in *Le Moyen orient: migrations, démocratisation, médiations*, Presses universitaires de France, 1994.

3.  See Chapter VII: "The Muslim Brothers' Holy (and Financial) War."

# Chapter XVIII

## ISLAMISM AS CONFRONTATION

> "Separating the Church from the State is not enough any more; religion must be separated from the identity, as well. And, specifically, if one wants to stop this amalgam from feeding fanaticism, terror and ethnic wars, the need for identity will have to be satisfied in some other way."
>
> Amin Maalouf

"What is striking is the Anglo-Saxon West's obstinacy in continually making the same errors," wrote Jacques Duquesne; "that is, they keep encouraging Muslim fundamentalism to the detriment of the Islamic countries that accept, or are trying to establish, a certain secularity. The reason is simple: it is because that form of Islam, while it is not fundamentalist, is nationalist and progressivist."[1] This duplicity is explained by a principle, which is also very simple: Islamism is based not on religion, but money. The Islamist ideology mainly seeks to accumulate capital and power. Its totalitarian search for a reinvented identity fits in with American projections particularly well since it coincides with the expansion of fundamentalism within the U.S., which has been perceptible for two decades. "This shift was facilitated by the extreme politicization of the televangelist sermon and the increasingly pronounced refusal to separate the spheres of the political and the religious," explains Denis Lacorne. "The very concept of the 'moral majority,' popularized by Jerry Falwell at the end of the 1970's, heralded the collapse of the old 'wall of separation' between the Church and the State that was instituted by the founders of the American Republic."[2]

This "revenge of God," to quote Gilles Kepel, postulates a fundamentalism that is no longer based on the individual who is seen as the basis of a citizenship to come, but on the collective, religious and identifying obligations of the various ethnic communities taken in their specificity.

What is called American "culturalism" or "communitarianism" is now being used as a model for certain Muslim communities of Europe, especially those that are linked to "associations" that come under the leadership of the Muslim Brothers. (They were especially involved in the various incidents relating to the "Islamic veil" that have become so common in France since the end of the 1980's.)

In every case you will find, behind the families of the girls who refuse to remove their veils in class, Islamist militants who are supported by all kinds of people who defend a right to be different. This sentiment may be generous, but it is dangerously vague. Upon closer examination, this "fuzzy generosity" often comes on top of absolute ignorance of the Islamist ideology and a bad conscience about former colonial exploitation. This is compounded, in American as in Europe, by an understanding of the rights-of-man that has been warped into a completely irresponsible individualism. Lenin called such "fellow travelers" ignoramuses and "useful idiots."

In fact, these "affairs" jeopardize not only the rules of operation that make a public school successful, but more broadly the exceptional case that a republic itself represents. The assertion of particular traits and preferences, in the long run, generate all kinds of apartheids that aim to "differentiate" the communities from each other. Here, we are touching not only on the Republic, but even more fundamentally on the principles of democracy when confronted with an assertive theological-political order in the making. François Burgat, a researcher at the CNRS and a political scientist, author of *L'Islamisme en face*, (roughly, *Islamism as Confrontation*), is an ardent defender of this apology for a "communitarianism à la Française."[3]

We should stop for a moment, and even quote this publication several times over — not so much to answer the author word for word, but to spell out the opposition that underlies our whole investigation: the emergence of a theocratic ideology opposing secularity. This attack against the founding principles of the Republic is particularly alarming, given that it is carried out by propagandists who advance under cover and take advantage of our guilty conscience with regard the Third World. (In France, this is particularly the case since the end of the Algerian war). In fact, self-abnegation and self-hatred contribute to the obstruction, not only of a relevant analysis of the Islamist ideology, but also of any objective approach to the phenomenon. The Muslim Brothers and those who promote their views (who are very active in certain Muslim communities) exert an absolute intellectual terrorism, establishing an aggressive monopoly over the "politically correct" expression of Islam.

In the case of François Burgat, it is not so much this professional researcher's knowledge of the Islamic world that is questionable, here, but the ideological use to which it is put. Indeed, he adopts and justifies, without any critical judgment, the viewpoint of the movements that he is supposedly studying. While it is not very common to see a researcher step through the mirror to the other side this way, it is rarer still to observe a scientist express such Messianic certainty. His title states the thesis: implying an Islamism that blocks the horizon and sets its own rules for an inescapable dialogue, an obligation to make things clear, a requirement that cannot be evaded. Islamism, according to Burgat, continues the labor of an unfinished de-colonization. Ultimately, it is a new type of liberation movement founded on the claim of "cultural identity." It is an old saw to say that religious fanaticism thus justifies its excesses through identity and "the right to be different."

Every theocratic ideology founds this "differentiation" on a "reconstruction of identity," producing intensely attractive myths. "'The law of God,' here, is endogenous more than celestial. Admittedly, there are many 'religious' categories that overtly carry out their reconciliation with the system of representation. But it includes a way of dressing or of decorating one's home; ways of speaking or of thinking; philosophical, literary or political references; modes of legal reasoning; in fact all those identifying markers that the advent of Western models had discredited and that, escaping the ghetto of their folklorization, are irrepressibly retrieving their lost appeal and their credibility," writes Burgat. He seems to be describing the Islamist trajectory as a return to a sort of paradise lost, pre-colonial, primordial if not ahistorical.

The strength of Islamism supposedly lies in this "irrepressible" capacity to restore the myth of an original Islam; an origin whose purity was fatally perverted by the insults of history. "The details of Islamist discourse and a good part of its effectiveness come, on the other hand, from its use of stock symbolic references that are perceived as being virgin to any external influence." The external is inevitably suspect, if not hostile, because it is foreign, and implicitly this refers to Western intrusions, part of an undifferentiated and atemporal view of the outside world.

The explanation then goes on to clarify this ideological rejection of any history. "To the *Homo politicus* who appropriates it, Islamist rhetoric also makes it possible to effect a beneficial reconciliation with the categories (real or mythical, it doesn't matter) of his culture as it is lived and intuitively experienced." Characteristic of totalitarian ideologies, this wonder-filled confusion between "reality" and "the mythical" is all the more disturbing since, here, it is supported by a researcher who, at the beginning of his work, claims to be following the methodological rationality of the social sciences.

Characteristic of all the quacks of the "new Right" and other everyday revisionists, this "irrepressible will" to insert historical reality into the always reinvented categories of founding myths sends a chill down the spine. Take another look at *Le Matin des magiciens* (The Morning of the Magicians) by Louis Pauwels and Jacques Bergier[4] to see how, in the same way, the legend of Thule and many other mythological constructs were used to invent the purity of the Aryan race and the other monstrosities of the Nazi ideology. Fascism always starts with contempt for history. Burgat adds three other forms of hatred: that of the West, that of women and that of secularity. The same as in the most militant Islamist literature, Burgat always regards the West as one of "the universals" of medieval metaphysics, a compact and undifferentiated substance deprived of any accident, of any space-time, like a non-being repulsive to the only being worthy of truth: the Islamist.

From this point of view, the West can be considered only as a bloc, as a crisis, confronted with an "irrepressible" decline. "What, in fact, does today's distress of the Western intelligentsia express?" wonders Burgat. His conclusion, in the final analysis, is to propose Islamism as the miracle solution to this "distress." It is conceivable that "hyperbolic doubt" or "disenchantment with the world" as a method of investigation escapes the philosophical culture of our researcher. On the other hand, that he adheres so much to the automatic assumptions of Islamist ideology is all quite striking. This automatism, which consists in resorting to a particular belief in order to save one's community of origin (if not all of humanity), is characteristic of the cult approach which, through a very specific type of redemption, generally aims to introduce a new political order and the redistribution of power and wealth.

Ghassan Salame wrote, "Others (Islamists) see in Islam the only possible alternative to the declining culture of the West and think that the adhesion of Westerners to Islam is delayed only by the incapacity of the Muslims to display their faith appropriately."[5] Other research works explain very well how the Islamist ideology developed, not by proposing an affirmative approach to Islam, but by cultivating hatred of the West, for instance during the first crusades. In addition to Burgat, several researchers have adopted this messianic approach, which is shared by the warlords of the Algerian GIA and by Afghan theologians. How can we have arrived at such self-hatred, if not by cultivating the certainty that the West is the bearer of an original sin that requires expiation, or even radical revenge?

On women, as on all crucial questions, Burgat adopts and supports the images of Islamist ideology, justifying the abolition of their rights in the name of their authentic liberation. In the very beautiful text "Islam fini et infini" ("Finite and Infinite Islam"),[6] Fethi Benslama answers this sophism directly. "Taking the case of women who voluntarily choose servitude (here, I intentionally take the formula used by La Boétie, who showed us what the assent to one's own servitude means) as a solution to distress, he tries to show that 'Islamism' is a means of emancipation for all the women in the Muslim world and that they mostly share this view. He does not specify that the consequences include the canonical veil, repudiation, polygamy, inequality before the courts of law and inheritance (one man = two women), and that many women fight against this intention." We are becoming inured to hearing all the cheerleaders of "the right to be different" justifying sexual mutilation and other attacks on the fundamental and universal rights of man in the name of cultural particularism, but it still is shocking to justify the relinquishment of women's rights in the name of their liberation.

Lastly, the third frame of this strange triptych has to do with secularity and the political Left. "The Left, supposed more amenable to accepting the advent of "another," retreats behind the rampart of its persistent (fundamentalist?) attachment to the symbols of secularity and appears today to be captive to its inability to admit that the universalism of republican thought might be questionable and that one might dare some day to try to write a piece of history in a vocabulary other than that forged by the Left."[7] While he is hardly a practitioner of philosophical doubt, François Burgat has a perfect command of dialectical inversion. Therefore he charges "the secular Left" with exactly the offense for which the latter reproaches the religious fanatics.

It would be a sophism to say that this enterprise consists in establishing a false symmetry between Islamist fundamentalism and a secularity that is expressed only on a fundamentalist plane. If that were all there is to it, how would the fundamentalism of the second justify that of the first?

What is at stake goes far beyond Burgat's *L'Islamisme en face* and raises the question of "democracy in opposition to Islamism," and in opposition to all forms of religious fanaticism. And the fact that certain Arab regimes, confronted with Islamism, choose the brutal eradication of the phenomenon in an authoritative defense of secularity, does not mean that democracy and secularity must necessarily be opposed. The latter condition is necessary, and certainly insufficient, to the establishment of the first.

Secularity is one of the great achievements of human liberty. By separating the political from the religious, it not only guarantees the cohabitation of several beliefs, but allows the accession to political citizenship regardless of belief. Secularity and democracy are interdependent in the currents of a still-evolving history, and their respective partisans can still invent new twists that respect the beliefs of various groups without contravening the common requirement of "living together."

As Robert Fossaert rightly recalled, "More than democratization, secularization is an integral factor in the pacification of the world system."[8] From this point of view, it would be unacceptable indeed for citizens to be obliged to practice their religion in hiding . . . Islam must be given the same access rights to the public sphere that the institutions of the other religions enjoy. Consequently, we must not talk bilaterally with Islamism as an "either/or" as Burgat would like to have us believe, but take into account specific and complex political situations.

Islamism *en face* is a curious reversal, for the question is not whether Islamism can be dissolved into democracy rather than into secularity, nor the converse — obviously, the answer is negative either way — but whether Islamism can be dissolved into Islam itself. Clearly, it is up to the Muslims themselves to interpret the original message of their faith and to decide what must be retained and what must be reformed of their rich patrimony, a fourteen-century heritage of history and culture.

"In Muslim law, there is no citizen, only the subject. The State is not distinct from the society, the prince is. That is the only version of Islam that is current today. The application of the Family Code in Muslim law is insanity," wrote Soheib Bencheikh, Mufti of Marseilles. "And yet, in Algeria, the Islamists and the anti-Islamists agree in saying that it is a divine dictation. They are wrong! It is not Islam, but an interpretation of Islam by a patriarchal society. In the event of divorce, the woman went to her father's family. Can one apply that in the public housing projects? No. As long as Muslims do not reform their law and do not read the Koran again with intelligence, we will always live this lacuna."[9]

Similarly, I recall with great emotion a visit with Muhammad Saïd Al-Ashmawy, who regularly receives death threats from the Egyptian Islamists and lives as a recluse in his apartment in Cairo. He passionately enjoined to me not to confuse Islamism with Islam, the Islam of faith and tolerance. "Islamism is above all our problem, we Muslims, because it is we who created it, encouraged it and too often used it for local political ends," he insisted.

"In the wake of the historical heritage of the Enlightenment, which belongs to us as much as it does to you, and to every free man, many Muslims make a distinction between what is political and what is religious," this former judge explained to me. "We want to posit that political action is a simple mortal act, neither holy nor infallible, and that governments are elected by the people and not by God. Attempting to qualify this secularist (that is, atheistic) distinction can only be an act of partisan fanaticism that muddies the waters and confuses different issues. For this distinction can only serve and elevate Islam, prevent its exploitation for political ends and avoid the repetition of the many errors that delineate its history."[10]

By inventing a means of dissociating the political and the religious, in accordance with the requirements of its own tradition, Islam will not undergo what François Burgat would call imperialism or the *diktat* of Western culture. It would achieve (as Soheib Bencheikh and Muhammad Saïd Al-Ashmawy explain, of their own volition), a beneficial reconciliation with its own history. At the risk abolishing itself in the cult-like and fascistic trends of moderate or radical Islamism, the result is the same. Islam, like the other human belief systems, cannot be satisfied with a history that is limited, closed, and circumscribed by the coercive interpretations of theologians who are hungry for power and money.

With Islamism, as with all forms of religious fanaticism, one principle is non-negotiable: that of the separation of the political and the religious; the separation of the Church and the State; the separation of theology and philosophy.

In 1665, Spinoza interrupted his writing of *Ethics*, his life's work, and indignantly threw himself into the writing of the *Tractatus Theologico-Politicus*. His friend and protector Jean de Witt would be assassinated by religious fanatics. He further explained his thinking in a letter to Oldenburg:

— First: to deal with those who would like to apply to philosophy the prejudices of theology;

— Second: to counter the general suspicion that he was an atheist;

— Third: to defend the freedom to philosophize against the zeal of the preachers.

This work was written under the pressure of circumstances similar to those of the assassination of the writer Farag Foda in Cairo on June 8, 1992; the massacre of the 258 inhabitants of the Raïs in the suburbs of Algiers during the night of August 27-28, 1997; the slaughter at Luxor on November 17, 1997; and the too many anonymous victims of religious fanaticism. The text was the inauguration of political philosophy, a weapon against the watchdogs of the revealed religions, an assertion that philosophy is in no way constrained by theology and that reason is in no way constrained by religion; that the State is in no way constrained by the Church.

Spinoza uses a very strict logical development to show that the Scriptures, the Bible, has nothing to do with philosophy; that revealed knowledge has no other goal but obedience and subservience; that the Bible was written under particular historical circumstances. He shows that religious freedom is well-founded, that freedom to think is incompatible with any revealed knowledge and that, consequently, it cannot be threatened without endangering the State. To give up the freedom to think would be the equivalent of giving up the protective nature of the State as Spinoza conceives it.

The *Tractatus Theologico-Politicus* ends on this note: "1) It is impossible to take away from man the freedom to say what he thinks; 2) this freedom can be accorded to the individual without endangering the right and the authority of the sovereign, and the individual can wield it without endangering this right, if he does not use it as license to change in any way the State's recognized rights or to do anything to overthrow the established laws; 3) the individual can enjoy this freedom without disturbing the peace of the State and (on the condition) it does not generate any problems that would be difficult to resolve; 4) the enjoyment of this freedom given to the individual does not endanger piety; 5) the laws established on matters of a speculative nature are entirely useless; 6) we have proven, finally, that not only can this freedom be granted without endangering the peace of the State, piety, and the rights of the sovereign, but that, to preserve them, this freedom must be established. . . . We thus conclude that what is required above all for the security of the State is that piety and religion be considered only in the exercise of charity and fairness, that the right of the sovereign to regulate all things, holy as well as profane, must relate only to actions and that, otherwise, every man is granted the right to think as he wishes."

This proof was offensive not only as a counterattack intended to convince the religious and political authorities that they are not threatened by philosophy; it is above all an assertion of an infinite power of liberation. With Islamism, as with any fanaticism whatsoever, we should revisit the *Tractatus* and reinterpret it for today's world. We should remind ourselves that freedom inherently brings, according to its own requirement, rights and duties. Liberation unfolds on the plane of immanence. It is nothing more than the expression of the society itself. It is a sign of itself and does not require external, much less transcendent, interpretation. It is not up to the clerics and theologians to describe its measure and its quality. Liberty in action is its own interpretation.

Footnotes

1. La Croix-L'Evènement, December 30, 1998.

2. "La politique du soupcon d'immoralité: comparaisons Franc-Americain," in *Pouvoirs*," No — 65 Presses Universitaires de France, 1993. Editions La Découverte, 1995. Gallimard, 1960.

3. Ghassan Salame, *Appels d'empire: Ingérences et résistances à l'age de la mondialisation*, Fayard, 1996.

4. In the magazine *Lignes*, No 30, February 1997, Editions Hazan.

5. François Burgat, "L'Algérie, des 'Fellaghas' aux 'intégristes,'" in *Le Genre humain*, Le Seuil, 1991

6. "Eglise et géopolitique," in the magazine *Hérodote*, La Découverte, 1st quarter 1990.

7. Soheib Bencheikh, *Marianne et le Prophète — L'Islam contre la France laïc*, Grasset, 1998.

8. Read (and read again!) Muhammad Saïd Al-Ashmawy, *L'Islamisme contre l'Islam*, La Découverte, 1991.

9. Spinoza, *Œuvres II — Traité théologico-politique*, translation and notes by Charles Appuhn, Flammarion, 1965.

Conclusion

THE CIA AT THE NEGOTIATING TABLE

> "Strategy certainly remains the art of vanquishing the
> enemy, but it also becomes the art of shaping the
> world system."
>
> Alain Joxe

Kabul, September 13, 1998.   The Taleban announce they have
taken over the town of Bamiyan, the capital of Hazarajat. This mountainous area in the heart of Afghanistan was the last significant bastion
of the domestic forces that had continued the fight against the Taleban
militia.  The Hazaras, a Shiite population (Persian-speaking like the
Iranians), are despised and hated by the Sunni Taleban who regard
them as dangerous heretics.  Their Mongol features lend credence to
the legend that they are descended from the hordes of Gengis Khan. In
1989, after the Soviets' departure, Iran encouraged all the Hazaras to
join Hezb-i-Wahdat — the Unity Party. Thus, the fall of Bamiyan was
seen not only as a stinging setback for Iran, but it took on a symbolic
value.  It completed the undivided Sunni domination of Afghanistan,
and guaranteed the return of the Pashtun administration (the Taleban's
ethnic group) in these mountains from which it had been expelled in
1979.  There were many testimonies that women were being abducted
and adults and children slaughtered (as with the Algerian GIA), accel-
erating Iran's response; Iran massed tens of thousands of Revolutionary
Guards at the Afghanistan border.  At the end of September, it supplemented its defense force and carried out military maneuvers involving
more than 200,000 soldiers.

Undoubtedly alarmed by this turn of events at the Afghan border — and not wanting to displease either of the two parties, Saudi Arabia asked Tehran and Kabul, in the name of "Muslim fraternity," to show restraint and to avoid any resolution by force. According to various diplomatic sources, the United States officially asked Riyadh to exert a moderating influence on the Taleban government.

Since then, the threat of an Iranian military intervention in Afghanistan has faded. Iran never had strategic objectives in Afghanistan, even during the war against the Russians. Tehran has no more ties in the area, and it lacks the financial means to pursue a conflict, even of low intensity; in any case, public opinion is opposed to any idea of war. Today, the Iranian government is trying to cash in, on the international level, for this policy of appeasement and non-intervention. Anxious to be reinstated in the international community, it seeks to be accepted as a moderate partner, a victim of terrorism, ready to pursue a rapprochement with Saudi Arabia, if not the United States, in order to isolate Pakistan and the Taleban.

For their part, the Taleban now have only one goal: international recognition. To achieve it, they have to modulate the theological fanaticism that is the foundation of their political legitimacy. Thus, they are betting mostly on their control of the Afghan territory, and they manifest a more permissive attitude with regard to the NGO's and U.N. agencies, while affirming their intention to fight against the drug traffic. Lastly, they are trying to deflect onto the Pakistani mercenaries all responsibility for the most obvious attacks on human rights. The Pakistanis have been set up as scapegoats for many civilian massacres. The "theology students'" new approach, however, raises one key question: what fate is reserved for Osama bin Laden?

This cumbersome guest has caused a cooling of relations with the "Saudi big brother." Whereas the Crown Prince Abdallah was still in favor of recognizing the Taleban regime, Prince Turki brutally broke off with Kabul. The all-powerful head of the Saudi secret service felt humiliated by Mollah Omar, the chief of the Taleban, who refused to expel bin Laden. He is untouchable since he has married his host's daughter. Tangled up in this affair, the "students" are seeking, through delaying tactics, to find a way out that would satisfy Saudi Arabia. Thus, according to the newspaper *Al-Charq Al-Awsat* of October 4, 1998, Kabul "proposed that Riyadh should try Osama bin Laden before an Afghan Muslim court. . . . The Taleban authorities planned to send a delegation of Afghan *ulemas* to Riyadh of in order to examine, with their Saudi homologues, the prospects for a Shari'a-based solution that could be supported by the ulemas of both countries." In the mind of the Taleban, expelling bin Laden was absolutely out of the question. Regarded as a stateless person, the interested party would have to be tried, in any event, on Afghan soil.

Thus the bin Laden affair continues to poison relations, not only between Kabul and Riyadh, but also with Washington. Now the Saudis are trying to convince their American partners that they are doing everything they can to control the Saudi billionaire's ability to cause harm. According to Al-Charq Al-Awsat again,[1] a financier who got out of the bin Laden networks went to the Saudi secret service in 1997 and gave them detailed information on the movement's bank accounts and funds transfers. This bit of information is quite amusing when you realize that Osama bin Laden was trained by the CIA and Prince Turki's agencies. This detail, reported in the daily newspaper that is considered to be the monarchy's semi-official mouthpiece, sends a double message. If the Saudi services pursue their investigation, Osama bin Laden is no longer one of their agents; and, the Riyadh authorities want to show that they deny any responsibility in the latest operations he financed. Nonetheless, he made his fortune and built his organization with the assistance of the most influential members of the Saudi royal family and with the complicity of the CIA.

Saudi and American sponsorship of Islamism reached its limit with the Nairobi and Dar es Salaam attacks, the more so as the FBI investigation progresses. Every day, the implication of the Pentagon and the CIA in the bin Laden networks becomes clearer. *The International Herald Tribune* of October 31 revealed that a former Green Beret was directly involved in the billionaire's clandestine organization. Egyptian by origin, Ali Mohamed, 46 years old, served for three years (1986 to 1989) in the Special Forces based in Fort Bragg, North Carolina, where it was affected with the training of the American commandos committed to the Middle East. During the same period, he took part in the military training of Islamist militants in several camps in the New York area. Even though the FBI refuses to make any official comment, its investigators are now working to verify the various links between an Islamist community in Brooklyn and the CIA instructors.

"Bin-Ladengate" is unfolding, and there is no escape. If it blows up one day, this scandal will reveal exactly how the various American intelligence agencies were involved in the process that led to the Nairobi and Dar es Salaam bombings. The FBI leaders are perfectly well-aware of the politically explosive dimension of their investigation, and so is the CIA.

The threat of this new scandal that hangs over the CIA's head (a CIA whose reputation has already suffered) explains its activism in the Middle East since the Israeli-Palestinian peace process has ground to a halt. Indeed, for two years, the CIA has endeavored to play a leading role in getting the Oslo agreements implemented. During this period George Tenet, the new director, has met with Yasser Arafat at least six times. On many occasions the CIA outpost in Tel-Aviv has organized coordinating meetings between the Israeli and Palestinian security chiefs. Its local staff ran multiple operations on the ground and has settled disputes between the Israeli and Palestinian police. Several Palestinian officers even had training courses in Langley, Virginia, at the Agency's headquarters. The CIA's objective is clear: to make itself technically and politically essential in this matter that is vital for the United States. That will certainly not stop the FBI investigation, but it will surely attenuate the political fall out of "Bin-Ladengate."

At the Wye Plantation, although the urgent search for a new agreement between the Israelis and Palestinians came up short, the American information agency was propelled onto the diplomatic scene a few days before the unhoped-for signature (which occurred the night of October 23, 1998). Yasser Arafat's Palestinian Authority should, in the long run, recover an additional 13% of the territory of the West Bank, in exchange for abrogating the passages in the Palestinian Charter that deny the right to the existence of the State of Israel. A compromise was found for the liberation of Palestinian prisoners held in Israel, and for security questions touching, in particular, on the fight against terrorism. This last item was discussed directly by Mossad and the CIA in Washington. A "Memorandum on Security" had been hammered out in December 1997. It was accepted by Arafat but refused by Netanyahu; the text was then bounced back and forth between Tel-Aviv, Gaza and Washington, until the Wye Plantation discussions. As a consultant and obligatory intermediary for the various versions of this text, the CIA quickly recognized that it could derive an advantage from this political game.

As technical guarantor of this "Memorandum on Security," the CIA could assert itself at the negotiating table and extract the final decision at the very moment when the political discussion threatened to break down. Intervening officially at the request of the White House, the director of the CIA undoubtedly took advantage of the distress of the presidency (totally immersed in the "Lewinsky" business) to pose as the savior of Israeli-Palestinian peace in the Middle East. "Spies, in theory, are used to collect and analyze information, not to conduct diplomacy in broad daylight," worried a CIA veteran. He added, "This is a first for the CIA, and it is likely that the President will return the favor when it needs it." Several foreign embassies share this analysis. The day when the FBI investigators present their final conclusions on the Nairobi and Dar es Salaam attacks, showing the CIA's implication in the bin Laden networks, the White House will remember October 23, 1998.

Two months earlier, by bombing military camps in Afghanistan, the United States apparently broke with the totalitarian regime of the Taleban that the CIA had contributed to establishing. The American gas company Unocal, which had provided armaments and mercenary soldiers to the Taleban, temporarily suspended its plan for a gas pipeline in Afghanistan "in consideration of the political conditions," in the words of a company spokesman on August 24, 1998.

But beyond these specific regional effects, the longstanding American-Saudi Arabia alliance was liable to suffer. Even though Riyadh remains, with Washington's complicity, the principal backer of global Islamism, the problems inherent in the unclear succession to King Fahd are far from being solved. It could be that the "Quincy Pact" that guarantees America's oil supply in exchange for Saudi security and sovereignty will hit troubled waters. By gradually opening up again to trade with Iran, the United States is likely to upset the Sunni Muslim world even more and to incur the wrath of its radical activists once again.

This evolution does not, therefore, presage an imminent inversion of alliances nor an end to the United States' sponsorship of any form of military-political expression of Islamism (or at least the movements that continue to suit their economic-strategic plans). Independently of the latest terrorist developments, Islamism continues to keep the Israeli administration off balance. In the long run, Israel is relying on its ability to start an intra-Palestinian war, and on its inexhaustible capacity to destabilize all the nation states in the Arab-Muslim world.

Islamism and Zionism are two complementary enemies, two different sides of the same process that obstructs the search for a fair peace in the Middle East and the beginnings of an equitable resolution of the Palestinian question. More specifically, Islamism has strongly contributed to the "digestion" of the Palestinian question — the eminently political question of the right to existence of a people that is, today, the victim of an aggressive policy of colonization and of ethnic cleaning. By transposing the question of the Palestinians' right to existence onto the religious ground, Islamism has only consolidated the theocratic bases of the Hebrew State (which has not given up its plan of a "Greater Israel" that would squeeze back the last Palestinians toward Jordan.

Thus, with the assistance of the radical Islamists, Zionism is on the path to success in fulfilling its great geopolitical intention: the destruction of the Arab world, in the sense of an "Arab space" that is organized around the existence and the cooperation of the Arab nation states. The new alliance contracted between Israel and Turkey, and the thawing relations between the United States and Iran, reinforce this evolution at a time when what remains of the Arab world is confronted with the problems of a power vacuum. In Saudi Arabia, King Fahd's succession is still an open question. That of the late King Hussein of Jordan, of Hafez el-Assad in Syria, the late King of Morocco and of Yasser Arafat were also far from being undisputed. At the end of 1998, more than thirteen states in the Middle East were approaching the critical moment in resolving their succession issues. The most acute is probably that of the Palestinian Authority.

At the extreme, and in spite of the new agreement signed at the Wye Plantation, the Palestinian question appears to be definitively buried, digested, voided. Edward Saïd is right in saying that this new text is "sterile, hopelessly sterile," and in deploring that "Now the Palestinians are bound by security provisions in favor of Israel, which continues to deprecate and degrade their existence — to say nothing of their aspirations, which have been completely overlooked. The catastrophe of 1948 has been erased, the same as the conquests of 1967 and 1982. The refugees will remain refugees and the Palestinians will be always be watched by Israeli soldiers. . . . The twelve strokes of midnight have already sounded."[1] It's a terrible but incontrovertible observation: the duty to remember does not apply to the mutilations of the Palestinian people, whereas it is asserted daily by the World Jewish Congress.

From now on, the international community has been devoting all its attention to Afghanistan under the Taleban and the "new great game" tied to Central Asia, the area everyone covets, the locus of all the Utopias and all the crises of the next millennium.

In this new great game, the businessmen and their lawyers, the heads of the great oil and gas companies, the mercenaries and the security guards take center stage, relegating diplomatic and other political actors to playing secondary roles. The Saudi billionaire is the perfect incarnation of this mutation of privatized Islamist terrorism that is practically quoted on the stock exchange, going hand-in-hand with the great economic restructuring that is in progress.

As Abou Nidal, in his time, permitted the fragmentation of the Palestinian camp, bin Laden and his networks are working toward the destruction of what remains of Arab nationalism, while promoting the globalization and the conversion of armed Islamism into an Islamism of business.

The "real God" hidden behind the "illusory God" of Islamist ideology is none other than finance and business. The central nerve of Islamism is not Islam, but money. The money and the businesses of Islamism are rooted these days in the impenetrable global economic networks. This redistribution, which generally takes place with help from "organized crime" channels, takes advantage of the increased liberalization of investments and financial flows that further restricts the parliamentary procedures and the democratic practices that still remain in Western countries. The same type of alienation that is effected via the Islamist ideology is also gaining momentum via the mechanisms of the global economy. Blending perfectly into the new matrices of "organized crime," this neoliberal trend is also accompanied by an accelerated privatization of the foreign policies of the great powers.

The trend toward the privatization of foreign policy is further intensified in the U.S. since the various special-interest decision-makers can work, on the domestic level, through trade associations and ethnic and religious lobbies that are increasingly powerful. Encouraging a transformation of the relations of power, these new actors are increasingly atomizing the process of political decision-making, with a result that is rather similar to that of Islamism. On top of this comes the progressive abandonment of the social protection provisions that formed the pillars of the welfare state for some thirty years. The relations between the political sector, the economic sector and the citizens have been profoundly upset. This trend, which started with a questioning of the State and a negation of the separation of the political and the religious, now has a profound impact on the possibility of safeguarding a republican public space where various modes of thought and beliefs can coexist.

The intoxication of the dollar — "In God We Trust" — sweeps away everything that stands in its path: national borders, institutions, cultures, states and nations. Now the future seems to belong only to McDonald's and to prophets with guns. We definitely have the Taleban we deserve — new forms of totalitarianism are watching for the right moment. Averroès, Spinoza, Rousseau, wake up! They've gone mad. . .

## Footnotes

1. October 4, 1998, edition.
2. *Le Monde*, Nov. 4, 1998

# Also from Algora Publishing:

CLAUDIU A. SECARA
*THE NEW COMMONWEALTH*
*From Bureaucratic Corporatism to Socialist Capitalism*

The notion of an elite-driven worldwide perestroika has gained some credibility lately. The book examines in a historical perspective the most intriguing dialectic in the Soviet Union's "collapse" — from socialism to capitalism and back to socialist capitalism — and speculates on the global implications.

IGNACIO RAMONET
*THE GEOPOLITICS OF CHAOS*

The author, Director of *Le Monde Diplomatique*, presents an original, discriminating and lucid political matrix for understanding what he calls the "current disorder of the world" in terms of Internationalization, Cyberculture and Political Chaos.

TZVETAN TODOROV
*A PASSION FOR DEMOCRACY –*
*Benjamin Constant*

The French Revolution rang the death knell not only for a form of society, but also for a way of feeling and of living; and it is still not clear as yet what did we gain from the changes.

MICHEL PINÇON & MONIQUE PINÇON-CHARLOT
*GRAND FORTUNES –*
*Dynasties of Wealth in France*

Going back for generations, the fortunes of great families consist of far more than money—they are also symbols of culture and social interaction. In a nation known for democracy and meritocracy, piercing the secrets of the grand fortunes verges on a crime of lèse-majesté . . . *Grand Fortunes* succeeds at that.

CLAUDIU A. SECARA
*TIME & EGO –*
*Judeo-Christian Egotheism and the Anglo-Saxon Industrial Revolution*

The first question of abstract reflection that arouses controversy is the problem of Becoming. Being persists, beings constantly change; they are born and they pass away. How can Being change and yet be eternal? The quest for the logical and experimental answer has just taken off.

JEAN-MARIE ABGRALL
*SOUL SNATCHERS: THE MECHANICS OF CULTS*

Jean-Marie Abgrall, psychiatrist, criminologist, expert witness to the French Court of Appeals, and member of the Inter-Ministry Committee on Cults, is one of the experts most frequently consulted by the European judicial and legislative processes. The fruit of fifteen years of research, his book delivers the first methodical analysis of the sectarian phenomenon, decoding the mental manipulation on behalf of mystified observers as well as victims.

JEAN-CLAUDE GUILLEBAUD
*THE TYRANNY OF PLEASURE*

The ambition of the book is to pose clearly and without subterfuge the question of sexual morals -- that is, the place of the forbidden -- in a modern society. For almost a whole generation, we have lived in the illusion that this question had ceased to exist. Today the illusion is faded, but a strange and tumultuous distress replaces it. No longer knowing very clearly where we stand, our societies painfully seek answers between unacceptable alternatives: bold-faced permissiveness or nostalgic moralism.

SOPHIE COIGNARD AND MARIE-THÉRÈSE GUICHARD
*FRENCH CONNECTIONS –*
*The Secret History of Networks of Influence*

They were born in the same region, went to the same schools, fought the same fights and made the same mistakes in youth. They share the same morals, the same fantasies of success and the same taste for money. They act behind the scenes to help each other, boosting careers, monopolizing business and information, making money, conspiring and, why not, becoming Presidents!

VLADIMIR PLOUGIN
*INTELLIGENCE HAS ALWAYS EXISTED*

This collection contains the latest works by historians, investigating the most mysterious episodes from Russia's past. All essays are based on thorough studies of preserved documents. The book discusses the establishment of secret services in Kievan Rus, and describes heroes and systems of intelligence and counterintelligence in the 16th-17th centuries. Semen Maltsev, a diplomat of Ivan the Terrible's times is presented as well as the much publicised story of the abduction of "Princess Tarakanova".

JEAN-JACQUES ROSA
*EURO ERROR*

The European Superstate makes Jean-Jacques Rosa mad, for two reasons. First, actions taken to relieve unemployment have created inflation, but have not reduced unemployment. His second argument is even more intriguing: the 21st century will see the fragmentation of the U. S., not the unification of Europe.

ANDRÉ GAURON
*EUROPEAN MISUNDERSTANDING*

Few of the books decrying the European Monetary Union raise the level of the discussion to a higher plane. European Misunderstanding is one of these. Gauron gets it right, observing that the real problem facing Europe is its political future, not its economic future.

EDITOR: BERNARD-HENRI LÉVY
WHAT GOOD ARE INTELLECTUALS?
*44 Writers Share Their Thoughts*

An intimate dialogue with some of the world's best minds, in the form of essays, interviews and responses to the oft-asked question, "What good are intellectuals?" 44 of the world's most respected authors reflect on life, death and meaning.

Authors include: Nadine Gordimer, Ivan Klima, Arthur Miller, Czeslaw Milosz, Joyce Carol Oates, Cynthia Ozick, Octavio Paz, Salman Rushdie, Susan Sontag, William Styron, Mario Vargas Llosa, etc.

DOMINIQUE FERNANDEZ
PHOTOGRAPHER: FERRANTE FERRANTI
ROMANIAN RHAPSODY
*An Overlooked Corner of Europe*

"Romania doesn't get very good press." And so, renowned French travel writer Dominique Fernandez and top photographer Ferrante Ferranti head out to form their own images.

In four long journeys over a 6-year span, they uncover a tantalizing blend of German efficiency and Latin nonchalance, French literature and Gypsy music, Western rationalism and Oriental mysteries. Fernandez reveals the rich Romanian essence. Attentive and precise, he digs beneath the somber heritage of communism to reach the deep roots of a European country that is so little-known.

PHILIPPE TRÉTIACK
ARE YOU AGITÉ?
*Treatise on Everyday Agitation*

"A book filled with the exuberance of a new millennium, full of humor and relevance. Philippe Trétiack, a leading reporter for *Elle*, goes around the world and back, taking an interest in the futile as well as the essential. His flair for words, his undeniable culture, help us to catch on the fly what we really are: characters subject to the ballistic impulse of desires, fads and a click of the remote. His book invites us to take a healthy break from the breathless agitation in general."
—*Aujourd'hui le Parisien*

"The 'Agité,' that human species that lives in international airports, jumps into taxis while dialing the cell phone, eats while clearing the table, reads the paper while watching TV and works during vacation – has just been given a new title."
—*Le Monde des Livres*

Richard Labévière
DOLLARS FOR TERROR
The U.S. and Islam

"Book of the Week: Dollars for Terror. Richard Labévière dissects the financial ties of the Islamic terrorist networks. On the basis of four years' research, this television journalist traces funds around the world, from Washington to Caribbean tax havens and, often, to peaceful Switzerland, depicting a new form of terror that is privatized and listed on the stock exchange."
—Le Point

"Nevermind the well-known ties between Uncle Sam and the Saudi emirs; Labévière shows that despite the violent attacks and virulent anti-American rhetoric, the world's greatest democracy is playing a leading role in propagating Islamic fundamentalism. Here is an audacious view of the globalization so loudly promoted by the U.S."
—Le Figaro Magazine

PAUL LOMBARD
## VICE & VIRTUE
*From Richelieu to Jacques Chirac*

Personal passion, in the course of history, has often guided powerful people more than the public interest. With what result?

From the courtesans of Versailles to the back halls of Chirac's government, from Danton — revealed to have been a paid agent for England — to the shady bankers of Mitterand's era, from the buddies of Mazarin to the builders of the Panama Canal, Paul Lombard unearths the secrets of the corridors of power. He reveals the vanity and the corruption, but also the grandeur and panache that characterize the great. This cavalcade over many centuries can be read as a subversive tract on how to lead.

JEANNINE VERDÈS-LEROUX
## THE "SAGE" AND THE POLITICIAN
*An Essay on the Sociological Terrorism of Pierre Bourdieu*

Sociologist Pierre Bourdieu went from widely criticized to widely acclaimed, without adjusting his hastily constructed theories. Turning the guns of critical analysis on his own critics, he was happier jousting in the ring of (often quite undemocratic) political debate than reflecting and expanding upon his own propositions.

Verdès-Leroux has spent 20 years researching the policy impact of intellectuals who play at the fringes of politics. She suggests that Bourdieu arrogated for himself the role of "total intellectual" and proved that a good offense is the best defense.

A pessimistic Leninist bolstered by a ponderous scientific construct, Bourdieu stands out as the ultimate doctrinaire more concerned with self-promotion than with democratic intellectual engagements.

HENRI TROYAT
## TERRIBLE TZARINAS

Who should succeed Peter the Great? Upon the death of this visionary and despotic reformer, the great families plotted to come up with a successor who would surpass everyone else — or at least, offend none. But there were only women — Catherine I, Anna Ivanovna, Anna Leopoldovna, Elizabeth I. These autocrats imposed their violent and dissolute natures upon the empire, along with their loves, their feuds, their cruelties.

Born in 1911 in Moscow, Troyat is a member of the Académie française, recipient of Prix Goncourt.

JEAN-MARIE ABGRALL
## HEALERS OR STEALERS
*Medical Charlatans*

Fear of illness and death: are these the only reasons why people trust their fates to the wizards of the pseudo-revolutionary and the practitioners of pseudo-magic?

We live in a bazaar of the bizarre, where everyday denial of rationality has turned many patients into ecstatic fools. While not all systems of nontraditional medicine are linked to cults, this is one of the surest avenues of recruitment, and the crisis of the modern world may be leading to a new mystique of medicine where patients check their powers of judgment at the door.

Jean-Marie Abgrall is Europe's foremost expert on cults and forensic medicine.